APPLIED WELFARE ECONOMICS, TRADE, AND AGRICULTURAL POLICY ANALYSIS

APPLIED WELFARE ECONOMICS, TRADE, AND AGRICULTURAL POLICY ANALYSIS

G. Cornelis van Kooten

University of Toronto Press
Toronto Buffalo London

ISBN 978-1-4875-0607-0 (cloth)   ISBN 978-1-4875-3324-3 (EPUB)
ISBN 978-1-4875-2409-8 (paper)   ISBN 978-1-4875-3323-6 (PDF)

Library and Archives Canada Cataloguing in Publication

Title: Applied welfare economics, trade, and agricultural policy analysis / G. Cornelis van Kooten.
Names: Van Kooten, G. C. (Gerrit Cornelis), author.
Description: Includes bibliographical references and index.
Identifiers: Canadiana (print) 20210145684 | Canadiana (ebook) 20210145714 | ISBN 9781487506070 (cloth) | ISBN 9781487524098 (paper) | ISBN 9781487533243 (EPUB) | ISBN 9781487533236 (PDF)
Subjects: LCSH: Agriculture and state. | LCSH: Agriculture – Economic aspects. | LCSH: Welfare economics. | LCSH: International trade.
Classification: LCC HD1415 .V36 2021 | DDC 338.1—dc23

University of Toronto Press acknowledges the financial assistance to its publishing program of the Canada Council for the Arts and the Ontario Arts Council, an agency of the Government of Ontario.

Canada Council   Conseil des Arts
for the Arts   du Canada

ONTARIO ARTS COUNCIL
CONSEIL DES ARTS DE L'ONTARIO
an Ontario government agency
un organisme du gouvernement de l'Ontario

Funded by the   Financé par le
Government   gouvernement
of Canada   du Canada

CONTENTS

3 Externalities and Nonmarket Valuation   49

4 International Trade and Applied Welfare Analysis   66

5 Governance, Rent-Seeking, Global Trade, and the Agreement on Agriculture 88

6 Analysis of Agricultural Policy: Theory   108

TABLES

FIGURES

ACRONYMS

ACRE   Average Crop Revenue Election (US)

AIDA   Agricultural Income Disaster Assistance (Canada)

AMS   aggregate measurement of support (as related to the WTO)

ANS   allowable net sales

AoA   Agreement on Agriculture (as related to the WTO)

A&O   administrative and operating costs

AR5   Fifth Assessment Report (released in 2014, it is the latest IPCC report assessing scientific, technical, and socioeconomic information regarding climate change)

ARC   Agriculture Risk Coverage (US)

ARC-CO   ARC-county option

ARC-IC   ARC-individual farm coverage

BCR   benefit-cost ratio

Brexit   British exit from the EU (2020)

BRM   business risk management

BSE   bovine spongiform encephalopathy (disease that strikes cattle that have been fed meat and bone meal containing the remains of other cattle and then spontaneously develop the disease or develop it by eating scrapie-infected sheep products)

CAIS   Canadian Agricultural Income Stabilization program

CAP   Common Agricultural Policy (EU)

CAPM   Capital Asset Pricing Model

CARA   constant absolute risk aversion

CBA   cost-benefit analysis

CCC   Commodity Credit Corporation (US)

CCP   counter-cyclical payments (US)

CGIAR   Consultative Group on International Agricultural Research

CRD   consumption rate of discount

CRP   Conservation Reserve Program (US)

CVD   countervailing duty

CVM   contingent valuation method (an approach to nonmarket valuation)

CWB   Canadian Wheat Board (1935–2012)

de minimis   Limits to support permitted under the WTO's Agreement on Agriculture (5% of agricultural production value for developed countries, 10% for developing countries)

DICE	Dynamic Integrated Climate and Economic (an integrated assessment model developed by William Nordhaus that employs a constrained optimization, economic growth approach to determine optimal investment in mitigation of climate change, with the social cost of carbon one of its outputs)
DMC	Dairy Margin Coverage (US)
EAFRD	Agricultural Fund for Rural Development (Pillar 2 support for EU agriculture)
EAGF	European Agricultural Guidance and Guarantee Fund (Pillar 1 support for EU farmers)
ECS	equilibrium (or effective) climate sensitivity (temperature increase associated with a one-time doubling of atmospheric CO_2 compared to pre-industrial times, but only after all climate system components have been able to adjust and come to a new equilibrium, which might take several centuries)
EEC	European Economic Community
EEP	Export Enhancement Program (US)
EQ	Environmental Quality (account)
EU-27	European Union 27 countries (prior to Brexit refers to EU-28 minus the UK)
FAO	Food and Agriculture Organization (UN)
FCI	Food Corporation of India
FIPA	Farm Income Protection Act, 1991 (Canada)
FTA	free trade agreements
FUND	Climate Framework for Uncertainty, Negotiation and Distribution (an integrated assessment model developed by Richard Tol that uses simulation to derive information similar to the DICE model)
GATT	General Agreement on Tariffs and Trade (replaced by WTO in January 1995)
GDDs	growing degree days
GDP	gross domestic product
GE	genetically engineered
GF	Growing Forward (name given to Canada's farm legislation that focused on a suite of business risk management programs; in place during 2008–2013 and replaced by GF2)
GF2	Growing Forward 2 (extension of Canada's GF legislation with some modifications; in place during 2013–2018; replaced by the Canadian Agricultural Partnership in 2018)
GHG	greenhouse gas (primary GHGs are water vapor H_2O, carbon dioxide CO_2, methane CH_4, nitrous oxide N_2O, and ozone O_3)
GM	genetically modified
GRIP	Gross Revenue Insurance Program (Canada)
IAM	integrated assessment model (computer models that integrate physical and economic components to investigate the costs and benefits of taking action to mitigate climate change)
IRR	internal rate of return
IPCC	Intergovernmental Panel on Climate Change (created by the UN and World Meteorological Organization to investigate the human influence on climate)
LCA	life-cycle assessment

LDCs   least developed countries

max ER maximizing expected revenue

max EU maximize expected utility

MC   marginal cost

MCDM   multiple-criteria decision-making

MFF   Multiannual Financial Framework of the European Union (essentially the EU budget)

MIRR   modified internal rate of return

MPI   milk protein isolates (a product of ultra-fine filtered milk)

MPP   Margin Protection Program (US)

Mt   one million metric tonnes

MYA   marketing year average (average US national price for a crop in a given marketing year)

MWh   megawatt hour (measure of *energy* produced by generating electricity equal to one million watt hours)

NAFTA   North American Free Trade Agreement between the US, Canada, and Mexico

NAP   Non-insured Crop Disaster Assistance Program (US)

NED   National Economic Development (account)

NGO   non-governmental organization

NISA   Net Income Stabilization Account (Canada)

NPV   net present value

NRA   Nominal Rate of Assistance to agriculture (% by which the domestic price exceeds or falls below the border price)

OECD   Organisation for Economic Co-operation and Development

OSE   Other Social Effects (account)

OTC   over-the-counter (transactions that occur outside of established markets)

P&G   Principles and Guidelines (replaced P&S for evaluation of US water projects in 1979)

P&S   Principles and Standards (US Water Resources Council's guidelines for project evaluation)

PA   principal–agent (relationship between higher and lower levels of decision makers)

PERT   political-economic resource transaction (agricultural programs that are considered to be efficient and of benefit to society)

PES   payments for environmental services

PEST   political economic-seeking transfer policy (agricultural programs that redistribute income to farmers but are inefficient as they do not benefit society)

PIK   Payments-In-Kind program (US)

PLC   Price Loss Coverage (US)

PSE   producer support estimate (OECD measure of the level to which a country subsidizes its agricultural sectors)

QOV   quasi-option value (a nonmarket value)

RCP	Representative Concentration Pathways
R&D	research and development
RED	Regional Economic Development (account)
ROW	rest of the world
SCC	social cost of carbon (equals the marginal damage from climate change)
SCM	Subsidies and Countervailing Measures (rules regarding whether or not a WTO member country can offer a subsidy to agriculture or another sector)
SCO	Supplemental Coverage Option (US)
SFP	single farm payment (EU)
S&H	shipping and handling
SM	supply management
SMP	skim milk powder
SPE	spatial price equilibrium
SSP	Shared Socioeconomic Pathways (climate change storylines used by the IPCC for determining future CO_2 emissions)
SURE	Supplemental Revenue Assistance Payments (US)
tCO_2	tonne (metric ton), or 1,000 kg, of CO_2
TEV	total economic value
TRQ	tariff rate quota (a low tariff is charged on below-quota imports, a prohibitive tariff thereafter)
VCS	voluntary coupled support (EU countries were permitted to use some of their *de minimis* limits allowed under the Agreement on Agriculture to subsidize farm programs that distorted production)
USDA	US Department of Agriculture
USMCA	US–Mexico–Canada Agreement that replaces NAFTA
VMP	value of the marginal product
WGSP	Western Grain Stabilization Program (Canada)
WRC	US Water Resources Council (interagency organization that deals with water resource management in the US)
WTA	willingness to accept (sometimes referred to as compensation demanded)
WTO	World Trade Organization
WTP	willingness to pay (equivalent to the area under a demand function, whether for a market traded good or service or an environmental amenity or service)

ACKNOWLEDGMENTS

The author wishes to thank Roel Jongeneel, Martijn van der Heide, Vincent Smith, David Orden, Lysa Porth, and Andrew Schmitz for helpful comments and suggestions; Alyssa Savage, Alyssa Russell, and Brennan McLachlan for research and technical support; and especially Linda Voss, without whose assistance this book would not have been possible.

1

INTRODUCTION

Despite nearly 75 years of development, there remains confusion about how to evaluate economic policies from an economics perspective. We see this in debates about the environment and climate change, where sometimes outrageous claims are made on the basis of economic arguments. We see this in the determination of compensation for the elimination of certain agricultural programs, and in discussions pertaining to raw log exports that are opposed by environmentalists. The purpose of this book is to help students in agricultural and forest economics, policy makers in various governmental and non-governmental organizations (NGOs), and others understand why people lobby in favor of certain public policies, something economists refer to as rent-seeking, and to understand the role of economics in analyzing government intervention in these and other situations.

To understand how government policies and interventions affect economic well-being, it is important to study how economists use applied welfare economics in an international context to measure the costs and benefits, as well as the income transfers, associated with existing and proposed policies. The aim of this book is not to provide complete coverage of the nuances of welfare economics, nor is this a book solely about international trade; rather, the focus is on selected key elements of applied welfare economics and trade that are useful for analyzing policy, especially in agriculture.

In selecting issues for inclusion in this text, three points were considered: (1) the available literature on applied welfare economics, also referred to as cost-benefit analysis, and issues that might still be considered contentious; (2) the methods used to analyze the implications of trade intervention (which is common in agriculture and forestry); and (3) the application of the tools of applied welfare economics and trade in analyzing government policy in agriculture and, to a lesser extent, climate change and forestry. In developing the cost and benefit measures used in welfare economics, several issues of current relevance are also considered, including the valuation of ecosystem services, the so-called precautionary principle, the use of a multiple accounts approach and its limitations, discounting, and climate change.

In agriculture, farmers encounter all kinds of uncertainty related to price and production risk. Investments in machinery and equipment are costly to make but are required to achieve economies of scale; yet such investments are easily stranded because they cannot be employed in other sectors of the economy. As a result of price and production uncertainty and the need for specialized inputs, governments intervene to support farm incomes, whether through price subsidies, supply restrictions (quotas), or subsidized crop insurance premiums. The benefits of government intervention tend to get capitalized in land and sometimes other asset values, leading to escalating costs of production that require further income support, thereby resulting in spiraling costs and payments. Further, government agricultural policies have been an obstacle to the conclusion of multilateral and bilateral trade agreements.

In forestry, government policies have resulted in log export restrictions in Russia, Canada, the United States, and elsewhere, even though economists have argued that raw log exports can increase the value of standing timber (sometimes referred to as stumpage), thereby incentivizing landowners to protect forestlands. There are US restrictions on Canadian softwood lumber exports, despite agreements between these countries that should prevent such restrictions. More recently, governments have provided subsidies aimed at using wood biomass to generate electricity, which has resulted in market distortions and the redistribution of wealth, while doing little to mitigate climate change.

1.1 Setting the Agricultural Stage

Agriculture is a vital sector of the global economy even if it plays a minor role in the economies of most countries, especially the developed countries and a developing country such as China. Given its importance, and since it is the primary subject of this book, we provide some background information about global agriculture and, in more detail, the agricultural sectors and farm policies of selected countries and regions, including in particular the United States and the European Union, which are the major players on the international agricultural stage. We begin with a surprise: despite a land mass of 3.37 million hectares (ha) and only 1.89 million ha of agricultural land (about 0.46% of that of the United States), the Netherlands is the second largest exporter by value of agricultural commodities in the world after the US, as indicated in Table 1.1. While one might think this is due to high-value products, such as flowers, cheese, cocoa, and many food products that come from processing imported raw agricultural commodities, this is only part of the story. While processing of imports and their subsequent export does occur, a great deal of Dutch exports is based on home-grown farm commodities. The Dutch export annually $25–$30 billion more food products than they import. The other surprise is that Brazil is the fourth largest exporter of agricultural commodities while China is sixth. Further, six other developing countries appear in the list of top 20 exporters.

The top exported food commodities by value for 2018 (the latest year for which data were available at time of writing) are provided in Figure 1.1. Soybeans, wheat, and maize (corn) are the most important grains that are traded; indeed, as grains, they are ranked first, second, and third, respectively, by weight in trade. Beef and veal constitute the largest primary source of animal protein that is traded. Note the importance of alcohol: together, wine (ranked fifth although not shown) and distilled alcoholic beverages (seventh) come second after "Food prep nes"—a category of unspecified food preparations—as the most important category of traded food products.

Table 1.1 Twenty largest exporters of agricultural commodities by value, 2018

Rank	Country	US$ billion	Rank	Country	US$ billion
1	United States	$149.122	11	Argentina	$37.172
2	Netherlands	$92.845	12	India	$36.730
3	Germany	$86.827	13	Indonesia	$35.389
4	Brazil	$78.820	14	United Kingdom	$32.255
5	France	$74.287	15	Australia	$31.984
6	China	$63.491	16	Thailand	$30.848
7	Spain	$50.961	17	Poland	$27.695
8	Canada	$49.490	18	Malaysia	$26.008
9	Belgium	$43.904	19	Mexico	$25.097
10	Italy	$43.756	20	New Zealand	$24.350

Source: Food and Agricultural Organization (FAO) of the United Nations (http://www.fao.org/faostat/en/#data/ [accessed July 9, 2020])

Figure 1.1 Top export commodities by value (US$ billions), 2018

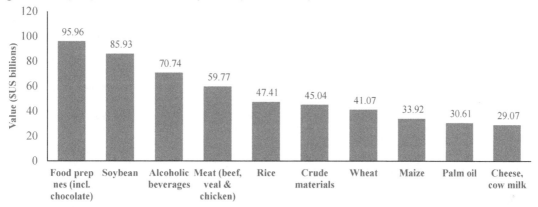

Notes: nes—not elsewhere specified; crude materials—such items as livestock sperm used for breeding
Source: FAO (http://www.fao.org/faostat/en/#data/ [accessed November 9, 2020])

1.1.1 Top Agricultural Commodity Producers

Exports provide some notion of a country's ability to produce more than it consumes. Countries with large populations are less likely to be exporters if arable land per capita is small, at least when it comes to raw agricultural commodities (primarily grains). Thus, for example, we would not expect the Netherlands to be a major exporter of grains and live animals given its high population density. The same might be true of China. If a country is a major exporter of some agricultural product, it likely has high value-added. Meanwhile, we should see land-rich countries such as Russia, Canada, Argentina, and the US produce more in the way of unprocessed (raw) commodities, such as grains. The only proviso pertains to climate; for example, Canada and Russia might not be able to grow much maize (corn) or sorghum because arable land in these countries is located where there is insufficient heat prior to planting and/or during the growing season. These observations are borne out in Tables 1.2 and 1.3.

The United States is the leading producer of soybeans, sorghum, and maize, and the fourth leading producer of wheat, which is a less valuable crop grown principally on the Great Plains. Canada is a top-ten producer of wheat, soybeans, and barley, and the world's largest producer of rapeseed (canola), which requires long days of sunlight (found in northern latitudes). Russia is the largest producer of barley, the third largest producer of wheat, and a top-ten producer of soybeans. Like Canada, it produces too little or no sorghum or maize to be a top producer, and unlike Canada, it is also not a top producer of rapeseed. Perhaps not surprisingly given their large populations (each exceeding one billion), China and India are top-ten producers of six of the seven crops listed in Table 1.2; the exception is barley (a coarse grain). China is the top producer of wheat and rice and second in rapeseed and maize, while India is one rung below China in four of the six crops, several steps behind in maize production, and two rungs ahead in sorghum. Brazil and Argentina are also important producers of soybeans, maize, and sorghum, while Ukraine is a top-ten producer of all grains but sorghum and rice.

Table 1.2 Ten largest producers of grains by weight (tonnes), 2017

Rank	Wheat	Soybeans	Sorghum	Rapeseed	Maize	Barley	Rice
1	China	USA	USA	Canada	USA	Russia	China
2	India	Brazil	Nigeria	China	China	Australia	India
3	Russia	Argentina	Mexico	India	Brazil	Germany	Indonesia
4	USA	China	Ethiopia	France	Argentina	France	Bangladesh
5	France	India	India	Australia	India	Ukraine	Vietnam
6	Australia	Paraguay	Sudan	Germany	Indonesia	Canada	Thailand
7	Canada	Canada	China	Poland	Mexico	UK	Myanmar
8	Pakistan	Ukraine	Argentina	Ukraine	Ukraine	Turkey	Philippines
9	Ukraine	Russia	Brazil	UK	S. Africa	Spain	Brazil
10	Germany	Bolivia	Niger	Romania	Romania	Denmark	Pakistan

Source: FAO (http://www.fao.org/faostat/en/#data/ [accessed July 9, 2020])

Again not surprisingly, China and India are the leading producers of fresh vegetables (respectively, first and second) and eggs (first and third), as indicated in Table 1.3. The US is a leading producer of eggs, butter, cheese, and meat products, as indicated in Table 1.3. It ranks first in all categories, except eggs and pork, where it is second. Brazil is a major producer of meat, eggs, and fresh vegetables, while Argentina is a major beef producer. Much of what Brazil and Argentina produce is meant for export (see Table 1.1). Russia is the only country appearing in each column of Table 1.3.

If we consider the 14 products identified in Tables 1.2 and 1.3, we find that China and the US are listed as top-ten producers of ten or more of these products. They are followed by Russia, India, and Brazil with nine placements in the top ten, France with eight, Germany with seven, and Argentina, Canada, Mexico, and Ukraine with five each. Despite having one of the largest economies in the world and a country that supports and protects its farmers to a greater extent than most other countries, Japan only makes the top ten in three categories—fresh vegetables, eggs, and chicken. Although it is a top producer of most major agricultural commodities, Russian farm output and food processing appear to be aimed primarily for domestic consumption, because it is not a top-twenty exporter of food commodities (Table 1.1), although it is a major exporter of wheat.

Table 1.3 Ten largest producers of vegetables, cow milk products, eggs, and meats by weight (tonnes), 2017

Rank	Vegetables	Butter	Cheese	Eggs	Pork	Beef	Chicken
1	China	USA	USA	China	China	USA	USA
2	India	New Zealand	Germany	USA	USA	Brazil	Brazil
3	Vietnam	Germany	France	India	Germany	China	China
4	Nigeria	France	Italy	Mexico	Spain	Argentina	Russia
5	Philippines	Russia	Netherlands	Japan	Brazil	Australia	India
6	Myanmar	Turkey	Poland	Brazil	Vietnam	Mexico	Mexico
7	Nepal	Poland	Argentina	Russia	Russia	Russia	Indonesia
8	S. Korea	Ireland	Czechia	Indonesia	Canada	France	Japan
9	Brazil	Iran	Russia	Turkey	France	Germany	Iran
10	Japan	UK	UK	France	Poland	S. Africa	Turkey

Source: FAO (http://www.fao.org/faostat/en/#data/ [accessed July 9, 2020])

Canada has a relatively small population but a large area of arable land that is farmed extensively (as opposed to intensively) to produce grains for export—primarily wheat, canola, and soybeans—the latter two are oilseeds that can be used for bioenergy and not only for food. Canada is also a major pork producer and a more minor player in terms of beef, selling both products in competition with US producers. Because of its marketing boards in milk, poultry (chicken and turkey), and eggs, it has no presence in export markets for these products as output is limited to supply the domestic market (see Chapter 7.3).

Finally, the Netherlands is only a top-ten producer in cheese (ranked fifth) despite being a power-house exporter. The domestic market for agricultural commodities is even smaller than that of Canada, so any commodity it produces that ranks in the global top ten must necessarily have a major export component. Further, the Netherlands sells a large variety of agricultural commodities, most of which have high value-added. While it might not be a world leader in the production of any single commodity, it certainly is in overall terms.

1.1.2 Food Security: Green Revolution and Crop Yields

The World Bank estimated that, in 2013, 766 million people globally lived in extreme poverty, defined as those living on less than US$1.90 per day in terms of purchasing power parity (PPP). This represented nearly 11% of the world's population, or 12.6% of those in developing countries. For comparison, in 1993, 33% of the world's population and 40% of those in developing countries lived in extreme poverty. The proportion of those considered ultra-poor (living on US$0.95/day or less) fell from 9.6% to 2.6% in the decade 1993–2013 (Barrett et al., 2019, p. 2). Much of the reduction in poverty was the result of economic growth in China. Poverty meanwhile continues to plague sub-Saharan Africa in particular. Yet the problem of global poverty is not a story about lack of agricultural production; rather, it is a story about abject poverty related to such factors as opportunity, education, adverse income distributions, et cetera. There is certainly enough food to feed the global population.

Agricultural research and technology transfers that began around 1950 and continued through the 1960s led to a sharp increase in crop yields throughout the world, but most particularly in developed countries. High-yielding varieties of various cereal grains were produced through selective crop breeding, with plants tending to be shorter, producing less stalk and more seed. In addition, plant breeders produced crops that were more responsive to synthetic nitrogen fertilizers; at the same time, various pesticides and herbicides were developed to control insect pests, fungus, and weeds, and irrigation and enhanced management techniques further contributed to greater production. A leading scientist of this so-called green revolution, Norman Borlaug, was granted the Nobel Prize in 1970 for saving perhaps one billion people from starvation. The green revolution continued after its initial impetus as it spread to developing countries, and its basic approach continues everywhere to this day. This is evident from Figure 1.2, which indicates that the yields (not just crop output) of four major grains have increased unabated since the 1960s, much more than doubling during the past half century.

Figure 1.2 Global productivity gains, major grains, five-year moving average of yields, 1961–2018

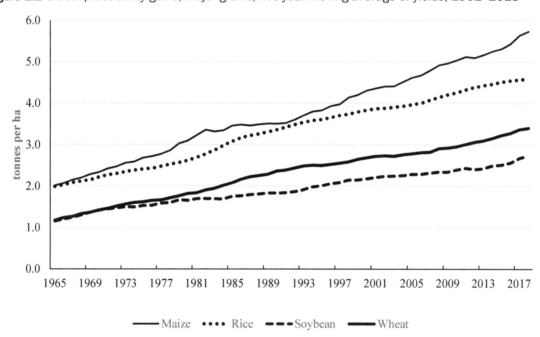

Source: FAO (http://www.fao.org/faostat/en/#data/ [accessed November 30, 2020])

There is concern that the green revolution is coming to an end and that, perhaps aggravated by climate change, crop yields will no longer increase or even decline, thereby potentially leading to frequent incidents of famine. What is ignored in such prognostications is the role of technological change and a fertilization effect caused by increased carbon dioxide in the atmosphere. As indicated in Figure 1.2 (and in Chapter 8.2), crop yields have not declined in recent years despite predictions to the contrary. The agricultural sector has seen major technological breakthroughs in the past several decades that have already altered the farming business in a positive way.

In developed countries, satellites coupled with computer technology can be used to determine globally what crops are being grown at any time and their prospective yields. Hence, in July 2020, the FAO predicted that global cereal production for the year would reach a record high of 2,790 million tonnes (Mt).[1] Technology can also aid in the creation of new financial products (e.g., weather-indexed insurance) that help farmers adapt to climate change. Global positioning satellites are used to guide equipment movement, while drones identify fungal and other pest invasions during the growing season, thereby enabling swift and effective targeting of chemical and fertilizer applications and optimal timing of harvests. New irrigation technologies that rely on swift and timely computer analyses, and water harvesting from early-morning fog (which occurs in some arid regions), are further examples of technological advances. These and other farm management technologies improve agricultural, financial, and environmental outcomes.

The same technologies might someday be employed in the developing countries. Already improved technologies reduce spoilage during storage, while mobile telephony enables farmers to determine where and when to sell crops to maximize returns. Better stoves for heating and cooking reduce deforestation and the need for crop residues and manure, which then improves soil quality. High-yielding crops currently grown in temperate latitudes are increasingly adapted to tropical conditions where hours of sunlight are shorter but temperatures higher.

The greatest potential of future technological changes will likely come from biology. Plant breeding and genetic engineering will lead to different crops and crop varieties that produce higher yields and are more resilient to weather extremes, such as droughts, and offer protection against pests, fungus, and disease. Likewise, research can be expected to provide chemicals or biological agents that target weeds and insect pests while being more benign in their environmental impact. The same is true for food technologies that may lead to meat substitutes that will have a lower impact on the environment than do livestock.

While it is difficult to predict what the future might hold for agriculture, one can be optimistic that technological changes will greatly improve the ability of agricultural producers to adapt to various changes that might affect them. Only when the scope for technological improvements is ignored might the future see a return to famines and starvation of those in developing countries.

1.2 Structure of the Book

The book is structured as follows. In Chapter 2, we introduce private financial methods of evaluating projects, and include a discussion of the main ranking criteria that are employed (e.g., net present value, internal rate of return, benefit-cost ratio). However, the major focus is on development of the theory behind social cost-benefit analysis (CBA). We demonstrate how total economic value can be decomposed into use and non-use values. We examine an approach for evaluating projects that originated in the United States called multiple accounts analysis; the multiple accounts framework is a helpful device for introducing considerations into social CBA that are relevant but difficult or impossible to quantify. Alternative approaches to project

---

[1] Grain Central, July 7, 2020, Record Global Cereal Production to Boost Stocks: FAO, https://www.graincentral.com/news/record-global-cereal-production-to-boost-stocks-fao/ [accessed July 14, 2020].

evaluation, including cost-effectiveness analysis and life-cycle analysis, are also discussed, although economists tend for the most part to ignore these methods. The chapter also includes an examination of how extreme events, and potential irreversibility, are handled in project evaluation.

Because choice of a social as opposed to a private rate of discount is so important to the outcome of cost-benefit analysis, an important section within Chapter 2 is devoted to discounting. In particular, because climate change and policies to mitigate it have impacts over a period of 100 or more years, we examine the rate used to discount costs and benefits accruing to future generations. Therefore, we distinguish between a social rate of time preference (also referred to as the utility rate of discount) and a consumption rate of discount in determining the overall discount rate, employing the well-known Ramsey discounting formula. Further, given that we deal with climate change policies, it is important to consider carbon dioxide (CO_2) emissions to and removals from the atmosphere. Does it matter if CO_2 emissions are reduced today or in the distant future? If so, should society place a greater weight on carbon fluxes—that is, discount future carbon fluxes—and, if so, at what rate? In Chapter 10, we argue that it is appropriate for policy to discount physical fluxes of CO_2 as to when these occur. Indeed, we argue that there is an important difference between a monetary discount rate and a rate used to discount (weight) carbon fluxes as to when they occur.

The environmental benefits of mitigating climate change are often considered to be most important in justifying the high costs of reducing global society's reliance on fossil fuels. But how does one define and then measure the costs to the environment of increasing levels of CO_2 in the atmosphere? At a more mundane level, what is the value of the ecosystem services that farmers provide to society when they choose not to drain wetlands or when they convert cropland to grassland, thereby reducing soil erosion while enhancing wildlife habitat? Ecosystem services, visual amenities, wildlife, clean air and water, open spaces, and such, are not traded in markets, which is why economists talk about nonmarket goods and services. The valuation of nonmarket and environmental goods and services is the topic of Chapter 3.

Because trade is important for the agricultural and primary sectors of an economy, we examine how to measure welfare in the context of international trade. In Chapter 4, we develop the concepts of excess supply and demand, and how the welfare impacts of domestic policies need to consider trade impacts. Specifically, we examine how trade considerations affect agricultural and forestry policies, and discuss how spatial price equilibrium (SPE) models can be used to analyze policies. SPE trade models assume that prices differ between countries or regions because of shipping and handling costs, plus import tariffs or export taxes, but they also assume that changes in the markets under investigation have little impact on the demand for goods and services produced in other sectors. Such trade models are useful for analyzing policies in agriculture and forestry because these sectors are sufficiently small in terms of their total impact on global gross domestic product (GDP); if that were not the case, then partial equilibrium analysis would need to give way to general equilibrium analysis, which is less detailed at the sub-sector level and less useful for examining policies related to specific commodities. We also consider welfare measurement in vertically and horizontally linked markets. To illustrate the concepts developed in this chapter, two examples are provided. These relate to EU protection of durum wheat and Canadian bans on log exports.

Institutions and good government are important to policy development. Governance and rent-seeking are discussed in Chapter 5 as these affect the types of agricultural legislation that politicians enact. Further, because agricultural policies have been a major impediment to the conclusion of international trade agreements, we also provide a broad-brush review of international trade. We focus on agricultural trade since agricultural policies have to be modified if the latest global trade agreement under the auspices of the World Trade Organization (WTO)—the Doha Development Agenda—is ever to be concluded. In particular, we examine the Agreement on Agriculture that was struck upon completion of the Uruguay Round of the General Agreement on Tariffs and Trade (GATT) in 1994 with the formation of the WTO in 1995. The Agreement on Agriculture continues to be slowly worked out, and it has implications for agricultural policy. These issues are discussed in the latter half of Chapter 5.

In Chapter 6, we develop the theories used most often by agricultural economists to analyze policy. Economic analysis examines how surplus measures (consumer and producer surpluses and government-created rents) are impacted by various agricultural policies. In doing so, we rely on the notions of excess supply and demand derived in Chapter 4. We indicate what impact agricultural policies have on prices and economic well-being. In particular, we examine the main policy tools that have historically been used to intervene in agricultural markets, and what their implications are for society. We examine the implications of price floors, buffer funds that store excess production in one period followed by disposal in a subsequent period, supply restrictions to support prices, tariff rate quotas and trade, liberalization of trade, price discrimination, and the introduction of genetically modified organisms.

The United States and the European Union are the most important agricultural regions in the world, accounting for a large proportion of global production of food and for the vast majority of exports. These jurisdictions have subsidized agricultural producers to a greater extent than farmers in most other places, thereby distorting trade and commodity prices globally. Since the European Union did not exist before the 1950s, we first examine agricultural policies in the US as it was the first modern state to implement agricultural support on a grand scale. As such, it was able to experiment with programs to a much greater degree than other nations; the US experience could thus inform EU agricultural policy. Therefore, we begin in Chapter 7 by discussing and analyzing in detail US agricultural policies, employing the tools of applied welfare economics. Because of Canada's proximity to the US and because much of its agriculture is intertwined with that of its neighbor (particularly the livestock sector), we also examine Canadian agricultural policy in Chapter 7. Canada's institutions and agricultural policies serve as a contrast to those of the US. In particular, Canada relied on state trading and continues to protect its supply-restricting marketing regimes in dairy, poultry, and eggs. Canada had also subsidized the transportation of grains to port facilities under one of the oldest and longest-lasting agricultural programs, known as the Crow Rate subsidy.

In Chapter 8, we consider agricultural policies in Europe. In all cases (Chapters 7 and 8), we consider policies that have failed, in the sense that they have been abandoned, and ones that are more successful, at least in the sense that countries continue to rely on them. Often a policy that is abandoned at one point in time is resurrected at a later date, albeit in an altered form. In Chapter 8, we also briefly discuss agricultural policies in emerging and developing countries, with a particular focus on China. One objective is to determine whether an emerging country has learned from experiences in developed countries or whether it is following its own route, perhaps repeating errors made earlier in other countries. We also examine India because it employs policies related to food security that were introduced more than a half century ago and have been successful in feeding a nation whose population will soon surpass that of China. Agricultural policies in other developed countries (e.g., Australia, New Zealand) and developing ones (e.g., Brazil) are only mentioned in passing where they might shed light on the discussion.

Given the cost of agricultural support programs, many countries have increasingly turned to business risk management programs and the potential of financial products to protect farmers and landowners against the vagaries of weather. One focus is on index-based insurance and financial weather derivatives that can be traded on existing markets, such as the Chicago Mercantile Exchange, or over-the-counter through private-sector companies, although futures markets and options trading are also examined as background. One financial product is crop insurance, which comes in two variants: crop yield and crop revenue insurance, with the latter protecting farmers against both production and price risk. The problem with many business risk management programs, particularly crop insurance, is that participation is often quite low unless premiums are highly subsidized. This issue and others related to risk management are the topic of Chapter 9. Business risk management programs in the US and Canada are examined in detail, because these countries, unlike Europe and elsewhere, now rely on such programs as the primary means to deliver agricultural support.

Finally, the focus of Chapter 10 is on climate change. The chapter begins with a discussion of the challenges that economists face in evaluating the welfare impacts of climate change. These relate to uncertainty about a future climate and the potential damages that one might expect, the types of models employed and how economic and climate models are integrated (if at all), and the meaning of welfare measures at that scale. In particular, we examine the integrated assessment models that are used by economists and how these relate to climate models. Then, we examine how economists use information on the relationship between weather variables and agricultural land values to measure changes in land rents that, in turn, represent the costs and benefits of change in the agricultural sector. Finally, we look at forestry because signatories to the Paris climate accord hope to rely on wood biomass for generating carbon-neutral electricity and sequestration of carbon in various ecosystem and post-harvest product pools to meet some of their targeted emissions reductions. A key factor in all of this is the rate used to discount streams of carbon, a subject shown to be of great importance for climate change mitigation.

Guide to Literature

Cost-Benefit Analysis: For more conceptual foundations of cost-benefit analysis, its theoretical underpinnings, and a framework for general application, see, for example, Just, Hueth, and Schmitz (2004), Boardman et al. (2011), and Hanley and Barbier (2009). Arguably the best reference work is Boadway and

Bruce (1984), who provide the economic theory underlying welfare analysis and a clear discussion of what economists should measure in conducting cost-benefit analyses.

Economics of Climate Change: There is now an enormous literature on the economics of climate change. For debate about the costs and benefits of mitigating climate change, see Stern (2007), Tol (2006), Weitzman (2007), and Heal (2009). Pindyck (2013) questions the use of integrated assessment models for calculating costs of climate change. Other discussions pertaining to climate change and economics can be found in McKitrick (2010) and van Kooten (2013).

Forest and Agricultural Economics: An introductory textbook in forest economics is by van Kooten and Folmer (2004), while Amacher, Ollikainen, and Koskela (2009) is a good graduate text. An excellent text on agricultural policy is by Schmitz et al. (2021), although readers might also benefit from the earlier editions (Schmitz, Furtan, and Baylis 2002; Schmitz et al. 2010). At a graduate level, Vercammen (2011) provides a more technical perspective that goes beyond agricultural economics. Background articles by Huffman (2016), Wallace (1962), Gardner (1987), and Rausser (1992) are well worth reading.

2

PROJECT EVALUATION CRITERIA

It is important to distinguish between private and social cost-benefit analysis (CBA). If, as Boardman et al. (2011, p. 2) propose, we "consider all of the costs and benefits to society as a whole, that is, the social costs and the social benefits," we refer to this as "social cost-benefit analysis." Economists employ social CBA for evaluating public policies because it is solidly grounded in economic theory, with many of the controversial aspects having been sorted out over a period of some 75 years. In the jargon of economics, a full social CBA of an environmental, energy, climate change mitigation, or any other project or policy that has effects beyond those directly incurred or captured privately balances all benefits, to whomsoever they accrue, against all costs, regardless of who bears them. Any redistribution of income brought about by the project is ignored and no distinction is made between rich and poor; it does not matter if a dollar accrues to a rich person or a poor one, it is treated the same.[1] Further, it is assumed that the project is sufficiently small so that prices elsewhere in the economy are unaffected. If only prices of substitutes and/or complementary goods and services are affected, the effects in the markets of those goods can be taken into account. These constitute the proper indirect effects of the project. If prices elsewhere in the economy are impacted, however, general equilibrium modeling would be necessary.

Social cost-benefit analysis is built on financial analysis, or private methods of evaluating projects. Therefore, we begin with the private perspective, as private costs and benefits are a component of social costs and benefits.

2.1 Private Financial Analysis

Consider the perspective of the private firm. For example, if an electricity system operator is considering the construction of an additional thermal power plant, the costs of the project equal:

- the up-front construction costs related to land, labor, and materials;
- annual operating (e.g., fuel, labor), maintenance, and (routine) replacement costs, usually referred to as the operating, maintenance, and replacement costs;
- estimates of the costs of unscheduled breakdowns and risks imposed by changes in fuel prices (and other input costs) over time;
- costs of meeting environmental regulations; and
- any costs related to the eventual mothballing of the facility.

---

[1] This is the assumption of constant marginal utility of income. Some argue that income distribution is the domain of macroeconomic policy (e.g., tax policy). Others apply weights to measures of economic well-being depending on who in society bears the costs or receives the benefits. Social theorists argue that this can be done by specifying appropriate utility functions (that might include altruism as a parameter) or social welfare functions, but in practice such decisions are political and beyond the purview of project evaluation, except that project evaluation or CBA can help identify the gainers and losers of a policy.

All costs are discounted depending on when they are incurred. Benefits are provided by the discounted stream of expected revenues from sales of electricity to households and industry, plus any "salvage" value at the end of the facility's useful life. As long as financial benefits over the lifetime of the project exceed costs, the private investor determines the investment to be feasible. That is, the rate at which the system operator weights the streams of costs and revenues is the rate of return that he or she hopes to earn on the investment. Thus, if the weighted stream of benefits exceeds that of costs, the project earns a higher rate of return on the investment than could be earned elsewhere.

Private project evaluation excludes spillovers unless the authority specifically requires the firm to pay for access to natural resources, to pay compensation to those "harmed" by the firm's activities, to pay an environmental tax, to purchase "pollution rights," or requires the firm to post a bond to offset society's potential future need to mitigate environmental damage caused by the firm's activities. These costs would be included by the firm in its financial analysis of a project. Further, a private evaluation uses market prices for natural resources, labor, land, and other inputs instead of the opportunity costs to society of those resources. Regardless of these limitations, it is important that public projects are valued from the perspective of private firms. For example, if the government wants to implement a given project and a financial evaluation considers it to be attractive from a private perspective, it might be wise just to let the private sector pursue it.

2.1.1 Financial Ranking Criteria

Private projects are usually ranked on the basis of financial criteria such as net present value (NPV), benefit-cost ratio (BCR), internal rate of return (IRR), and/or modified internal rate of return (MIRR).

Net Present Value (NPV)

For ranking projects on the basis of NPV, the following assumptions are needed:
- the discount rate is given and usually taken as the market interest rate;
- capital is always readily available;
- the interest rate for borrowing is the same as the interest rate for lending;
- cash flow projections include all relevant costs and benefits, and taxes; and
- projects are mutually exclusive (so that they can be evaluated separately). Any combination of projects should be considered as a separate option.

If these assumptions are valid, the NPV is the sum of the project's discounted benefits minus the sum of the discounted costs over the project lifetime:

$$(2.1) \qquad NPV = \sum_{t=0}^{T} \frac{B_t - C_t}{(1+r_t)^t},$$

where B_t represents the benefits derived from the project in period t, C_t refers to the costs in period t, T is the lifespan of the project, and r_t is the interest or discount rate in period t. Because it is difficult to forecast future interest rates, the discount rate is generally assumed to remain constant in each period. If we are evaluating a single project and NPV is greater than zero, the project is worth undertaking. If we are evaluating several projects, the one with the highest NPV should generally be chosen, although that will depend on factors unique to each project. For example, some projects may be riskier than others, or projects have different lifespans (in which case one might wish to annualize the net discounted benefits of each project in order to make the comparison).

Benefit-Cost Ratio (BCR)

This is the ratio of the discounted total benefits from a project divided by the discounted total costs of the project:

$$(2.2) \quad BCR = \frac{\sum_{t=0}^{T} \dfrac{B_t}{(1+r_t)^t}}{\sum_{t=0}^{T} \dfrac{C_t}{(1+r_t)^t}} .$$

If the BCR for a single project is larger than one, then the project increases real wealth. When comparing different projects, however, the problem of scaling appears. For example, a project with total benefits of $1 million may generate a greater increase in real wealth than a project with total benefits of $100, but the ratio of benefits to costs may not be as high. Thus, projects must have an equal outlay basis if they are to be compared.

Payback Period

For the vast majority of projects, costs are incurred before any benefits are realized, which is why the term "cost-benefit analysis" is preferred here to "benefit-cost analysis." During the construction phase of a project, a firm incurs costs only—costs are front-loaded. Benefits do not usually accrue until construction is complete. The payback period, therefore, is the point in time when a project's total benefits exceed its total costs (including interest payments). At that time, the project has paid back its initial investment. Both costs and benefits should be discounted when estimating the payback period. The major problem with the payback method is that it ignores cash flows (costs and benefits) that occur beyond the payback period. If this is the only financial criterion taken into account, it is possible then to accept a project that has a negative NPV. Nevertheless, the payback period is a useful indicator for firms that are unsure about future cash flows and their position in the market. Obviously, firms tend to prefer projects with a shorter payback period.

Internal Rate of Return (IRR) and Modified Internal Rate of Return (MIRR)

The IRR is a popular criterion for private project appraisal. The IRR is the discount rate for which the NPV is zero—where the project's discounted benefits exactly balance discounted costs. It is found by setting NPV=0 in equation (2.1) and solving for r (assuming r does not change over time). The project with the largest IRR is generally preferred, subject to the proviso that the IRR exceeds the discount rate. Despite its popularity, the IRR criterion needs to be used with caution. First, for complex cash flows, there might be more than one IRR for a single project. And second, the IRR approach assumes that the project can both borrow and lend at the internal rate of return. In other words, excess funds generated by the project can be invested externally at the IRR. This is certainly not the usual case.

The modified IRR (MIRR) is the average annual rate of return that will be earned on an investment if the cash flows are reinvested at the firm's cost of capital. Therefore, MIRR more accurately reflects the profitability of an investment than does IRR. To determine the MIRR, it is necessary to solve the following equation:

(2.3) $K_0 (1+\text{MIRR})^T = \text{FV}_{\text{cash flow}},$

where K_0 is the capital investment (effectively calculated at time zero), T is the project's lifespan, and $\text{FV}_{\text{cash flow}}$ is the future value of the cash flow—it is the value of the cash flow compounded to time T using the discount rate that reflects the firm's cost of capital.

2.1.2 Conclusion

A number of different criteria are used by private firms and even government agencies to evaluate whether a particular course of action—construction of a new manufacturing facility, purchase of another business, investment in a sports facility, and such—meets the entity's goals or more specifically defined objectives. In this section, we considered only financial criteria, such as net discounted returns (discounted profits), internal rate of return, or the time required for an investment to be paid back. We have ignored such intangibles as the contribution that an action makes to a firm's goodwill. For example, some forest companies have been known to pay for research into the effect of logging practices on amphibians, and how practices can be changed to take any adverse impacts into account. Clearly, there is no financial benefit that can be readily identified; indeed, those research results suggest logging costs might increase to take into account goodwill. However, the firm may prevent erosion of market share if this activity leads a retailer to treat the company's wood products more favorably than those of a rival.

The narrow focus on the firm's purpose is what characterizes private evaluation, whether such an evaluation is based on financial or non-financial factors, or some mix of the two. The criteria used by these economic agents or entities in making decisions ignore the impacts that their decisions have on other elements in society. They ignore social costs and social benefits more broadly. They ignore spillovers and distributional impacts. It is important to recognize that it is not only private firms that fail to include social costs and benefits in their analyses. Often government agencies (e.g., Bureau of Land Management in the US), publicly owned (crown) corporations (BC Ferries), and government departments have their own clientele and are generally more concerned with their survival than they are with the overall public good. Yet taking into account all costs and benefits, social and private, is the task of applied welfare economics—of social CBA.

2.2 Society's Perspective: Social Cost-Benefit Analysis

The private perspective is not ignored in social CBA. In many cases, the private decision is adequate, and there is no need for public intervention. The only reason why the public authority would be involved in private investment decisions is if there are important externalities or spillovers, which are costs (negative externalities) or benefits (positive externalities) imposed upon others that are not taken into account by the decision maker (see Chapter 3). If spillovers are small, the transaction costs of rectifying them might be too great to warrant intervention. If the externality is sufficiently large, a case can be made for public intervention. Intervention might take the form of regulations that prevent the project from going forward, or regulations that modify the project (and change the cost-revenue balance sheet for the private investor) so that spillovers are addressed. An example of the latter might be a requirement to install scrubbers to remove SO_2 and other harmful pollutants from a power plant's smoke stack, or an up-front insurance payment by a pipeline operator in case of an oil spill.

Alternatively, some investments that are considered worthwhile from a public standpoint might not proceed without subsidies or direct involvement by the authority. For example, the public authority might consider providing a subsidy to biodiesel producers to encourage substitution of biodiesel for fossil fuels, thereby reducing CO_2 emissions. On the other hand, mandates that require a certain proportion of diesel sold at the pump to include biodiesel might be just as effective in encouraging biodiesel production, but at lower cost to the public purse. In either event, such interventions must pass a social cost-benefit test, where a benefit of the action/policy is the reduction in CO_2 emissions.

2.2.1 Benefits and Costs as Rent and Surplus

Social cost-benefit analysis does not ignore financial costs and benefits, but it does proceed differently than private evaluation of costs and benefits. As discussed in section 2.6 below, it employs a social rather than a private rate of discount, with the former generally lower than the latter. Further, social CBA considers opportunity costs (shadow prices) of resources as opposed to market prices. For example, the market wage rate might be higher than the social wage rate because of market impediments that cause the wage rate to exceed the marginal value product—the value of the additional output that the next unit of labor produces. In other words, the amount that labor is paid at the margin exceeds the value of what it produces. In that case, the economist recommends either that the wage rate be lowered (its shadow value is less than what is actually paid) or that less labor be hired as this will raise its marginal productivity, thereby increasing its marginal value product. If a large pool of unemployed workers exists, the shadow price of labor might well be zero from a social standpoint; indeed, a project that reduces unemployment likely reduces costs to the public coffers.

In economics, costs and benefits constitute a surplus that is either lost (cost) or gained (benefit). There are four types of economic surplus.

(1) *Consumer surplus* is the difference between the value that consumers place on goods and services and the actual expenditure required to obtain those goods and services. In essence, it is the difference between the total benefit that consumers derive from purchasing Q and what they actually have to pay (which equals $P \times Q$). It can be measured by the area below the marginal benefit (demand) function and above price. This is illustrated in Figure 2.1.

Consumer surplus is not always directly measurable. Consider the case where a project does not affect consumer surplus because the market price is unaffected. It is unlikely, for example, that decisions concerning the harvest or protection of a single commercial forest landscape, or the development of a wind energy project, will affect the prices of timber products or electricity. Thus, the direct consumer surplus associated with such a project is unlikely to change; indeed, unless the project lowers price, the consumer is not going to gain surplus from the project. In that case, consumer surplus becomes relevant only in some other market, but not the market for lumber or energy. Suppose that, in addition to the market for lumber or energy, there is a demand for an environmental amenity that is somehow impacted by the logging decision or energy project. In that case, there may be surplus that needs to be taken into account in evaluating the logging or energy project. This would be an indirect cost or benefit associated with the project, which is discussed below as the fourth type of surplus.

(2) *Producer surplus* or *quasi-rent* constitutes the difference between total revenue and total variable cost. It can also be measured by the area below price and above the marginal cost (supply) function, as indicated in Figure 2.1.[2] While constituting a true welfare measure, producer surplus constitutes a rent accruing to fixed factors of production and entrepreneurship. That is, in the construction of Figure 2.1, the supply curve is taken to be a short-run supply function, which means that returns to the fixed factors of production must come from producer surplus. Hence, attempts to tax this quasi-rent will adversely affect firms' investment decisions.

One can think of consumer and producer surpluses from another perspective that does not require assumptions about the derivation of demand, a perspective that ignores the utilitarian foundations of demand. Think of the supply function as the minimum amount that a seller is willing to accept (WTA), at the margin, to part with the item in question. Any amount above minimum WTA constitutes a surplus to the seller. Likewise, the demand function can be thought of as the maximum amount a buyer is willing to pay. Suppose that person A is willing to sell an article at any price above $9, while person B is willing to pay upwards of $17 for that item. If they agree to a price of $12, person A gains a surplus of $3 while B gains a surplus of $5, so the total surplus shared between them is $8. If the trade had occurred at $15, A would have realized a surplus of $6 and B a surplus of $2, but again the benefit to society (the two people) is still $8. Even if A was coerced to sell at $7, so that B gained $10, the total surplus of this exchange would remain $8 (=$10–$2).

---

[2] Of course, the supply (marginal cost) function is much flatter before the project is built than afterwards. Once the project is built, the construction cost is ignored in the determination of quasi-rent, as bygones are bygones.

Figure 2.1 Consumer and producer surplus

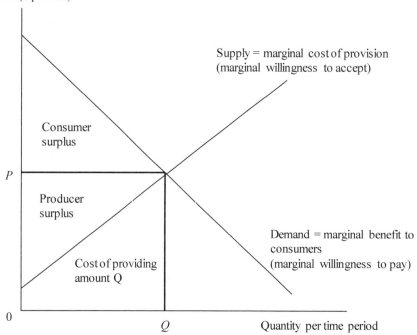

Measurement in the case of environmental or nonmarket goods can be troublesome in this framework. What is required in this case is a payment mechanism. Such a mechanism requires two conditions. First, *privateness* implies that a hypothetical payment mechanism requires a market-like environment where people, acting individually, buy or sell private correlates of the public good to be valued. Second, *pay-as-you-go* requires payment based on actual participation rather than hypothetical participation in the market. For example, in planning a new bridge, the analyst must estimate user numbers *ex ante*, but surplus measures should be based on actual users and fees that are paid to cross the bridge. In this regard, public–private partnerships might be better in providing public goods as opposed to public provision alone. The measurement of nonmarket values in a utilitarian framework is discussed in Chapter 3.

(3) *Resource rent* accrues to natural resources and consists of two components that are often indistinguishable from each other in practice and difficult to separate from the second type of surplus—the quasi-rent (producer surplus). We illustrate the concept of resource rent with the aid of Figure 2.2, noting in particular that the supply curve in this figure differs from that in Figure 2.1.

The first component of resource rent is *differential* (or *Ricardian*) *rent* that arises because of inherent or natural advantages of one location relative to another. Consider oil production. The price is such that the marginal oil sands producer earns at least an internal rate of return higher than the market interest rate. In comparison, Middle East producers earn a huge windfall, which constitutes a differential rent. Likewise, a woodlot located near a sawmill or transportation corridor (such as a highway or water route) earns a windfall relative to an identical woodlot that is located farther from the sawmill or transportation corridor.

Figure 2.2 Scarcity and differential components of resource rent

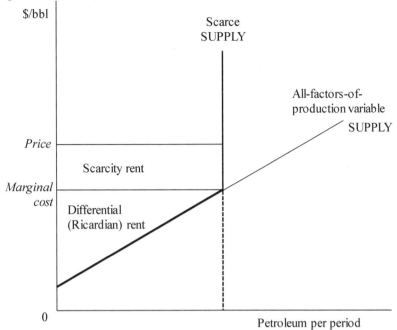

Second, there is a *scarcity rent* that results simply from oil scarcity or a limit to the number of stands with commercial timber. That is, if the oil sands or timber producer, despite being the highest cost producer, earns a windfall over and above what could be earned elsewhere in the economy, there is a scarcity rent because price exceeds the marginal cost of production.

Resource rent is the sum of the differential and scarcity rents, and it is often the greatest benefit in decisions about whether to harvest a forest, develop an energy project, or invest in a biofuel refinery. The benefit is that government can tax resource rents without adversely affecting private investment decisions. However, because measurement of resource rents is difficult, governments must be careful in taxing such rents lest quasi-rents be taxed instead.

(4) Finally, the *indirect surplus* refers to benefits or costs that accrue in markets for substitute and/or complementary goods and services. However, indirect benefits occur only if price exceeds marginal cost in one of the affected markets. Whenever price exceeds marginal cost, this implies society values the good or amenity more than it costs to provide it. Hence, if there is an increase in the demand for the good so that more of the good or amenity is purchased, there is a benefit given by the difference between price (marginal willingness to pay) and marginal cost for each unit purchased; this occurs until the declining marginal willingness to pay equates to a rising marginal cost as more is produced. Conversely, there is a cost if the opposite is true—when demand shifts inward and less is bought. Note that there is only an indirect benefit if individuals are free to increase or decrease the quantity they purchase; if not, there is nothing to measure in the market for substitutes or complements. Further, if price equals marginal cost in each of the markets for substitutes and complements, there are no indirect effects even if purchases change.

2.2.2 The Fundamental Equation of Applied Welfare Economics

We can summarize the foregoing results using a simple relationship. Consider Figure 2.3 where a policy (some type of subsidy) shifts the supply curve for good q_1 from S^0 to S^1, causing the price to fall from p_1^0 to p_1^1. The direct benefit is measured in market 1, which is targeted by the policy; it is given by the change in the consumer surplus plus the change in quasi-rent (producer surplus). Indirect benefits accrue in associated markets for complements and substitutes, but only if these markets are not perfectly competitive so price does not equal marginal cost.

Consider Figure 2.3 where some policy (viz., research and development (R&D) that led to technological improvement) increases the supply of good q_1 (shifting supply to the right), thereby causing its price to fall. The demand for products that substitute for q_1 falls (shifts inward) while that of complements is increased (shifts out). In market 1, there is a gain in welfare given by area $(a+b)$.

Figure 2.3 Surplus gain due to government policy that increases supply

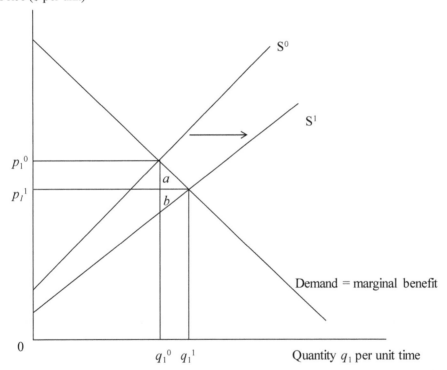

If instead a policy (viz., tax) reduces the supply of q_1 (shifting supply from S^1 back to S^0), there is a deadweight loss in market 1 equal to $(a+b)$. In both cases, the area $(a+b)$ is a direct surplus. To the welfare gain (loss) in market 1, one must add (subtract) the indirect surpluses that are measurable in related but distorted markets. The total welfare effect, ΔW, can be decomposed into its direct plus indirect welfare areas. Assuming fixed producer prices, the change in welfare is given by:

$$(2.4) \quad \Delta W \approx \int_{q_1^0}^{q_1^1} [D(q) - S(q)] dq \pm \sum_{j=2}^{n} [P_j - MC_j] \Delta q_j, \qquad \text{(Fundamental Equation)}$$

where q_1^0 is the initial consumption in market 1 before the policy and q_1^1 is the final consumption, and there are n relevant markets. Equation (2.4) is due to Robin Boadway and Neil Bruce (1984) and might be considered the fundamental equation of applied welfare economics. The welfare change given by (2.4) is approximate because P_j and MC_j are assumed to be fixed as q_j changes.

If $q_1^0 < q_1^1$, the outcome of the integral in the first term in (2.4) is positive, while the sign on the second term is negative. Conversely, if $q_1^0 > q_1^1$, the integral in the first term is negative, and the sign on the second

term is necessarily positive. In the case of Figure 2.3, we find that $\int_{q_1^0}^{q_1^1} [D(q) - S(q)] dq = \text{area}(a+b)$.

Now consider the second term in equation (2.4). It refers to the indirect benefits measured in the $n-1$ markets impacted by the change in the price of q_1—that is, the distorted markets of goods and services that are complements or substitutes with respect to q_1. Notice, firstly, that, since prices in other markets are assumed to remain fixed, the indirect welfare measures are approximate. Second, it is possible that a distortion in an affected market takes the form of a subsidy so that marginal cost exceeds price, in which case a reduction in the output of an affected market is socially desirable because the good or amenity costs more to produce than its value to society as given by its price. Third, the indirect surplus might be negative or positive depending on whether the affected markets are substitutes or complements of q_1.

Finally, depending on whether the policy impacting market 1 shifts supply to the right (Figure 2.3) or to the left, the indirect welfare changes will usually offset the direct welfare change measured in market 1, because the distortions in related markets indicate that the policy analysis is in the context of the "second best." However, the indirect surpluses measured by the second term in (2.4) should not offset the direct welfare change measured by the first term, because this would imply that the original budget allocation was not optimal. Yet, some argue that, because we are in the realm of "second best" and if markets are sufficiently distorted, including market 1, it might be possible that the indirect surpluses offset the direct surpluses. In the context of Figure 2.3, this would imply that the direct benefit of the subsidy (ignoring its cost), which equals area $(a+b)$, could be offset so that ΔW is negative—the overall benefit of subsidizing q_1 is negative. Although unlikely for the reason already noted, the mathematics do not prevent this possibility.

It is important to note that environmental spillovers, such as global greenhouse gas emissions, also fall into the category of indirect surplus. Since markets are absent, price cannot possibly equal marginal cost. Therefore, it is necessary to determine the costs (benefits) in those markets using nonmarket valuation. It is also important to recognize that environmental damage is measured as a loss to consumers similar to lost consumer surplus.[3] The cost of environmental damage is measured as lost surplus, which becomes a benefit (i.e., the damages avoided) of a project that reduces the environmental "bad" (concentration of CO_2 in the atmosphere). When all of the changes in surpluses resulting from a project are appropriately summed, the net (discounted) social benefit must exceed the capital cost of the project.

Finally, the criteria for judging whether one project is preferred or somehow better than another from society's perspective are the same as those used under private CBA. That is, the equations above remain valid. What then is the difference between the private and social perspective? The difference is determined by what one measures and includes as costs and benefits, and the discount rate that one employs (which is considered further in section 2.6).

2.2.3 Total Economic Value

Another way to look at social CBA is via the concept of total economic value (TEV), which is the sum of direct use values, indirect use values, non-use values, and the values associated with remaining flexible in the face of risk and uncertainty. A summary of the various types of values that comprise TEV is provided in Figure 2.4. In the figure, it is clear that many of the values that economists attribute to natural resources are ignored in private valuations, and even in the evaluation of public projects. In particular, the focus is generally on the far left branch of the figure, namely, on consumptive direct use values. From Figure 2.4, TEV is given by:

(2.5)   TEV = Total use value + total non-use value + value of remaining flexible,

where the value of remaining flexible is related to risk and uncertainty. All values are discounted so that they are in present value terms.

Consider the example of a policy regulating biofuel content in gasoline that causes wetlands, native rangeland, and/or forested areas to be converted to crop production. Let E_t refer to the net environmental benefits that these lands provide in their original state at time t. These benefits include ecosystem services of wetlands in reducing soil salinity and seepage of nitrogen from adjacent cropped lands into ground and surface water, benefits of wildlife habitat, and so forth. Of these environmental benefits, ecosystem services may be the most difficult to measure, while other benefits are easier to measure. For example, nonmarket valuation surveys and other evaluation techniques can be used to determine the values that recreationists place on wildlife viewing, hiking, hunting of waterfowl and ungulates, and so on; but the benefits of reduced soil salinity and nitrogen seepage can only be measured using a great deal of detective work and sophisticated theory and estimation techniques.

---

[3] Technically, consumer surplus is not the theoretically correct measure in the case of nonmarket environmental amenities; rather, the correct measures are compensating and equivalent surplus (variation).

Figure 2.4 Components of total economic value (TEV)

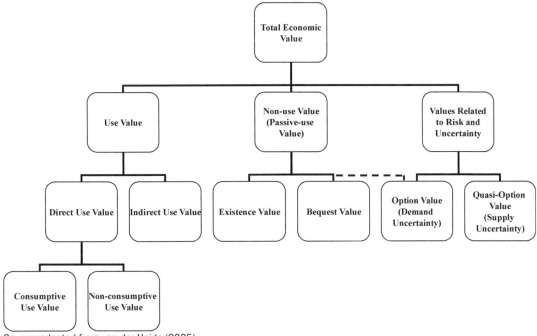

Source: adapted from van der Heide (2005)

In the context of Figure 2.4, E can be thought of as the various use values that the wetland, native grassland, and forested areas provide; it consists of values related to consumptive use (hunting, grazing services), non-consumptive use (wildlife viewing, hiking), and indirect use (ecosystem services such as waste assimilation and water quality control). Then the cost-benefit rule for implementing a biofuels regulation that adversely affects marginal land currently in its natural state is:

$$(2.6) \quad \sum_{t=0}^{T} \frac{B_t - C_t - E_t}{(1+r)^t} > 0,$$

where B_t are the benefits from the policy in each period t; C_t are the operating, maintenance, and replacement costs plus capital costs of investments brought about by the regulation; and r is the social rate of discount. Benefits in this case would include the value of reduced CO_2 emissions brought about by the policy. The time horizon is T, which is the expected life of the project. In period T, there may be salvage benefits and/or environmental or other clean-up costs.

The variable E is treated as a cost separate from C in order to emphasize that the environmental costs are different from the commercial operating costs of regulating biofuel content in gasoline, with the commercial costs but not environmental costs borne by the energy provider. Depending on the project or policy, the environmental costs might include costs associated with the transport and storage of hazardous wastes, potential radiation from and terrorist threats to a nuclear power facility, and the loss of visual amenities when a landscape is converted from its more natural state to the monoculture of energy crops such as corn. While one expects E to be positive because it measures lost environmental benefits, there might be situations where it is negative and not a cost to society (e.g., tree planting on denuded land with biomass used to reduce CO_2 emissions from fossil fuels).[4]

In the context of the conversion of wetlands, native grassland, and/or forest to crop production, there are two further considerations. First, even in a deterministic world with no uncertainty about their potential future loss, natural areas have existence and bequest value. People attribute value to the knowledge that these natural areas exist and can be passed to the next generation, even though they themselves do not visit or intend to visit them. In Figure 2.4, we refer to such value as non-use value.

Second, there is likely to be uncertainty both with regard to supply and demand. Demand uncertainty is related to people's concern about the future availability of environmental services that may be threatened by the loss of wetlands due to a policy that converts the natural area to crop production. It results because future income and preferences are uncertain, such that individuals might value the environmental amenity more in the future. Option value (OV) is the amount a person would be willing to pay for an environmental amenity, over and above its current value, to maintain the option of having that environmental asset available in the future. Option value is usually measured in conjunction with existence and bequest value (as indicated by the dashed line in Figure 2.4); indeed, nonmarket valuation techniques generally elicit all three at the same time making it difficult to separate them, although this can be done in surveys by asking questions that specifically focus on separating option value into its various components.

Supply uncertainty is related to irreversibility, and its measurement is known as quasi-option value (QOV). The idea behind QOV is that, as the prospect of receiving better information in the future improves, the incentive to remain flexible and take advantage of this information also increases. Having access to better information results in the revision of one's initial beliefs, so it is "greater variability of beliefs" rather than "improved information" that leads one to choose greater flexibility over potentially irreversible development (say, as a result of cropping marginal agricultural land). Thus, QOV is always positive.

The problem with QOV is that it is also difficult to measure in practice, so its use in cost-benefit analysis is limited.[5] Rather, the concept provides support for the notion of a safe minimum standard of conservation, which suggests that an irreversible development should be delayed unless the costs of doing so are prohibitive. This concept is discussed in more detail in section 2.5 below.

The cost-benefit model is extended to account for all of these costs and benefits. The decision rule to allow the conversion of natural land, which currently serves as habitat for waterfowl and ungulates, to energy-crop production is now:

$$(2.7) \quad \sum_{t=0}^{T} \frac{B_t - C_t - E_t}{(1+r)^t} - (TNUV + OV + QOV) > 0,$$

where $TNUV$ refers to total non-use value, and the remaining terms in parentheses refer to the existence value

---

[4] An example of an integrated social cost-benefit analysis that relies on TEV is provided in Chapter 6.6.
[5] For marginal agricultural land that provides wildlife habitat benefits and visual amenities, OV and $TNUV$ (total non-use value) are measured using contingent valuation (Chapter 3), while QOV can be determined using an optimization procedure for addressing uncertainty known as stochastic dynamic programming.

of the marginal land and the benefits of keeping the land in its current state and remaining flexible as opposed to developing land by growing crops on it. This formulation takes into account all social costs and benefits associated with the proposed project.

2.2.4 Total (Average) Value versus Marginal Value

Several caveats remain. What is neglected in the preceding framework is the impact that the existence of alternative sites for producing energy crops and the availability of alternative amenities have on nonmarket (environmental) values. For example, what someone is willing to pay for an option to visit a particular wetlands area is sensitive to the availability of similar sites in other locations. If there is an abundance of wetlands, one expects option value to be small; if there are few wetlands elsewhere, option value is much larger. Hence, it is not the total or average environmental value that is important, but the marginal value. Too often the focus is on total or average value as opposed to marginal value.

Making decisions on the basis of average or total value leads to loss of economic welfare, as illustrated with the aid of Figure 2.5. In the figure, the curve labeled AB represents the average benefits from the environmental amenity (not to be confused with the demand function for the amenity), and is determined as the total area under the marginal benefit (demand) curve, labeled MB, divided by the levels of the amenity. The marginal cost (MC) of providing the environmental amenity increases as more of the amenity is provided; for example, if the costs of providing wetlands equal the foregone net returns from cropping, it is necessary to convert increasingly higher-quality cropland into wetlands, which increases the per hectare costs of providing the next wetland area. A decision based on average (total) value would lead to the provision of g^* amount of the amenity (determined from point x), while the correct amount to provide as determined by economic efficiency considerations is g^E. If the decision is based on total value, the social cost of providing the last unit of the amenity is given by c^*, but the marginal benefit to society of this unit is zero. The total loss in economic well-being from providing too much of the amenity (the cost to society) is therefore given by area ($xyzg^*$).[6]

This thinking cuts both ways. Suppose, rather than an environmental amenity, the object is the output of energy crops. If a decision is made on the basis of average and not marginal returns, the last acre planted to energy crops would cost more to plant and harvest than it yields in revenue from the sale of the energy crops.

---

[6] In Figure 2.5, this is the difference between the area under MC (which equals total costs) and that under MB (total benefits) between g^E and g^*. It is the net social cost of providing g^* of the environmental amenity.

Figure 2.5 Marginal vs. average benefits of decision-making

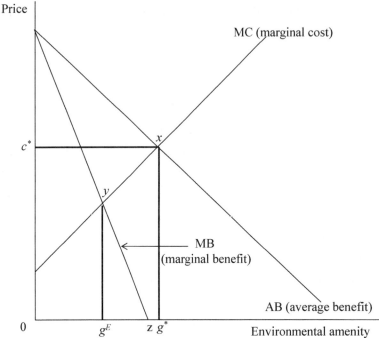

2.2.5 Conclusion

Social cost-benefit analysis assumes that everything of interest to the decision maker can somehow be measured in monetary terms. Yet, there remain some things of importance to society that simply cannot be included in the money metric. Since these items are only important if they are somehow (directly or indirectly) affected by the project, these intangibles must be evaluated or judged against the money metric. If the focus is on employment (which is not a true economic welfare measure), any gain in employment that a policy/project brings about needs to be evaluated in terms of the change in the apparent surpluses that result when jobs are created. This is preferably measured in terms of the forgone opportunities (loss in economic surpluses) per job created. If the focus is on CO_2 emissions, a project that reduces CO_2 in the atmosphere needs to be evaluated with respect to the change in a society's surpluses (economic well-being broadly defined). Society might accept a project that removes CO_2 from the atmosphere at a cost of $25 per tonne of CO_2 (tCO_2), but perhaps not at a cost of $250 per tCO_2.

Finally, the dynamics of wildlife and the agriculture–nature ecosystem will affect both the value of the agricultural crop and the environmental service benefits. If wetlands can be recreated on cropped land after a short period of time, so that the former attributes of the natural area are regained, planting energy crops is not irreversible and the quasi-option value is negligible. If it takes a very long period of time to recover the wetlands, the development of cropland may essentially be irreversible, but the benefits of planting energy crops and converting marginal agricultural lands may still exceed costs and be a worthwhile undertaking.

There is a conundrum here because the irreversibility of wetlands conversion to production of energy crops needs to be balanced against the potential irreversibility caused by the climate change that energy crops seek to mitigate. This issue is considered further in the final subsection of this chapter.

In the next subsection, we examine the issue of so-called intangibles in the context of what has been referred to as multiple accounts analysis. In such an analysis, the surplus and rent measures discussed in this section constitute one account, while various intangibles constitute the other accounts. These intangibles may nonetheless be measured in monetary terms, but one must take care not to include such measures in the cost-benefit account, which is considered to be the economic efficiency account (or the net economic benefit account). The separateness of accounts is clearer in the case where measurement is in non-monetary units, because the distinctiveness of accounts is clear, and aggregating across accounts is not possible.

2.3 Multiple Accounts and Alternative Criteria

The multiple accounts framework departs from social cost-benefit analysis in subtle ways, but two points remain relevant: First, social CBA and the measurement of spillovers or externalities form an integral component of multiple accounts analysis. Second, because some stakeholders will have greater affinity for one account over the others, the existence of several accounts should not become an excuse for denying the need to trade off intangibles against the money metric of social CBA. When no account is taken to be the standard against which all other accounts are to be judged, reaching consensus among stakeholders can be difficult.

Project evaluation originated in the United States as legislators sought guidelines to determine whether publicly funded resource development projects were likely to achieve their aims. One guideline developed by US legislators in the Flood Control Act of 1936 required that the benefits of water development projects, "to whomsoever they may accrue," should exceed all the social costs related to the project. This requirement subsequently developed into the US Water Resources Council's (WRC) Principles and Standards (P&S) for water project evaluation, which appeared in the US Federal Register in 1973 and 1979. In 1973, the WRC identified four objectives for project evaluation:

1. All the benefits and costs of a project had to be considered in the evaluation, regardless of who bore the costs and who received the benefits. This is the objective of national economic development (economic efficiency).
2. Impacts on the environment had to be calculated and included in the cost-benefit analysis. This implied that the nonmarket benefits of recreation, environmental degradation, et cetera, had to be taken into account.
3. The regional benefits of resource development projects were to be included explicitly in the analysis, making it possible to justify a project on the basis of its regional development benefits.
4. Finally, the impact of a project on social well-being had to be taken into account. For example, the analyst or planner was to take into account the impact of the project on certain groups in society (e.g., on African Americans or on those with lower incomes). This objective, then, required explicit consideration of social issues in evaluating resource development projects.

The 1973 P&S for evaluating projects focused only on the first objective. The 1979 P&S attempted to extend the evaluation methodology to the second objective by including methods for monetizing some nonmarket values, particularly recreational values (viz., water recreation on reservoirs) and some environmental values related to improved water quality. Unlike in 1973, the 1979 P&S included detailed instructions for evaluating projects. However, the last two objectives were not addressed, perhaps because the WRC did not feel these could be handled within the P&S framework then proposed.

The 1979 P&S were subsequently replaced by Principles and Guidelines (P&G). Since it was imperative to include items two, three, and four into the evaluation process, the 1983 P&G did so by recognizing non-commensurability among the various objectives, which was not explicitly done in the earlier P&S. Thus, the WRC adopted a *multiple accounts* approach to project evaluation.

Four accounts are identified in the P&G, and these are similar to the four categories indicated in the P&S. The important difference between the approaches is the recognition that the various accounts deal with different objectives and are not commensurable. Thus, the 1983 P&G include a description of methods for displaying the different accounts. The four accounts are as follows:

1. National Economic Development (NED) Account
2. Environmental Quality (EQ) Account
3. Regional Economic Development (RED) Account
4. Other Social Effects (OSE) Account

Cost-benefit analysis is used only to evaluate those items that can be monetized, namely, those found in the NED account and the components of the EQ and RED accounts that could be quantified in monetary terms. This is not to suggest, however, that the monetary values are commensurable (as shown in the discussion about employment and multipliers below). Items that cannot be monetized are to be presented in each of the EQ, RED, and OSE accounts and are briefly described in the following paragraphs.

2.3.1 Environmental Quality

According to the P&G, environmental items that are to be displayed in the EQ account are ecological, cultural, and aesthetic attributes. Ecological attributes include functional aspects of the environment (e.g., assimilative capacity, erosion, nutrient cycling, succession) and structural aspects such as plant and animal species; chemical and physical properties of air, water, and soil (e.g., pH of rainfall); and so on. Cultural attributes are evidence of past and present habitation that can help in understanding and propagating human life. Aesthetic attributes include sights, scents, sounds, tastes, impressions, and so forth of the environment. It is clear that, while these attributes could be measured in monetary terms (using nonmarket valuation methods), it may be too costly or difficult to do so (hence the term "intangibles"). However, they can be measured in other ways that include both quantity indicators that employ numeric and non-numeric scales and quality indicators such as "good" and "bad." It is obvious that the EQ attributes need to be presented in a clear and concise fashion if they are to be of use in the decision-making framework.

Several principles govern the enumeration of items within the environmental quality account. Both an interdisciplinary approach and public input are required in this process, although the means for involving the public is left to the discretion of the planning agency. In all cases, however, the EQ attributes are to be displayed in a way that highlights the comparison between the "with project" and "without project" scenarios.

2.3.2 Regional Economic Development and Employment: Indirect Benefits

There is much confusion in cost-benefit analysis about the regional impacts of resource development projects and the use of multipliers to take into consideration so-called (but misleadingly labeled) indirect benefits (including job creation).[7] Regional impacts are the purview of the RED account, and these have historically been addressed using input-output models, because such models can be used to develop activity and employment multipliers. Input-output models and similar regional accounting frameworks are only able to identify changes in value-added throughout the regional economy (i.e., changes in GDP) brought about by the project or policy, but variations in value-added are a measure of changes in economic activity and not a measure of economic surplus (benefits or costs) per se. Rather, value-added represents an upper limit on the opportunity cost of the resources employed in the various activities that generate the value-added. The RED account recognizes that it is wrong to sum the regional and national economic benefits—increases in GDP brought about by government expenditures cannot in and of themselves be considered a benefit measure because the opportunity costs of using the funds in another fashion are neglected. Simply because two items (efficiency and changes in GDP) are measured in monetary terms does not imply that they are commensurable.

One possible approach to valuing the opportunity cost of a project is to compare the effects of the alternative use of the funds (as determined from an appropriate input-output model) with the effects generated by the proposed spending on the project. The former might be thought of as project-specific opportunity costs and might be positive or negative—or inconsequential. These opportunity costs need to be included on the basis of the with-without principle of project evaluation. It is necessary to subtract the benefits of the alternative project from those of the proposed project, in which case the proposed project's net indirect benefits might actually be negative.

The takeaway point is this: The economic efficiency of the resource development project is overstated if changes in value-added are included while ignoring the potential value-added generated by using the funds in an alternative endeavor (perhaps even leaving the funds with taxpayers). Use of an appropriate general equilibrium model would prevent this kind of confusion.

When labor resources are not fully employed, their shadow (true) value is not given by the observed wage rate. If there is persistent unemployment of resources, particularly labor, the opportunity cost of such resources (their shadow price) is essentially zero and an argument can then be made to include the value-

---

[7] These are not indirect benefits (as discussed in section 2.2.1), because they are not a welfare measure. These might more appropriately be considered indirect "impacts" as opposed to "effects."

added benefits of a project in the CBA. But there are a number of arguments against this view.

First, it needs to be determined if unemployment is indeed persistent, and, if it is, whether the cause is structural (e.g., a poorly trained labor force) or not. If it is structural, a publicly funded regional development project aimed at job creation will not help local residents as it will attract workers from outside the region. From a national perspective, job losses in other regions need to be counted as a negative impact of the project.

Suppose high unemployment is not structural. This does not imply, however, that a proposed resource development project is the best means for creating jobs. Macroeconomic policies may be much more effective in reducing unemployment. Indeed, there is a built-in problem with capital intensive resource development projects. Several years to more than a decade is often needed to obtain authorization for proceeding with a resource development project, and this is also true for many other projects (e.g., replacing an old bridge, building a sewage treatment plant). The macroeconomic situation might change dramatically between the time of project conception and construction. Unemployment may no longer be a problem and, as construction begins, the project may simply bid up labor costs, perhaps even making the project uneconomic. Relying on large projects to deal with unemployment could turn out to be wrongheaded.

Finally, if the shadow price of labor is zero, the opportunity cost of capital must also be higher than is evident from the observed rate of return to capital. The reason is that returns from capital must be diverted to support unemployed labor. Therefore, since the discount rate is determined by the opportunity cost of funds used in the project, the discount rate to be employed in the analysis must be higher than would otherwise be the case. The higher discount rate militates against resource development projects, and offsets the supposed benefits due to secondary or regional impacts.

If a public project is funded by an increase in local taxes, an interesting question that arises is whether or not the same multiplier is used to measure the contractionary impacts of those taxes as is used to measure the expansionary impacts due to the project itself. Use of the same multiplier leads to offsetting impacts, although the overall impact would likely be negative as a result of leakages—the revenue required to fund the project will be greater than the project costs because of transaction costs and inefficiencies inherent in tax collection and government bureaucracies. Likewise, spending public funds on projects to create jobs, while popular with politicians, ignores the jobs lost elsewhere due to the contractionary impact of higher taxes.

The RED account recognizes that, despite being valued in monetary terms, regional impacts (changes in economic activity) are not the same as economic efficiency or national economic development. Benefits to a region may be costs to the nation as a whole. The existence of a separate RED account simply recognizes that regional income transfers are important (just as the OSE account recognizes that income transfers among various groups in society might be important). By separating the NED and RED accounts, the incompatibility between national economic development and income distribution among regions is explicitly recognized.

2.3.3 Other Social Effects

The OSE account includes items that are not included in the other three accounts but are important for planning. While the P&G provide no procedures for evaluating other social effects, it does indicate that such effects include "urban and community impacts; life, health, and safety factors; displacement; long-term productivity; and energy requirements and energy conservation" (US Water Resources Council 1983, p. 12). The guidelines also call for the inclusion of the effects that a project has on income distribution, employment, the fiscal impacts on state and local governments, quality of community life, and so on. While some of these effects can be measured in monetary terms and are to be included in the economic efficiency (NED) account, others need to be displayed using guidelines similar to those of the EQ account. It appears that public agencies have substantial freedom within the planning process to include whatever items they wish in the OSE account and how they are to be displayed.

2.3.4 Concluding Observations about Multiple Accounts

A problem occurs with the multiple accounts approach when all of the accounts are given equal status—i.e., when no account is given precedence over any other account. In that case, proponents of any one account are not required to seek compromise, conceding to trade off one benefit for another, but they tend to become entrenched in their position. The WRC's P&G are clear that environmental quality, regional economic development, and other social effects need to be compared against or in terms of the economic efficiency account. That is, trade-offs between non-monetized effects (or intangibles) and economic efficiency must be made clear. This implies that social CBA takes precedence over other considerations, or that, at the very least, the cost of any deviation from an economically optimal decision must be identified in terms of its welfare loss.

It is important to recognize that project appraisal must always compare the situation "with and without" the project, program, or policy in place. Thus, a proper CBA will take into account all opportunity costs, including indirect costs associated with market failure (e.g., monopoly, unpriced environmental impacts), whose measurement was discussed in the previous section. Social CBA will ignore items that cannot be measured in monetary terms, not because these items are unimportant, but because they cannot be integrated into the money metric of applied welfare economics. They are an aside, addressed in descriptive terms, if at all. The multiple accounts framework, on the other hand, requires first off that a proper social CBA be completed, but then that intangibles be explicitly considered, with changes in such intangibles explicitly traded off against changes in economic efficiency. Such an approach would identify the social cost of creating a local job, for example, thereby enabling the decision maker to determine whether it is worthwhile undertaking a project that leads to local jobs.

Although the difference between cost-benefit analysis and the multiple accounts approach is a subtle one, it is nonetheless important enough to warrant the adoption of a multiple accounts approach for the evaluation of public projects, programs, and policies. This recommendation comes with a warning, however:

Application of a multiple accounts approach to evaluation should never become an excuse for neglecting a proper social cost-benefit analysis. The reason is that, outside of the surplus and rent measures employed in cost-benefit analysis, there is no other consistent, theoretically appropriate means of judging projects. The alternative is that one ends up trying to compare apples and oranges, in which case any decision can be justified.[8]

2.4 Alternative Methods for Evaluating Projects

There exist many alternatives to social cost-benefit analysis. Some of these are quite sophisticated and address some of the weaknesses associated with the use of money metrics. While there is nothing wrong with many of the alternatives examined below, since project evaluation refers, after all, to any consistent set of criteria for analyzing decisions, our view is that the cost-benefit criterion based on economic surpluses is the most theoretically sound and consistent approach. Nonetheless, this does not mean that information available from some of these alternative evaluation methods could not inform the decision-making process.

2.4.1 Cost-Effectiveness Analysis

Where an objective can be realized by alternative means but the objective itself cannot be valued in monetary terms, cost-effectiveness analysis (CEA) can be used to determine the least-cost means of achieving the objective. CEA is often used for evaluating health, education, environmental, and defense programs and policies, because program/policy benefits are generally not easily or accurately measured in monetary terms. CEA aims at identifying the least-cost strategy for achieving a non-economic objective and involves comparing the costs of various mutually exclusive, technically feasible project options and selecting the one with the lowest costs—i.e., the most cost-effective one.

Most of the CEA literature is in the context of the health sector, where stakeholders are reluctant to measure health impacts and human lives saved (or bettered) in monetary terms. Nonetheless, CEA can be applied in other sectors just as easily.

Recommendations for the use of CEA generally warn that the conclusions of CEA must be weighed against a variety of political and distributional considerations. The information that CEA contributes is often summarized by the cost-effectiveness ratio, which is the cost per unit health effect achieved by using a particular health intervention. The cost-effectiveness ratio ranks health interventions so that health resources are deployed in the most efficient manner. CEA starts by identifying the proposed intervention and its alternatives, including the alternative of doing nothing. Alternatives are then compared using the cost-effectiveness ratio:

---

[8] As an example, suppose you rank the potential purchase of an automobile by examining characteristics and rating each. Cost, fuel efficiency, color, power, and other attributes are rated on a scale of 1 to 10. Cars are ranked according to the sum of the attribute scores. Would a person really choose the car with the highest score? Perhaps, but it is unlikely as the ordinal ratings are not comparable unless they are converted to a common, cardinal metric.

$$(2.8) \quad \text{CE ratio} = \frac{C_0 - C_k}{E_0 - E_k},$$

where subscripts 0 and k describe, respectively, the intervention under consideration and the alternative to which it is compared; C_0 and C_k are associated present values of costs; and E_0 and E_k are the respective health outcomes (measured in some fashion). When performing a cost-effectiveness analysis, the cost-effectiveness ratio of the intervention in question is compared to the cost-effectiveness ratios of other commonly used forms of medical care. If it is relatively low, the intervention is considered to be a good value.

The art of CEA is proper accounting of costs and health outcomes. Typical measures of health outcomes are years of life saved or years of quality-adjusted life saved. These values are obtained from statistical medical experience. When dealing with environmental issues, the denominator from the cost-effectiveness ratio would contain the relevant variable for the environmental problem of concern—it could be emissions, concentration of pollutants, energy savings, or nuclear waste produced. For example, policies to reduce atmospheric levels of CO_2 might be compared in terms of their cost per tonne of CO_2.

One challenge in using CEA is the choice of a cost-effectiveness ratio cutoff for decision-making. Further, CEA may not be welfare enhancing because it often ignores all possible options (only binary and not multiple comparisons are made) and mixed strategies. Nonetheless, it is a rigorous method for bringing economic considerations into decisions regarding health care, and it has the advantage of acceptance by different stakeholders. However, our view is that, for taking into account intangibles (items that cannot be measured in monetary terms), both multiple-criteria decision-making (next subsection) and multiple accounts analysis are preferred over cost-effectiveness analysis.

2.4.2 Multiple Criteria Decision-Making

Another alternative is to employ multiple-criteria decision-making (MCDM). This tool provides decision makers with the trade-offs among all of the different objectives, so that the explicit effects on other accounts can be clearly identified when a choice is made. These are the opportunity costs as expressed in both monetary (foregone economic efficiency) and non-monetary terms. This is both the major advantage of MCDM and its weakness. As long as trade-offs are made with respect to the money metric of cost-benefit analysis (i.e., economic efficiency), MCDM adheres to the multiple accounts criteria we considered above. In the context of energy projects, if trade-offs are made relative to other metrics (e.g., jobs versus carbon uptake without regard to efficiency), consistency in the evaluation of energy projects will flounder as society may end up not pursuing the "best" suite of energy projects available.

Nonetheless, MCDM can serve a very important purpose within the multiple accounts framework. The reason we favor the use of MCDM within multiple accounts analysis is because not all possible spillovers can be measured in monetary terms—some are truly intangible in this regard. MCDM can deal with objectives that are not commensurable in a consistent and scientifically sound fashion. It enables the analyst to identify positions that are sub-optimal in the sense that two or more objectives can be improved simultaneously. For example, MCDM might suggest an alternative energy project to the one under investigation, one that generates more jobs and more carbon benefits while retaining the same levels of biodiversity, economic efficiency, and so on. The advantage is that, in making comparisons with the money metric, MCDM yields shadow prices (i.e., monetary values) for the intangibles, which could not be done in another framework of analysis.

One area of increasing interest in the development of MCDM is the use of fuzzy logic, which has an advantage in quantifying language (see section 3.3.4). This approach recognizes that many of the concepts involved in decision-making are far from clear or precise; in essence, they are fuzzy. Fuzzy sets provide an explicit way of representing vagueness about what objectives are and how one might quantify them. However, implementing fuzzy MCDM in practice is challenging, and the approach has not been accepted by governments or NGOs.

2.4.3 Life-Cycle Assessment

Life-cycle assessment (LCA) evaluates the effects that a product has on the environment over its entire life (hence it is sometimes referred to as cradle-to-grave analysis). The objective is to trace the product after its usefulness has ended and it has been discarded; thus, it has the potential for increasing resource efficiency and, more importantly for private owners, decreasing liability. It can be used to study the environmental impact of either a product or the function the product is designed to perform. As LCA is a continuous process, companies can begin an LCA at any point in the product/function cycle.

LCA can be used to develop business purchasing strategies, improve product and process design, set eco-labeling criteria, and otherwise communicate about the environmental aspects of products. The key elements of LCA are to identify and quantify the environmental loads involved throughout the product cycle (e.g., energy and raw materials consumed, emissions and wastes generated) and to evaluate the potential environmental impacts of these loads.

Over the last ten years there has been a rapid expansion in the demand for and use of LCA, fueled by both industry and government. For industry, a major use is in characterizing current operating practices with a view towards how industry stands in relation to current and proposed legislative measures. A series of LCA performed by any company over consecutive years will fully determine that company's operating practices as well as establish manufacturing trends. LCA can be used to identify potential resource savings and/or savings related to compliance with government regulations. Governments, on the other hand, can use LCA to heighten awareness of the implications of proposed legislation, especially in cases where the effects of legislation run counter to original intentions, so that legislation can be amended before it is adopted. An example of this has occurred in the setting of realistic recycling targets, with some countries having tempered recycling requirements so that they were more effective in achieving ultimate as opposed to proximate objectives. Companies in both the developed and developing world have used LCA to meet ISO 14000 series environmental standards.

How does life-cycle analysis relate to cost-benefit analysis? Clearly, LCA could be useful in identifying (external) costs, which are often ignored in standard social CBA, not because they are unimportant but because they are not recognized. For example, when personal computers and many other sorts of home electronics became readily available, their disposability was never on the radar screen of most analysts, regardless of the evaluation method they employed. Nonetheless, an LCA would have identified this as an environmental problem that only now is being addressed.[9] The EU has passed legislation requiring that automobiles must be made of environmentally friendly materials that are either entirely recyclable or capable of completely deteriorating and becoming benign to the environment.

LCA might fail to estimate the real value of externalities, however, when dealing with non-uniform pollutants. LCA sums emissions independently in the place where they are released. This works fine with greenhouse gases like CO_2, because the marginal damage of one tonne of CO_2 emissions is the same regardless of where it has been released.[10] But for pollutants such as SO_2, NO_x, lead, and particulates, the marginal damage from pollution is highly dependent on location. For instance, one tonne of lead released in the center of a city results in greater damage to society than one tonne of lead released in a sparsely populated area. Since LCA gives the same value to emissions regardless of where they are released, it could provide misleading information when non-uniform pollutants are released at different locations.

2.4.4 Cumulative Effects Analysis

Economists have long considered the problem of cumulative effects in an externality context. For example, many municipalities have waste treatment plants that have a limited capacity. Efficient pricing requires that residents pay the marginal cost of waste treatment, and this is usually done. However, as more residents are connected to the system, the capacity is eventually exceeded. The dilemma for efficient pricing is that the last person/firm added to the system (the marginal user) would need to pay the entire cost of building the new plant. This would be blatantly unfair as the infra-marginal users (those whose use eventually leads to overcapacity) are just as responsible for overloading the system as the last user. But how then does a new treatment plant with greater capacity get funded? One way is to charge a system development fee whenever a new user is connected to the system, in the eventuality that the plant's capacity is exceeded.

Such a case is reasonably straightforward to analyze because measurement of cumulative effects is possible, although municipalities often fail to implement system development charges (or do so simply to generate revenue that is spent elsewhere). From the perspective of energy development projects and their environmental impacts, cumulative effects analysis seeks to measure the point at which the "stream of

---

[9] Many discarded electronic products ended up in China, because the Chinese government was willing to receive these wastes for a fee (although China recently began to stop this practice). This does not solve the environmental problem, but only shifts it from one jurisdiction to another.
[10] Scientists track carbon released as a result of wood burning for energy. The carbon enters the atmosphere but CO_2 is then removed by growing trees and stored in biomass; however, a distinction is made as to whether the carbon is sequestered in forest ecosystems, oceans, or other carbon sinks.

wastes" or environmental damage becomes sufficiently great that investments in conservation and environmental improvements are warranted. Determining cumulative effects is beneficial (and can inform a cost-benefit analysis), but a cumulative effects analysis cannot say anything about policy design.

2.5 Extreme Events and Irreversibility

There are three means for addressing extreme events and the possibility of irreversibility resulting from a decision either to do something or not to do something. The first is to determine the cost of the extreme event or irreversibility and the probability of its occurrence, and then include the expected cost in cost-benefit analysis. If the probability of the event and its cost, or some combination of the two, is sufficiently high, the expected cost may be sufficiently great that avoiding the extreme event or irreversibility will be the optimal decision. In other cases, the cost will be small and the cost-benefit criterion will indicate that the project should proceed. In cases where the probability of the extreme event/irreversibility is not known and/or the cost associated with it is vague, Monte Carlo cost-benefit analysis (simulation across the range of probabilities and possible costs) can be used to determine the probability that the social CBA criterion is violated.[11] This is a consistent approach (as argued below).

Second, economists have long debated another criterion that is invoked only when dealing with extreme events and irreversibility, namely, the notion of a safe minimum standard of conservation. Begin by ignoring the probability of the occurrence of any event and consider the maximum potential loss (maximum cost) associated with any strategy under some state of nature. We could choose the strategy that minimizes the maximum loss—the min-max strategy. The problem with such a decision criterion is that it would prevent us from choosing a project whose net benefit to society might be very large simply because there is a very small risk of an extreme event that imposes large costs. It is also possible that we avoid choosing the "best" strategy because it has a potential loss that is only slightly larger than the loss that would occur by doing nothing. That is, the min-max criterion could lead us to choose in favor of a strategy with a high probability of large loss simply because the alternative is a project (which might be to do nothing) with an extremely low probability of a similar but only slightly greater loss.

Clearly, the min-max strategy is not in the best interests of society because it fails to take into account event/outcome probabilities and the scale of cost differences. The safe minimum standard of conservation addresses this and other shortcomings via the following decision rule:

> *Safe minimum standard*: Choose in favor of the strategy that provides the greatest flexibility and smallest potential loss, unless the social cost of doing so is "unacceptably large."

This rule places development of natural resources beyond routine trade-offs, although the safe minimum standard does not permit deferral of resource development, say, at a cost that is intolerably high. The problem

---

[11] For example, under the social CBA criterion, a project is desirable only if the benefit-cost ratio is greater than 1.0. Monte Carlo CBA might generate 10,000 benefit-cost ratios, of which some proportion are less than 1.0. Knowing the probability that irreversibility can lead to a negative B–C ratio informs the decision.

lies with the term "unacceptably large." Who decides when the cost is unacceptably large? In some cases, society can readily agree to accept risks that are extremely small but the potential benefits are large. In other cases, it is difficult to make such a decision and it must be made in the political arena, with all of the facts made available to citizens.

The third criterion for situations where there exists the potential for extreme events and/or irreversibility is the most commonly applied: the precautionary principle. Environmentalists define it as follows: "When an activity raises threats of harm to human health or the environment, precautionary measures should be taken even if some cause and effect relationships are not fully established scientifically."[12] The EU has taken the lead in promoting the precautionary principle as a basis for making decisions about the environment, using it to prevent research, development, and adoption of genetically modified organisms in agriculture under the Cartagena Protocol on Biosafety (2000) to the 1992 UN Convention on Biodiversity.

The precautionary principle is logically inconsistent, however. For example, a decision based on the precautionary principle would prevent a country from building nuclear power plants, even though doing so would reduce environmental and health problems associated with acceptable means of generating electricity. For example, wind turbines kill bats and raptors, and disturb sleep, while biomass burning leads to pollution and might actually increase emissions of CO_2 that contribute to climate change. Indeed, wind turbines would not have been allowed had the precautionary principle been invoked. As Cass Sunstein (2005b) states, "Taken seriously, [the precautionary principle] can be paralyzing, providing no direction at all. In contrast, balancing costs against benefits can offer the foundation of a principled approach for making difficult decisions."

The use of either the safe minimum standard or the precautionary principle implies that one no longer employs social cost-benefit analysis as the decision criterion. In the case of safe minimum standard, the social CBA criterion is jettisoned when the costs of avoiding irreversibility are considered intolerable, regardless of the size of any net benefits identified by a proper CBA. In the case of the precautionary principle, no other criteria are employed unless there is no risk whatsoever of damage to human health or the environment. The chances of that in the case of energy projects is small—wind turbines endanger birds, fossil fuels lead to global warming, hydro dams endanger fish, biomass energy encourages destruction of wildlife habitat because marginal lands are brought into crop production, there is a risk of nuclear meltdown if nuclear energy is used, and so on.

Again, the proper way for dealing with extreme events and irreversibility is to estimate all of the costs and benefits of a project, taking into account all possible spillovers. Risks and people's perceptions of risk, and expert judgments of health and environmental risks and the ranges of costs associated with spillovers, can be employed in Monte Carlo simulation to determine the probability that an energy project results in losses to society, and the distribution of those losses. This information can then be used to determine whether

---

[12] Wingspread Statement on the Precautionary Principle, 1998, available at The Global Development Research Center, http://www.gdrc.org/u-gov/precaution-3.html [accessed December 3, 2020].

the risks are worth undertaking—whether the benefits associated with accepting the risk (of building a nuclear power plant or oil pipeline, say) are sufficiently great enough.

The problem is that environmental groups often invoke the precautionary principle to block resource and other development projects, while no analysis of the potential environmental costs has ever been undertaken. If provided with transparent cost-benefit information, society might well be willing to accept the small risk of a major oil spill or nuclear accident in return for significant expected net benefits.

2.6 Discounting and Choice of Discount Rate

Because one dollar received today is worth more to an individual (or society) than the same dollar received at some future date (say, even next year), it is necessary to discount future costs and benefits relative to current ones—future dollars are weighted so that they are worth less today. Discounting is necessary to measure and compare the stream of benefits and the stream of costs at a single point in time, whether that is at the beginning or at the end of the time horizon, or even at some intermediate point. The problem is to choose an appropriate discount rate that reflects society's preferences for current over future consumption. A project's desirability or that of some course of action is highly sensitive to the rate of discount. What, then, is the appropriate rate of discount to use in weighting future costs and benefits? This turns out to be a rather difficult question to answer.

2.6.1 Dilemmas in Choosing a Discount Rate in Cost-Benefit Analysis (CBA)

Before getting into complications regarding the treatment of future generations, consider some practical issues. Contemplate first whether a nominal or real rate of discount is to be employed. It is generally preferable not to use a nominal rate of discount because it requires that inflation be taken into account. The allocation of investment and consumption over time is uncertain and based on expectations, and, since it is not possible to predict inflation over the life of a project that could well exceed 100 years, real and not nominal monetary flows should be discounted at a real rate of discount. There is already enough uncertainty about the future to warrant using real rather than unpredictable money flows.

There is also a dilemma concerning the arbitrary advocacy of a very low or zero discount rate to justify large current public investments in highways, waterways, schools and universities, climate change mitigation, and so forth that have high up-front costs but provide large benefits far into the future. They have intergenerational consequences (as discussed below). What happens when public projects are discounted at a very low rate while the rate of return in the private sector, or the market rate of interest, is high? One could argue that, if rates of return in the private sector are high, an optimal strategy might be for the government to delay, perhaps indefinitely, a public project, investing funds earmarked for such a project in the private sector. The future returns from such investments could then be used to compensate those adversely impacted by not going ahead with a project or, in the case of climate change, to subsidize adaptation to climate change. Thus, the use of an arbitrarily low or even zero rate of discount is not a panacea for justifying high current expenditures. Indeed, a proper accounting of opportunity costs (what else can be done with the funds?) might lead to a different conclusion. This has led economists to advocate the use of discount rates for evaluating public projects that are based on the opportunity cost of funds.

Funds to finance public projects could come from income taxes (displacing an equal amount of consumption) or from increased public-sector borrowing. Borrowed funds could displace an equal amount of private investment, so it might be appropriate to use the rate of return in the private sector, which is probably between 7% and 8%; this is known as the *opportunity cost of capital* rate. If borrowed funds originate with private savings or if income taxes are used, a lower interest rate might be justified; this might be referred to as the consumption rate since the interest rate on savings indicates the rate at which an individual trades future consumption for present consumption. In practice, however, public funds come from a variety of sources, so the *opportunity cost of the funds* can be calculated. Suppose that a public investment project costs $100, and that $40 displaces private investment and $60 consumption. If the rate of return to private investments is 8% and the consumption rate of interest is 2%, then the opportunity cost of the funds is 4.4% (= 0.40×8% + 0.60×2%). The main difficulty in deriving the opportunity cost rate is that it is not easy to determine where the *marginal* funds originate. Further, not all government revenues come from income taxes and/or domestic borrowing, as governments earn income through charges, royalties on resource extraction, tariffs on imported goods, and so on.

People clearly behave as if they discount the future because they prefer something today (the sure thing) rather than tomorrow (because it is unsure)—they exhibit an implicit rate of time preference with respect to consumption, so it makes sense as a principle for choosing a discount rate to focus on consumption. Then, the consequences of a government program or regulation should be converted into monetary effects on consumption as opposed to investment, with the consumption effects then discounted at the consumption rate of interest—the rate faced by consumers when they save, rather than businesses when they borrow.

In the United States, the real rate of return on investments by large companies over the period 1926–1990 was about 7% after taxes, while it was 8% over the period 1926–1998. Given a corporate income tax rate of about 35%, the pre-tax rate of return is thus about 11% to 12%. Since individuals in the US pay up to 50% in income taxes, the rate of return to individuals as owners of companies is closer to 4%, which might then be considered the consumption rate of interest—the rate at which people trade off spending over time. Interestingly, the US Office of Management and Budget requires the use of 7% for valuing costs and benefits external to the government and 3% for internal costs and benefits. However, despite this straightforward reasoning for deriving the consumption rate of discount from market data, the consumption rate of interest is difficult to measure. For example, people willingly invest their savings in Treasury bills and other guaranteed investments that yield as little as 2% or less after taxes; but these are riskless investments that might be considered safe havens during times of financial crisis.

Individuals not only have different rates of time preference, but even the same individual employs different discount rates depending on the situation. It is difficult to reconcile the fact that different people use different rates to discount the future (although practically speaking, individual rates are equated to the market rate at the margin). Evidence from behavioral economics indicates that people commonly discount future losses at a lower rate than future gains, and that they use higher rates to discount outcomes in the near future than those in the distant future. In one survey, half of respondents were asked for the largest sum of money they would be willing to pay to receive $20 a year from now, while the other half was asked to provide the smallest sum of money they would accept today to give up receiving $20 a year from now: "The rate used to discount the future gain was, on average, about three times higher than the rate used to discount the future loss" (Knetsch 2000, p. 283).

There are other quirks associated with discounting, although these also relate to risk perceptions. People express greater willingness to discount future environmental benefits from a government program at a lower rate than the benefits of a program that enhances future consumption of material goods. Individuals are willing to pay more to avoid an extremely small risk of dying from a nuclear accident, say, than they are to avoid a much higher risk of death associated with something with which they are more familiar (e.g., drinking and driving).

Finally, society may choose to save more collectively than the sum of all individual savings decisions. The government is considered a trustee for unborn generations, whose wealth will (at least in part) depend on the state of the environment that they inherit, so real consumption (and rates of return on investments) may not grow, and may even decline, when we degrade the environment. Further, because of risk and uncertainty (giving rise to so-called risk premiums), society's rate of time preference will be lower than that of individuals, as society as a whole is better able to pool risks; certain individual risks are mere transfers at the level of society. While individuals face a real chance of dying, society does not really face such a risk. All in all, these more or less ethical arguments suggest that society's rate of discount is lower than that of individuals making up the society. The social rate of discount is lower than the opportunity cost of the capital rate (real rate of return on investments) or the opportunity cost of funds rate, but it is not immediately clear how much lower. Indeed, any rate between 2% and 8% might be justifiable, although perhaps not on ethical grounds. On ethical grounds, future generations must be taken into account.

2.6.2 Risk Adjusted Discount Rates

Before considering intergenerational equity, we examine decisions that do not immediately affect future generations. If outcomes are unknown but estimable with some probability, the decision maker faces a risk that is measured by the expected variability in outcomes. If variability of returns from one project is higher than for another project, it is said to be riskier. The variance and standard deviation are measures of variability or spread and, thus, measures of risk. Most decision makers are risk averse—i.e., reluctant to take risks. Given equal expected net returns, a risk-averse individual will choose the project with the perceived narrower distribution of payoffs as there is more certainty about the outcome.

There are ways to account for risk in investment projects. A commonly applied method is to use risk adjusted discount rates. The Capital Asset Pricing Model (CAPM) requires that riskier projects have higher rates of return, surely greater than the market rate of return (market rate of interest). Otherwise, no agent would invest in them. The fundamental equation of the CAPM is:

(2.9) $\quad r_i = r_f + \beta\,(r_m - r_f)$,

where r_i is the required return for risky asset i, r_f is the risk-free rate of return (say, the rate on Treasury bills), r_m is the market rate of return, and β measures the investment's contribution to risk relative to the market. Returns are assumed to be normally distributed, so β is estimated as the ratio of the covariance of the asset and market returns to the variance of the market return:

(2.10) $\quad \beta = \dfrac{\mathrm{cov}(\,r_i, r_m\,)}{\mathrm{var}\,(\,r_m\,)}$.

βs are usually calculated from past behavior and market returns. If time series data are available on rates of return, β is the regression coefficient that compares the responsiveness of the investment returns with changes in the market returns. Published data on βs can be useful for private and public projects. For example, Merrill Lynch and Value Line publish βs for stocks of a large number of companies. For project evaluation, asset βs instead of stock βs are required, although the latter can be converted into the former by recognizing that the asset value of a firm equals debt plus equity. Thus, the β of an asset is the weighted sum of the stock β plus the debt β.

Consider an example of the use of CAPM in the energy sector. Suppose a North American investor is considering the construction of an electric generating plant similar to ones operated by others. By checking βs published by Merrill Lynch for other electrical generating companies, some idea of the relevant β for the project can be obtained. The average β for 23 large utilities in the US is 0.45. Assume that the investor has 40% of her assets as debt and the debt β is zero. Then, the asset β for the project would be 0.27. If the nominal risk-free rate is 9% and the market rate is 8.8 percentage points higher, the required return for the new investment project using the above formula is: $r = 9\% + 0.27(8.8\%) = 11.4\%$. This means that the energy investment is worth undertaking only if its expected net present value is positive when future costs and benefits are discounted at a rate of 11.4%.

Risk is often relevant when dealing with externalities. For example, the benefits of mitigating global warming depend on so many variables that analysts cannot accurately estimate costs or benefits. Also, it is often the case where the emission reductions resulting from a carbon mitigation project are risky (e.g., carbon sequestration in agricultural soils). Therefore, it is reasonable to think that private investors involved in carbon mitigation investments might require a rate of return that is higher than the risk-free rate.

2.6.3 Discounting in an Intergenerational Context

A particular controversy about the discount rate relates to how much importance we attach to the well-being of future generations compared to the current one. This is particularly important for climate change policy where future generations are thought to benefit the most from the current generation's mitigation efforts.

However, the future generation also bears costs: mitigation reduces future incomes and today's investments could lock a future generation into a technology that might be inappropriate to their circumstances. Whatever society does today will have an impact on future generations; there is an ethical dimension to the choice of a rate to discount the future benefits and costs of climate change mitigation.

It is generally accepted that it is ethically indefensible to discount the utility (as opposed to consumption) of future generations. The argument is as follows: cost-benefit analysis converts costs and benefits into consumption units and discounts them at the rate at which society would trade consumption next year for consumption in the current year. In doing so, and assuming no uncertainty, the Ramsey discounting formula is a useful starting point to think about the choice of a discount rate. The Ramsey formula distinguishes between the *utility rate of discount* (also known as the *social rate of time preference* or *generational discount rate*) and the *consumption rate of discount* (CRD)—it is important to distinguish between the rate at which utility is discounted (welfare of future generations is discounted) and the rate at which consumption is discounted. If there is only a single consumption good, the Ramsey formula is given as:

(2.11) $\quad \delta = \alpha + \varepsilon \times g_t,$ (Ramsey Discounting Formula)

where δ is society's consumption discount rate, α is the utility rate of discount, and g_t is the rate of change of consumption, c'_t $(=dc/dt)$, weighted by the negative of the elasticity of the marginal utility of consumption, ε $= -c_t u''/u' > 0$, where $u' = du/dc > 0$ and $u'' = d^2u/d^2c = du'/dc < 0$. This elasticity ($\varepsilon$) tells us how fast the marginal utility of consumption, u', falls over time as consumption rises. The Ramsey formula says that society's consumption discount rate is equal to the social rate of time preference plus the rate of change of consumption (c'_t) multiplied by the negative of the elasticity of the marginal utility of consumption, $\varepsilon(c_t)$. In essence, then, there are two discount rates to consider—the utility rate of discount and the consumption discount rate.

The Ramsey formula can be interpreted as a prescriptive approach to discounting, with parameters α and ε considered to be policy choices, or as a descriptive approach to discounting, with parameters α and ε based on market rates of return (decisions in financial markets). Under the prescriptive approach, α and ε are chosen on the basis of ethical deliberations. With the descriptive approach, the value of the social rate of time preference (α) can be based on the real rate of return on long-term government bonds, while the consumption rate of discount could be based on the rate of return on risk-free investments, the opportunity cost of capital, or the opportunity cost of funds (as discussed in the previous subsection).

The long-run rate of growth in per capita consumption is often used as a starting point for calculating the discount rate to use in comparing inter-temporal costs and benefits related to climate change. It indicates by how much the material well-being of the future generation can be expected to rise above that of the current one. The change in per capita consumption over time, c'_t, can be determined using historical data, although we have no guarantee that consumption will continue to grow in the future as it has in the past. Suppose that the growth in per capita consumption is 1.3% and that, once adjusted by the negative elasticity of marginal utility of consumption, it remains at 1.3%.[13] To this is usually added a social rate of time preference of 1% or 2%. Suppose the rate on long-term government bonds best represents society's utility discount rate; then, the rate of discount to employ would be 2.3% to 3.3%.

There is nothing to prevent the policy maker from setting the pure rate of time preference to zero (α=0) for ethical reasons—that we cannot discount the utility of future generations. This does not, however, imply that society's consumption discount rate is also zero. The choice of the rate used to discount future costs and benefits is identical to the choice of a consumption rate of discount (δ), which hinges on the choice of generational discount rate (α) and the choice of the elasticity of the marginal utility (ε). In the case of climate change, for example, the choice of the (α,ε) combination varies greatly among economists. For example, in the climate literature, economists have used α=0.1% and ε=1 to show that damages from climate change are very high, and that mitigation should be undertaken immediately.[14] These values were employed in the UK government's *Report on the Economics of Climate Change*, often referred to as the Stern Review after its lead author, economist Nicholas Stern, with the result that future damages appeared much larger in current terms than under a more realistic assumption about the discount rate.

Others have used α=1% and ε=3 to come to a more conservative conclusion about damages. For example, in his Dynamic Integrated Climate and Economics (DICE) model for determining economic policies related to climate change (see Chapter 10), the Nobel laureate William Nordhaus employs a generational discount rate of 1.5% and an elasticity of the marginal utility of consumption ε=1.45, with the result that there is less urgency to mitigate climate change compared to the Stern result. Even with α=0.1%, a high value of ε=3 leads one to recommend delaying action to mitigate climate change.

The marginal cost of emitting an additional metric ton of CO_2 (tCO_2) into the atmosphere at any time is given by the stream of future damages discounted to the year in which that emission occurred. This is the marginal damage from atmospheric CO_2 and is referred to as the social cost of carbon (SCC). A higher SCC is indicative of the need to take action now to mitigate fossil fuel emissions rather than delaying. Estimates of the SCC can be derived using the DICE model, which is done in Table 2.1 where the SCC is dependent on the values of three parameters. First is the equilibrium climate sensitivity (ECS), which is the expected increase in temperature (measured in °C) if the concentration of CO_2 doubles from what it was in pre-industrial times (about 280 parts per million, or ppm). The Intergovernmental Panel on Climate Change (IPCC) places this value between 1.5°C and 4.5°C; we choose to examine 2°C and 3°C—the latter value is employed by Nordhaus.

---

[13] This implies ε = 1. If consumption were falling over time rather than increasing, the second term in (2.11) would be negative, and the consumption discount rate could potentially be negative, in which case the value of an increment of consumption would be rising over time rather than falling.

[14] Lower values of ε imply that society chooses to save a larger proportion of its output to improve the welfare of future generations. When ε=0, any proportional increase in consumption by someone today is equal to the same proportional increase of a person at any future date, regardless of whether they are rich or poor. For ε=1, any proportional increase in consumption by someone equals the same proportional increase of a person living at the same time; taking $1 from someone earning $1,000 is the same as taking $1 million from someone earning $1 billion.

Second, Nordhaus employs a value of the elasticity of the marginal utility of consumption of 1.45, but values of 1.0 and 3.0 are also considered. Finally, the social rate of time preference is taken to be 1.5% by Nordhaus and 0.1% by Stern. If the SCC is less than about $50/tCO_2$, there is not a great deal of urgency in reducing emissions and certainly not the sort of action recommended in IPCC's 2018 report on controlling the mean global temperature rise to 1.5°C above pre-industrial times when it is already 1°C above that mark. Perhaps surprisingly, the results in Table 2.1 are most sensitive to the assumed elasticity of marginal utility of consumption and much less sensitive to the intergenerational discount rate and equilibrium climate sensitivity parameter. William Nordhaus's view might best be represented by the results in the first column, while that of the Stern Review by the results in the fourth column.

Table 2.1 Estimated optimal social cost of carbon ($/tCO_2$), various scenarios and selected years, 2015–2100

	ECS = 3.0°C				ECS = 2.0°C	
	Elasticity of the marginal utility of consumption					
	1.45	3.0	1.45	1.0	1.0	1.45
	Social rate of time preference (intergenerational rate of discount)					
Year	1.50%	0.10%	0.10%	0.10%	0.10%	1.50%
2015	29.48	12.99	113.48	252.62	144.33	17.14
2020	35.25	15.35	136.66	295.15	170.67	20.41
2030	49.10	22.03	187.36	376.15	220.71	28.19
2040	66.32	31.76	245.65	460.25	271.95	37.75
2050	87.25	45.14	312.98	554.77	326.91	49.27
2060	112.25	62.84	390.75	659.72	386.64	62.90
2070	141.66	85.56	481.92	772.46	452.37	78.80
2080	175.79	114.03	587.60	890.71	524.19	97.14
2090	214.94	148.92	706.04	1,012.09	600.09	118.08
2100	259.38	190.85	835.73	1,134.03	678.50	141.76

Source: Author's calculations using the DICE model, version R2016.

The derivation of the Ramsey discounting formula is based on a single consumptive good that subsumes environmental (nonmarket) goods and services. If, on the other hand, consumption is disaggregated so that environmental services are treated separately, and under the assumption that these are greatly endangered by climate change, even mid-range values for α and ε will lead one to recommend immediate albeit expensive action to mitigate climate change.

Notice that in the Ramsey formula, ε is written as a constant parameter, but in actuality it is a function of time because consumption might change over time: $\varepsilon_t = -c_t u''/u'$. Thus, if there is uncertainty concerning the rate of growth in per capita consumption, an additional term needs to be subtracted from formula (2.10), which will cause the social planner to save more today to the benefit of future generations. The Ramsey formula (2.11) then needs to be modified as follows:

(2.12) $\delta = \alpha + \varepsilon\, \mu_g - \frac{1}{2}\, \varepsilon^2\, \sigma_g^2$,

where μ_g and σ_g^2 are the mean and variance, respectively, of an independent, identically distributed normal distribution of the change in consumption over time. The last term is a precautionary term that reduces society's consumption discount rate. Historical estimates of the mean and variance are μ_g=1.8% and σ_g^2=3.6%, which results in a precautionary effect of 0.26%, which would lower a certain δ value of 3.60% to 3.34%.

Now it is quite possible that per capita consumption growth slows over time, which will affect the consumption rate of discount. Indeed, if shocks to consumption are correlated over time, or if the values of μ_g and σ_g are unknown, the consumption rate of discount will likely decline over time. Further, an individual may require a payment of $1.05 next year to forgo receiving $1 today, which implies a discount rate of 5%. However, the same individual may be willing to give up $1 in 20 years' time to obtain $1.01 in 21 years, implying a discount rate of 1%. In other words, the discount rate declines as costs and benefits accrue in the more distant future—i.e., the discount rate declines as the time horizon increases. This is referred to as *hyperbolic discounting*, in contrast to exponential discounting, which uses a constant rate of discount. While the use of a declining discount rate leads to time-inconsistent decisions because the mere passage of time causes an individual to modify their choice, in an uncertain world there is always the possibility that good *ex ante* decisions turn out to be regrettable *ex post* (once nature is revealed).

Using Monte Carlo simulation and historical information on the pattern of inflation-adjusted interest rates, and assuming the stochastic process for interest rates is not mean reverting (does not trend towards a mean in the absence of exogenous shocks), one study finds that the value of $100 received 400 years in the future is worth many orders of magnitude more today if interest rate uncertainty is taken into account than if a constant discount rate is used (see Table 2.2). Because actual discount rates vary in unpredictable fashion (i.e., follow a "random walk"), the discount rate to be employed should be lower than in the absence of this consideration. That is, an additional term needs to be subtracted from the revised Ramsey discounting formula (2.12), and this term depends on time and the number of observations used to estimate μ_g and σ_g. Clearly, there is a strong case to be made for the use of a declining discount rate in the evaluation of climate change mitigation policies and natural resource and energy projects.

Table 2.2 Value today of $100 received in 200 and 400 years: Comparison of constant vs. random walk discounting, selected discount rates

Discount rate	Constant discounting		Non-mean-reverting random walk	
	200 years	400 years	200 years	400 years
2%	$1.91	$0.04	$7.81	$3.83
4%	$0.04	$0.00	$1.54	$0.66
7%	$0.00	$0.00	$0.24	$0.09

Source: Adapted from Newell and Pizer (2003, Table 2).

Using the Ramsey formula (2.11) with an additional term to reflect uncertain consumption, one gets a declining discount rate. Suppose that α=0, ε=2, σ_g=3.6 percent, and the mean rate of growth in consumption,

μ_g, equals 1% and 3% with equal probability. Then the rate used to discount future costs and benefits should decline from 3.8% today to 2.0% in 300 years. While the US Office of Management and Budget employs constant (exponential) discount rates of 3% and 8%, France and the UK employ declining discount rates. The French rate declines much as described above, declining from about 4% in discounting near term consumption to about 2.5% in discounting consumption 200 years or more from now.

The discount rate used in the UK declines in steps of 0.5 percentage points from 3.5% to 1.0%; costs and benefits are discounted at 3.5% if they occur within 25 years of the present, at 2.5% if they occur from about 75 and 125 years from the present, at 1.5% between 200 and 300 years, and at 1.0% beyond 300 years. Thus, $1,000 accruing in 100 years is worth $84.65 today, while it is worth $50.53 if it is realized in 300 years. The case for using a declining discount rate is a strong one, at least in the case where consumption of future generations (those 100 years or more from now) is affected. The only remaining issue relates to the determination of the parameters of the Ramsey formula, and whether to use a prescriptive or descriptive approach.

Guide to Literature

The assumptions underlying cost-benefit analysis are spelled out in Zerbe and Dively (1994). However, the work of Harberger (1971, 1972) is most important in providing the theoretical underpinnings of welfare economics, especially his three postulates of welfare economics. Arguably, the best textbook on welfare economics is by Boadway and Bruce (1984, especially pp. 252–255). The alternative approach to thinking about surplus areas, which does not require utilitarianism, is due to Sugden (2003, 2005).

A clear discussion of quasi-rent, scarcity rent, compensating and equivalent variations, and compensating and equivalent surpluses is provided in van Kooten and Folmer (2004, pp. 13–30). The concept of total economic value and its components is discussed by many authors. Nontechnical summaries are found in Pearce and Warford (1993), van der Heide (2005), and the Millennium Ecosystem Assessment (2003, 2005), which seeks to identify the ecosystem services and their value. Technical discussions of option value and quasi-option value are provided by Ready (1995) and Graham-Tomasi (1995), respectively, while Bulte et al. (2002) measure QOV using stochastic dynamic programming in an application to tropical forest protection in Costa Rica.

The application of cost-benefit analysis and its evolution, and the origins and proper use of multiple accounts, are provided in various reports by the US Water Resources Council (1973, 1979, 1983). Confusion about multipliers and indirect benefits was addressed by Stabler, van Kooten, and Meyer (1988) and Hamilton et al. (1991), although Boadway and Bruce (1984) had earlier clarified this in a theoretical context.

In terms of other decision criteria, Krcmar et al. (2001) and Krcmar, van Kooten, and Vertinsky (2005) provide applications of multiple criteria decision-making, including the use of fuzzy techniques. An excellent synthesis of multiple objective decision-making and the use of fuzzy methods is provided by Krcmar and van Kooten (2008). The definition of the precautionary principle was adopted by 32 individuals at the Wingspread Conference, Racine, Wisconsin, 23–25 January 1998 (see http://www.gdrc.org/u-gov/precaution-3.html [accessed July 15, 2020]). Sunstein (2005a, 2005b) discuss problems related to the precautionary principle.

Prasad (2014) examines the role of riskless investments during financial crises. The CAPM model is discussed, among other places, by Zerbe and Dively (1994), who provide an example from the energy sector.

The discussion on intergenerational discounting and the Ramsey formula is based on Arrow et al. (2012) and Heal (2007, 2009, p. 277). Knetsch (2000) finds that people discount future losses at a higher rate than equivalent future gains. Similarly, psychologists find that people oppose policies that expose them to very small risks yet exhibit highly risky behavior (e.g., Fischhoff et al. 1981). Discussions of hyperbolic discounting and declining discount rates are found in Weitzman (1998, 1999), Dasgupta (2002), Newell & Pizer (2003), and Arrow et al. (2012). Much of section 2.6.2 is based on Arrow et al. (2012).

Information on the DICE model is found in Nordhaus (2013). For further references see the Guide to Literature in Chapter 10. The UK government's Stern Review is summarized in Stern (2007) and is found at https://webarchive.nationalarchives.gov.uk/+/http://www.hm-treasury.gov.uk/sternreview_index.htm [accessed January 21, 2021]. Also see IPCC (2014).

Food for Thought

2.1. Discuss what is meant by von Thuenen rent. How does it differ from Ricardian rent? (Hint: see van Kooten and Folmer 2004, pp. 39–41).

2.2. Discuss how multiple accounts analysis might lead to policy deadlock if each stakeholder represents a particular account and is not required to evaluate the trade-off between their account and the efficiency account. Why is it necessary to make explicit the trade-off between any account and efficiency?

2.3. The Cartagena Protocol on Biosafety is a supplementary agreement to the Convention on Biological Diversity that was adopted January 29, 2000, and entered into force on September 11, 2003. It deals with the movement of living organisms in an era of genetic modifications and essentially invokes the precautionary principle to prevent genetic engineering of crops. What have been the repercussions of the protocol on the agricultural sector and on developing countries in particular? Discuss.

2.4. Based on the discussion in this chapter, what do you think is meant by the extensive and intensive margins of cultivation?

2.5. If the government imposes a rent restriction on apartments, how does one measure the economic impacts? That is, what does one measure? Under what circumstances would one measure changes in other sectors?

2.6. Provide a brief explanation of each of the following (use illustrative diagrams if necessary):
(a) marginal benefit function   (b) resource rent   (c) quasi-rent

2.7. Suppose the production function for crop Y is Y=f(A, B), where A and B are inputs. Further, suppose the price of Y increases by 10% and the price of input A increases by 15%, while the price of B remains unchanged. Should the farmer increase or decrease her use of A? How about the use of B?

2.8. In his report on the economics of climate change, Lord Nicholas Stern used a very low rate of discount of 1.4%, while the Yale economist William Nordhaus (see Chapter 10) uses a rate exceeding 2% in his analysis. What would be the implications of using a low rate versus a high rate?

2.9. Discuss what is meant by "hyperbolic discounting."

2.10. Assume that a 30-year-old is injured in an accident and the insurance company wants to determine the compensation required to cover the discounted income loss resulting from the accident. It is assumed that the individual earned $50/hour as a farmer and that, as a result of the accident, the farmer had to reduce the number of hours that could be worked each week by 12. What level of compensation should be awarded? In making the case, you need to state clearly your assumptions regarding discount rates, length of time that the person is incapacitated, et cetera. You might wish to provide different scenarios; for example, the farmer might need to hire someone to do the work she would have done otherwise. Does it matter if you are presenting the case on behalf of the injured individual or on behalf of the insurance company that has to make a payout? Would a litigant be disadvantaged if the insurance company acted on behalf of both the farmer and the person who injured him?

3

EXTERNALITIES AND
NONMARKET VALUATION

Indirect costs and benefits occur when projects have negative or positive spillovers (externalities) that are not taken into account in private decisions about resource use. Interestingly, externalities are often ignored by public decision makers, who are supposed to look after the well-being of all citizens in society but tend to focus on their own agendas or on the clientele they serve. An externality occurs, for example, when surface water used for secondary or enhanced recovery in oil wells is not priced to take into account the value of water in other uses. Surface water injected into oil wells reduces stream flow, thereby affecting water recreation (e.g., swimming, boating), fish and other wildlife habitat, irrigators, and downstream generation of hydroelectricity. Likewise, farmers may not pay the true marginal cost of the water they use because losses to recreational users, the hydroelectric generation facility, and so on are neglected. Carbon dioxide emissions that result in climate change are a significant externality because costs are imposed on global society, but no individual agent or country has the incentive to reduce CO_2 emissions. The focus in this chapter is on the problem of measuring the externality effects.

In the example of enhanced oil recovery using water, the surplus lost to agriculture and the electrical grid can be measured, with some effort, using market data, but the loss to water recreationists and the negative effects on aquatic species cannot easily be determined. These losses can be measured using a variety of nonmarket valuation methods that are now generally accepted and, in some countries, even mandated.

It is possible to distinguish approaches for measuring the value of nonmarket amenities according to whether changes in the environmental amenity leave traces in markets, whether market information can be used indirectly to estimate surplus values.[1] Choice-based models employ information about a related activity to provide estimates about the value of an amenity. In particular, it may be possible to estimate a *cost function* or an *expenditure function* that includes both market goods and the environmental amenity as variables, and from it draw inferences about the demand for the amenity. Theoretically, if it is possible to estimate a cost function (in the case of production economics) or an expenditure function (in the case of consumer theory), so-called duality theory can then be used to derive the input or output demand functions, respectively. Since

---

[1] The term *environmental amenity* is used in a generic sense to refer to any good or service that is unpriced or priced well below its marginal cost of provision, whether that is wildlife habitat, water/air quality, wilderness areas, recreation sites, visual landscapes, risk of exposure to radiation, etc. All of these have value because individuals would be willing to pay something to have more (or less) of it, or require compensation to put up with or lose it. Of course, this presumes that the individual has some property right over the amenity affected by the action of others.

the price of the environmental amenity is effectively zero in most cases, the entire area under the relevant demand function between the amenity's with-and-without-project levels will constitute the surplus measure of benefit or cost (depending on whether the amenity increases or decreases). The best known of these methods are the *hedonic pricing* and *travel cost* methods, but they also include *damage functions*. Each of these is briefly described below.

In many situations, market information cannot be relied upon to derive a cost or expenditure function because the environmental amenity is not directly related to other goods and services—it is separable in individuals' utility functions. That is, increments or decrements in the environmental amenity are valued by individuals because it affects their well-being (utility), but such changes do not affect how they allocate their budgets. For example, suppose a forest that can be viewed from the road is now harvested. For the person who travels this road, utility has gone down—she has been negatively impacted by the loss of the visual landscape and would likely be willing to pay some amount to prevent the clear-cut. Nonetheless, since she does not pay, she does not change the way in which she allocates her spending on market goods and services. To determine the value of her loss, we would need to ask her directly about the value she placed on the forested landscape versus the clear-cut. We require a survey instrument to elicit directly her *willingness to pay* (WTP) for the scenic amenity or her *willingness to accept* (WTA) compensation to forgo the amenity (put up with the clear-cut), with the latter sometimes referred to as the *compensation demanded*.

Notice that WTP and WTA are alternative measures of consumer surplus, something discussed in more detail below. Here we simply point out that, since this approach requires individuals to respond to hypothetical questions, it is referred to as the *contingent valuation method* (CVM) if actual values are requested, or the contingent behavior method if a behavioral response is desired. Alternative approaches in this genre include contingent ranking; choice experiments (or *stated preferences*), which require respondents to state their preference between situations (much like in marketing surveys); conjoint analysis; and other techniques that are briefly discussed below.

3.1 Cost Function Approach

The cost function approach for measuring environmental values relies on the estimation of a relationship between the output of some market-traded commodity and the level of the environmental amenity. For example, the output of an energy crop, such as corn for ethanol or switchgrass for biodiesel, might be adversely impacted by soil salinity. By estimating what is known as a damage function, it is possible to determine the effect that different levels of soil salinity have on yields. Using this relationship and the per unit price of the energy crop, it is possible to estimate the costs that different levels of soil salinity impose. If salinity is related to certain land-use practices, the externality (spillover) costs of such practices can be determined. Suppose an increase in salinity occurs as a result of cropping marginal land, which is brought about by a regulation requiring greater use of biofuels. The damage function approach could then be used to value one component of the environmental cost of the bioenergy regulation.

Another example of a damage function relates to soil conservation. Agricultural economists have estimated relations between soil depth and crop yield similar to that illustrated in Figure 3.1. The damage function intersects the vertical axis above zero because crops can grow in subsoil. Notice also that a drop in soil depth from D_0 to D_1 leads to a reduction in yield from y_0 to y_1, with the damage obtained by multiplying the crop loss by its price. If there is less soil on the site, a similar degree of soil erosion leads to a much greater loss in yield, as indicated by the downward arrow. Finally, technology can mask the adverse impacts of soil erosion, making soil conservation appear less attractive, as indicated by the increase in yield from y_0 to y_2 when soil depth declines from D_0 to D_1. The reason is that technological change has shifted the relationship between soil depth and crop yield upwards. The true loss in yield is measured by the difference between y_2 and y_1. While this is a simple example, it illustrates the difficulty of measuring environmental damages. In Chapter 10, we employ a similar device to examine climate impacts, with soil depth replaced by temperature and crop yield with a variety of goods or services that are traded in markets.

Figure 3.1 Damage function between soil depth and crop yield

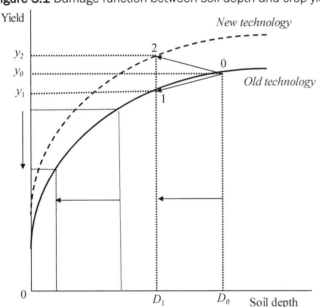

Also falling into the category of nonmarket valuation are the costs of averting damages. Whenever people take action to avoid the adverse effects of spillovers (e.g., pollution in a big city, risk of exposure to radiation), the costs of such actions provide information about the value of the spillover. For example, if the municipal drinking water supply contains dissolved minerals or is contaminated with nitrogen, purchases of bottled water can be used to provide one estimate of the benefits of improving water quality. However, it would be difficult to separate purchases of better quality water compared to what comes from the water faucet from those related to convenience, the trendiness of bottled water, and so on. Purchases solely to avoid the poor water quality provided by the municipality are an averting expenditure.

3.2 Expenditure Function

3.2.1 Hedonic Pricing

Hedonic pricing relies on market evidence related to property values to determine the value that people assign to improvements in access to public and quasi-public goods (e.g., police and fire protection, local parks) and environmental quality. It is assumed that individuals choose the amount of public goods and environmental quality they want by the choices they make concerning residential property purchases. People choose to live in areas that have cleaner air or less crime; they choose to live near airports or along highways; and they choose to live on quiet or busy streets. The choice is determined by what they are willing and able to pay for housing. Hedonic pricing exploits these choices by estimating implicit prices for house characteristics that differentiate closely related housing classes. In this way, it is possible to estimate demand functions for such characteristics and for public goods such as air quality and noise. The hedonic technique requires that the following three methodological questions are answered in the affirmative.

- Do environmental variables systematically affect property prices?
- Is knowledge of this relationship sufficient to predict changes in property values from changes in air pollution or noise levels, say?
- Do changes in property values accurately measure the underlying welfare changes?

If any of these is not answered in the affirmative, the methodology cannot be applied.

Hedonic pricing is a two-stage procedure: In the first stage, the hedonic or implicit price function is obtained by regressing various property characteristics (such as lot and house size, number of bedrooms and bathrooms, etc.), neighborhood factors (e.g., nearness to schools, parks, fire hall), and environmental characteristics (e.g., air quality) on the property's price. The implicit price of any attribute is found by differentiating the hedonic price function with respect to that characteristic. But, in order for the price of the characteristic to vary with the level of the attribute, the hedonic price function must be nonlinear in the characteristic; otherwise, one cannot proceed to stage two and estimate a demand function for the attribute.

In the second stage, the implicit prices of the attribute are regressed on income, quantity of the characteristic, and other (instrumental) variables. This constitutes the inverse demand function. The area under the demand function between the current and proposed levels of the characteristic constitutes a measure of the (consumer) surplus associated with the proposed change.

Empirical studies that have used the hedonic pricing method to determine the effect of aircraft and traffic noise on residential property prices find that there is a measurable effect. For aircraft noise, a one-unit change in the measure of noise (as related to human hearing and discomfort) resulted in prices that were 0.5% to 2.0% lower, while traffic noise reduced house prices by 0.1% to 0.7% per decibel (Lesser et al., 1997, p. 281).

3.2.2 Recreation Demand and the Travel Cost Method

To assess benefits from recreation, the travel cost method emerged as perhaps the first technique for valuing nonmarket benefits. The travel cost method is a type of revealed preference model where:

- individuals are observed to incur costs so as to consume commodities related to the environmental amenity of interest; and
- the commodities consumed are not purchased in a market where prices are determined by supply and demand.

A number of different approaches are available for estimating welfare gains/losses in the travel cost framework. In general, the travel cost method assumes that costs incurred to travel to a site are identical to an onsite entry fee. This knowledge along with the number of visits to a site (and in some variants visits to multiple sites on the same trip) can be used to construct a demand function for the site(s) in question. Again, the area under the demand function yields information about the consumer surplus, which is then used as a measure of benefit or cost.

The hedonic pricing method can also be used to estimate the demand for recreation, but the problems involved are complex. Simply, total household expenditures on recreation at a particular site take on the role of property values in the hedonic (implicit) price function. Expenditures by a large number of households engaged in recreation at more than one site are regressed on a variety of private and public characteristics of the various sites. Again, by differentiating the hedonic price function with respect to any public attribute, an implicit price for that attribute is obtained. In the second stage, the implicit prices for the attribute are regressed on household characteristics, particularly income, and the amount of the attribute available, however it is measured. The resulting equation is the demand function for the attribute. The area under the demand function can then be used to measure the benefit of a change in the attribute in question.

3.3 Contingent Methods or Direct Approaches

It is generally thought that the damage function, travel cost, and hedonic pricing methods provide reasonable estimates of true values because they rely on market data—observations of people's behavior. Hence, they are best employed to estimate use values (see Figure 2.4), which relate to the unpriced benefits that environmental amenities provide in the production or consumption of some other good or service. For instance, a forest provides ecosystem services such as flood control, water storage, and waste assimilation, as well as recreational and other consumptive and non-consumptive (e.g., wildlife viewing) use benefits.

Measures of non-use or passive-use values, on the other hand, cannot be derived from market data. Non-use values include existence, bequest, altruism, and other inherent values that are independent of people's spending on market goods and services. Existence value is the value of simply knowing that an environmental asset exists; for example, people express a willingness to pay simply for the knowledge that whales exist. Bequest value refers to people's willingness to pay to endow the future generation with the asset, while altruism refers to the benefit that a person places on the benefit another person gets from the environmental asset (and not explicitly identified in Figure 2.4). Additionally, option value is often indistinguishable from bequest and existence values; it too cannot be derived from market data. Indeed, existence, bequest, and option values are together often referred to as preservation value, which is determined primarily with contingent methods.

Contingent methods are required whenever the amenity to be valued leaves no behavioral trail in the marketplace. Therefore, contingent devices involve asking individuals, via surveys or in experimental settings, to reveal their personal valuations of increments (or decrements) in an unpriced good. Because people are asked directly to reveal their values, the method is referred to as the stated preference approach, even though the market is contingent. A contingent market defines the good or amenity of interest, the status quo level of provision and the offered increment or decrement therein, the institutional structure under which the good is to be provided, the method of payment, and (implicitly or explicitly) the decision rule that determines whether and how to implement the offered program. Contingent markets are highly structured to confront respondents with a well-defined situation and to elicit a circumstantial choice upon the occurrence of the posited situation. But such markets remain hypothetical, and so too are the choices people make within these markets.

Because the constructed markets used by economists to elicit value are hypothetical, some argue that the values obtained using the methods described below are imperfect. In most cases, contingent valuation devices are used to value natural and ecosystem capital, and such capital clearly has value; indeed, natural and ecosystem capital may be of utmost importance to the long-term survival of society. Thus, it would be a grave error for decision makers to ignore the nonmarket services provided by forests, rangelands/grasslands, wetlands, lakes, rivers and riparian zones, and even croplands, whether these services entail carbon storage and sequestration, commercial timber harvests, food production, maintenance of water quality, provision of wildlife habitat/refuge, or recreational and scenic amenities. The question is how best to measure and include nonmarket values into the decision calculus.

3.3.1 Contingent Valuation Method

The contingent valuation method (CVM) was initially proposed some 50 years ago in an effort to value nonmarket amenities. Subsequently, CVM was approved by the US Department of the Interior for implementing regulations under the 1980 Comprehensive Environmental Response, Compensation, and Liability Act (CERCLA) as amended in 1986. In 1990, the US Oil Pollution Act extended liability to oil spills (as oil was not considered a hazardous waste). A 1989 decision by the District of Columbia Court of Appeals involving CERCLA in the case of Ohio v. Department of Interior affirmed the use of CVM and permitted inclusion of non-use values in the assessment of total compensable damages. In the early 1990s, an expert panel led by two Nobel prize-winning economists (Kenneth Arrow and Robert Solow) supported the use of stated preferences (CVM) for valuing nonmarket amenities. Thus, in the US at least, CVM is used both for determining compensation when firms or individuals damage the environment and in cost-benefit analyses.[2]

Surveys are used in CVM to elicit information regarding the minimum level of compensation required by an individual to forgo an environmental amenity or public good (compensation demanded) or the maximum amount the individual would be willing to pay to obtain the nonmarket amenity. As shown next, these measures are rooted in economic theory and constitute a surplus measure equivalent to consumer surplus.

Consider Figure 3.2. Suppose the current level of an environmental amenity is given by E_0 and we wish to know the benefit of a policy that causes the level to increase to E_1. In Figure 3.2(a), the initial well-being (utility) of a respondent to a valuation question is given by u_0 at E_0. The combination of income m and amenity E_0 results in a utility of u_0. All combinations of income and the environmental amenity that lie on the u_0 curve lead to the same level of utility. However, if income is reduced from m to $m-k$ while the level of the amenity is increased from E_0 to E_1, the person's well-being increases to u_1. That is, the person is made better off by giving up k amount of income to move from point M to point d, thus gaining E_1-E_0 amount of the amenity. The maximum amount she would be willing to pay for the move from M to d is measured by the distance cf; any proposed loss of income less that cf, such as amount k ($=df$), would be accepted.

Despite the fact that environmental amenities are not traded in a market, we draw three demand curves in Figure 3.2(b). These can be thought of as shadow demand curves that exist in theory but not in practice. Consider first the ordinary demand function. As discussed previously, the benefit of a policy that increases the amount of the environmental amenity is given by area **A+B**, which is the consumer surplus. However, since prices do not exist, we cannot estimate such a demand function. The other two demand curves are called compensated demand functions because the individual either gives up or gains income in order to remain at the same level of utility as the level of the amenity is varied. As noted above, if a person starts at point M in panel (a) and moves to point d, her income would need to be reduced by amount cf to keep her at u_0; this keeps her on the compensated demand curve $D(u_0)$. The equivalent of cf in panel (a) is area **A** in panel (b). This is known as the *compensating surplus*.

Notice that in the above analysis the individual is assumed to have a right to E_0 but not E_1. However, if the person had the right to E_1 but was only able to access E_0, we would need to ask her what the minimum amount of compensation she would demand to put up with E_0 rather than the E_1 to which she is entitled. The minimum amount she is willing to accept (WTA) as compensation is given by distance RN in panel (a) and it too constitutes a surplus measure akin to consumer surplus. In this case, the appropriate compensated demand function is $D(u_1)$ and the appropriate surplus measure is given by area **A+B+C** in panel (b), which equals RN in panel (a). This area is known as the *equivalent surplus*.

---

[2] In court cases, CVM can be used to estimate compensatory damages, but not the punitive damages that the court might assess.

Figure 3.2 Willingness to pay (WTP) and willingness to accept (WTA) compensation (compensation demanded) as surplus measures, with $D(u_0)$ and $D(u_1)$ compensated demand functions

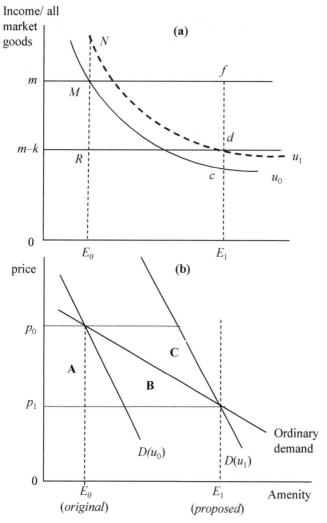

In the case of environmental amenities, therefore, there are three measures of surplus from the standpoint of "consumers"—consumer surplus (CS), compensating surplus (WTP), and equivalent surplus (WTA). These are given in Figure 3.2(b) by areas **A**+**B**, **A**, and **A**+**B**+**C**, respectively, so that WTP < CS < WTA. In theory, areas **B** and **C** are considered to be very small, so that WTP ≈ CS ≈ WTA—the three measures are approximately equal. However, studies consistently find that compensation demanded (WTA) is significantly greater than WTP, so that the initial endowment or one's property right matters a great deal.[3]

---

[3] We could just as well examine the case where the "original" level of the amenity in Figure 3.2 is E_1, and then ask what the associated measures would be. In this case, WTP would be a negative value (indicating that compensation is required), while WTA is positive (indicating the respondent would need to pay). By switching the subscripts in the figure, we then find that WTA < CS < WTP.

In the absence of market data, a stated preference approach, whether CVM or some other approach that relies on direct elicitation of value, is needed to determine the surplus from changes in the availability of an environmental amenity. To implement the CVM, for example, the analyst must design a survey that provides information about the contingency to be valued and then asks a respondent to state their maximum WTP or their minimum WTA for a specified change in the amenity. Anchoring can be a problem because a respondent may have no idea what the amenity might be worth, so the value they provide might be considered unreliable. An alternative that is generally preferred to this open-ended sort of question is to provide a value (determined in a pre-test stage of survey construction) to which the respondent is required to respond yes or no. The proposed value is for an anticipated increment or decrement in the availability of wildlife habitat, say. The contingent valuation question would ask whether the respondent would be willing to contribute $x to a project that would increase wilderness area by w hectares, or whether they would accept $y to prevent a logging company from harvesting w hectares of wilderness. Statistical models can then be used to estimate the overall value of the wildlife habitat based on responses from many people, who face different payment schemes for the contingency.

While primarily used to determine non-use values, the stated preference approach can also be employed to value market-traded goods and services, which is useful for testing how well responses to hypothetical purchasing questions correspond to actual ones.

An important use of contingent valuation surveys is to determine preservation values for such things as tropical rain forests and wildlife. CVM studies found that US residents are willing to make a one-time payment of $1.9–$2.8 billion to protect an additional 5% of the globe's tropical forests; preservation of wildlife was estimated to provide benefits in the neighborhood of $68 million per year for Alberta residents; and preservation of old-growth forests was valued at perhaps $150 per household per year. This suggests that ignoring these values in the management of natural resources can lead to substantial misallocation of resources.

3.3.2 Choice Experiments/Stated Preferences

Unlike CVM, the choice experiments approach does not require survey respondents to place a direct monetary value on a contingency. Rather, individuals are asked to make pairwise comparisons among environmental alternatives, with the environmental commodity in question (one of the alternatives) characterized by a variety of attributes. For example, a survey respondent is asked to make pairwise choices between alternative recreational activities, with each distinguished by attributes such as the probability of catching a fish, the type of fish, the amenities available to fishers (e.g., whether or not there are boat rentals), distance to the site, and so on. It is the attributes that are important, and it is these that are eventually assigned monetary value. In order to do so, one of the attributes must constitute a monetary touchstone (or proxy for price). Distance to a recreational site might constitute the proxy for price (as in the travel cost method), but, more generally, one of the attributes will be a (hypothetical) entry fee or an associated tax. Once the values of all attributes are known (from the value of the one and the pairwise rankings), the overall value of the amenity is determined by assuming additivity of the attributes' values. Of course, it is possible that the total value of the amenity is greater than the sum of its components, or vice versa.

While the methodology has been used primarily to value recreational sites, the earliest studies applied the choice experiment approach to the estimation of non-use values. Choice experiments avoid the "yea-saying" problem of dichotomous choice surveys as respondents are not faced with the same all-or-nothing choice, although recent advances in CVM questionnaire design have addressed this issue.

Another advantage of choice experiments over CVM occurs when it comes to the transfer of benefits (e.g., transfer of estimated benefits for water quality improvements in one jurisdiction to those in another). This issue is discussed further below. Yet another advantage is that repeated questioning of the same respondent in the choice experiment approach enables consistency testing that is not possible in CVM where one valuation question is usually asked. Choice experiments may also be a means of getting around the embedding problem of CVM. Embedding describes a situation where people state they are willing to pay $40 per year to protect grizzly bears, for example, but they are also willing to pay no more than $40 per year to protect wildlife per se. Of course, if asked to break down the latter into the valuation of various species or categories of wildlife, grizzly bears are worth much less than $40. Finally, by allowing some attributes to take on levels both above and below the status quo, the choice experiment approach enables one to estimate both WTP and WTA compensation.

The choice experiment approach differs from conjoint analysis because, with the latter, respondents are asked to rank all of the alternatives from highest (best) to lowest (worst). Such a ranking can then be used to infer the importance of the attributes that characterize each alternative within one's preference function. Conjoint measurement is a marketing technique that uses revealed choice among goods with different characteristics (as in hedonic pricing) with a survey that asks people to choose among or rank hypothetical alternatives (contingent ranking) to impute the values of the characteristics. It is used primarily to predict the potential for new products.

3.3.3 Constructed Preferences/Stakeholder Method

Some decision theorists have proposed a multiple attribute, utility-theory contingent valuation (MAUT–CV) approach to address the inability of respondents in standard CVM to make holistic assessments about environmental resources. Individuals do not know the value of the resources they are asked to consider, but are constructing values "with whatever help or clues the circumstances provide" (Gregory, Lichtenstein, and Slovic 1993, p. 181). Thus, rather than attempting to uncover environmental values, the analyst's task is to help individuals discover those values by having them work towards "a defensible expression of value" (ibid., p. 179). In essence, this approach requires the analyst to work with stakeholder groups, with the purpose of getting them to develop comprehensive, hierarchical attribute trees and then ranking attributes on a 0 to 100 scale.

The MAUT–CV method is also able to address uncertainty as components with probabilities can be built into the model, so that the final calculation is an expected value. It is unlikely that it can address disparities between WTP and WTA (between the value placed on gains versus that on losses) as the results are path dependent, varying by the path used to help people discover their values. Since the approach is designed primarily to enable groups of stakeholders to come to a decision about a preferred course of action, as opposed to seeking to estimate a measure of well-being (namely, a surplus measure), it provides little in the way of useful information for social CBA, but does provide information about how a group of disparate stakeholders would rank projects, programs, or policies.

3.3.4 Fuzzy and ad hoc Methods for Determining Nonmarket Values

Given the difficulty that people have in valuing environmental amenities or public goods like wildlife, several researchers have employed a number of ad hoc methods for incorporating such difficulty or uncertainty into the valuation process. As a consequence, some have suggested that verbal language be used in contingent valuation frameworks. Conversion of verbally relayed preferences to monetary value is difficult and can, in our view, only be done using fuzzy set theory. Research along these lines has made some progress, but no one has yet employed only verbal language to derive values for nonmarket amenities. The fuzzy methods used to date have estimated values similar to those found by approaches more solidly grounded in economic theory. However, there remains the feeling that, while a fuzzy method can lead to the mitigation of many of the problems encountered with CVM, the link between economic theory and the values derived using the fuzzy approach is perhaps too weak for such values to be taken seriously. Nonetheless, the fuzzy approach is more solidly grounded in economic and measurement theory than ad hoc methods (see van Kooten, Krcmar, and Bulte, 2001).

3.4 Benefit Transfer

Use of nonmarket valuation techniques to estimate economic surpluses for use in social cost-benefit analysis can be quite expensive and time consuming. The decision maker needs to determine whether the expense is warranted. A question that arises is: Can one use the values estimated elsewhere and apply them to the situation under consideration? It may be possible in some circumstances to avoid large transaction costs associated with the valuation of spillovers and yet provide reasonable values for decision-making. While debate over existing techniques for monetary valuation of environmental goods and services continues, the search for new and simpler approaches remains.

Benefit transfer is an area of research that continues to develop. Benefit or value transfer involves "borrowing" monetary environmental values estimated at one site (the study site) and applying them to another (the policy site). The attraction of benefit transfer is that it avoids the cost of conducting primary studies whereby the benefits of natural or environmental assets, or the damages associated with degradation of the environment, are measured with one or more of the techniques described above.

There are two main approaches to benefit transfer—unit value transfer and function transfer. Unit value transfer is the easiest as one simply transfers the environmental values from a study site to the policy site. The valuation estimates may be left unadjusted or may be adjusted in some way. Although transferring unadjusted estimates is undesirable, since the values experienced at the study site may not be the same as those at the policy site, it is a widely practiced approach. For example, in a study of the value of natural capital in settled regions of Canada, environmental values from a variety of sources and jurisdictions were transferred as an approximation of the value of natural capital. If funds are not available for detailed analyses, this approach is often preferred to ignoring ecosystem service values altogether.

A more sophisticated approach is to transfer the entire benefit function. In this case, instead of transferring only the benefit estimates, the researcher transfers an estimated benefit function, substituting information about the independent variables at the policy site into the regression equation based on the study site.

Meta-analyses can also be used to adapt direct values and even value functions from multiple studies so they can be used at the policy site. Meta-regression analysis can be used to take the results from a number of studies, synthesize research findings and analyze them in such a way that the variations in unit values or value functions found in those studies can be explained.

As noted, the advantage of benefit transfer is that it is both pragmatic and cost-effective and, therefore, the method is an attractive alternative to expensive and time-consuming original research. Benefit transfer enables the analyst to quickly inform decision makers about the environmental costs or benefits of projects and policies. In some policy contexts, however, the benefit transfer method remains controversial. The major reason for this relates to the accuracy of transferred estimates since validity tests show that the uncertainty could be quite large, both spatially and inter-temporally. This is especially the case for complex goods, such as biodiversity related to agricultural and landscape values. Nonetheless, the benefit transfer approach is recognized as a valid technique for valuation of agricultural and forest ecosystem biodiversity, but only if the circumstances at the study site are close to those at the policy site, which is often unlikely to be the case. This does not necessarily imply that the application of benefit transfer should be restricted to use within the same region. Nonetheless, there are many issues that must be addressed when conducting benefit transfers between different regions, and even between countries (which is controversial), especially as these concern landscape values.

Recent initiatives have sought to facilitate the use of benefit transfers. These have relied on meta-regression analysis of data from various studies of the same resource, such as the meta-analysis of wetland services. An example of the types of values available for use in benefit transfer studies is provided in Table 3.1 for wetland services.

3.5 Concluding Discussion

The use of surveys to obtain information about environmental and other nonmarket values remains controversial. In his book, the *New Holy Wars: Economic Religion versus Environmental Religion in Contemporary America*, Robert Nelson (2010) argues that, by developing the contingent valuation method and other approaches to nonmarket valuation, economists were able to avoid becoming irrelevant in debates about the environment. They were thereby able to usurp the high ground from biologists and other environmental scientists. Many ecologists then adopted nonmarket valuation to make the case that the world's ecosystems are so valuable that they should be protected regardless of the cost.

Table 3.1 Value of wetland services for benefit transfer purposes ($/ac of wetland)

	United States				Canada
	Northeast	Southeast	Inter-mountain	Pacific	Canada
Min	$33	$0.41	$6	$124	$51
Max	$908,492	$6,494	$456	$5,657	$198
Average	$49,873	$448	$80	$1,555	$137
Median	$618	$21	$17	$718	$149

Source: Woodward and Wui (2001)

Environmental scientists estimated that, in 2011, the globe's ecosystems provided services valued at between $125 trillion and $145 trillion annually (measured in 2007 US dollars). In 2007, all of the economies in the world produced goods and services, as measured by GDP, worth $56.7 trillion; between 2000 and 2016, global GDP increased from $50.0 trillion to $77.6 trillion (measured in real 2010 US dollars). Incredibly, these authors valued the Earth's ecosystem services as greater than the value of all the goods and services produced globally. This is similar to arguing that the value of the labor used to produce something is greater than the thing produced, which is impossible!

There are two potential problems with this type of analysis. First, the environmental scientists confuse total and marginal benefits (see Chapter 2.2). The total value of the Earth's ecosystems is vastly underestimated! If the globe's ecosystems were to be completely destroyed, humans would cease to exist; hence, ecosystem value must be infinite. However, humans choose whether or not to harvest the next hectare of forestland and convert it to agriculture, replant it to forest cover, or develop it. Even if the choice is to protect or develop large swaths of an ecosystem, the choice is never to destroy all of it; indeed, as more pristine forest is lost, for example, what remains becomes increasingly more valuable to society and the pressure to protect it will rise accordingly. This is the difference between total and marginal value. Of course, large values of the Earth's ecosystems lead ecologists to advocate for environmental policies that seek to protect ecosystems well beyond the point where the marginal costs of protecting ecosystems exceed their marginal benefits.

Second, the extension of local estimates of ecosystem services to the global level fails to recognize that there are income constraints that prevent stated benefits from exceeding GDP. The estimated value of the services provided by the Earth's ecosystems is based on a benefit transfer approach; benefits from various studies using the methods discussed in section 3.4 have been applied to the evaluation of ecosystems for which no information is available—the majority of the globe's ecosystems. Because the estimated total value is more than double the value of global GDP, it is clear that the global willingness to pay for the unpriced services of ecosystems, including the ability to satisfy compensation demanded, would violate the global budget constraint. In other words, the estimates are essentially meaningless. This type of study might best be likened to an attempt to value the Earth's atmosphere: What is the benefit of the atmosphere? That is, what would be the cost (forgone benefit) of removing the Earth's atmosphere? Such a question is meaningless, of course.

Finally, there is a problem with the use of surveys to monetize environmental amenities. Regardless of how well a survey is structured, respondents are required to value a contingency. The Nobel laureate Daniel Kahneman distinguishes between two systems that determine the way we think. System 1 is fast, intuitive, and emotional, while system 2 is slow, deliberate, and logical. System 1 dominates because we tend to be lazy and avoid engaging system 2 to the largest extent possible. In responding to the types of surveys economists use to elicit monetary values for ecosystem services, protection of wildlife, and so forth, respondents will rarely if ever engage their system 2. Research shows, for example, that respondents are then easily primed—their response to any hypothetical question is determined by what engaged them prior to being confronted by a survey. Researchers can then easily prime respondents to give answers that favor what the researcher desires, but respondents can also be primed to give answers that will differ significantly from one occasion to another. In each case, the values elicited might not be helpful or representative of the true value of the non-traded goods or services in question.

Can questionnaires be structured to provide the real value that people place on ecosystem services and the environment? Some economists argue that the state of the art has reached a point where, with adequate pre-testing and proper procedures, surveys can obtain reasonable monetary estimates of nonmarket goods and services. However, Kahneman and others are skeptical, arguing that, despite many efforts, proponents of surveys have not been able to overcome problems associated with priming, anchoring, framing, and other problems, including the so-called endowment effect. The endowment effect implies that people value something more when they own it than if they have to purchase it; thus, in the jargon of economics, there is a discontinuity in the indifference curve at the endowment. This violates the underlying theory of cost-benefit analysis, leading economists to conclude that nonmarket valuation methods are at odds with neoclassical economic theory and CBA.

The theory underlying the valuation of nonmarket amenities is not in question. Rather, it is the practice of estimating and then employing such values in applied welfare analysis. Results from contingent valuation studies are frequently used to tip the balance of cost-benefit analyses towards the environment and against development. Without large nonmarket values, the benefits of many development projects, from construction of pipelines to the draining of mosquito-infested swamps, would be given the green light. Without presumed high nonmarket damages, climate change is unlikely to be the problem many fear it to be. For the most part, while the theory of nonmarket values is well developed, the practice is much less so. Despite some four decades of experience with surveys and questionnaires, one cannot be totally confident that the nonmarket (environmental) values derived from surveys are sufficiently robust to employ straightaway in cost-benefit analysis. The reasons are the three mentioned above: Average values are estimated when marginal ones are required, budget constraints are violated, and the problems identified by Kahneman (and others) are simply unresolvable.

To argue that nonmarket amenity values should not be included in cost-benefit analyses does not imply that nonmarket values are unimportant, however. Rather, it recognizes that externality values based on responses to questionnaires that do not involve actual purchases, payments, or transfers of funds are not the same as values derived from actual market transactions and should, therefore, not be treated as if they are the same. In cost-benefit analysis, environmental values based on responses that involve no actual transactions of money (i.e., no consequences) should be treated more like one of several multiple accounts, much as regional economic benefits (see Chapter 2.3). Changes in the availability of a public good, or the stream of ecosystem services from a landscape, should be balanced against the opportunity costs that such changes imply in terms of a project's net present social value. That is, contingent values should perhaps not be included directly into the efficiency calculation—that the estimated surplus measures from surveys are not comparable to the surpluses derived from market information. Environmental amenities should then be included as a separate account in a project evaluation (even if they are measured in monetary terms) and compared to the economic efficiency account. In that case, a political decision is required to determine the trade-off between economic opportunities and the environment.

Guide to Literature

The valuation of public/environmental goods and services that are not traded in markets might be the most important topic in environmental economics. The literature is vast, but classic summaries of the theory and methods are by Freeman (1979, 2003). The first travel cost models were developed by Clawson (1959) and Thrice and Wood (1958). The hedonic pricing method followed later; it is described in Freeman (1995) and Smith (1997). In a classic paper, Krutilla (1967) recognized that some environmental goods/services are strongly separable in the utility function and have no effect on the demand for market goods, so changes in their availability leave no trace in markets. To determine their value economists were required to elicit values directly using contingent valuation surveys; a discussion of these methods is provided in Cummings, Brookshire, and Schulze (1986) and Mitchell and Carson (1989).

As a result of criticism of the contingent valuation method, a blue ribbon panel (Arrow et al. 1993) was struck to resolve large observed differences between WTP and WTA compensation, but failed to do so partly because research found that the initial endowment (i.e., the property rights) affected outcomes when they were not supposed to (Horowitz and McConnell 2002). The choice experiment/stated preference approach to valuation was introduced by the University of Alberta's Wiktor Adamowicz (Adamowicz 1995; Adamowicz et al. 1998). Studies by Kramer and Mercer (1997), Phillips et al. (1989), and van Kooten (1995) provided CVM-based estimates of the benefits to US citizens of protecting tropical forests, wildlife in Alberta, and old-growth forests, respectively.

Gregory, Lichtenstein, and Slovic (1993) propose a method of constructing preferences.

Studies applying fuzzy methods to the valuation of public goods are due to the current author (van Kooten, Schoney, and Hayward 1986; van Kooten, Krcmar, and Bulte 2001; van Kooten 1998). In particular, the method has been used to address respondent uncertainty (van Kooten, Shaikh, and Suchánek 2002; Sun and van Kooten 2009). Evans, Flores, and Boyle (2003) were the first to suggest using only verbal as opposed to numeric responses in CVM surveys. A review in the context of respondent uncertainty is provided by Shaikh, Sun, and van Kooten (2007).

The section on benefit transfer is largely based on van der Heide, Powe, and Navrud (2010), while a special issue of *Ecological Economics* examines the state-of-the-art and science of benefit transfer (Wilson and Hoehn 2006). An Organisation for Economic Co-operation and Development (OECD) (2001) study is one example where unadjusted values from one study are applied to a different situation, a technique Olewiler (2004) also used to provide rough estimates of the value of ecosystem services to Canadians. Examples of meta-regression analyses that have sought to identify benefits include studies of biodiversity value (Navrud 2001), residential water demand (Dalhuisen et al. 2003), and the costs of CO_2 sequestration in forests (van Kooten, Laaksonen-Craig, and Wang 2009). Good reference books on benefit transfer are by Garrod and Willis (1999) and Navrud and Ready (2007). John Loomis (now retired) initiated a benefit transfer toolkit that appears to be maintained by Colorado State University and is found at: http://dare.agsci.colostate.edu/outreach/tools/ [accessed January 13, 2020].

Costanza and his colleagues (1997, 2014) have provided estimates of the nonmarket value of the Earth's ecosystems. Nelson's book *The New Holy Wars* (2010) argues that, by developing nonmarket valuation techniques, economists took back ground gained by environmentalists.

In the concluding section, questions are raised about the validity of the nonmarket values obtained from surveys. In this regard, Kahneman's book *Thinking, Fast and Slow* (2011) is a must read. He identifies priming (pp. 52–55) as a problem, but also anchoring (pp. 126–127), joint versus single valuation (p. 359), and framing (pp. 366–369). Other research skeptical of contingent valuation surveys includes Kahneman and Tversky (1979, 1984), McFadden and Leonard (1993), and Knetsch (2000). Hausman (2012) argues that nonmarket valuation methods are at odds with cost-benefit analysis. Finally, Lewis (2017) provides an excellent overview of the analysis of Kahneman and Tversky in this regard, while Kay and King (2020) call the whole exercise into question.

Food for Thought

3.1. Provide a brief explanation of each of the following (use illustrative diagrams if necessary):
(a) nonmarket valuation
(b) damage function
(c) travel cost method
(d) hedonic pricing
(e) contingent valuation
(f) choice experiments
(g) benefit transfer

3.2. An economist with Victoria's planning department has recently estimated the inverse compensated demand for clean water from the city's water source to be:

$P_Q = 250 - 0.25\, Q$,

where Q is measured as the reduction in nitrogen contamination. What is the benefit of increasing Q from 100 to 250 units—that is, of reducing nitrogen pollution by a corresponding amount? Is this measure the consumer surplus? If not, what is it?

3.3. Mail surveys are often used to elicit the values that individuals place on resources that are not traded in markets (e.g., scenic amenities, wildlife habitat). The most common technique used, one that is strongly defended by its practitioners, is the contingent valuation method (CVM) and its derivatives. However, a famous UBC professor once noted that the only way you will ever determine the value of wilderness is to put a fence around it and charge people for entry. Would this capture the value that CVM seeks to address? What is that value?

3.4. *True, False, or Uncertain? Make sure to indicate why.* The safe minimum standard of conservation is a conservative policy that requires choosing the policy that minimizes the maximum potential loss.

3.5. What is the difference between compensating variation and compensating surplus? Why do we use the compensating variation rather than consumer surplus? Under what conditions is compensating surplus used as the welfare measure rather than compensating variation?

3.6. Environmental amenities that are "strongly separable" in the utility function do not leave a trace in other markets because changes in their availability do not affect the way we spend our money. Yet, knowledge that there exist polar bears, elephants, whales, etc. does affect our utility—our sense of well-being. To measure the value individuals attach to these amenities, economists have employed contingent valuation methods (CVM), namely, questionnaires that present the contingency (the hypothetical change) that is to be valued and then ask a valuation question using either an open-ended or dichotomous-choice format. What is the difference between these types of questions? What are the advantages or disadvantages of each?

3.7. *True, False, or Uncertain? Indicate why.* Whenever there is a market failure (e.g., tropical deforestation occurs at a higher rate than socially desired, farmers' agronomic practices lead to high rates of soil loss), government intervention (either through regulation or taxes/subsidies) can help society "regain" economic efficiency.

3.8. Cruise ships heading to Alaska often dock in the James Bay area of Victoria, BC. Auke van der Berg is a natural resource economist who has recently estimated the following hedonic or implicit price function for clean air in the James Bay district near downtown:

$$P_{House} = 400{,}000 + 9{,}250\,X_1 + 20{,}000\,X_2 - 800\,Q + 50\,Q^2,$$

where P_{House} is the house price (in $s) obtained from real estate listings, X_1 is the lot size (measured in square meters), X_2 is the number of rooms, and Q is the amount of pollution (in tonnes of particulate fallout per hectare measured at the nearest monitoring station, with such sites located every few km).

(a) What does the addition of one more room add to the price of the average house in the James Bay area?

(b) What does an additional square meter of lot size add to the house price?

(c) What effect does an increase in particulate fallout of 1 tonne/hectare have on the price of this house?

(d) What should Mr. van der Berg do next if he wishes to estimate the benefits of reducing particulate fallout that affects James Bay residents?

4

INTERNATIONAL TRADE

AND APPLIED WELFARE ANALYSIS

Economic welfare measurement can fruitfully be applied to the evaluation of trade policy pertaining to natural resources, including agriculture and forestry. In this chapter, we demonstrate how tools of applied welfare analysis can be used to evaluate government policies in agriculture and forestry within the context of international trade. Applied welfare economics is employed to identify and measure the economic costs and benefits of projects and/or public policies, as well as the income (re)distributional effects that government projects or policies bring about. Because of the richness of the various agricultural policies that have been implemented by the United States, the European Union, and other countries over more than 50 years of intervention (see Chapters 7 and 8), the agricultural literature offers an excellent place to look for insights into policy. Quantitative assessments of various policies depend on the development of an appropriate theoretical framework for conducting the analysis. In this chapter, such a framework is developed and some examples of how this approach can be used to analyze trade policies are provided; illustrations focused on agricultural policy more specifically follow in Chapter 6.

4.1 Spatial Price Equilibrium Trade Modeling

Trade in any product can be analyzed using a spatial price equilibrium (SPE) model of international trade. Because this is a partial equilibrium model, changes in countries' policies regarding the commodity in question will affect only a select number of upstream and downstream commodities, and markets for substitutes or complements if they are characterized by market failure (recall equation 2.4), but have essentially no impact on relative prices elsewhere in the economy. SPE models assume that any differences in prices between regions are the result of shipping and handling costs (e.g., freight, insurance, exchange rate conversion fees, other transaction costs), plus tariffs and non-tariff barriers. Thus, in the absence of these costs, prices would be the same in every region as a result of spatial arbitrage—the law of one price holds.

As an example, the development of a spatial price equilibrium trade model for durum wheat is explained with the aid of Figures 4.1 and 4.2. Canada is a major producer and exporter of durum wheat, which has a high protein content and is used in the production of pasta. Canada accounts for between 10% and 20% of world durum production and, for the period 2012–2016, accounted for nearly 40% of global exports; thus, changes in Canadian durum production and exports will impact world prices.

The derivation of the excess demand (ED) and excess supply (ES) functions for durum for any given region is illustrated in Figure 4.1. In the absence of trade (referred to as autarky), domestic consumption, production, and price are determined by the intersection of the domestic supply (S) and demand (D) schedules. In the figure, the autarkic equilibrium quantity and price are Q^* and P^*, respectively. A country will generally engage in trade if the world price of durum is greater or less than the domestic price plus (if exporting) or minus (if importing) the shipping and handling (S&H) costs. If the world price is higher than the domestic price, the country will export durum (as is the case for Canada); if the world price is lower, it will import the good even if it produces more than the amount produced in the exporting country. How much will it supply or demand?

Figure 4.1 Determining excess supply and excess demand for durum wheat

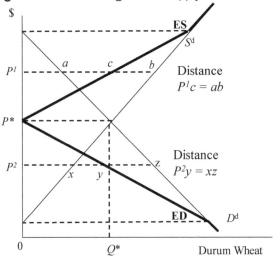

Suppose that the world price is P^1 (as shown in Figure 4.1), which is what firms can get by selling abroad (after S&H costs plus any tariffs). The amount the country will supply to the world market is equal to the difference between what domestic producers are willing to supply at P^1 (given by point b on the domestic supply curve S^d) and what domestic consumers will buy at that price (point a on D^d). The difference between what producers are willing to supply and what domestic consumers are willing to buy at each price above P^* constitutes excess supply, with the ES function tracing out this excess supply at various prices. Thus, ES at P^1 equals ab (= distance P^1c). Likewise, if the world price is below P^*, it is the difference between what consumers are willing to buy and what producers are willing to sell that constitutes excess demand; it is these differences at various prices that trace out the ED schedule. At P^2, ED $= xz = P^2y$. The ES and ED curves are shown in Figure 4.1.

The ES and ED schedules can be derived mathematically if one assumes linear (inverse) demand and supply as in Figure 4.1:

(4.1) $P^D = \alpha - \beta q$, α, $\beta \geq 0$, and

(4.2) $P^S = a + bq$, a, $b \geq 0$.

The excess demand and supply curves in the figure are then given by:

(4.3) $ED = \gamma - \delta q$, and

(4.4) $ES = \gamma + mq$,

where $\gamma = P^* = \dfrac{a\beta + b\alpha}{\beta + b} \geq 0$ and $m = \delta = \dfrac{b\beta}{\beta + b} \geq 0$. Notice that γ is the equilibrium domestic price, so that, in

the absence of shipping and handling costs and tariffs, the excess supply and demand curves start at the same point on the vertical (price) axis. Further, the absolute slopes of the ED and ES curves are identical (although ED slopes down and ES slopes up).

Now consider durum trade between Canada and the rest of the world (ROW). The problem with this simplification is that Canada exports durum to a wide variety of countries, so a trade model should really take into account bilateral trade among various countries or regions, such as Canada and China, the US and Indonesia, the EU and Africa, Argentina and China, and so on. There is also market fragmentation so that some countries in the EU might export durum wheat outside the EU (say France to China), while others import durum (say from Russia or Ukraine). Nonetheless, the Canada-ROW example offers an excellent way to illustrate how SPE trade models can be used to analyze policy. Further, the principles used in the case of two trading partners can be extended to include multiple countries engaging in bilateral trade, although a numerical trade model will be required in that case.

A durum wheat trade model for Canada and the rest of the world is illustrated in Figure 4.2. In the figure, the domestic demand functions for durum in Canada and the ROW are given by D_C and D_R, respectively, while respective supply functions are given by S_C and S_R. Under autarky (no trade), an amount q_c^* of durum wheat will be consumed in Canada at a domestic price of P_c in panel (a); in the ROW, autarkic consumption will be q_R^* at a price P_R in panel (c). Note that for trade to take place the difference between the autarkic prices must exceed the S&H costs plus tariffs—the transaction costs of getting the good from one market to another, that is, $P_R > P_c +$ S&H (trans) costs.

The well-being of citizens in each country is determined by the sum of the benefits they receive as consumers (consumer surplus) and as producers (producer surplus). Economic welfare is always determined as the sum of surpluses (e.g., net revenues rather than gross sales).[1] In the absence of trade, the consumer surplus associated with durum production is given by area ($a+b+c$) in Figure 4.2(a) for Canada and area α in Figure 4.2(c) for the ROW. The producer surplus is measured, in the absence of trade, by ($e+d$) for Canada and by ($\beta+\gamma$) for the ROW. Total welfare is the sum of producer and consumer surpluses, and is simply given by the area between the demand and supply curves. For Canada, total surplus in the absence of trade is given by ($a+b+c+d+e$), while it is ($\alpha+\beta+\gamma$) for the rest of the world.

---

[1] According to economic theory, the area between the demand and supply functions up to the point where they intersect provides the greatest welfare, and, according to Arnold Harberger's First Theorem of Welfare Economics, perfect competition will always lead to the maximization of welfare if demand intersects supply from above.

Figure 4.2 Model of international trade in durum wheat

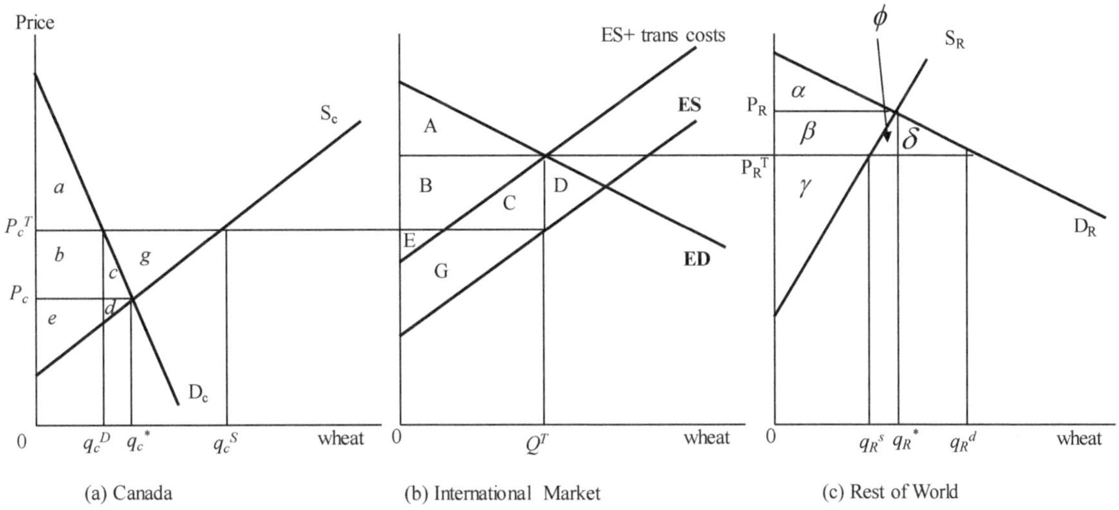

(a) Canada   (b) International Market   (c) Rest of World

^{T} refers to post-trade and * to autarky

4.2 Unrestricted Free Trade

To demonstrate that trade improves the welfare of citizens in both countries, it is necessary to show that total surplus in each country increases. This is done using Figure 4.2. Since, in the absence of trade, the price in the ROW is greater than that in Canada, Canada will export durum wheat to the ROW as long as the difference in price between the two regions exceeds the S&H costs plus tariffs.

With trade, the price in Canada rises from P_c to P_c^T, while the ROW price falls from P_R to P_R^T. Canadian processors (consumers of durum) lose as a result of the price increase and make less pasta; consumption in Canada falls from q_c^* to q_c^D and the consumer surplus falls from $(a+b+c)$ to area a only. However, Canadian farmers receive a higher price ($P_c^T > P_c$ in panel (a)), causing them to increase production from q_c^* to q_c^S. An amount $q_c^S - q_c^D$ ($=Q^T$) is sold to the ROW, while producer surplus increases from $(d+e)$ to $(b+c+d+e+g)$. The well-being of Canadians as a whole increases by area g, with durum farmers the main beneficiaries from trade.

The situation in the rest of the world mirrors that of Canada. The fall in ROW prices causes the food industry (consumers) to purchase more wheat (from q_R^* to q_R^D) and increase their overall surplus by an amount given by ($\beta+\phi+\delta$). Durum wheat growers in the ROW now face a lower price and curtail output to q_R^S, giving up a producer surplus of β in the process. However, the gain to consumers is greater than β, with the net gain to citizens in other countries given by ($\phi+\delta$).

The main results can be summarized in the international market of Figure 4.2(b). The amount traded between Canada and the ROW is $Q^T = q_c^S - q_c^D = q_R^D - q_R^S$. The net gain to the ROW is area A, which is equal to ($\phi+\delta$) in panel (c); this net gain accrues to ROW consumers and therefore is measured under the excess demand curve ED. The gain to Canada equals the area above the excess supply curve ES and below the demand price, or ($B+C+E+G$), but S&H costs of ($B+C$) are incurred. Hence, the net gain from trade is ($E+G$), which is equal to area g in panel (a). Note that both Canada and the ROW are better off with trade in durum wheat than without trade.

For the purposes of analyzing policy, a back-to-back representation of the trade model in Figure 4.2 can also be used. This is done in Figure 4.3, where q_c^* and q_R^* again refer to the autarkic quantities in Canada and the rest of the world, respectively, while P_c^* and P_R^* are the associated autarkic prices. Canada's excess supply curve can be represented in the ROW diagram (right-side panel in Figure 4.3). With trade in this case, the ES adjusted for S&H costs plus tariffs of $\$t$ per unit of wheat (ES+t) is added horizontally to the domestic ROW supply to find the relevant total market supply S^T in the ROW market. The market clearing price in the ROW market is then P_R^T, while the price in Canada is P_c^T ($=P_R^T-t$). Canada exports Q_c^E ($=q_c^S-q_c^D$) amount of durum to the ROW.

Figure 4.3 Back-to-back representation of the durum wheat trade model

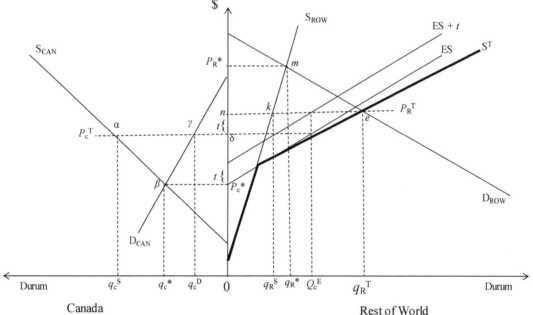

The gains from trade and the gainers and losers in each of the two regions can be readily identified. In Canada, consumers lose a surplus equal to the area bounded by $P_c^*\delta\gamma\beta$ in the left panel of Figure 4.3, while wheat farmers gain a surplus given by area $P_c^*\delta\alpha\beta$; the net welfare gain to Canada thus equals area $\beta\alpha\gamma$. There are gainers and losers in the ROW as well. The losers in this case are foreign durum wheat producers, whose surplus falls by the area bounded by points P_R^*nkm; durum consumers gain the surplus area bounded by P_R^*men. Summing the loss in producer surplus and the gain in consumer surplus leads to an overall gain in welfare in the ROW equal to the area bounded by mke. The global increase in welfare from trade in durum wheat is given by the area bounded by points $\beta\alpha\gamma$ in the left-side panel plus the area bounded by points mke

in the right-hand panel minus the transaction costs, which equal $t \times Q_c^E$. The overall gain must, however, be positive because trade would not otherwise take place.

The approach in Figure 4.3 is somewhat richer than that in Figure 4.2, and it is usually used to analyze policies affecting trade, particularly in agriculture and forestry. We use a similar diagrammatical analysis to investigate the (qualitative) impacts of various policies that governments use to favor domestic farmers, processors, manufacturers, or consumers.

4.3 Trade and the Measurement of Well-Being in Multiple Markets

In the previous discussion, we focused on trade in a single commodity. Many trade models include multiple commodities. It is not always clear how welfare measurement occurs when links among commodities constitute a vertical chain or commodities are horizontally related. In conducting welfare measurement in this case, it is important that we work with equilibrium demand and supply functions that take into account how price changes in one market reverberate through related markets back to the original market.

In this section, we employ general equilibrium demand and supply functions (discussed in section 4.3.2) to examine the measures needed to analyze policy in an international context. In doing so, we distinguish between net welfare changes and changes in welfare surpluses that are considered to be income transfers. Net welfare changes are calculated along the lines discussed in Chapter 2.2 in conjunction with the fundamental equation of applied welfare economics (equation 2.4); that is, the net welfare change constitutes the sum of the direct costs/benefits measured in the market immediately impacted by the policy plus the indirect costs/benefits in all affected markets where price exceeds marginal cost. To motivate the discussion, assume a government policy is enacted to reduce the production of flour from wheat.

4.3.1 Vertical Chains

Consider the case of the vertical chain in Figure 4.4, where wheat and flour markets are vertically integrated. It is assumed that the supply functions in the upstream $n-1$ market, which supply wheat producers with fuel, fertilizer, seed, tractor services, and labor, are horizontal or perfectly elastic ($\varepsilon_s = \infty$); likewise, it is assumed that the demands in the downstream markets for bread and pasta (the $n+1$ market) are perfectly elastic ($\varepsilon_D = \infty$). These two assumptions imply that changes in the demand for inputs into wheat production do not affect the prices of inputs (denoted r_{n-1}), and that changes in the supply of flour do not affect the prices of downstream bread and pasta (denoted P_{n+1}). These are realistic assumptions since, for example, the cost of flour in the production of bread is a very small portion of the total cost of producing bread. Given these assumptions, the consumer surplus in the wheat market can be measured by the producer surplus in the flour market.

Consider a government regulation that reduces the production of flour from F^0 to F^1 in panel (c). There is a change in consumer surplus in the upstream wheat market in panel (b) as the derived demand for wheat shifts downward from $D_{wht}(P^0)$ to $D_{wht}(P^1)$. Due to this lower demand for wheat, the price falls from r^0 to r^1, causing a change in consumer surplus equal to $(u-v)$; surplus u is lost because of the inward shift of the demand function, but v is gained because of the lower price. Since it is assumed that all wheat is used to produce flour, the change in consumer surplus in the wheat market is equal to the change in quasi-rent (producer surplus) in the downstream flour market. Thus, the change in consumer surplus in the wheat market equals the loss $(c+d)$ in Figure 4.4(c). Notice that the general equilibrium, competitive supply curve for flour S^*_{flr} takes into consideration the effect of the new wheat price, r^1, on flour supply; thus, it is not necessary to have S^*_{flr} shift as a result of this price change as it is inherently incorporated through its derivation.

There remain two additional surplus measures that need to be taken into account. First, in the wheat market (Figure 4.4b), the loss in quasi-rent to farmers is equal to $(v+w)$, which is equivalent to the change in consumer surplus of area z in the upstream market for fertilizer and feed, labor, fuel, equipment rentals, and so forth (Figure 4.4a). Again, this area must only be measured once, either in the wheat market or in the upstream market; double counting must be avoided. In applied work, the upstream $n-1$ markets (Figure 4.4a) are not modeled, and therefore it is only the quasi-rent in the wheat market that is measured.

Finally, in the flour market (Figure 4.4c), a scarcity rent is created equal to $(a+c)$, as supply is constrained to be lower than demand due to policy intervention. Producers of flour may capture the scarcity rent if it were created through a quota on production, while, if it arose due to an ad valorem tax, the government captures it as tax revenue.

The point of the above analysis is this: The welfare measures appropriate for a vertically integrated chain are the consumer surplus, producer surplus (quasi-rent), and scarcity rent. This result hinges on the assumption that remaining upstream and downstream markets are characterized by perfectly elastic output demand and input supply, respectively. It is also predicated on the assumption that markets for bread and pasta, which are horizontal markets, are characterized as a single market and that this market is the only user of wheat. If, for example, beer producers require wheat as an input, it is then necessary to assume that the demand function for beer is also perfectly elastic. We now consider what happens if this is not the case.

4.3.2 Vertical and Horizontal Chains

Now suppose that there are producers of other commodities that compete with flour for wheat. Assume that wheat is purchased only by breweries that produce wheat beer and by mills that grind wheat into flour. The demand for wheat in this case is the sum of the separate derived demands for wheat by flour and beer producers. In essence, the demand for wheat is the horizontal sum of the value of the marginal product (VMP) functions of wheat in making beer and wheat in producing flour. This is illustrated in Figure 4.5.

Figure 4.4 Welfare measurement in a vertical chain

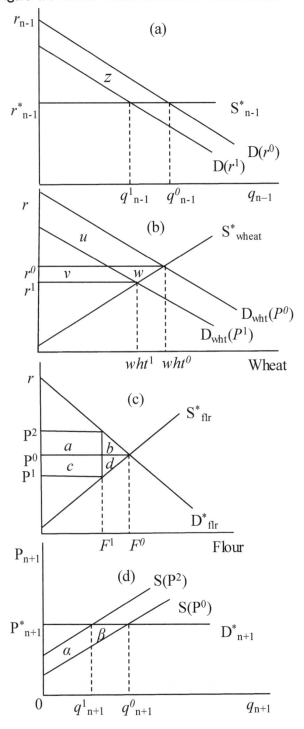

Figure 4.5 Combining the vertical and horizontal welfare chains

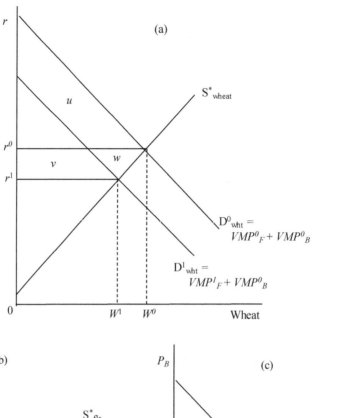

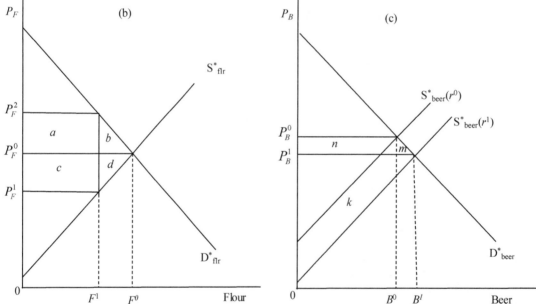

Let * denote a general equilibrium demand or supply function, but only in a restricted sense. In Figure 4.5(b), we again assume a policy is implemented that restricts the amount of flour produced (this figure is equivalent to Figure 4.4c). The change in the price of flour will reduce the price of wheat, which in turn will increase the supply of flour; yet this feedback is not explicitly shown because it is already taken into account in the construction of the general equilibrium supply function S^*_{flour}. The same is true of S^*_{beer}; if there is an exogenous shift in supply or demand in the beer market that results in a change in its price, the price of wheat is impacted but the feedback from this price change on the supply of beer is already taken into account in the general equilibrium supply function. However, the general equilibrium supply function for beer does not take into account the feedback resulting from a lower price of wheat ($r^1 < r^0$ in Figure 4.5a) caused by the reduced production of flour. Therefore, the policy affecting the flour market will impact the beer market through changes in the price of wheat.

What is the welfare impact of a policy-induced increase in the demand price of flour but a reduction in the supply price? The welfare impacts on the downstream bread and other markets remains the same, as does the welfare impact in the upstream wheat market, at least as drawn. However, there is an additional welfare consideration as a result of the horizontally related beer market. Assume the beer market is also a final consumer market, so that, unlike the case of flour, there is no further downstream market to consider. The decrease in the price that producers receive for flour reduces the value of the marginal product of wheat used to produce flour ($= P_F \times MP_{wheat\ in\ flour}$) from $VMP^0{}_F$ to $VMP^1{}_F$, thus shifting the demand for wheat inwards as indicated in Figure 4.5(a). The price of wheat falls, thereby causing the supply function for beer to shift from $S^*(r^0)$ to $S^*(r^1)$. Suppliers of beer lose a producer surplus equal to area n, but they gain k, while consumers of beer benefit by ($n+m$). Therefore, the net welfare change in the beer market is given by ($k+m$).

What is the overall change in well-being? Upon applying the fundamental equation of applied welfare economics (equation 2.4), the overall change in welfare is given by ($b+d$) in Figure 4.5(b). All of the other welfare measures are income transfers. That is, once one sums up all of the welfare measures in the preceding analysis, and assuming all markets are perfectly competitive, the only welfare change resulting from a policy that restricts the production of flour is given by ($b+d$) in Figures 4.4(b) and 4.5(c). Yet, the income transfers that result from the policy are an important consideration.

Assumptions regarding markets within vertical and horizontal chains are central to spatial price equilibrium trade models. In the remainder of this chapter, we illustrate the use of the foregoing concepts with some examples. These illustrate the important need to take into account international trade impacts in policy analysis.

4.4 Economic Policy and Trade: Examples

In this section, two examples of how to use SPE trade models to analyze economic policy are examined. In the first, European restrictions on Canadian imports of durum wheat are explored, followed by an illustration of the use of partial equilibrium trade models to examine the impacts of log export restrictions from British Columbia.

4.4.1 EU Import Restrictions on Canadian Durum Wheat

Consider again the case of trade in durum between Canada and, in this case, the European Union. Suppose the EU first imposes an ad valorem import duty on Canadian wheat and then replaces it with an import quota.

The situations are illustrated in Figures 4.6 and 4.7, respectively, for the import duty and quota. The demand for wheat in both regions is a derived demand by flour and pasta producers. Since the autarkic price for durum is lower in Canada than in the EU, under free trade the EU would import Canadian durum wheat.

Figure 4.6 Durum wheat trade: Imposition of an import duty on Canadian durum exports to Europe (arrows indicate direction of changes in consumption and production)

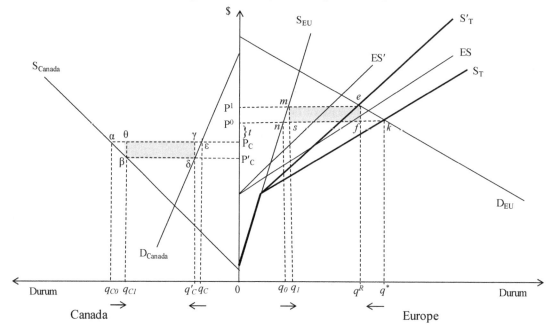

In the right-side panel of Figure 4.6, the European domestic supply function is denoted S_{EU}, while ES represents the Canadian excess supply function, which includes the S&H costs, symbolized by t. S_T then denotes the horizontal sum of S_{EU} and ES, with equilibrium occurring at point k where European demand D_{EU} intersects S_T. Under free trade, quantity q^* would be consumed in the EU and the European price would be P^0; q_0 would be produced domestically, with q^*-q_0 imported from Canada. In Canada, the free trade price would be P_c, q_{c0} is produced, and q_c is consumed, with the difference exported to the EU.

An ad valorem duty by the EU on imports of Canadian durum causes the excess supply curve to pivot from ES to ES'. The horizontal sum of ES' and S_T is now S'_T, so the intersection of the effective European supply and demand functions occurs at point e, where an amount q^R is now consumed. This is less than the q^* consumed under free trade. European farmers increase durum wheat production from q_0 to q_1, while Canadian exports fall from q^*-q_0 ($=q_c-q_{c0}$) to q^R-q_1 ($=q'_c-q_{c1}$). Canadian production declines and consumption increases as indicated because price falls from P_c to P'_c. Conversely, the European price rises from P^0 to P^1.

Figure 4.7 Durum wheat trade: Implementation of a quota on Canadian durum exports to Europe (arrows indicate direction of changes in consumption and production)

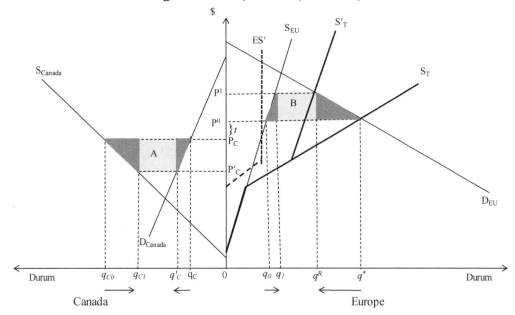

The tax revenue accruing to the EU is given by sum of the two shaded areas. Notice that the burden of this transfer falls on European consumers and Canadian farmers. Further, there is a deadweight loss due to inefficiency from not producing durum wheat in an optimal fashion that is given by four small triangles—the area bounded by points $\alpha\beta\theta$ plus $\varepsilon\delta\gamma$ in Canada, and efk and mns in Europe.

Now consider the case where the EU employs a quota on Canadian imports of durum wheat. This is illustrated with the aid of Figure 4.7. Here the quota is set so that the excess supply curve is given by ES'. The supply function facing Europeans is now given by S'_T in Figure 4.7 so that the price difference between Europe and Canada is P^1–P'_C rather than P^0–P_C as under free trade. The results are similar to those in Figure 4.6, but the diagram illustrates (despite the use of similar labeling) a quota restriction that leads to lower imports from Canada than under the ad valorem tax. The quota rent equals the sum of the light-shaded areas A and B in Figure 4.7; area A represents the burden paid by Canadian farmers and area B the loss to European consumers. The quota rent is up for grabs—it might accrue to European importers (who are granted a license to import durum), Canadian exporters, or some other agent able to collect this rent (e.g., a shipping firm). Whether the quota rent is greater than the tax revenue in Figure 4.6 depends on the elasticities of supply and demand. As the deadweight losses (dark areas in Figure 4.7) increase, this causes the income transfers (light-shaded areas) to fall.

4.4.2 Incentivizing Antidumping and Countervailing Duty Complaints: Byrd Amendment

As a trade measure aimed at foreign suppliers of agricultural commodities and other products, the US

Congress at one time passed an amendment to the Agriculture, Rural Development, Food and Drug Administration, and Related Agencies Appropriation Act (2001). The amendment was the Continued Dumping and Subsidy Offset Act of 2000, commonly referred to as the Byrd Amendment. The Byrd Amendment allowed any "manufacturer, producer, farmer, rancher, or worker representative" that was party to an antidumping or countervailing duty investigation to qualify for the disbursement of funds collected as a result of that investigation. The funds would then be disbursed as compensation for expenditures in any of the following areas: manufacturing facilities, equipment, R&D, personnel training, acquisition of new technology, health care benefits to employees, pension benefits, environmental expenses, raw materials and inputs acquisition, and working capital. Because the affected party could claim expenditures in such a large variety of areas, this was a clear, albeit perverse, incentive for any US agent to bring trade cases before the US Department of Commerce.

The Byrd Amendment incentivized US agricultural producers, lumber manufacturers, and others to initiate countervailing duties (CVD) against countries exporting to the US. Potentially, a successful trade complaint leading to the imposition of countervailing duties on a foreign supplier results in higher domestic US prices that benefit the complainant (increasing producer surplus and perhaps other rents) and potential CVD payouts. Thus, the Byrd Amendment provided a double jeopardy that encouraged US producers to continue trade action against foreign sellers. For example, trade actions were subsequently directed at Canadian suppliers of wheat and lumber.

The Byrd Amendment prompted a series of dispute resolution panels at the World Trade Organization (WTO), initially called for by Australia, Brazil, Chile, the EU, India, Indonesia, Japan, Korea, and Thailand, and later supported by Canada and other countries. A WTO panel ruled in September 2002 that the Byrd Amendment violated at least nine WTO articles covering a host of fair trade practices, and this ruling was subsequently upheld on appeal in January 2003 with the US directed to make changes accordingly. Due to lack of timely US action, the WTO authorized Canada to impose 15% ad valorem duties on certain US products (cigarettes, oysters, and live hogs) in retaliation for countervailing duties imposed on softwood lumber until it recouped $11.16 million USD in the first year. Likewise, Japan was authorized to impose duties of 15% on imports of US steel.

The Byrd Amendment was finally repealed in 2006, but its provisions remained in effect until October 1, 2007. However, according to Wikipedia, the EU estimated that some $1 billion of antidumping duties imposed by the US government were redistributed to various companies under this legislation. For example, one pasta company apparently received $3.0 million in 2006 and, despite its repeal later in the year, $4.6 million in 2007.

4.4.3 Restricting Log Exports

Forest companies in British Columbia can only export logs from federal or private lands if logs are declared surplus to domestic requirements; this implies that no domestic buyer of logs is forthcoming or that an offer to purchase surplus logs is deemed inadequate. In the latter case where there is a large disparity between offers to sell logs and bids to purchase them, a provincial Timber Export Advisory Committee determines whether the seller of logs will be permitted to export them. Not surprisingly, log exports from the province have historically risen when lumber markets were weak, falling again as demand picked up. Naturally, lumber manufacturers and other log processors have opposed exports since they result in higher domestic prices.

Many economists have argued against log export restrictions on the grounds that free trade in logs yields the greatest welfare benefits to the provincial economy (as some 95% of Canadian forestlands are owned by provincial governments). This may not be the case, however, because export restrictions may well be preferable to either a total restriction on log exports or complete free trade. For example, by acting as a monopolistic seller, Canada could and perhaps should voluntarily restrict lumber exports to the United States in order to capture the policy-induced scarcity (i.e., monopoly) rents that would be created. The same is true with respect to British Columbia's log export policy. The policy requires that, before logs can be exported, logging firms must demonstrate that there is no local demand for logs or that the price local processors are willing to pay for logs is unreasonably low. Since changes in the supply of BC logs on the international market have an impact on global log prices (i.e., the excess demand function for BC logs is downward sloping), it might be optimal to restrict log exports from the perspective of maximizing welfare to the province, and that a move away from that policy toward freer trade would lead to a loss in well-being. This case is investigated somewhat further in what follows.

Log exports from BC are an important part of the province's external trade. In 1987, log exports amounted to somewhat less than 4 million cubic meters (m^3), but a decade later they were less than ½ million m^3. Log exports rose dramatically after 1997; by 2005, they reached nearly 5 million m^3, falling to about 3 million m^3 by 2009 as a result of the global financial crisis, and then rising rapidly to well over 6 million m^3 in 2013. Given that global log trade amounts to about 35 million m^3, it is clear that changes in BC exports have an impact on world log prices.

Log trade between British Columbia and the rest of the world can be analyzed with the aid of Figure 4.8. In panel (a) of the figure, British Columbia's supply and demand functions are denoted S_{BC} and D_{BC}, respectively. The respective price and quantity under autarky are then given by P^A and q_A. With trade, the province faces an excess demand for logs from the rest of the world given by ED, while ES is BC's excess supply. However, $ES' = ES + T$ is the relevant excess supply as it includes S&H costs of T/m^3 (no country imposes tariffs on log imports). If BC restricts log exports to the amount Q^R ($= q_1 - q_0$ = quota level of log exports), this shifts ES to ES^R in panel (b) representing the international market. Logs are sold internationally at price P^1, but domestically they are sold at the lower price P^0 as a result of S&H costs.

Compared to no log exports, British Columbia's consumers lose ($a+b+x$) but producers gain ($a+b+x+c$) for a net gain of $+c$. In addition, ($j+f$) is a surplus created by the policy-induced scarcity (i.e., not allowing free trade in logs) and could be wasted through the export process or captured by the log exporter or the (public) landowner. If log exports are now freely permitted, the world price P^W becomes relevant and BC would export Q^W logs ($= q_s - q_d$ = free trade level of log exports).

Figure 4.8 British Columbia's log trade: Analysis of log export restrictions

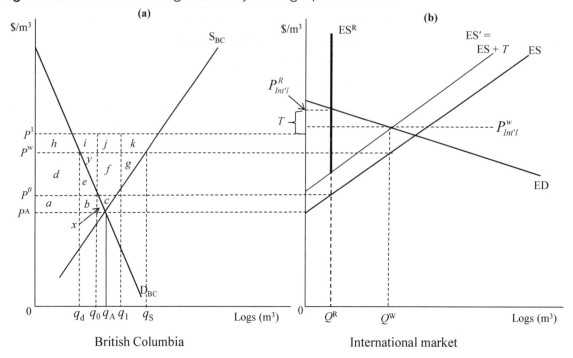

British Columbia   International market

Compared to the restricted log export situation, BC wood processors (consumers of logs) lose $(d+e)$ and timber owners gain $(d+e+y+g-j)$, assuming areas f and j initially accrued to the forest owners. The net gain to BC is thus $(y+g-j)$ with j lost because of the price decline in the international market. This is the correct area that can easily be measured if the elasticities of supply and demand in each of the markets are known—that is, if there is information to construct the equations for the demand and supply functions.

The evidence suggests that British Columbia's log export policy has resulted in a level of exports that led to higher provincial well-being than would be the case if free trade in logs were allowed. It also led to higher well-being compared to autarky. Indeed, the actual level of permitted log exports might even be somewhat greater than the level that would result in the highest monopoly rents.

The problem with the analysis above is that it is static. Suppose, instead, that the goal of government policy is to generate jobs or to create the largest possible wood processing sector in the world. Then it may be necessary to implement industrial policies that would prevent loss of manufacturing potential to other countries. Following the discussion in Chapter 2, the economist would then need to compare the net benefits under an industrial policy that prevents all log exports against the net benefits of a policy that permits log exports; this means that the analyst would need to state explicitly the benefits forgone (the costs) of creating jobs. This would enable the policy maker to compare industrial strategies for creating manufacturing jobs across sectors. If the industrial policy is more concerned with retaining manufacturing ability (avoiding loss of manufacturing capacity to other countries) for strategic reasons, it might also be necessary to examine other economic strategies that create scarcity rents, such as import duties or export taxes. Again, the models discussed here could prove helpful in providing information on one of the aspects the decision maker must take into account—the aspect related to the economic efficiency of policy.

4.5 Concluding Discussion

Spatial price equilibrium models are an alternative to general equilibrium models although many economists prefer the latter. SPE trade models are simply able to provide much greater product detail than general equilibrium models. The latter take into account all of the relative price changes that a policy induces; they take into account all of the potential changes that a policy could bring about. In contrast, SPE models assume that the impact of any given policy is confined to a particular sector, and that changes in the prices in that sector have little or no impact elsewhere in the economy. In some senses this is true in agriculture and forestry. Supply management in the dairy sector of one country is unlikely to have a large effect on prices in other sectors of that country and, if so, it is doubtful that markets in these other sectors are characterized by market imperfections on a scale that requires the analyst to take these into account. Although dairy prices in other countries might be affected, again the welfare measures that need to be taken into account in the non-dairy, non-agricultural sectors in these countries are too small to be of concern. The same holds for forestry: The impact of a US countervailing duty on softwood lumber from Canada is too small to change relative prices elsewhere in the economy. Indeed, changes in lumber price probably do not even affect house prices in Canada or the United States.

An SPE model is able to consider different types of softwood lumber, for example, and thereby whether lumber from Canada is a substitute for US lumber, or whether it is a complement. To what extent is cedar lumber decorative compared to US lumber? Is Canadian spruce–pine–fir lumber preferred to US lumber in the construction of multi-story housing? What role does US lumber play in such construction? There is generally too little disaggregation in general equilibrium models to address these sorts of issues.

Policy analysis can be diagrammatical, analytical or numeric, or some combination of these. In the chapters that follow, we rely primarily on diagrammatical analysis. However, both the diagrammatical and analytical approaches can only be indicative of the directional shifts that policies can bring about. To estimate the costs and benefits, it is necessary to develop empirical, numerical models. Once functional forms are specified, the model parameters can be empirically estimated; alternatively, one could use information about model parameters, such as elasticities of supply and demand, from other studies. One can then analytically solve for the quantities and prices shown in the diagrams and calculate the welfare areas, although this is more challenging if more than one market and several constraints or policies are involved. The other option is to model the functions indicated in the diagrams using mathematical programming, where an objective function (usually maximization of producer plus consumer surpluses) is maximized subject to various constraints representing the policy changes. Either of these approaches enables the identification of welfare measures and income transfers as suggested by the diagrams.

The issue of functional form can also be important. The models and diagrams that we have considered thus far, and ones that will be constructed in the following chapters, assume linearity of supply and demand functions. While quadratic and Cobb-Douglas functional forms have also been used, research indicates that policy outcomes are quite robust to functional form.[2] Linear functional forms are simple to use for diagrammatical analyses of policies. In the appendices to this chapter, we examine supply restrictions using linear functions and the form of the objective function in spatial price equilibrium (law of one price) models. As shown in Chapter 2, producer and consumer surpluses are given, respectively, by areas below the demand function and above market price, and below price and above the supply function. With linear functions, these areas result in a quadratic objective function, as shown in Appendix 4.B, while constraints tend to be linear. This implies that one can use quadratic programming to solve SPE models. This is a great advantage over more complicated functional forms, because it is easier to solve and, especially, to interpret outcomes from a quadratic programming model than from another nonlinear mathematical programming model. This is particularly true when an SPE model, for example, includes a large number of regions along with several related products.

In the chapters that follow, we employ diagrammatical analysis to examine the welfare implications of agricultural policies that have been used in various jurisdictions to support farm incomes. The use of numerical approaches is explored in exercises that are found in the Food for Thought section at the end of each chapter. Because trade is a major driver of agricultural policies, we begin by focusing on global and domestic institutions and trade.

Appendix 4.A: Mathematics of Supply Restrictions

Suppose that the inverse supply and demand functions are linear as follows:

Supply: $\qquad p^s = a + b\,q$, $a, b > 0$

Demand: $\qquad p^d = \alpha - \beta\,q$, $\alpha, \beta > 0$

Solving for the competitive equilibrium quantity gives: $q_c = \frac{\alpha - a}{b + \beta}$ and $p_c = \frac{a\beta + b\alpha}{b + \beta}$. We can also write supply and demand, respectively, in their normal form as: $q_S = -\frac{a}{b} + \frac{1}{b}p$ and $q_D = \frac{\alpha}{\beta} + \frac{1}{\beta}p$.

The elasticities of supply and demand can be determined from their formulae as:

$$\varepsilon_S = \frac{dq_S}{dp}\frac{p}{q} = \frac{1}{b}\left(\frac{a+bq}{q}\right) = \frac{a}{bq} + 1 \text{ and } \varepsilon_D = \frac{dq_D}{dp}\frac{p}{q} = \frac{1}{\beta}\left(\frac{\alpha-\beta q}{q}\right) = \frac{\alpha}{\beta q} - 1$$

Now consider two cases used to support price: (1) a supply restriction or quota (q_R) and (2) a price support (p_s).

$\underline{\text{Supply restriction}}$: Let $q_R = \gamma q_c$, where $0 \leq \gamma \leq 1$. Then

---

[2] Respective quadratic and Cobb-Douglas demand functions are written as: $p^d = \alpha - \beta\,q + \gamma\,q^2$ and $p^d = \alpha\,q^{-\beta}$, $\alpha, \beta > 0$, γ free. In the Cobb-Douglas function, the elasticity of demand is $-\beta$.

$$p_R = \frac{(1-\gamma)\alpha\beta + \alpha\beta + \gamma\ a\ \beta}{b+\beta}, \quad q_R = \gamma\left(\frac{\alpha-a}{b+\beta}\right).$$

Notice that $p_R = p_c$ and $q_R = q_c$ if $\gamma=1$.

Price support: Let $p_S = \delta p_c$, where $\delta \geq 1$ (price support/deficiency payment). Then

$$q_S = -\frac{a}{b} + \frac{1}{b}\delta\left(\frac{a\beta + b\alpha}{b+\beta}\right) = \frac{-ab - a\beta + \delta a\beta + \delta b\alpha}{b(b+\beta)} = \frac{(\delta-1)a\beta + b(\delta\alpha - a)}{b(b+\beta)}.$$

If there is no price support, then $\delta = 1$, which implies $q_S = \frac{\alpha-a}{b+\beta} = q_c$.

Appendix 4.B: Calculation of Objective Function in SPE Models

The approach used in this appendix is to calculate the consumer surplus as the area under the excess demand function. To this we add the net revenue of supply regions. Assume the excess demand function for wheat, say, is linear:

(B1) $P^d = \alpha - \beta\ Q$, where $Q = \sum_{r=1}^{N} q_r$ and N = number of regions.

Assume that the individual regional marginal cost (supply) functions are given by:

(B2) $P_r^S = a_r + b_r\ q_r \Rightarrow q_r = \frac{P_r^S - a_r}{b_r} \Rightarrow Q = \sum_{r=1}^{N} q_r = \sum_{r=1}^{N} \frac{P_r^S - a_r}{b_r}.$

Then the total revenue is

(B3) $TR = P^d\ Q = (\alpha - \beta\ Q)\ Q,$

while the consumer surplus is

(B4) $CS = \frac{1}{2}(\alpha - P^d)\ Q = \frac{1}{2}\beta\ Q^2.$

The total benefit of selling wheat in any period is given by the sum of TR and CS.

(B5) $TR + CS = (\alpha - \frac{1}{2}\beta\ Q)\ Q$

To obtain the net global surplus in the wheat market, it is necessary to subtract from total benefit the sum of the individual regional total costs. For any given period, the total cost of supplying wheat is:

(B6) $TC = \sum_{r=1}^{N}(a_r q_r + 0.5\ (P_r^S - a_r)q_r) = \sum_{r=1}^{N} 0.5\ (P_r^S + a_r)q_r)$
$= \sum_{r=1}^{N} 0.5\ (a_r + b_r q_r + a_r)q_r\ = \sum_{r=1}^{N}(a_r + 0.5\ b_r q_r)q_r$

The net surplus in the international market for wheat in a given period is then:

(B7) $NS = TR + CS - TC = [\alpha\ Q - \frac{1}{2}\beta\ Q^2] - \sum_{r=1}^{N}(a_r + 0.5\ b_r q_r)\ q_r.$

Guide to Literature

In addition to the applied welfare economics literature indicated in the preceding chapters, a good place to start looking at spatial price equilibrium models of trade, and the law of one price on which they are based, is the textbook by Vercammen (2011, Chapter 2). See Harberger (1971, 1972) concerning three theorems of welfare economics. Just, Hueth, and Schmitz (1982, pp. 177–199) illustrate how price changes in one market reverberate through related markets back to the original market (see also Just, Hueth, and Schmitz 2004).

Further discussion of how welfare is measured in applied trade models and the structure of such models, including a method of calibrating components of a bilateral trade model, is provided in van Kooten and Johnston (2014). Van Kooten and Voss (2021) also examine trade in forestry and agriculture using SPE models as well as econometric methods (gravity and Global Vector Autoregressive, or GVAR, trade models), while providing computer code written in R and GAMS for solving a variety of trade models.

Margolick and Uhler (1992) and Fooks, Dundas, and Awokus (2013) argue for free trade against log export restrictions. However, if an exporting country can exercise market power in the world market, it might well pay to restrict exports. Van Kooten (2002) argues that Canada should resolve the softwood lumber dispute with the US by forming the exporting provinces into a trade cartel, and van Kooten (2014) demonstrates that BC's policy to restrict log exports makes economic sense. An example of robustness of policy implications to functional form is provided by Carter and Mérel (2016).

Food for Thought

4.1. In Figure 4.4, we found that a restriction on output of flour led to a loss that could be measured in the market for inputs into the production of wheat—equal to area Z in Figure 4.4(a). This area equals the change in quasi-rent accruing to wheat producers, which was given by area $(v+w)$ in Figure 4.4(b). The derived demand for flour is given in Figure 4.4(c). As a result of the restriction on flour production, suppliers lose quasi-rent given by area $(c+d)$, although they could gain some of it back as a quota rent. What area could they possibly gain back as quota rent? Would they gain more than this amount? Is there another market in which area $(c+d)$ might be measured? If so, identify the area in that market which would give an equivalent welfare measure.

4.2. Assume a country is a net importer of eggs, although it also produces some eggs itself. To protect egg producers and raise their incomes, the government places an effective quantity restriction on imports and at the same time puts a quota scheme on domestic producers. Illustrate the situation diagrammatically. Who are the gainers and losers? Make sure to identify the potential areas in the diagram that constitute losses and/or gains, and to whom they accrue. Is some form of a "quota rent" created? Is there more than one quota rent? Who gets these and how large are they? (HINT: Draw a back-to-back diagram showing the excess supply curve of the foreign suppliers on the left and the sum of the domestic plus foreign excess supply on the right to determine your free trade equilibrium. Then impose your constraints on domestic production of eggs and the restriction on import quantity.)

4.3. Discuss the economic welfare distortions that the Byrd Amendment might have on trade and the benefits that those initiating an antidumping or countervailing duty petition with the US's International Trade Commission. HINT: See Schmitz and Schmitz (2012).

4.4. Countries A and B trade commodity q. The stylized explanation of the trade between the countries is given by the figure where S&H refers to the shipping and handling costs, P and p to price, S and D to supply and demand, respectively, in the countries, and ES and ED to the excess supply and demand functions for countries A and B, respectively.

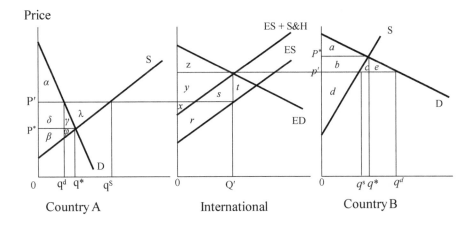

Price

Country A   International   Country B

(a) What areas in the far right panel constitute the net gain to country B?

(b) What is the gain or loss to producers in country A as given by areas in the far left panel?

(c) In the center panel, identify the net gain to country A.

(d) There are two ways that the S&H costs can be measured. In the center panel, identify at least one of the areas that constitutes a measure of the S&H costs.

4.5. What is the difference between an ad valorem tariff and a per unit tariff? What is the effect on a country's excess demand curve for a particular commodity?

4.6. Suppose that a large country exporter applies a domestic input subsidy. In general, how does this program affect competing producers in the importing country and what is the appropriate trade remedy required to counteract this subsidy?

(a) Show the effects of the input subsidy on producer and consumer prices in the domestic market and on the world price. What happens to production and consumption in the importer's market and the exporter's market? What happens to volume of trade?

(b) Now suppose that the importing country imposes a countervailing duty (CVD) that is applied to imports and just equals the level of the per unit subsidy. Does the CVD exactly compensate for the effect of the subsidy or does it create a distortionary effect?

(c) If the subsidizer were a small country exporter, what would be the appropriate countervailing duty?

(d) What are the two stages of the countervailing duty case? The analysis above relates to which stage of the CVD case?

4.7. Although there have been several successful regional trade agreements, WTO negotiations are still underway with respect to agricultural trade. Not many are optimistic that there will be a new WTO agreement, but most trade analysts would prefer to see one multilateral agreement rather than several regional trade agreements.

(a) What are the advantages and disadvantages of the multilateral approach relative to regional trade negotiations (preferential trade agreements)? What are three main major areas (pillars) that are under negotiation with respect to the WTO Agreement on Agriculture? What are the issues with respect to liberalizing tariffs?

(b) Will the same formula be used for all types of products?

(c) What problems are encountered in attempting to liberalize tariff rate quotas?

(d) With respect to export competition, what measures are considered to be indirect subsidies? What are the current proposals with respect to export subsidies?

(e) With respect to domestic subsidies, what are the major issues being negotiated?

(f) Would it be better to have a WTO agreement or the Trans-Pacific Partnership Agreement (which has now been signed but excludes the US and China)?

4.8. What is the difference between an antidumping (AD) case and a countervailing duty (CVD) case? The US has used both strategies to impose duties on Canadian softwood lumber, for example. What are the steps of the process of initiating these types of measures? What are problems with establishing dumping margins and subsidy levels? Are the remedies appropriate? To whom does the injury test apply? Who would benefit from an import duty?

4.9. As an economic analyst for the World Fish Organization, you assume the domestic demand and supply for cod fillets in Iceland are given by the following linear demand functions: $P^d = \alpha - \beta q$
$\alpha, \beta \geq 0$ and $P^s = a + bq, a, b \geq 0$

Subsequent econometric analysis leads to the following domestic Icelandic supply and demand functions: $p^d = 120 - 2q$ and $p^s = 2/5\, q$.

Now, Iceland exports cod all over the world. The excess supply function for Icelandic cod is the quantity difference between supply and demand at each given price and can be calculated as follows:

$$ES = \frac{\beta a + \alpha b}{b + \beta} + T + \frac{b\beta}{b + \beta} q \, ,$$

where T is the transportation cost. You also assume a linear excess demand function, $ED = A - Bq$, with the elasticity of ED given by:

$$\varepsilon_{ED} = \frac{dq}{dp}\frac{P^W}{q} = \frac{-1}{B}\frac{P^W}{q}, \text{ so that } B = \frac{-1}{\varepsilon_{ED}}\frac{P^W}{q} \text{ and } A = p^W\left(1 - \frac{1}{\varepsilon_{ED}}\right).$$

Finally, you determine the following:

Item	Parameter	Value
Domestic price with no trade ($/kg)	p^A	20
Domestic consumption/supply no trade (kg)	q^A	50
Elasticity of ED (measured at world price)	ε_{ED}	-2/3
World price ($/kg)	p^W	60
Transportation cost ($/kg)	T	10

As the economist at World Fish, you are asked to:

(a) Determine the effect of international trade on Iceland; that is, what is the gain to trade compared to autarky?

i. What are the formulae for the equations of ED and ES?

ii. Construct a diagram consisting of domestic and international trade panels (not necessarily back-to-back). Plot the domestic supply and demand equations in the domestic trade panel and plot the excess demand and excess supply functions on the international trade panel. Show the gains and losses from trade in each of the panels and provide an actual measure of the net gain to Iceland from trade.

(b) Suppose that Iceland sets an export quota of 36 kg of cod fillets. (Using a separate diagram is useful.)

i. Compared to autarky, calculate the total gains and/or losses.

ii. Is Iceland better off with an export quota or with free trade? Why or why not?

4.10. Mathematically derive equations (4.3) and (4.4) from equations (4.1) and (4.2). See also Appendix 4.A.

5

GOVERNANCE, RENT-SEEKING, GLOBAL TRADE, AND THE AGREEMENT ON AGRICULTURE

In modern societies, the production of natural resource and agricultural commodities, and the consumption of food, do not occur in an institutional and policy vacuum. Institutions and government policies have an enormous impact on a country's primary sectors. In this chapter, we examine the role of institutions and governance, especially as it applies to agriculture. In addition to domestic institutions and governance, we also consider global institutions that affect international trade. Along with the previous chapters, this chapter forms a foundation for analyzing the welfare impacts of government policies and international agreements, which are the primary subject material of the following chapters.

5.1 Institutions and Governance

5.1.1 Models of Government

Adam Smith opposed government intervention in the economy, arguing that the welfare of society was enhanced if everyone acted in their own self-interest. The "invisible hand" of the market would result in greater overall economic benefits than if government had intervened to direct the market in a particular direction; even if government intervened to alleviate the suffering of the least well-off, the poor would have been better off if the invisible hand of the market had been allowed to run its course. Nor did Adam Smith believe people would squander away their rising incomes by bearing more children—i.e., that population growing at an exponential rate would outstrip food production rising at an arithmetic rate, thereby condemning the working class to perpetual poverty. This was Thomas Malthus's idea, although it was probably not his greatest insight. Malthus's more important contribution was his idea that consumers (mainly workers) might not demand all that was produced by the capital-owning class. Investment would then be inadequate to absorb all savings, and recession would be the outcome.

Of course, the "recessionary" problem identified by Malthus never materialized in any important sense until the Great Depression of the 1930s. John Maynard Keynes's solution to this severe recession was for government to step into the breach, investing unspent savings on public projects whether those were infrastructure projects, investments in education, or some other form of government spending. However, Keynes remained a capitalist, urging that government intervention occur only during times of recession so as to create employment. When the economy recovered, he expected governments to pay off the debts incurred during recession (from borrowing the unspent savings); he certainly did not expect governments to run deficits during times when the economy was not in recession. Clearly, Keynes's advice has not always been heeded, partly because economists take different stances regarding the role of government.

What are some models of government's role? Too often it is assumed that governments act only in the best interests of society. This notion has been referred to as the "helping hand" model of government. Under this model, the main purpose of government is to produce public goods and correct market failures, although doing so often leads to a redistribution of income; intervention is often justified nonetheless by arguing or demonstrating that the gainers from the intervention could compensate the losers and still be better off, even though compensation is not actually provided. Unfortunately, "policy failure" is a frequent outcome. Policy or government failure occurs when state intervention in the economy to reduce unemployment (increase aggregate demand by public spending), provide public goods, correct market failure, or redistribute income leads to an even greater misallocation of resources.

Policy failure is a central theme of a second model of government, the "grabbing hand" model. Government departments consist of individuals who are not always interested in the well-being of society but, rather, act in their own self-interests, pursuing their own agendas rather than the common good. Governments consist of bureaucracies that take on a life of their own, with individuals inside government departments or other government agencies working to protect their own turf as much or more so than seeking the welfare of the citizens who pay their wages. Bureaucrats often fail to deliver even what their political taskmasters desire because the objectives of the two parties diverge.

This is a particular case of the principal–agent (PA) problem in economics: the principal (politician/citizen) expects the agent (bureaucrat) to carry out her agenda—the agent is expected to maximize the principal's objective function. However, the agent's objective or desire not only differs from that of the principal, but the agent also has information not available to the principal. Thus, the PA problem is not only one of misaligned objectives, but also one of asymmetric information.

In addition to the PA problem, corruption is often associated with the grabbing hand. Corruption is said to occur when decision makers (elected or otherwise) do someone a favor in exchange for something (e.g., acquiesce to a zoning change, change a farm support program), and/or sell a government service or commodity (e.g., passport, driver's license, employment visa, building permit) in return for a bribe. A bribe consists not only of an under-the-table payment of money, but might take various subtle forms, including gifts, free meals, implicit acceptance of abuse, and so on. The flip side of corruption is private-sector lobbying to get government to do something that creates rents and/or distributes rents in the direction of the lobbyist. Rent-seeking occurs, for example, when the US Lumber Coalition lobbies to restrict imports of softwood lumber from Canada so that, in their language, "more American homes can be built with American lumber milled by American workers."[1] Other examples include lobbying by Canadian dairy producers to retain supply management (SM) that ensures stable farm gate prices and quota rents, and lobbying by private-sector financial firms in the US to be the sole conduit for providing subsidized crop insurance to farmers. Lobbying can also come from inside government bureaucracies, where civil servants lobby to protect or expand their own interests.

In contrast, the invisible hand model of government argues for a reduced role of the state. Market failures are considered to be small, and certainly much less of a problem than "big government." By minimizing the role of the state, many problems will resolve themselves, or so it is thought. In this regard, the Nobel laureate Ronald Coase's famous insights about externalities were less directed at the role of government in correcting such environmental spillovers than at the role of the state in defining property rights and then relying on markets and/or the courts to resolve remaining externalities.

Nonetheless, whether or not there should be a minimal role for the state is a moot point. It is simply unrealistic to think that the role of government in modern societies can be rolled back. State intervention in the economy is here to stay; the helping hand model of government is the one that dominates. It forms the basis of cost-benefit analysis (see Chapter 2), which has become instrumental to policy making; it can also serve as a check on state intervention but is rarely used in that capacity. Perhaps the greatest casualty of big government has been reduced individual freedom, which is seen when government actions affect property rights—as in the case of takings, for example.

5.1.2 Takings

The Fifth Amendment to the US Constitution (November 1791) states: "… nor shall private property be taken for public use, without just compensation." This amendment is frequently called the "takings clause." Takings occur, for example, when governments expropriate property to make way for a new road. Such takings are known as a *titular taking*—literally a taking of title to the property (*expropriation* of private property)—and are accepted as long as the owner is provided with fair market value, or *direct compensation*. Taxes to pay for the armed forces or police protection provide compensation in the form of security, while taxes used to build roads, sewers, and so on similarly provide indirect benefits. Redistributing income by taxing the better off to provide for the less fortunate also provides *in-kind compensation* in the form of social stability, while also satisfying altruistic motives (and the recognition that one could be in a similar situation to that of the less fortunate). Social stability or even a social sense of fairness might justify universal medical coverage, for example.

A social safety net provides in-kind compensation to those who pay the bill. However, there is no in-kind compensation when social programs encourage abuse, constitute an income transfer from poor to rich (or even rich to rich), impose one group's idea of what is best for society upon others with an alternative

---

[1] US Lumber Coalition, 2020, About Us, https://uslumbercoalition.org/about-us/ [accessed December 4, 2020].

view, or when the military or police are large and pose a threat to innocent citizens of one's own country (or even those of another country). While there are many ingenious arguments for taking things from individuals, political philosophers question whether or not some government actions justified under the takings clause are indeed constitutional.

Another form of taking results from legislation that is meant to address environmental externalities or the provision of public goods. Such legislation could lead to *regulatory takings*. Environmental activism might result in regulatory takings. For example, a landowner might purchase a property near a city with the intent of selling it to a developer in 15 years. The land is not well-suited for farming, so the owner has a realistic expectation that his investment will pay off. However, with increasing urban development, citizens have identified this particular property as a particularly good location for a park. The overseeing government relents and, to avoid having to purchase the property and as a result of citizen lobbying, zones the property as agricultural land and subsequently purchases it at a much lower cost than had development been permitted. The landowner has effectively experienced a regulatory taking.

Most democratic countries have some provision to prevent the government from taking property from citizens without compensation. But regulatory takings are another matter. Often the agent affected by a regulatory taking is inadequately compensated or not compensated at all. There are three potential reasons for this: First, the bureaucracy is better able to fight lengthy legal cases than citizens, with litigants sometimes passing away before cases are resolved. Second, definitions of "property" and "compensation" are not always clear; for example, the term *property* refers not only to the physical asset but to what one can do with the asset. Third, the deck is often stacked against the party whose property rights were negatively impacted. More individuals may be on the side of the government, or powerful environmental lobby groups might be behind the regulations, while individual landowners lack the resources to stand up for themselves in court. In the case of industry, there may be little sympathy for paying compensation to large firms that have suffered a regulatory taking.

The true economic test of whether a public policy or project is economically worth pursuing is this: if those who benefit from the policy are able to compensate the losers and still be better off, the program is worth undertaking. Efficient outcomes do not, in principle, require that compensation be paid, but not requiring gainers to compensate losers will, in practice, give them an incentive to overstate the true value of their gains. For example, environmentalists have no economic incentive to limit their demands because they have no requirement to compensate those harmed (e.g., the poor who must pay a carbon tax to heat their homes, a landowner who cannot develop land because lobbyists have identified the land to be environmentally sensitive). Governments may be tempted to pursue programs or adopt policies only because they are able to shift the burden of their implementation onto private individuals who have no power to mitigate the costs or prevent "wipeouts." If governments had to pay compensation in all circumstances, they would be more likely to avoid policies that impose large costs on ordinary citizens but provide few benefits to society. Such outcomes are likely to be more efficient, and efficient outcomes are desired because they utilize less of society's scarce resources.

5.1.3 Institutions

A jurisdiction's institutional environment and its level of social capital are important drivers that facilitate economic efficiency and economic progress. While one line of economic research (located in the New Institutional Economics) deals with governance, another line of research pioneered by Oliver Williamson of Harvard University focuses on transaction costs.

The institutional environment consists of formal rules (constitutions, laws, and property rights) and informal rules (sanctions, taboos, customs, traditions, and norms or codes of conduct) that structure political, economic, and social interactions. Informal constraints are commonly referred to as social capital, which the Nobel laureate Elinor Ostrom defines as "the shared knowledge, understandings, norms, rules, and expectations about patterns of interactions that groups of individuals bring to a recurrent activity" (Ostrom 2000, p. 176).

Trust

Trust is perhaps the most important element of social capital, and it affects the costs of transacting: If one's confidence in an enforcement agency falters, one does not trust people to fulfill their agreements and agreements are not entered into. There is an element of trust in any transaction where one must decide (make a choice) before being able to observe the action of the other party to the transaction. One must assume that the other person is not acting with guile, keeping hidden information about themselves that can be used to their advantage at the expense of the other party to the transaction. Trust is the catalyst that makes an economy function efficiently.

When it comes to governance, three sets of institutions are critical: the state, rule of law, and procedural accountability. A state that is powerful without accountability is a dictatorship, while a weak state that is kept in check by subordinate political forces is ineffective and, at the extreme, unstable. Rule of law is required to protect property rights, enforce contracts, and ensure that the most powerful actors in the political system are bound by the same rules as other citizens. Finally, procedural accountability is required to ensure the quality of outcomes.

Despite democratic accountability, some countries lack a strong state and are characterized by pandering to various clientele and by corruption; other countries have a strong state but little in the way of rule of law, thereby exhibiting the same characteristics of clientelism and corruption. In yet other countries, the state may be strong but decision makers are not held to account. It is important that the state be effective and, yet, that the state leviathan is shackled by society—that it does not become despotic. It is not surprising that few countries score well on all aspects of governance. This is indicated, for example, by the World Bank's control of corruption index, which is provided for selected countries in Figure 5.1. Indexes for other aspects of governance are also available, but they are generally correlated with the control of corruption index.

Figure 5.1 World Bank's control of corruption index, selected countries, 2018

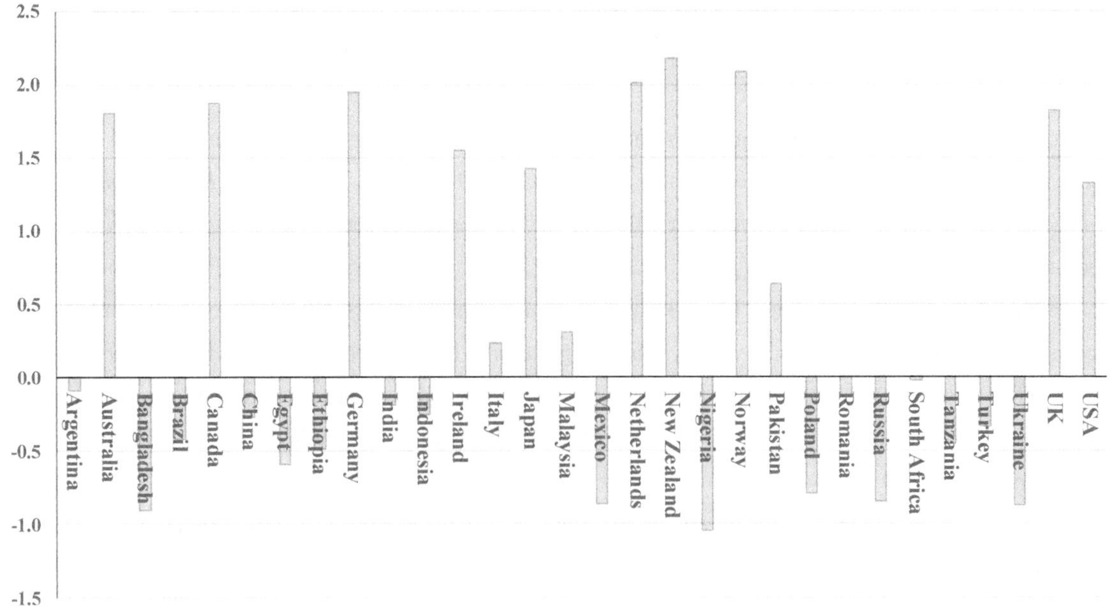

Scale: Very good =+2.5 to Very bad = −2.5
Source: World Bank, DataBank: Worldwide Governance Indicators at http://databank.worldbank.org/data/reports.aspx?
source=worldwide-governance-indicators# [accessed July 16, 2020].

International institutions typically work with nation states and require their co-operation; however, few states are able to contribute both strong laws and transparent governance. Consequently, it is unsurprising that international institutions that depend on state support also lack the capacity to effectively curtail production-distorting payments to agricultural producers, say, and more generally discipline multilateral agreements. Trust is often lacking and, as a result, international trade agreements include provisions for challenging countries that fail to comply.

Transaction costs

Transaction costs relate to the organization of a transaction—time and effort searching for a solution, brokerage fees, advertising costs, and so on. Transaction costs increase the costs of government policies, such as action to correct environmental externalities; indeed, transaction costs could be sufficiently large so that it is not optimal to correct an externality—transaction costs can prevent a policy from achieving its objective, resulting in a worse situation than that without the policy in place. If transaction costs are high enough, the overall costs of correcting an externality, or providing a public good or service, may exceed the benefits of doing so; then it is in society's interest not to correct the perceived market failure. Transaction costs also increase the social burden of supporting farm incomes, incomes that might not have been supported without rent-seeking (lobbying) on the part of agricultural producers.

5.1.4 Financing Government and Public Projects

Finally, we might consider how governments finance projects because, when all is said and done, financial constraints affect the ability of governments to pursue all of the policies and projects that they would like to implement. In other words, financing constraints will limit what the government does and require it to make trade-offs. This is the main lesson of Francis Fukuyama's (1992) book, *The End of History and the Last Man*—that a balance is needed between the role and size of the public sector and that of the private sector. Too large or too little a role for the public sector could lead to economic inefficiency and political unrest. One might add to this that a balance is needed between the primary sectors that produce wealth and all other sectors of the economy, whether the wealth generating sector is in private or public hands. Of course, history has shown that leaving the wealth generating sector in the public domain leads to inefficiency, partly because agents responsible for producing primary commodities are likely to pursue their own goals rather than those of the public.

The government can pay for its operations, including whatever projects and policies that it seeks to implement, in various ways:

- out of an existing budget surplus (if there is one);
- by borrowing on financial markets;
- through higher charges for services provided by the public sector (e.g., higher transportation fees, fees for doctor services at hospitals), and fees for use of natural resources (e.g., collecting a higher proportion of resource rents);
- out of profits, if any, from the operation of publicly owned companies;
- through increased taxes on incomes, properties, consumption, businesses, et cetera; and/or
- by printing money.

The latter option is open only to a federal government and only if the country is not in a currency union.

Any decision to raise funds is a political one—but no matter how funds are raised, there will be consequences. Unless there is compensation,[2] any public expenditure involves an income transfer; one consequence is that there will be people (or companies) that engage in rent-seeking behavior to ensure that they are the beneficiaries of income transfers. Likewise, there will be opposition to whatever revenue generating mechanism is employed, whether higher charges (say, for transportation or health care services) or taxes, or greater borrowing. Taxes and charges will be opposed because they increase the costs of those who must pay the tax or charge; they may also be opposed because people have an ideological predilection against charges or taxes, or a preference for private rather than public provision of services such as health care or crop insurance. But there is also another problem with charges and taxes: there is no guarantee that revenues actually increase as economic agents take counter measures to avoid the increased charges or taxes.

---

[2] As discussed in the section on takings, compensation takes various forms. For example, if one pays fees for public health care, compensation comes in the form of access to such care.

If corporate income and other taxes are raised, firms may leave for another jurisdiction where taxes are lower. This could reduce overall economic activity, lowering tax revenues from all sources while simultaneously increasing unemployment and other social welfare payments—these "automatic stabilizers" increase spending during downturns in the economy. Firms do have some ability to move to perceived tax havens. This led in the early part of the new millennium to a reduction in not only corporate but also income taxes in western Europe as eastern European countries that recently joined the EU attempted to attract investment and highly skilled labor by reducing taxes and simplifying the tax system. Thus, it could turn out that the elasticity of revenue with respect to the tax or charge is such that revenue falls with increased taxes/charges. A number of years ago, when the province of Saskatchewan attempted to raise revenues via a large hike in the provincial sales tax, it found that sales tax revenue actually declined.

Corporate and personal income taxes, along with consumption taxes (sales taxes), remain a major revenue source for most governments. Governments must, however, balance various tax sources to avoid a flight of investment and skilled labor, and the added costs when the economy underperforms as a result. The same applies to charges for public services. Indeed, it may turn out that the costs of public provision of such things as transportation services (bus, ferry, train) or health services could be lowered by letting the private sector provide them. The private sector has a greater incentive to reduce costs, so quality control becomes an issue with private provision of such services.

Finally, the government can borrow money to finance its programs, but this places a burden on future generations. Further, too much borrowing can increase the government's cost of borrowing—the interest that it needs to pay on the funds it borrows for the project or program in question plus what it pays on all other outstanding debt. If new borrowing triggers a change in the government's credit rating (and even governments can default on loans and thus are a credit risk), the cost of the project might increase significantly as it must pay more on its total debt as that debt is renewed.

A government must be careful as to how it raises funds as there are trade-offs. In the context of austerity measures needed to address high debts, *The Economist* points out that "fiscal adjustments that rely on spending cuts are more sustainable and friendlier to growth than those that rely on tax hikes. Studies show that cutting public-sector wages and [income] transfers is better than cutting public investment. Many cuts, from raising pension ages to slashing farm subsidies, have a double benefit: they boost growth both by improving public finances and by encouraging people to work harder or promoting more efficient allocation of resources."[3]

Raising taxes may harm growth, but there are some fiscal measures that can address budget deficits while still promoting the growth required to get a country out of debt. Nonetheless, if it is absolutely necessary to rely on taxes, the ones that do the least harm to growth are taxes on consumption and immobile assets such as land. Green taxes may also make sense, but one has to be careful as these might harm the poor more than is desired.

---

[3] *The Economist*, March 31, 2010, Fiscal Tightening and Growth: A Good Squeeze, https://www.economist.com/finance-and-economics/2010/03/31/a-good-squeeze.

5.2 Land Use and the Principal–Agent Problem

Farm operations inevitably lead to externalities. Residents living in rural areas or the urban-agricultural interface often complain about air and water pollution, smell, noise, and other spillovers from agricultural activities. In many cases, agricultural operations have been ongoing for decades or even centuries without conflict, but, as cities expand and crop and livestock operations intensify, conflict over environmental externalities increases. To protect farmers against nuisance complaints, potential lawsuits, and local regulations that would interfere with agriculture, many jurisdictions pass right-to-farm legislation.

In addition to right-to-farm legislation, governments might simply mandate farmers to implement so-called best management practices; these are practices that have been identified as having the least negative impact on the environment. Agricultural producers might not be eligible to participate in farm support programs unless they adopt best management practices. Many countries require farmers to implement certain soil conservation measures or, more often, set aside some of their land in a conservation reserve before they can receive farm support payments. A requirement to implement some environmentally friendly agricultural practice in order to qualify for farm support payments is commonly known as *cross compliance*. Cross compliance is considered a red-ticket policy as it forces farmers to comply with environmental standards to receive subsidies.

Governments might also provide subsidies to agricultural producers explicitly to target mitigation of environmental externalities (e.g., to ensure proper disposal of animal wastes), or to incentivize landowners to provide ecological/environmental goods and services (e.g., protect wetlands or plant trees). In essence, the government and sometimes non- or quasi-governmental organizations provide payments for environmental services (PES). This requires identification of a baseline or counterfactual land use or farming practice, with the producer provided a payment in accordance with a specified departure from the baseline. For example, a landowner might be paid for planting trees where none existed previously; a farmer might be paid to reduce the number of tillage operations on cropland to mitigate soil erosion and accompanying nutrient runoff into surface waters; or an agricultural producer is paid to protect bird habitat during breeding season by planting bird-friendly specialty crops or delaying harvests of hay. These types of programs are referred to as green-ticket environmental policies because they incentivize agricultural producers to meet or exceed certain environmental standards.

Monitoring and enforcement of regulations and counterfactual land uses can be a problem, however, the extent of which depends on institutions, governance, trust, and so on (as discussed in section 5.1). A PES program generally requires landowners to enter into contracts with government or a sponsoring non-governmental organization. Measuring and monitoring greatly increase the transaction costs of contracting but are necessary because the agent (landowner/farmer) has information that is unavailable to the principal (government/NGO). As noted above, the agent often acts in ways hidden from and contrary to the desires of the principal.

As an example, landowners might enter into a contract to plant trees that sequester carbon and create forest carbon offsets. The carbon offsets might become the property of the principal who then uses the carbon offsets to claim compliance with international climate treaties or sells the credits on a carbon market. Carbon offsets need to be certified before they can be sold, which creates an additional PA layer. There is a possibility that the carbon offsets certified for sale might not materialize because the agent who is supposed to carry out the land-use changes or forestry activities fails to do so for various reasons: In developing countries, the landowner (principal) may not have informed the peasant farming the land (agent) about the need to plant trees, the land may be unsuited for the trees specified in the contract, or the contract is broken the moment better crop opportunities arise. An up-front payment is needed to induce the land-use change, but this does not guarantee that the land will stay in forestry for the required length of time.

The effectiveness of contracts will depend on the ability to enforce contracts and the efficacy of rule of law, which tends to be weak in some countries (recall Figure 5.1). Resolving the PA problem—the need to align the incentives of the principal and the agents—probably poses the greatest challenge to contracting. Economists have addressed the PA problem related to PES by focusing on the payment mechanism. For example, to encourage landowners to participate in tree-planting projects, an up-front payment is clearly required to cover initial planting costs. Then a second and final payment would be made at the end of the contract period, with this final payment providing the needed incentive to keep agents from violating the contract by converting land to an alternative use. The difficulty here is that the principal does not have sufficient a priori information about carbon markets, the availability of alternative land uses, and how the opportunity costs of land might change during the contract period.

To reduce the risks of land conversion, the principal might provide a fixed per hectare payment plus annual payments that vary according to an index of agricultural prices. This turns out to be more efficient than tying variable payments to the price of carbon. Another suggestion is for contracts to provide two payments: one payment covers fixed costs while the other covers variable costs. The objective is to get the agents (landowners) to reveal truthfully whether they face high or low marginal costs of converting land to other uses—to reveal the onsite supply function for environmental services. In that case, the principal can design contracts that are incentive compatible with the principal's objectives. In theory, this then eliminates the PA problem; practice turns out to be quite different, partly because monitoring and enforcement remain an issue even if the contract itself is sound.

5.3 International Trade Negotiations and Agriculture

Agriculture has historically been and continues to be a particular obstacle in the negotiation of multilateral (and even bilateral) trade agreements. Agricultural policy distortions account for nearly 65% of all policy-induced trade distortions, and some 80%–90% of these are tariffs and tariff rate quotas (discussed below). The Uruguay Round of the General Agreement on Tariffs and Trade (GATT) began in 1986 and concluded with an agreement at the end of 1994. Then, beginning January 1, 1995, the GATT was replaced by the World

Trade Organization (WTO), which is an intergovernmental organization that regulates international trade. Conclusion of the GATT negotiations and establishment of the WTO was facilitated by an Agreement on Agriculture (AoA) and an Agreement on Subsidies and Countervailing Measures (SCM).

5.3.1 Agreement on Agriculture

The AoA was significant because it resolved or, at the least, found some way around the obstacles that countries' agricultural support programs posed in reaching an agreement on reducing overall tariff and non-tariff trade barriers. The conclusion of the Uruguay Round also included an agreement to continue negotiating on agricultural policy reform, which began in 2000.

The AoA permits some subsidies, classifying them according to three pillars—domestic support, market access, and export subsidies. Domestic support includes three main categories of agricultural support payments, referred to as boxes.

- *Green box* subsidies must not distort trade or, at most, cause minimal distortions. They have to be government funded and must not involve price support. Subsidies cannot target particular products but may provide direct income support for farmers if decoupled from current production levels or prices. Subject to certain conditions, environmental protection and regional development programs can be subsidized without limits. Supply-managed sectors do not fall into the green box because they are not government funded but, rather, the burden of such programs falls on consumers (so they are found in the blue box discussed below).
- *Amber box* subsidies include all domestic support measures considered to distort production and trade and that are not included in one of the other boxes. Included in the amber box are measures to support prices or subsidies that relate directly to how much is produced. Each of the 32 countries involved here have committed to limit the support they provide. These commitments are expressed in terms of a single total Aggregate Measurement of Support (AMS), which includes all supports for specified products together with supports that are not for specific products (and defined in Article 1 and Annexes 3 and 4 of the AoA). These limits to support are referred to as *de minimis* (minimal) levels, and are 5% of agricultural production value for developed countries and 10% for developing countries. Because amber box subsidies are trade distorting, countries are required eventually to reduce or eliminate them (see below).
- *Blue box* subsidies are perhaps best considered to be "amber box with conditions"—i.e., conditions designed to reduce distortions. Any support that would normally be in the amber box is placed in the blue box if the support also requires farmers to limit production. Thus, agricultural programs that require farmers to set aside land for conservation use in order to be eligible for subsidies—referred to as cross compliance—are included, as are production-limiting programs, such as supply restrictions (supply management), that might adversely affect trade. There are no limits on spending on blue box subsidies.

There are also exemptions for developing countries, sometimes referred to as the *S&D* or *development box*, because of its special and differential treatment of these countries. The reductions in agricultural subsidies and protection undertaken as a result of the conclusion of the Uruguay Round are provided in Table 5.1, although only figures for cutting export subsidies appear in the agreement.

Table 5.1 Agricultural policy reform as a result of the conclusion of the Uruguay Round of the GATT in 1994: Percent reductions in support payments by developed and developing countries and time frame for their implementation[a]

Item	Developed 1995–2000 (6 years)	Developing 1995–2004 (10 years)
Tariffs[b]		
Average cut for all agricultural products	-36%	-24%
Minimum cut per product	-15%	-10%
Domestic support[c]		
Total AMS cuts for sector (base period: 1986–88)	-20%	-13%
Exports		
Value of subsidies	-36%	-24%
Subsidized quantities (base period: 1986–90)	-21%	-14%

[a] Least developed countries did not have to make commitments to reduce tariffs or subsidies.
[b] The base level for tariff cuts was the agreed to (or bound) rate before January 1, 1995; or, for unbound tariffs, the actual rate charged in September 1986 when the Uruguay Round began.
[c] The other figures were targets used to calculate countries' legally binding "schedules" of commitments.
Source: Derived from World Trade Organization data and Hanrahan & Schnepf (2007).

Many of the targets in Table 5.1 have been met, but countries are still seeking further reforms; this is discussed in Chapters 7 through 9. Under existing WTO rules, and as argued by the US, direct payments to agricultural producers fall into the green box because they do not incentivize production nor distort trade. There is no limit on what a country can spend on green box subsidies. Subsidization of crop insurance premiums can affect output, however, and are thus trade distorting. The US has recognized that its yield and revenue insurance programs must be classified as amber box subsidies (see Chapter 9.2).

The objective of trade negotiations is to reduce or eliminate amber box subsidies, while green box programs continue to be exempt from trade reduction commitments. Trade commitments are expressed in terms of total aggregate measurement of support (AMS). In the current negotiations, various proposals deal with how much further these subsidies should be reduced, and whether limits should be set for specific products rather than continuing with a single overall aggregate limit for each jurisdiction. Blue box programs are tolerated, but they could be targeted by other countries for modification; for example, Canada's dairy and poultry marketing regimes have been singled out, although Canada has argued that supply management should be classified in the green box. Even so, some countries want to keep the blue box as it is because they see it as a crucial means of moving away from distorting amber box subsidies without causing too much hardship. Governments are still in the process of replacing crop-specific subsidies with ones that provide income support and target income volatility but no longer distort trade—programs that decouple support payments from output. Europe's basic farm payment (Chapter 8.1) and the use of base acres and base yields in 2014 US farm legislation (Chapter 7.2) are examples of attempts at decoupling.

During current WTO negotiations, proposals have sought to modify the amber box. One idea has been to set limits for specific products as opposed to continuing with single overall aggregate limits. On the other hand, if an overall limit is retained, proposals have looked at reducing the AMS by half—reducing the *de minimis* level from 5% to 2.5% for developed countries, say. It is unclear what will happen, but some countries appear to be taking into account such a possibility when reforming their agricultural support policies.

The Doha Round of the WTO, known as the Doha Development Agenda because it emphasized integration of the developing nations into the world trade system, was launched at the Fourth Ministerial Conference of the WTO held in Doha, Qatar, in November 2001. Agricultural negotiations are of great importance to the Doha Round because policies that distort agricultural trade account for two-thirds of all trade-distorting policies. Agricultural negotiations emphasize market access, particularly for developing and least developed nations. In addition to (1) market access, the focus of agricultural negotiations would be on (2) domestic support and (3) export subsidies—together these three issues are known as the three pillars of the agricultural negotiations (as noted above).

Based on WTO notification data for the period 1995–2001 prior to the start of the Doha Round, 24 of 36 countries (or trading blocs) that were eligible to use export subsidies actually used them, with the European Union accounting for nearly 90% of the total; for the same period, the EU, the US, and Japan accounted for 91% of domestic support (35 out of 149 countries reported using domestic support payments). However, all countries have implemented barriers to market access, making this a complex issue to deal with in trade negotiations. Indeed, tariffs and tariff rate quotas (defined below) account for some 80%–90% of the total cost of trade-distorting agricultural policies, with domestic support and export subsidies accounting for the remainder.

The EU and the US had agreed to a framework for negotiating agricultural trade liberalization by 2003. However, a group known as the G20 developing nations, which included Brazil, China, India, and South Africa, made a counter proposal for developed countries to reduce domestic subsidies and agricultural tariffs by a significant amount. At a meeting in Cancun, Mexico, in September 2003, parties failed to reach an agreement reconciling the two positions. A framework agreement was subsequently agreed to in July 2004, but negotiators could not complete a draft of the agricultural "modalities" (the ways or methods of doing something) by a July 2005 deadline. The framework agreement included, among other items, elimination of export subsidies; reductions in the *de minimis* exemptions, which were set at 5% of total value of agricultural production (TVP) for developed countries and 10% for developing countries; and a subsidy ceiling of 5% of product TVPs in the blue box category where none previously existed. An overall limit on total domestic subsidies (amber box plus blue box plus *de minimis*) was also proposed where none previously existed.

Subsequently, a Hong Kong (HK) Declaration on Agriculture adopted December 18, 2005, included the following key resolutions:

- Elimination of export subsidies by 2013. The EU met this target but other countries did not.
- Reduction in domestic support levels. The HK Declaration placed developed countries in three bands according to the extent of needed cuts. The EU was placed in the highest band, thus having to reduce its support levels by the greatest percentage. The US and Japan followed in the middle band, with remaining countries in the lowest band. The extent of the required reductions would be decided during the negotiations concerning modalities.
- Improvement in market access. Countries are to replace non-tariff barriers on sensitive products with quotas; tariffs on within-quota imports would be low (or non-existent), while those above the

quota would be formidable. This resulted in the tariff rate quota (TRQ) system, which is discussed in section 5.4. The process of substituting non-tariff barriers with a combination of quotas and discriminating tariff levels is known as tariffication, with tariff rates also to be negotiated as part of the modalities. However, developing countries are to be given preference in accessing developed country markets. For example, the EU abolished its supply management regime in sugar at the end of September 2017, replacing it with a TRQ that provides certain developing countries priority access to its sugar market.

- Immediate elimination of export subsidies on cotton.
- Development access. Developed and, to the extent possible, developing countries are to provide better access (e.g., specific TRQs) for agricultural products from the least developed countries (LDCs). Notice that this differs from "improvement in market access," which deals with developed countries providing developing countries with preferential access. Here, developing countries are to provide LDCs with preferential access to their markets.

Doha negotiations were suspended indefinitely on July 24, 2006, because a core group of countries—the United States, European Union, Brazil, India, Australia, and Japan, known as the G6—could not resolve issues related to agricultural trade. Indeed, one observer declared that the Doha negotiations are "effectively in a deep coma or dead" (Gantz 2013, p. 1). The main sticking points concerned the three agricultural pillars discussed previously: (1) trade-distorting domestic supports, (2) the potential elimination of export subsidies, and (3) increased market access for agricultural products (e.g., some countries protect import-sensitive products). In addition to agricultural reform, main issues at stake during Doha Round negotiations relate to developing countries—to ensure sustainable economic growth within a liberalizing world economy and increase developing countries' access to markets in developed countries. As noted above, developing countries play a much larger role in the Doha negotiations than they ever did in the Uruguay Round.

At a December 2015 meeting of WTO ministers in Nairobi, Kenya, an approach to making progress on agricultural trade was reached under the auspices of the Trade Facilitation Agreement reached at Bali in 2013. It included a proposal by the EU, Brazil, Uruguay, Paraguay, Argentina, Peru, New Zealand, and Moldova to reform agriculture. A main item was the elimination of export subsidies by the end of 2018 and limits after 2020 on the activities of state trading enterprises (which might be construed as providing an export subsidy). This applies as well to supply-managed commodities where imports are restricted through a TRQ but some products are exported. For example, Canada restricts imports of dairy products but exports skim milk powder (SMP) (for reasons discussed below and in Chapter 7.3), although this was to end by 2021. Meanwhile the EU ended all export subsidies from July 2013.

WTO members also agreed that negotiations would continue regarding trade-distorting public storage programs in developing countries; storage is incentivized with support payments that constitute a trade distortion. Attempts to have this activity included in the green box have been rebuffed because only non-distorting policies are considered in the green box. To get around the issue, the Bali position remains in place—a so-called peace clause whereby countries agree to exempt from legal challenges public storage policies in developing countries if storage is meant to enhance food security. Further, developing countries may also raise tariffs temporarily to address import surges or price declines—known as the Special Safeguard

Mechanism. Unfortunately, the suspension of formal negotiations under the Doha Development Agenda was not lifted in 2015 "due to differences among WTO members regarding the value of the previously made attempts to reach consensus" (EU 2016). Nonetheless, a Trade Facilitation Agreement, which included the aforementioned agricultural reforms, came into effect February 23, 2017, when two-thirds of the WTO membership ratified it.

In the meantime, the suspension of Doha Round negotiations opened the door for countries to pursue bilateral and regional free trade agreements (FTAs). This led to the Comprehensive and Progressive Agreement for Trans-Pacific Partnership signed on January 23, 2018, by 11 countries (but not the US or China); the Comprehensive and Economic Trade Agreement (CETA) between Canada and the EU; the US–EU Transatlantic Trade and Investment Partnership talks (not concluded as a result of President Trump's election); and other regional trade initiatives (e.g., Pacific Alliance in Latin America with Mexico, Peru, Chile, and Colombia).

The US, Canada, and Mexico renegotiated the North American Free Trade Agreement (NAFTA) at the request of the United States. The US felt that NAFTA disadvantaged US workers while enabling its partners to run up large trade surpluses. During negotiations, US president Donald Trump targeted Canada's supply-managed sectors (dairy, eggs, and poultry), arguing that they should be dismantled. Dairy was a particular target because Canadian imports of a new product, milk protein isolates (MPI) from Wisconsin, increased after the early 2000s, because they were classified in the Canadian tariff schedule as a protein rather than as a dairy product—MPIs were thus ruled to be outside the supply management regime. Canada countered with a new ultra-fine filtered milk product category that undercut MPI imports from the US. The US considered Canada's ultra-fine filtered milk to be a subsidized product because it indirectly benefits from supply management. Under the new US–Mexico–Canada (USMCA) trade agreement, which was signed September 30, 2018, but not ratified until 2020, Canada agreed to provide the US tariff-free access to 3.6% of its dairy market. Further, tariffs on milk protein concentrate (including MPI), skim milk powder, and infant formula are to be eliminated, thereby satisfying a major US demand that Canada remove its impediments to such imports. This should drive Canada's price for domestic skim milk powder toward the world price, thereby reducing what farmers get for milk as their price is a blend of the SMP and butter fat target prices. Nonetheless, as discussed further in Chapter 7.3, Canada remains committed to supply management.

Bilateral and regional trade negotiations have impacts on any country that continues to protect its agricultural sectors. This was obvious in the USMCA negotiations. As noted above, agricultural policy distortions account for the majority of all policy-induced trade distortions, with most related to tariffs and TRQs. Ongoing WTO negotiations will inevitably seek to eliminate tariffs and import quotas.

5.3.2 Agreement on Subsidies and Countervailing Measures

As noted above, an Agreement on Subsidies and Countervailing Measures was also agreed upon with the conclusion of the Uruguay Round of GATT negotiations and creation of the WTO. According to the WTO, the agreement "addresses two separate but closely related topics: multilateral disciplines regulating the provision of subsidies, and the use of countervailing measures to offset injury caused by subsidized imports" (WTO n.d.(a)). Although it appears that some direct export subsidies or subsidies to exporting enterprises might be tolerated, there are three types of adverse effects that enable another country to lodge a complaint. First, subsidized imports can cause injury to a domestic industry in the territory of the complainant. This is considered the sole basis for countervailing action. Second, serious prejudice arises when subsidies lead to adverse effects, such as export displacement, in the market of the subsidizing WTO member country or in a third country market. Finally, nullification or impairment of benefits can arise where subsidization undermines an impacted country's improved market access that is presumed to occur from a bound tariff reduction. The harmed country can be permitted to impose countervailing duties, expect the subsidization to cease, or receive restitution payments.

The best known example in agriculture occurred in 2002 when Brazil lodged a complaint with the WTO (dispute resolution case DS267) concerning US cotton subsidies. The case was resolved in 2014 with the US providing a one-time payment of $300 million to the Brazilian Cotton Institute and replacing its cotton subsidies with a different form of protection, the Stacked Income Protection Program (see Chapter 9.2).

5.4 Tariff Rate Quota

Instead of simply eliminating quota schemes wherever they are found, international trade negotiators have substituted import quotas with tariffs. This has resulted in a two-tiered tariff. For example, to protect its dairy quota regime, Canada limits the import of (specialty) cheese from other countries. The tariff applied to the quota is generally in line with tariffs other countries impose on similar goods; however, to prevent cheese imports above the quota, a prohibitive tariff is applied to over-quota imports. The quota is thus referred to as a tariff rate quota (TRQ). The purpose is that, as part of ongoing trade negotiations, countries bargain to have the import quota increased and above-quota tariffs reduced.

The TRQ and its welfare implications are investigated with the aid of Figure 5.2, which illustrates the situation for the US sugar industry. A quota amount of sugar is imported at a low per unit tariff rate of t_0, but remaining imports face a prohibitive tariff t_1. In panel (a), the world price of sugar outside the US is assumed to be p^* (left-hand panel), although the US quota is instrumental in determining this price. Indeed, the excess supply from the rest of the world will equal the US sugar quota $\bar{q} = q_x^S - q_x^D$. Assume there are no shipping and handling costs. Then the lightly shaded area in panel (c) represents the quota tariff revenue, which is captured by the US government, while the darker area is a policy-induced scarcity rent.

Figure 5.2 Illustration of tariff rate quota in US sugar sector

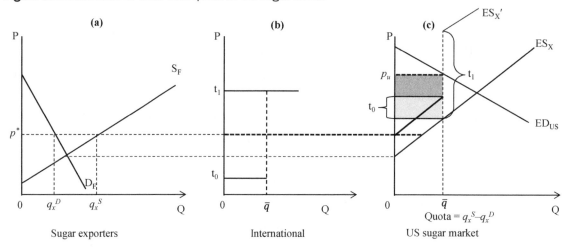

Sugar exporters   International   US sugar market

5.5 Concluding Discussion

The focus of this text is on the primary sectors, but most particularly agriculture and forestry. Unlike the extractive minerals and oil and gas industries, there is often less stigma attached to agriculture and forestry. Forestry has been targeted by environmental groups for the logging of old-growth timber and unsustainable forest practices, but complaints have been addressed through various agreements and, most particularly, certification schemes, such as the Forest Stewardship Council, which certifies sustainable forest management practices. Further, in a world concerned with CO_2 emissions from fossil fuels, wood biomass is generally viewed as a carbon-neutral renewable alternative energy source and alternative building material to concrete and steel, the production of which leads to large CO_2 emissions. This has placated much criticism directed at the sector.

Agriculture is in a different situation. Agriculture produces the food required to live, although this has not exempted it from criticism. Because people eat more meat as they become richer, there is concern that greater livestock production could lead to a future food shortage as animal rearing is an inefficient means to convert grain to energy. Further, an increase in ruminants will lead to greater emissions of methane, which is considered a potent greenhouse gas. As noted in this chapter, intensive agricultural activities result in externalities that might need to be addressed (see Chapter 6). One such externality relates to the use of fertilizers and herbicides, which increase greenhouse gas emissions. Climate change, agriculture, and food security are the topic of Chapter 10.

But farmers also face risks that are not found in other sectors of the economy. In addition to the usual risks of running a business, farmers face risks associated with weather, disease, pests, and so on (see Chapter 9). At the same time, they are required to invest in machinery and other costly equipment that cannot generally be used in another endeavor. Farm assets are stranded if a farm enterprise fails; the equipment can only be used in agricultural activities and not in other industries.

Finally, because of the importance of food in society and because farming is considered a noble activity, citizens are more inclined to support farmers than they would small businesses. Shortly after World War II the population of developed countries was mainly rural, so farm support programs were favorably looked upon by the majority of citizens. As the rural population and the number of farmers declined, agricultural producers remained a force to be reckoned with—in many countries rural voters had greater political clout than urban ones. As their numbers declined, farmers were better able to organize to lobby for various farm programs, whereas the transaction costs of organizing taxpayers to oppose the farm lobby were too great for any small number of them to bear. At the same time, because food had become a smaller component of people's expenditures, agricultural programs that increased food prices at the farm level had little impact on how consumers allocated their budgets, so consumers also had no incentive to oppose rent-seeking on the part of farmers. Indeed, concerns about food safety led citizens to accept higher subsidy rates for farmers than would otherwise be the case.

As we will see in the next few chapters, while institutions in developed countries favored agricultural producers to the extent that they were recipients of large (even vast) transfers of income from consumers and general taxpayers, the same institutions eventually resulted in the scaling back of such transfers. This was partly the result of international trade negotiations, but it was also the result of politicians and the financial needs of governments. To balance budgets or, at least, make funds available to politicians for other favored programs, farm support payments had to be scaled back. Appeasement of farmers had to come by other means, which included mandates to use biofuels in gasoline, increased access to foreign markets, greater reliance on business risk management programs, direct payments rather than payments tied to production, and so on. This transition is examined in greater detail as we examine the agricultural policies of the US, the European Union, Canada, and some other jurisdictions. To do so, we employ the standard techniques of applied welfare economics discussed in Chapters 2 through 4. We begin, however, with a theoretical overview of the policies that countries have employed—and often abandoned.

Guide to Literature

The discussion of early economists is based on Heilbroner (1999); discussion of institutions and good government is based on Hart, Shleifer, and Vishny (1997), Landes (1998), La Porta et al. (1999), Shleifer and Vishny (1999), De Soto (2000), and Fukuyama (1992, 2014); trust on Ostrom (2000); and takings on Epstein (1985). Acemoglu and Robinson (2019) discuss the trade-off between state power and society's power, noting that in the most successful countries, society has been able to shackle the state leviathan. Arguedas and van Soest (2011) and Engel et al. (2012) examine ways to mitigate PA problems in PES schemes.

Background to the WTO and the Agreement on Subsidies and Countervailing Measures is found in Coppens (2014, esp. pp. 27–38). More information on WTO negotiations and trade rulings are found in WTO (2002, 2003a, 2003b, 2005, 2015a, 2020). Brink (2014) provides an excellent analysis of the WTO and Agreement on Agriculture. Information on the status of agriculture in the Doha Development Agenda negotiations comes from the latter and various online sources (WTO 2014a, 2014b, 2015b, 2020, n.d.(a), n.d.(b)). Information about the 2014 US Farm Bill is found in Chapter 7.2.

Food for Thought

5.1. *True, False, or Uncertain? Make sure to indicate why.* Markets operate within an institutional structure of policies, rules, and regulations that establish the rights and obligations of the market participants.

5.2. With respect to the Agreement on Agriculture of the World Trade Organization, what is the difference between the amber and blue boxes? Why is there no red box?

5.3. Provide a brief explanation of each of the following:
(a) best management practice
(b) amber box subsidy
(c) autarky
(d) regulatory taking

5.4. *True, False, or Uncertain? Make sure to indicate why.* The three most important concerns of society that government needs to address are: (1) employment, (2) per capita income, and (3) economics and personal freedom.

5.5. What are the three pillars of the WTO's Agreement on Agriculture?

5.6. What is included for agriculture in the Comprehensive and Economic Trade Agreement (CETA) between Canada and the EU? What will be the benefits for Canada? What are the prospects that a US–EU free trade agreement will be concluded?

5.7. What are the non-tariff measures or barriers that countries use to affect international trade? Give an example of a situation in which a non-tariff barrier may be beneficial for social welfare even if it reduces trade compared to the situation where it is not applied.

5.8. Under NAFTA, agricultural trade between the US and Mexico and Canada has increased, and Mexico and Canada are among the largest destinations for US agricultural exports. NAFTA was renegotiated and is now known as the USMCA.

(a) Describe one important change that occurred in the renegotiation of NAFTA that would increase agricultural exports of the United States to Mexico or Canada.

(b) Describe one change in the USMCA that you think would cause agricultural exports of the United States to Mexico or Canada to decrease.

5.9. Provide a brief explanation of what is meant by a tariff rate quota (TRQ) and how the idea originated.

5.10. Which of the following actions would be legal under international trade rules (WTO), and which would not?

(a) A US tariff of 20 percent against any country that exports more than twice as much to the United States as it imports in return.

(b) A subsidy to Canadian wheat exports aimed at recapturing some of the markets lost to the European Union.

(c) A US tariff on Canadian lumber exports, not matched by equivalent reductions on other tariffs.

(d) A Canadian tax on lumber exports, agreed to at the demand of the United States to placate US lumber producers.

(e) A program of subsidized research and development in areas related to high-technology goods such as electronics and semiconductors.

(f) Special government assistance for workers who lose their jobs because of competition from imports.

5.11. Consider a small country, A, that applies a tariff, t, to imports of durum wheat.

(a) Suppose that A decides to *reduce* its tariff to t'. Draw a back-to-back diagram for the domestic supply and demand for A and the international market (derived excess demand curve of A) to illustrate this change. What happens to the quantity of durum wheat produced in A and its price? What happens to durum imports—i.e., foreign production of A?

(b) Are there gains or losses to domestic consumer surplus due to the reduction in the tariff? Are there gains or losses to domestic producer surplus due to the reduction in the tariff? How is government revenue affected by the policy change? Illustrate these on the figure.

(c) What is the overall gain or loss in welfare due to the policy change?

5.12. Tariffs are not the only method to protect a market. Analyze the following:

(a) Explain and show how a variable import levy works. How does this type of levy result in more export price variability than a fixed, specific tariff would when there are random shocks in the world market? Under what conditions are these levies allowed under the WTO Agreement on Agriculture (AoA)?

(b) If the variable levy is replaced by a two-tier tariff rate quota (TRQ), indicate how this mechanism works using a two-panel diagram that shows what happens in the world market and in the importer's market. Who gains from the TRQ?

(c) If the TRQ quota is binding there will be excess profits to be made by importing. Discuss two administrative methods to allocate this preferential access to the TRQ.

6

ANALYSIS OF AGRICULTURAL POLICY: THEORY

In the modern era, governments have been willing to support the incomes of farmers, partly to protect against income variability, but also for a variety of other reasons. These include a desire for food security (ensure adequate domestic food production capability) and food safety (e.g., avoid imports of contaminated food or diseased livestock), and to earn foreign exchange through exports, protect a "motherhood-and-apple-pie" lifestyle, and prevent the demise of rural communities. It also includes subsidies to raise farm incomes, which is a direct result of lobbying. These issues are all wrapped up in what has been referred to as the farm problem (e.g., Gardner 1987). As indicated in Figure 6.1, agricultural producers face price and production risks that are less common in other sectors of the economy, and society has intervened to protect farmers against such risks through various programs that effectively raise prices above free market prices ($P_S > P^*$).

Figure 6.1 Agricultural production and price risks (as indicated by the arrows) and government policy to support prices

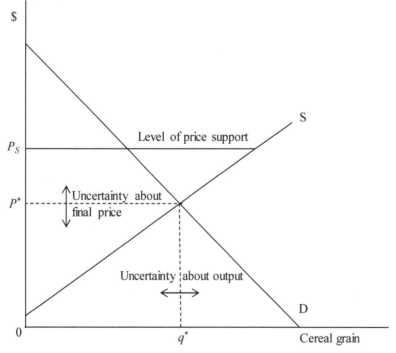

In this chapter, tools of applied welfare economics are used to evaluate various policies that governments have implemented to support the agricultural sector. Our approach is to compare the gains and losses across consumers and producers, and government, using the surplus measures introduced in Chapter 2.2. A policy is considered to be welfare enhancing if it satisfies the *compensation principle*, namely, that the gainers can compensate the losers and still be better off. In this chapter, a variety of approaches to agricultural stabilization are compared using the compensation principle. This is followed in Chapters 7 and 8 by a description of agricultural support in various jurisdictions. The objective is to examine how farm policies have been enacted in practice and what their welfare impacts have been. A discussion of crop insurance and agricultural risk management programs, which also involve various types of subsidies, is left to Chapter 9.

6.1 Background to Analysis of Agricultural Policy

Governments desire to support farm incomes, but this can only be done by providing a direct subsidy that is not tied to production, or by somehow raising the price producers receive. Direct payments to farmers that are unrelated to products are generally opposed by taxpayers. The focus here is on a support price, as illustrated in Figure 6.1. The problem is that support prices lead to overproduction and thereby limit the options available to policy makers. The option that is chosen depends partly on the eventual cost to the public treasury and the farm program's income redistributional consequences. The available options are illustrated with the aid of Figure 6.2.

Figure 6.2 Agricultural price support and disposal of surplus ($=q_1-q_0$): Options I (price P_D eliminates surplus) and II (surplus stored as $P_D=P_S$)

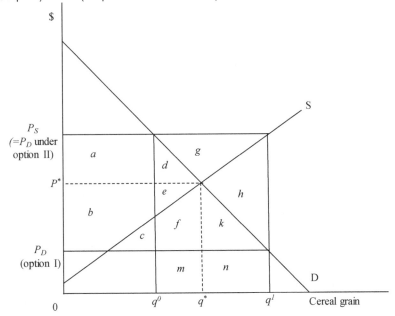

First, the government can set the support price at P_S and sell output at the price P_D to clear the market. Compared to the situation where the government does not intervene, consumers gain a surplus given by area $(b+c+e+f+k)$, producers gain $(a+d+g)$, and the cost to the treasury is the entire rectangle $(a+b+c+d+e+f+g+h+k)$. The deadweight loss in this case is given by area h, while the gains to consumers and producers constitute an income transfer from the general taxpayers.

Second, the authority can set the support price at P_S, sell what it can at that price (namely q^0), and store the commodity, perhaps for later sale to recoup costs. In this case, the cost to the treasury is $(d+e+f+g+h+k+m+n)$ plus any costs of storage (minus what might be recouped later). Producers gain the same area as in the first case, but consumers are made worse off by area $(a+d)$, which constitutes a transfer from consumers to producers, with area a constituting a savings to the treasury compared to the earlier situation. The problem is that the holding of stocks may not be sustainable, except in the case where the government can effectively use buffer funds to stabilize prices as opposed to increasing them (as discussed in section 6.2). In the past, the US and EU have employed various forms of storage as part of their agricultural policies.

A third option when the government supports the producer price at P_S is to export surplus production into the world market, as indicated in panel (a) of Figure 6.3. There, q^1 is produced, q^0 is sold domestically at the high price, and the remainder is exported at the world price P_W. The cost to the treasury in this case is $(b+g+h+k)$, while consumers lose area a because they cannot buy at the world price (although the measured loss would be smaller if the comparison is made to the autarkic situation). The problem with this solution is that, because the domestic price exceeds the world price, the country is charged with dumping, which is not allowed under international trade rules.

Figure 6.3 Agricultural price support and disposal of surplus ($=q_1-q_0$): Options III (panel a) and IV (panel b)

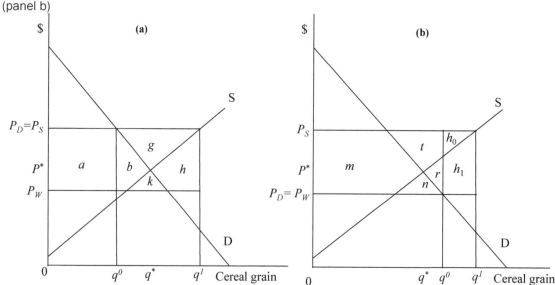

Finally, the government can support the producer price at P_S, leading to an output of q^1, as illustrated in panel (b) of Figure 6.3. In this case, $q^0 > q^*$ is sold domestically at the world price P_w, with the remainder exported abroad at that price. The cost to the treasury is then $(m+n+t+r+h_0+h_1)$, which is much greater (by area a in panel (a)) than in the previous case. However, the charge of dumping is avoided because the domestic price no longer exceeds the world price.

There are other ways to stabilize and protect the incomes of farmers using price support mechanisms. For example, producer prices can be tiered. As discussed in Chapter 7, the US has employed a tiered system: a low price to prevent producers from planning high production levels, but eventually supporting output at a higher price depending on past yields. Prices paid by domestic consumers could also be tiered, or support levels could be tied to various compliance measures. For example, producers could be required to reduce the area they crop by some percent below an average of previous years and/or set aside a proportion of total cropland as a conservation reserve. Lastly, the authority can support the price received by producers simply by restricting the supply of the commodity. The use of import or export quotas was discussed in Chapter 5.4, but is revisited below.

6.2 Stock-Holding Buffer Fund Stabilization

As noted above, the government can purchase a commodity when prices are low, store the commodity for a time, and then sell it when prices are high. The purpose in this case is to stabilize prices rather than raise them. The use of a storage scheme in the case of supply uncertainty can be illustrated with the aid of Figure 6.4 for a country that does not trade in the commodity—a closed economy. Since there are no true closed economies in today's world, the purpose is to illustrate how economists have historically looked at storage.

First, assume that the source of uncertainty is the price of an input such as fertilizer. Suppose the price of fertilizer can take on one of two values, each with equal probability. If the price of fertilizer is high, the supply function is S_1, but it is S_0 if the price of fertilizer is low; each of S_0 and S_1 occur with probability of ½. If futures prices embody knowledge of the demand function and also respond immediately to changes in the input price of fertilizer, the producer knows to use more fertilizer so as to produce q_0' when the price of fertilizer is low (S_0) and, by using less fertilizer, q'_1 if the fertilizer price is high (S_1). In the former case, the variable cost of production is given by the area bounded by ($0kmq'_0$), while it is ($0gnq'_1$) in the latter case (S_1). The expected consumer surplus in each period is ½($cmP_0 + cnP_1$), whereas the expected producer surplus or quasi-rent is ½($kmP_0 + gnP_1$).

When society intervenes to stabilize prices through a storage program, producers no longer face prices that fluctuate between a low P_0 and high P_1, but they can plan on a stable price P_e. To stabilize price at P_e, the authority buys the amount ($q_0 - q_e$) when S_0 occurs and sells ($q_e - q_1$) = ($q_0 - q_e$) when S_1 occurs. With stabilization, when S_0 occurs, consumers lose (P_0mbP_e) while producers gain (P_0mdP_e), with a net gain to society given by (bmd). When S_1 occurs, consumers would gain (P_ebnP_1) with stabilization while producers would lose (P_ehnP_1), with the net gain to society equal to (hbn).

Figure 6.4 Buffer stock stabilization under supply uncertainty

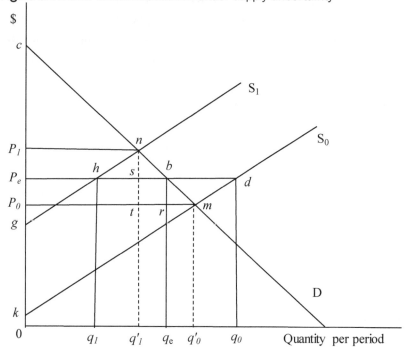

The storage scheme leads to an average annual net gain of $\frac{1}{2}(hbn + dbm)$ minus administration and storage costs. It is deemed welfare improving by the compensation principle. While producers are better off with the stabilization fund, their incomes are more variable than they would be in the absence of buffer fund stabilization. With stabilization, the surplus received by consumers is unchanged from one period to the next, equaling (cbP_e) each period; but it is less by area ($strb$) compared to no stabilization. In contrast, if the source of price variability is due to demand uncertainty, producers will prefer uncertainty to price stabilization while consumers will prefer stable prices.

The problem with the standard model of stabilization is that uncertainty does not originate with the price of fertilizer, or the price of any other input for that matter. Nor is the main concern uncertainty on the demand side, because demand for grains tends to be rather inelastic, dependent on population and incomes, neither of which is likely to change much from one year to the next. Rather, the uncertainty with which governments are most concerned is the result of weather, disease, fungus, or pests. If there is drought, crop yields are much reduced, while timely precipitation and adequate warmth can lead to bumper crops. Although the weather input affects supply and thereby welfare, it does not constitute a factor of production that agricultural producers can vary and combine in optimal fashion with other inputs. Quasi-rent cannot be attributed to weather factors!

If outcomes are the result of weather factors, the analysis in Figure 6.4 needs to be modified as shown in Figure 6.5. Acting independently and on expectations of the future price at harvest and normal weather conditions, the decisions of grain producers will lead to the planning supply function S_P. If expectations are realized, farmers will produce q_e, incurring variable costs equal to area $(0abq_e)$ and receiving a quasi-rent given by (P_eab). Regardless of the weather outcome, the variable cost incurred by producers does not change— weather affects yield outcomes and thus total revenue and what is available to offset against fixed costs. Generally, this would be the quasi-rent. Then, the difference between total revenue and total variable costs consists of components of quasi-rent plus rent, with the latter attributable to the weather factor.

Figure 6.5 Buffer stock stabilization under climate uncertainty

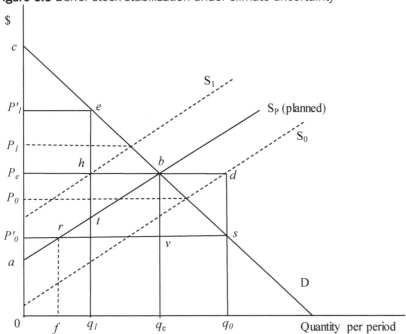

Consider first consumers. The expected consumer surplus is (cP_eb) except that the true consumer surplus will vary according to whether the weather-induced outcome is q_0 or q_1. Under q_1 the consumer surplus is (cP'_1e), while it is (cP'_0s) under q_0. If the government stabilizes price at P_e by storing amount $(q_0 - q_e)$ (= distance bd) when S_0 occurs and selling $(q_e - q_1) = hb = (q_0 - q_e)$ when S_1 occurs, the consumer surplus is (cP_eb) in every period. Because $(P_ebsP'_0) > (P_ebeP'_1)$, consumers are worse off with storage that stabilizes price at P_e than they are if prices were left to fluctuate.

On the producer side, the economic surplus is given by the difference between total revenue and total variable costs. In the case of bad weather (outcome q_1), the surplus is given by $q_1 \times P'_1 - (a0bq_e)$; in the case of good weather (outcome q_0), the surplus is given by $q_0 \times P'_0 - (a0bq_e)$. The first question to ask relates to whether there is even a surplus under each of these conditions. Under a good weather outcome, the surplus is positive if $(arP_0') + (q_evsq_0) > (rvb)$; under a bad weather outcome, the surplus is positive as long as $(ateP'_1) > (q_1tbq_e)$. Now there is no guarantee that there is a positive surplus in either case, although, from the diagram, it appears that it is more likely the case for the good weather outcome (q_0) than the bad one (q_1). It all depends on the elasticities of supply and demand and their functional forms. However, it is clear that, under storage, producers are better off as they are guaranteed an expected quasi-rent of (abP_e); indeed, they might well be better off than indicated in the standard analysis.

That analysis is much starker than the standard one, because it indicates that agricultural producers can fail to recoup their investment costs under good or bad weather outcomes. This insight is one factor that has driven the desire for government intervention through storage. Although agricultural producers have an incentive to lobby for storage schemes, governments in developing countries may also have an incentive to store grain for political reasons. Despite the result that consumers are better off with price instability, the fact that prices fluctuate to a much greater extent in the alternative model (Figure 6.5) than the standard one (Figure 6.4) relates to food security concerns. Because expenditure on food accounts for a large proportion of household income in developing countries, and especially among the poorest people, governments are more sensitive to high prices (bad weather outcomes) than to low prices (good weather outcomes). Indeed, in developing countries, agricultural policies seek to avoid bad outcomes in terms of high prices, whether the policy tool involves storage schemes or export bans, or both.

Under the WTO's Doha Development Agenda, developing countries play a key role (see Chapter 5.3). Therefore, no country can implement agricultural policies in isolation—trade implications must be taken into account. In developing countries, and especially in the least developed countries, one of the greatest sources of uncertainty pertains to the global price of an agricultural commodity rather than domestic supply or demand. In that case, stabilization and storage have to be considered differently. Consider Figure 6.6. Again assume that (P^*, q^*) represents the domestic price and quantity in the absence of trade—the intersection of domestic supply (S) and demand (D) occur at e. However, the country is a price taker, facing global prices for the commodity that vary between P_0 and P_1, with an expected value $E(P) = \bar{P}$. For simplicity, assume P_0 and P_1 occur with equal probability of ½.

Agricultural producers will produce q^S in each period because they base their decisions on the expected price $\bar{P}$. Thus, with price stabilization, if the global price is P_1, producers lose ($\bar{P}mnP_1$), but consumers gain ($P_1bd\bar{P}$). Conversely, if the global price turns out to be P_0, producers gain ($\bar{P}mhP_0$) while consumers lose ($\bar{P}drP_0$). Overall, consumers are worse off with price stabilization as they would lose an average of ½ × area (drg) in each year, while producers would be just as well-off with or without price stabilization.

While the above analysis applies to any small, open economy, the case of least developed countries might be different. The optimal policy for a developing country might yet be to stabilize prices, specifically because food purchases account for the majority of people's expenditures. Suppose that, at any price above $\bar{P}$, the poorest in society are no longer able to purchase enough food to avoid malnutrition or starvation. Suppose the domestic price consumers pay was allowed to fluctuate with the world price, while producers plan to produce according to the expected price $\bar{P}$—i.e., the situation with no price stabilization. Then, if the global price is P_1, domestic consumption would fall to q_1, with some citizens consuming too little food while producers would export $q^S - q_1$ (=distance bn).

To avoid this, the authority would need to ban exports while importing an amount given by md (=$q^D - q^S$). In practice, some countries have used a combination of export restrictions and purchases on global

Figure 6.6 Price stabilization in a small, open economy

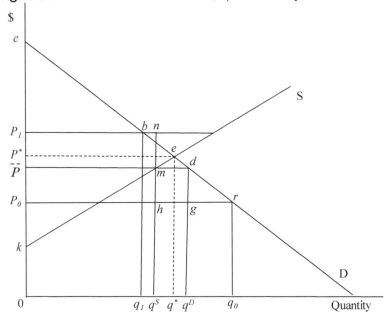

markets to prevent this situation, thereby avoiding malnutrition or starvation and urban unrest. A price stabilization program, perhaps even one that employs stockholding (operating much like that discussed in conjunction with Figure 6.5), may be adopted to forestall this.

6.3 Quotas and Supply-Restricting Marketing Boards

The authority can choose to increase the price that producers receive by restricting output. In that case, no cost is imposed on the public treasury, except perhaps expenses related to the implementation and governance of a quota scheme—the costs of maintaining a supply-restricting marketing board that sets production levels, allocates quota (output) across producers, sets rules for transferring quota, allocates quota to importers (if any), and monitors compliance. A supply management (SM) scheme essentially transfers income from consumers to producers.

The economic implications of an SM system can be demonstrated with the aid of Figure 6.7. A commodity marketing board would behave much like a monopolist and optimally restrict the supply of eggs, say, to q^R, where the supply or marginal cost function intersects the marginal revenue curve (MR). The relevant supply curve is then kinked as indicated by the dark supply curve S^R—producers are allocated egg quota to prevent output from exceeding q^R. With less output entering the market, producers receive P_S, which is also the price consumers pay, while producers' marginal (supply) costs are c. The deadweight loss is $(d+e)<h$, where h measures the deadweight loss associated with a price support program such as that of Figure 6.2. Whether this is true depends crucially on the elasticities of supply and demand.

Figure 6.7 Restricting supply and the need for quota

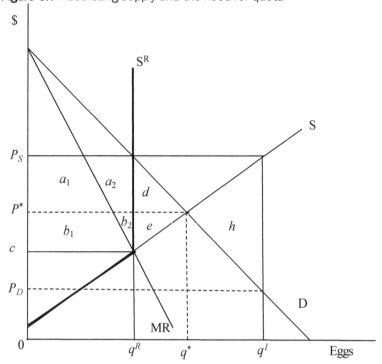

In going from free to restricted trade in Figure 6.7, consumers lose surplus (a_1+a_2+d), of which (a_1+a_2) constitutes an income transfer to producers and d is a deadweight loss due to inefficiency. However, because the marginal cost to the producer is c, the wedge between price and marginal cost results in a policy-induced scarcity rent equal to $[(a_1+a_2) + (b_1+b_2)]$, known as the quota rent. That is, the right-to-produce now has value, which is determined as follows. The annual rent R_A received by an egg producer is given by the producer's quota, say $\bar{q}$, multiplied by the difference between the market price and the marginal cost of production: $R_A = \bar{q} \times (P_s - c)$. If the quota scheme is assumed to continue into perpetuity, the quota value would equal $QV = R_A/r$, where r is the rate used to discount future quota rents. The value of one unit of quota would be $(P_s - c)/r$. Since the SM scheme is unlikely to continue into perpetuity, because there is always a risk that outside lobbying will result in the eventual demise of the quota regime, the rate r used to discount the annual stream of quota rents will be high, although r will vary from one producer to another.

The true value of quota can only be determined in a market where quota is bought and sold. If quota is not sold in a separate market, its value would be capitalized in another factor of production, such as land, equipment, or livestock (viz., milk cows). In that case, it would be necessary to estimate $[(a_1+a_2) + (b_1+b_2)]$ using empirical estimates of supply and demand elasticities, along with whatever information can be garnered from farm budget studies that enable one to calculate the costs of various factors of production. It is important to recognize that, if quota rent gets capitalized into factors of production, the costs of production are ratcheted upwards, with the original quota owners capturing the initial windfall. Finally, it is necessary to determine the discount rate producers might use in valuing their egg quota to determine QV.

There are other drawbacks to restricting the supply of a commodity. First, if the price of the commodity exceeds the world price after the implementation of the quota scheme, import restrictions will be required, which leads to lobbying by trading partners to gain access to the supply-restricted market. This was discussed in Chapter 5.4 in the context of a tariff rate quota. The quota system could also be an obstacle to producers who wish to export the supply-managed commodity; potential exporters might not own sufficient quota, although production for export could be exempted from SM. It might also be the case that the quota system promotes inefficiency that makes domestic producers less competitive in global markets. Alternatively, a country might be accused of dumping if it restricts access to its own market while selling similar commodities abroad. For example, Canada restricts imports of cheese, but was able to export skim milk powder (a milk protein) until such exports were prohibited under WTO rules. Finally, it is possible that quotas are used in a jurisdiction to limit the cost of disposing excess product on global markets. These considerations are addressed further below.

6.3.1 Quota and General Equilibrium Welfare Measurement

Applied welfare analysis is used to illustrate how the introduction of a quota scheme impacts other markets—to demonstrate how the fundamental equation of applied welfare economics (equation 2.4) is used in practice. From Figure 6.7, the deadweight loss of a quota regime is given by ($d+e$). However, indirect benefits or costs from the market intervention also need to be considered. When the price of eggs increases, the demand for complements shifts inwards and that of substitutes shifts outwards. Consider protein substitutes such as dairy and meat products, and assume that, at the time supply restrictions in eggs are implemented, supply of dairy is already restricted but meat is traded in a free market. The dairy and meat markets are illustrated in panels (a) and (b), respectively, of Figure 6.8. The increase in the price of eggs shifts the demand curves in the dairy and meat markets from D_{dairy} to D'_{dairy} and D_{meat} to D'_{meat}, respectively, increasing consumption of dairy and meat products.

In the dairy sector, the marketing board ensures that price is held constant at P^S_d by releasing additional quota to dairy producers. This increases the marginal cost of production from c to c', but there remains a wedge between price and marginal cost—the dairy market continues to be distorted because, at the margin, society's willingness to pay for more dairy products exceeds the cost of producing them. Hence, society is better off by producing more; indeed, more dairy products should be produced until the marginal benefit as measured by price equals the marginal cost of production. Therefore, according to the fundamental equation of applied welfare economics, a benefit from the outward shift of the dairy demand function caused by the increase in the price of eggs is given by ($\alpha+\beta$) minus ($\delta+\varepsilon$) in panel (a).[1] The result must be positive because whenever price exceeds marginal cost, there is a positive welfare gain from producing more, so ($\alpha+\beta$) > ($\delta+\varepsilon$). This benefit in the dairy sector offsets the loss in eggs from restricting supply. Notice also that dairy producers gain ($\delta+\varepsilon$) as quasi-rent, where δ is a transfer between one category of rent (quota) to another (producer surplus) and ε is a true increase in quasi-rent.

---

[1] Equation (2.4) is an approximation that, in Figure 6.8(a), would measure the gain in the dairy market as ($P^s_d - c$)×($D^1 - D^0$), using c rather than c' as the relevant measure of marginal cost.

Figure 6.8 Indirect welfare effects in meat market of implementing quota in dairy market

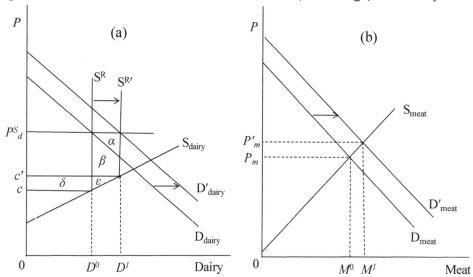

In the meat sector of panel (b), the market price and marginal cost of production continue to equate, before and after the intervention in the egg market. The meat market is not distorted and there are no welfare gains or losses to be measured there.

Overall, therefore, the cost of introducing supply management in eggs when the dairy sector is already distorted is given by ($d+e$) in Figure 6.7 minus ($\alpha+\beta-\delta-\varepsilon$) in panel (a) of Figure 6.8. Of course, the measured welfare gain in the dairy market cannot exceed the loss in the egg sector as this would imply that the introduction of supply management in eggs would enhance societal welfare—that the distortion introduced in the egg sector offsets the negative effects of the original distortion in the dairy sector. This is unlikely because it would imply that economic agents initially misallocated their income—that consumers did not maximize their welfare prior to the initiation of supply restrictions in the egg market.[2]

6.3.2 Quota Buyouts

The costs of a quota system are borne by consumers, with the original producers the major beneficiaries as they were already in the sector at the time that the scheme was first implemented and did not have to pay for quota. Subsequent producers have to pay the capitalized value of the quota rent to be able to produce the product. Quota constitute an input that raises output prices but also the cost of production, although in practice quota rent is not considered a cost the authority uses to calculate the cost of production.[3] The higher prices

---

[2] However, according to the theory of the second best, it might be possible for the gain in the dairy sector to exceed the loss in the egg sector.

[3] In Canada's dairy sector, the marketing authority conducts an annual survey to determine the cost of producing milk, which is then used along with other information to determine the wholesale price that processors pay. Since small, inefficient producers are likely overrepresented in the survey, costs tend to be high and ratchet upwards over time to the benefit of the efficient producers.

harm the poorest in society to a greater extent; further, they lead to inefficiencies, as the need to purchase expensive quota often prevents producers from realizing economies of scale and impedes trade negotiations. It is inevitable, therefore, that any quota scheme will eventually need to be abolished. To eliminate a quota program, it is necessary to ask: How does one dismantle a quota regime? How much does it cost?

Before answering these questions, consider the three policy levers that are available to the authority as it reforms the dairy sector over a period of time using a number of policy steps. First, the authority can slowly increase the quota so that prices fall and output expands to a new quota level at each step. Second, for an exporting country where the support price was initially greater than the world price, the authority can reduce the support price in steps that are not directly related to market outcomes. At each step, exports will need to be subsidized, at least until the final step when the jurisdiction's domestic price equals the world price. Since exports are already subsidized, an increase in the quota at a given step can reduce the export subsidy required as long as the reduction in the support price at that step is sufficiently large enough. Finally, the authority needs to determine the appropriate compensation it will provide at each step.

To the extent that producers have a right to or an investment in quota, governments might need to provide compensation to get them to acquiesce to changes in the SM regime. This might be required if the authority agrees to modify or eliminate SM as part of international trade negotiations, as was the case when NAFTA was renegotiated leading to the USMCA as discussed in Chapter 5.3. The authority might need to buy back quota, which requires a determination of a fair buyback price. If a market for quota exists, prices for quota can be used as a basis for setting compensation. But should farmers be compensated the value of the quota rent?

There are several reasons why producers should *not* be compensated the full amount of the quota rent. First and foremost, the quota rent in Figure 6.7, for example, is given by $[(a_1+a_2) + (b_1+b_2)]$, but this is not the loss that quota holders incur when SM is eliminated. Rather, producers lose (a_1+a_2-e), because they retain (b_1+b_2) as quasi-rent (producer surplus) and gain additional quasi-rent equal to e as production increases to q^*.

Second, many farmers have already recouped their investment in quota, although this depends on when they joined the marketing scheme. The quota system provides them a windfall at the expense of consumers. Nonetheless, even dairy producers whose quota investment has already been paid off will engage in rent-seeking to protect the quota windfall, although some will have squandered part of the windfall away by failing to take advantage of new technology, new market opportunities, and so forth.

Third, while recent entrants into the sector may be disadvantaged by less-than-full compensation, the new entrants are likely to be the most efficient producers, who might benefit if they could expand their operations without needing to purchase additional quota. In the absence of SM, they might be able to earn a great deal of surplus by accessing export markets. This could be the case in Canada, for example, which has not participated in the growing global demand for dairy products in developing countries.

Lastly, quota rents and deficiency payments accrue over time. The rate used to discount the periodic rents determines the value of quota. As noted above, if a market for quota exists, prices for quota can be used as a basis for setting compensation; they can also be used to estimate the discount rate dairy producers use to value quota. Because there is uncertainty regarding the survival of the quota regime, uncertainty about future milk prices, and uncertainty about the size of the rent to which the quota buyer is entitled, purchasers of quota generally employ a short payback period in making decisions.

Tobacco buyback programs have been used in the US and the Canadian province of Ontario in an attempt to reduce production for health reasons. The US buyback program was relatively successful, but the Ontario program was not very effective as production did not decline to the extent expected. In Europe, farmers were compensated when the EU eliminated dairy quota. This is discussed further in the next section.

6.3.3 Designing and Dismantling a Multi-Region Quota Program

Canada employs country-wide quota programs in the dairy and poultry sectors, while the EU operated with a dairy quota from 1984 to 2015. The EU quota was referred to as a "super levy" since it penalized a member state if its producers exceeded that country's quota level. In both cases, individual regions (provinces and member states) managed the quota schemes in their respective jurisdictions, allocating quota and setting rules for trading it. The main difference between the Canadian and EU schemes related to external trade: Canadian prices are above world prices so that imports need to be restricted; the EU exported dairy products before and after the quota regime was put in place. In Canada, the quota regime was designed to support producer prices by raising the domestic price; in the EU, prices were already supported with the quota simply used to reduce exports and thereby the subsidy required to dispose of excess production. In both Canada and the EU, internal trade was restricted to make SM function properly.

The mechanics of quota setting and dismantling are examined in this section. Given that the socially optimal production of a commodity is the free market outcome, the optimal allocation of quota depends on the objective of the supra authority. If the objective is to maximize the well-being of milk producers, the supra authority would allocate quota across regions so that the aggregate supply function (sum of the marginal costs of individual producers) equals the marginal revenue associated with the derived aggregate demand for milk (e.g., see Figure 6.7). With multiple regions, the analysis is somewhat more complicated. In the following paragraphs, we examine how a supra authority would optimally allocate quota across regions, while permitting sales between regions. We ignore the potential for the supra authority to price discriminate across regions (discussed in section 6.4 below).

Consider the case of SM in dairy. Assume two regions, A and B, and assume further that the supra authority seeks to set a quota where the marginal revenue associated with the total joint demand for milk products equals the joint supply function, as illustrated in Figure 6.9, which employs a back-to-back diagram. The overall quota is set at $\bar{q}_T$, where the total marginal revenue MR_T, associated with total demand D_T, equals total marginal cost (S_T). The respective quotas for regions A and B are then set at $\bar{q}_A$ and $\bar{q}_B$ so that each region produces milk at the same marginal cost (with circles in the diagram indicating the intersections where economic agents would make their output decisions). Because region A has a lower cost of production than region B, more quota is allocated to A than to B, even though consumers in A consume less than those in B (compare M_A in region A to M_B in region B). Recalling the above discussion, the quota rents in regions A and B are given by the light- and dark-shaded areas, respectively.

Figure 6.9 Allocation of dairy quota and the creation of quota rents

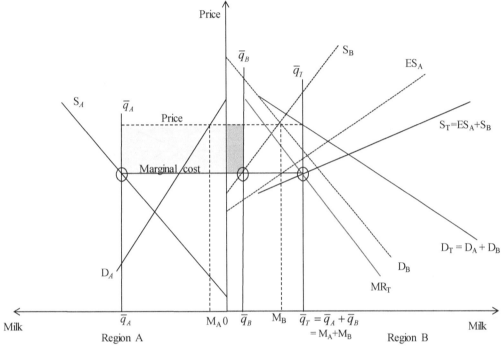

Neither the EU nor Canada used this approach to allocate quota across regions. Because the EU was interested solely in reducing the costs of subsidizing exports of dairy products, it imposed limits on the dairy products that each member state could export (measured in milk equivalents). Member states then set and allocated their own quota to prevent excess production; of necessity, trade between member states had to be restricted, which became an impediment to greater economic integration—an explicit objective of the EU. The need for greater economic integration and WTO rules concerning exports of a restricted commodity eventually led to the elimination of the super levy.

In Canada, production of milk for industrial purposes is regulated at the federal level, with provinces assigned quota according to historic production. Provinces then determine how much milk is produced in any period and allocate output to quota holders; fluid (fresh) milk is not traded across provincial boundaries, except as needed by processors for the industrial market; there is little concern about economic integration for political reasons.

The EU eliminated its quota scheme by first converting some of the quota rent into a deficiency payment. The authority reduced the price of milk, but compensation was only paid on the difference between the previous price ("old price") and the reduced price ("new price"). If the EU had allocated quota among states in optimal fashion, as in Figure 6.9, then the analysis would proceed as illustrated in Figure 6.10.

Figure 6.10 Intermediate step to eliminating a dairy quota scheme: gains, losses, and income transfer

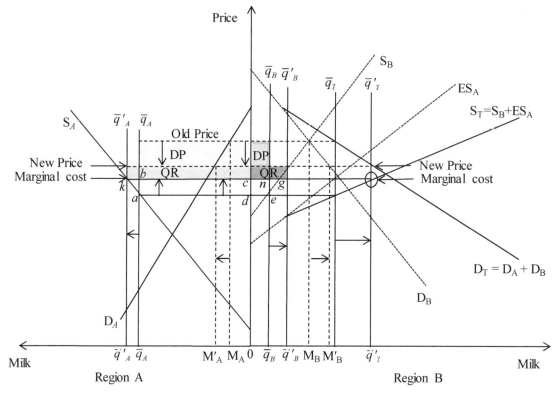

In Figure 6.10, arrows are used to indicate the directions in which shifts take place. The deficiency payment is based on a reference level of production, given by $\bar{q}_T$ (initial quota) and not the raised level $\bar{q}'_T$, which is the quota required to lower the price. In the figure, $\bar{q}'_T$ represents the new supra-level quota, with $\bar{q}'_A$ and $\bar{q}'_B$ denoting the new quota assigned to regions A and B, respectively. The deficiency payment in each region is given by the lighter of the two areas in each of the panels and is labeled in each as DP. The darker areas labeled QR represent the new quota rents—the quota rents associated with higher production levels, higher marginal cost, and a lower price.

Notice that the dairy producers in region A lose the area bounded by points (*abcd*), but gain it back as quasi-rent plus the small quasi-rent triangle (*kab*); they also lose the light-shaded area of quota rent given by $\bar{q}_A$ × (new price – marginal cost), but regain it as a deficiency payment. In addition, some of the quota rent is retained because there is still a wedge between price ("new price") and marginal cost. Further, they gain the small rectangle given by $(\bar{q}_A' - \bar{q}_A) \times$ (new price – marginal cost), which is the added quota rent attributable to the increase in output (quota); the new quota rent is the darker-shaded area denoted QR on the left side.

Likewise, for region B, the loss experienced by dairy producers equals the lighter-shaded area denoted DP plus (*cden*), with the latter regained as a quasi-rent and the former as a deficiency payment. In addition, a small triangle (*eng*) of quasi-rent accrues to the producers in region B plus the rectangle given by $[(\bar{q}_B' - \bar{q}_B) \times$ (new price – marginal cost)], so the new quota rent is given by the dark-shaded area denoted QR on the right side of Figure 6.10.

Overall, the deficiency payment (the lighter of the two shaded areas in each of the panels) now comes from the supranational government instead of consumers, unless of course the government taxes consumers to compensate producers; the darker-shaded area in each panel continues to constitute a transfer from consumers to producers.

At least one other step would be required to eliminate the quota system entirely, although in practice the process of eliminating the quota scheme likely occurs in more than two steps. In each subsequent step following the first, the original quota is used to determine the deficiency payment. One practical approach used in Europe is to prorate the compensation paid in each subsequent step as a proportion of the eligible deficiency payment. Thus, the second step might only provide for 70% of the loss, the third step only 50%, and so on. (This is discussed further in the context of EU agricultural policy in Chapter 8.1.) The point here is that dairy producers are not compensated the full amount of the quota value. Further, given that the rate producers use to discount the annual stream of quota rents is likely due to uncertainty regarding the expected life of the quota regime, a program of compensation might be limited to some five or perhaps ten years.

Decision makers might be concerned that the elimination of a quota program leads to the concentration of production in one or two regions. Figures 6.9 and 6.10 do not permit such a conclusion because producers in both regions A and B slide up their aggregate supply functions as the quota is relaxed. Because the supply price rises and the demand price falls as price and marginal cost converge, any supplier already in the market would remain in the market. One (or several) regions could dominate the dairy market once it is liberalized only if there exist significant economies of scale that are available in one region but not another, which is unlikely.

6.4 Price Discrimination

In an effort to stabilize incomes in the agricultural sector, policy makers have encouraged the establishment of product marketing orders, which are then allowed to practice price discrimination in contradistinction to what is permitted in other industries under antitrust legislation. Indeed, many countries encourage discriminatory pricing in the dairy sector, where it is simple to segregate markets for fresh (fluid) milk and industrial milk, providing farmers with a blended price. This is illustrated using Figure 6.11.

Figure 6.11 Price discrimination across fluid and industrial milk markets

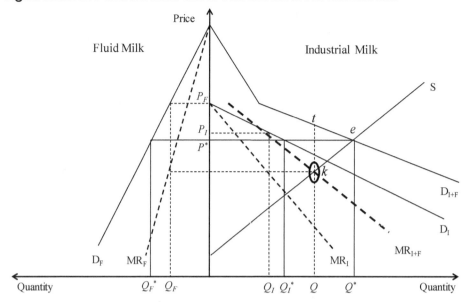

In the absence of price discrimination, the price in both the fluid and industrial milk markets is set equal to the intersection of the milk supply function S and the total (combined) demand for milk, denoted by D_{I+F}. This leads to a market clearing price of P^* with Q_F^* and Q_I^* consumed in the fluid and industrial milk markets, respectively; overall, Q^* ($=Q_F^*+Q_I^*$) amount of milk is consumed.

With price discrimination, the elasticities of demand in the two markets must differ. Then, if discrimination is permitted, the marginal cost of producing milk (given by S) is set equal to the marginal revenue MR_{I+F} associated with the total demand function. The intersection of S and MR_{I+F} (illustrated by the circled point k) is used to determine the marginal revenues in the separate fluid and industrial milk markets so that $S = MR_{I+F} = MR_F = MR_I$. To maximize profit, the marketing agency sets output in the fluid milk market equal to Q_F with the corresponding price, P_F, determined by the demand function in the fluid milk market. The same is done in the industrial milk market, where output and price are Q_I and P_I, respectively; total output is $Q = Q_F + Q_I$. The deadweight welfare loss to society from price discrimination is measured by the triangle (*tke*). Dairy producers receive the blended price, which is a weighted average of P_F and P_I.

Price discrimination alone proved insufficient support for dairy farmers in some developed countries. While Canada introduced supply management in the early 1970s, Europe and the United States introduced price supports in the dairy sector in addition to price discrimination. The economic consequences are illustrated with the aid of Figure 6.12. For a price support to be effective, however, the price floor must lie above the lowest of the prices in the markets for fluid and industrial milk, in this case P_I. In order to support the price, the government must purchase industrial milk (as fresh milk will spoil). With government purchases, the effective demand function becomes D (the dark kinked curve in Figure 6.12) with a horizontal segment at the floor price P_S.

Figure 6.12 Price discrimination in fluid and industrial milk markets with a price floor

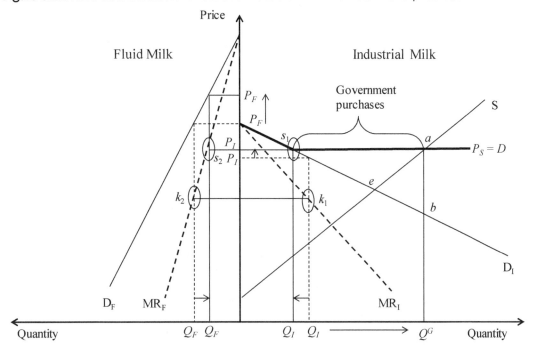

Prior to government purchases but with price discrimination, the marketing agency bases its sales on intersection points k_1 and k_2 (Figure 6.12), which were determined from point k in Figure 6.11 as described above. With government purchases, the new marginal revenue that the marketing agency faces is given by P_S. Optimal sales are determined by the intersection of marginal revenues and P_S, at points s_1 and s_2 for the industrial and fluid milk markets, respectively, while prices are found from the respective demand functions D_I and D_F. As shown by the arrows in Figure 6.12, consumption in each market is reduced because prices go up (eventually to P_I' and P_F'). The blended price also goes up. The initial purchase by government raises the blended price resulting in an output response, leading the government to purchase more to maintain price. The final result is that the blended (support) price equals the marginal cost of milk production S, with government holding more industrial milk than originally intended.

The cost to the public purse of this program is given by the rectangle bounded by points ($Q_I'Q^Gas_1$) minus the amount of surplus milk ($Q^G–Q_I'$) that the government might be able to sell abroad multiplied by the world price, which will necessarily be below P_S. The cost to the public purse also constitutes the net welfare loss; in this case, it is not measured by the usual deadweight loss triangle (*eab*) because it will depend on how much of the surplus $Q^G–Q_I'$ is disposed of in overseas markets and at what price.

As noted, both the US and the EU employed this support regime to protect dairy producers. The EU abandoned it in favor of supply restrictions in April 1984, while the US continued to employ this approach for a much longer period. Thus, during the 1980s, the US Commodity Credit Corporation (see Chapter 7.2) bought 5% to 30% of milk production as butter (fat) and milk powder (protein). However, during the 1990s, the US reduced the support price of milk and, along with a rise in the market price of industrial milk, overproduction was no longer a problem.

6.5 Agricultural Technology: Genetically Modified Organisms

6.5.1 Agricultural Research and Development

Historically and especially since the early twentieth century, technological advances in the agricultural sector have come from various sources: agricultural producers, private companies, universities, international agencies, and local and national governments. What are the major sources?

1. Farmers have long experimented with various plant varieties, crop and livestock management regimes, machine innovations, et cetera; for example, farmers have historically selected plant varieties that consistently perform best under local environmental conditions, and they will usually share such enhancements with other farmers.
2. Research and development (R&D) by private companies has led to improved plant varieties (e.g., hybrid corn), new and more environmentally friendly chemicals (fertilizers, herbicides, and insecticides), and advances in equipment design, including irrigation equipment, tractors and combines, drones, and transport vehicles. Private-sector research is limited by the need to earn a return. Therefore, it tends to focus on solving the most costly problems of the most economically important crops, the results from which can be patented to protect intellectual property.
3. Agricultural R&D is also conducted at universities and colleges, often in conjunction with farmers and private-sector partners, using public funding; agricultural faculties within postsecondary institutions are also engaged in extension, providing farmers and rural communities with a better understanding of scientific advancements in agriculture and rural development.
4. Likewise, national (and state/provincial) governments play an important role, both as a funder of R&D and, through public agricultural research stations, as a direct player in the development of new crops and plant varieties (e.g., rust resistant wheat), new agronomic practices (e.g., use of summer fallow to conserve soil moisture), identification of the best management practices, and programs that reduce risks related to drought, floods, pests, and infectious diseases in livestock. Many developing countries have established National Agricultural Research Systems that conduct research, with results usually made freely available to the public. Research that leads to public goods, which are not traded in markets and whose benefits cannot be captured by a private entity, is not of interest to the private sector; thus, it falls to the public sector to undertake such research.
5. Finally, international quasi- and non-governmental organizations conduct agricultural research, primarily under the auspices of the Consultative Group on International Agricultural Research (CGIAR), which constitutes a network of more than 3,000 partners from national governments, academic institutions, global policy bodies, private companies, and NGOs, and has some 10,000 researchers and staff. As indicated in Table 6.1, CGIAR consists of 15 centers, each working on regional agricultural problems related primarily to developing countries.

Another aspect of technological advances in the agricultural sector relates to the dissemination of knowledge—i.e., outreach, or extension. Extension refers to the function of educating farmers and facilitating the transfer of improved technology. In the United States, extension is a function of land-grant universities (see Chapter 7.2) that is funded partly by the federal government and partly by states—hence the term "cooperative extension." In Canada, extension is primarily the function of provincial ministries of agriculture. In addition to public extension activities, there is also a role for the private sector. Many accounting and farm management services can be delivered by the private sector, as can information and education regarding new equipment, seed varieties, weather forecasting, availability of various chemicals, their purpose and rates of application, and so forth.

Table 6.1 CGIAR international agricultural research centers and locations

	Center name (acronym)	Location
1	Africa Rice Center (WARDA)	Cotonou, Benin
2	Bioversity International	Rome, Italy
3	Centro Internacional de Agricultura Tropical (CIAT)	Cali, Colombia
4	Center for International Forestry Research (CIFOR)	Bogor, Indonesia
5	Centro Internacional de Mejoramiento de Maiz y Trigo (CIMMYT)	Mexico City, Mexico
6	Centro Internacional de la Papa (CIP)	Lima, Peru
7	International Center for Agricultural Research in the Dry Areas (ICARDA)	Beirut, Lebanon (Aleppo, Syria)
8	International Crops Research Institute for the Semi-Arid Tropics (ICRISAT)	Patancheru, India
9	International Food Policy Research Institute (IFPRI)	Washington, DC, US
10	International Institute of Tropical Agriculture (IITA)	Ibadan, Nigeria
11	International Livestock Research Institute (ILRI)	Nairobi, Kenya
12	International Rice Research Institute (IRRI)	Los Banos, Philippines
13	International Water Management Institute (IWMI)	Colombo, Sri Lanka
14	World Agroforestry Centre (ICRAF)	Nairobi, Kenya
15	World Fish Center	Penang, Malaysia

Source: CGIAR, Research Centers, https://www.cgiar.org/research/research-centers/.

6.5.2 Genetically Modified Organisms

Classical plant breeding was based on visual selection methods that were first adopted in scientific fashion by the Augustinian friar Gregor Mendel (1822–1884), although history is replete with examples of crossbreeding to develop new crops and varieties. The most notable example likely concerns the development of various varieties of corn in pre-Columbian Mexico and Peru. But Mendel was the first to talk about dominant and recessive traits, which are now commonly known as genes. The original green revolution began with the Nobel Laureate Norman Borlaug's crop research in Mexico in the late 1940s, although it began to take off in the 1960s with the transfer of technologies to developing countries. It relied on crop breeding to develop hybrid varieties of maize, adapted to each local maize-producing area. This was followed by improvements in wheat and rice, with the latter particularly important for the least developed countries, leading to short stature, high-yielding, fertilizer-responsive varieties. It was the new cost-reducing technologies related to nitrogen fertilizers and other chemicals, which killed or controlled weeds and pests, that were important supplements to crop breeding, although machinery technologies and increasing atmospheric CO_2 also contributed to increases in crop yields, with CO_2 perhaps accounting for some 15% to 20% of yield increases experienced during the latter half of the twentieth century, when the green revolution seemed to have ended; however, global yields of many crops have not stagnated, as expected, but continue to increase (see Chapter 10).

The potential productivity enhancements due to green revolution technologies now appear to have been mostly exploited. Reaching the limits of the green revolution, a second green revolution is needed to meet the challenge of doubling world food production. This revolution is possible through biotechnology, which has the potential to open new frontiers that could:

- improve nutritional content of grains;
- increase crop tolerances to drought, wetness, temperature, salt, aluminum toxicity, and so forth;
- increase yields and/or planted area under adverse or variable geographic and climate conditions;
- internalize resistance to diseases, viruses, and insect pests;
- reduce pesticide use, especially insecticides;
- reduce other chemical use through the development of herbicide-resistant varieties; and
- slow down product deterioration.

The development of genetically engineered (GE) crops in 1996 ushered in a new agricultural revolution. For example, African rice was low yielding, but had four desirable properties: resistance to viruses and disease; drought and salt tolerance; high protein content; and excellent taste and aroma. Contrariwise, Asian rice was characterized by high yield potential and excellent responsiveness to fertilizer applications, and very good harvest and milling properties. Because the two species would not cross sexually in classical plant breeding, a combination of classical plant breeding and biotechnology enabled scientists to combine the best traits of each for African rice growers, which yielded great benefits.

Elsewhere farmers rapidly adopted a technology package that involved planting of glyphosate-resistant crops (corn, canola, soybeans, cotton, sugar beet, alfalfa)—plants tolerant to a broad-based herbicide that would kill weeds but not the food crop. The technology was hailed for its financial, soil conservation, and carbon sequestration benefits, with crop area under zero tillage rising dramatically from 45 million hectares (ha) to 111 million ha between 1999 and 2009. The glyphosate-resistant crop technology reduced the costs of machine operations (plowing) with little or no impact on yields, lowered runoff of nitrogen and other chemicals into surface waters because soil erosion declined, and increased soil organic matter and carbon storage. The success of this simple and flexible technology led not only to widespread adoption (beyond all expectation), but to long-term continuous use.

Needless to say, the widespread adoption turned out to reveal a negative aspect of GE. In this case, integrated weed management strategies, such as mechanical (manual) weeding and deep plowing to bury weed seeds, were abandoned while weed resistance to glyphosate applications increased. In response, farmers increased herbicide application rates and frequency, and applied additional herbicide active ingredients, rather than turning to traditional weed management techniques. Meanwhile, weed tolerance to glyphosate grew at an average annual rate of 22.3%, rising even more rapidly in recent years.

The response of farmers was to rotate different types of genetically modified (GM) crops. For example, rather than plant only glyphosate-tolerant canola developed by Monsanto and sold under the trademark Roundup Ready canola, farmers would grow glufosinate-tolerant canola developed by Bayer Crop Science and sold under the trademark LibertyLink canola. Along with rotating other non-GE crops in a rotation with the two types of genetically modified canola, farmers have been able to ward off weed resistance to these chemicals in many cropping regions. Farmers are resistant to mechanical strategies because these are expensive and because they find the soil quality benefits of growing GM canola to be extremely worthwhile.

The response of industry to potential weed resistance to glyphosate or glufosinate has been to develop GM crops that are tolerant not only to the herbicide in question, but also to 2,4-D, dicamba, and other herbicides. The idea is to stack two or more herbicide resistant traits in GE crops, thereby reducing the probability that resistant weeds emerge to an estimated 1.0×10^{-19} to 1.0×10^{-20}. Indeed, the very tactic is the same as that used in the treatment of cancer patients, where a cocktail of chemicals is used to kill cancer cells.

Is genetically modified food safe to eat? Over 250 million Americans and millions more in other countries have been eating GM foods for several decades with not a single illness attributable to GM organisms. Most beer and cheese consumed in the world are already genetically engineered, as are innumerable pharmaceuticals (e.g., immunizations against Hepatitis A and B). GM foods are subjected to an unprecedented amount of testing before being put on the market.

Nonetheless, consumers remain resistant to GM foods. They are concerned that they will harm the environment by speeding the development of weed and insect resistance to chemicals, transfer genes to wild relatives, and harm non-targeted organisms. Most notably, the EU has opposed GM crops at home and their development internationally, in essence blocking funding of GE agricultural research at international research centers that are part of CGIAR. The EU opposes GE crops on the grounds of the precautionary principle adopted by the Cartagena Biosafety Protocol (discussed in Chapter 2.5).

The welfare impacts of genetic engineering can be examined with the aid of Figure 6.13. S^0 and D^0 are the supply and demand functions before the technological advance; q^0 is produced and consumed, and the price is p^0. The consumer surplus is given by the area bounded by (ap^0u) and the producer surplus by (cup^0). The development of the GM crop shifts the supply curve to S^1, thereby increasing quantity to q^1 and lowering price to p^1. The new consumer surplus is given by (awp^1) and the new producer surplus by (dwp^1); the net gain to society is then equal to ($cuwd$).

Figure 6.13 Welfare impacts of genetically modified crops

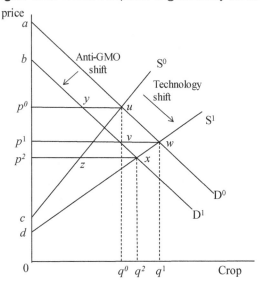

Now suppose there is a backlash against the GM crop that causes demand to shift to the left from D^0 to D^1, so quantity falls from q^1 back to q^2 with price falling as well from p^1 to p^2. Compared to the situation where there is no backlash, the loss in consumer surplus is given by $(awvb - p^1vxp^2)$, while producers lose (p^1wxp^2). The net loss is simply the area between the two demand curves, that is, the area bounded by $(awxb)$. Overall, the technology leads to a change in consumer surplus from (ap^0u) to (bp^2x), and producer surplus from (p^0uc) to (p^2xd). The net gain or loss to consumers is given by $(p^0yxp^2 - auyb)$; the net gain or loss to producers is $(p^2xd - p^0uc)$, which constitutes a gain as long as $(czxd) > (p^0uzp^2)$.

Clearly, the consumers' response to the new technology will determine whether the producer benefits from research and the resultant technological change. Further, the precautionary principle signals against investments in improved technologies; likewise, signals by consumers, food safety advocates, or environmental lobbyists will reduce incentives to conduct research to increase yields via genetic engineering.

The welfare analysis in Figure 6.13 seems straightforward, but is it really? We assume that, prior to the technological change, consumers allocate their incomes in optimal fashion. The technology first shifts the supply function and, assuming that consumers view the food crop the same before and after the genetic modification, the welfare changes identified above hold. But then there is a shift in demand—there is a change in the preference for a food product because it is no longer perceived to be the same product as previously. This explains the loss of $(auyd)$. But the price of the "not-quite-the-same" product drops as a result of the increase in supply and decline in demand, so consumers benefit by area (p^0yxp^2). By the fundamental equation of applied welfare economics (equation 2.4), there is nothing to measure in other markets. The only glitch, if it can be called that, is the change in consumer preferences that reallocated income from the market depicted in Figure 6.13 to other markets. The assumption of fixed preferences is violated, although justified if the good in question has changed in chameleon-like fashion. Consumers treat the GM crop as a different product than the non-modified crop. While the approach to measurement can still be useful for analyzing policy, care needs to be taken to ensure welfare changes are properly adjudicated in these situations, because the analysis needs to take into account that we are dealing with a "new" product.

6.6 Measuring Externalities in Agriculture

Agricultural activities generate many benefits to society, but there are also costs. Although net value-added can easily be calculated as the quasi-rent (producer surplus) attributable to agriculture, there are positive and negative externalities that are neglected or not properly accounted for in determining the overall contribution that agriculture makes to society. Consideration of externalities would be important in countries where industrial agriculture and exports dominate. In countries such as the Netherlands, which is the second largest exporter of agricultural commodities by value in the world after the United States, the externality costs and benefits need to be balanced against value-added to get a sense of whether the agricultural sector provides an overall benefit to society. This is not to suggest that, if the externality costs exceed value-added, agriculture should be abandoned entirely. Rather, it might be necessary to cut back some agricultural production to reduce the externality costs, but not entirely cease farming activities. With this in mind, a number of studies have attempted to measure the external costs and benefits of agriculture in various countries. In these studies and the discussion that follows, consumer surplus is considered but not actually measured because doing so would be very difficult.

In several studies of agricultural spillovers in the UK (Pretty et al. 2000, 2001, 2005; O'Neill 2007), total externality costs were calculated to be £233 million annually, or 89% of average net farm income in 1996. To encourage farm activities that would result in positive externalities, which are under provided in the marketplace, subsidies and regulatory measures were recommended, whereas regulation and economic incentives (levies/taxes) were recommended to correct negative externalities. However, to compare the externality costs to average net farm income in a particular year is a bit misleading, partly because net farm income often tends to be low and might be particularly low for the year in question. Using gross value-added in UK agriculture as the standard for comparison, the externality costs appear small—only about 3% of gross value-added.

For the US, the external costs of agricultural activities were estimated to range from $5.7 to $16.9 billion annually (Tegtmeier and Duffy 2004). Based on 168.8 million hectares of cropland in the US, the external costs could vary from $29.44 to $95.68 per ha, which appears quite dramatic. Again, it is perhaps better to compare the externality costs against gross value-added in the US agricultural sector; the externality costs constitute some 5% to 15% of this standard, which suggests that some action might be needed to address agricultural-sector externalities. One response might be to reform agricultural policy, but this would require careful consideration as some policies to address certain types of externalities may lead to adverse consequences elsewhere (including high transaction costs). Further, the US already has a number of policies in place that address externalities (see Chapter 7.2).

The UK and US studies were conducted by agronomists, who provided no theoretical basis for the measures they employed. So, what constitutes agricultural externalities, negative or positive? Both livestock operations and crop production impose external costs. Both have a negative impact on the soil. In many developed countries, there are regions where manure from livestock is spread on the land, causing excessive deposits of nitrogen that gets converted to nitrates (NO_3), phosphates, and zoonosis (diseases that are transferable from animals to humans), while crop production employs pesticides and fertilizers that negatively impact the soil. These forms of chemical pollution of soil adversely affect plant and animal biodiversity. Likewise, changes in land use and how land is managed also impact the composition of the soil, thereby affecting its future productivity and biodiversity. (In developing countries, manure is used to promote crop growth as fertilizers are often applied at sub-optimal rates or not at all; indeed, sometimes manure and other nutrients, such as crop residues, are removed from the land and used to fuel cooking stoves.) Finally, certain land-use practices (e.g., planting of trees, zero tillage, and permanent grasslands) can sequester carbon from the atmosphere, thereby mitigating climate change—a positive externality.

Livestock enterprises and arable farms have an impact on water quality, primarily because chemicals that first enter the soil subsequently leach into groundwater or run off into surface water. Phosphates and nitrogen can adversely affect lakes, making them less suitable for supporting aquatic life, while polluted water can have a negative effect on biodiversity more generally. Chemicals in ground and surface waters can also affect human health. To improve water quality involves costs, with any estimates of these costs providing information about the negative externality effects of agricultural activities.

Livestock operations emit methane (CH_4), CO_2, nitrous oxide (N_2O), sulphur dioxide (SO_2), and ammonia (NH_3) to the atmosphere, while arable farms emit CO_2 and nitrogen. Emissions of N_2O and SO_2 are a concern because N_2O rapidly oxidizes to become nitrogen dioxide (NO_2), which results in smog, while SO_2 leads to acid rain. CH_4 and CO_2 emissions from agricultural activities are important contributors to global warming (see Chapter 10). The impacts of CH_4 and CO_2 can be measured using information on the shadow price of carbon and knowledge about emissions from livestock operations and crop production.

The impacts of agriculture go beyond the traditional environmental impacts on soils, water quality, and the atmosphere. They also concern the impacts on biodiversity, wildlife habitat, landscapes, animal welfare, food security, and human health. Farming reduces habitat for some animals (e.g., large ungulates), but creates habitat for others (e.g., meadow birds); it destroys some amenities (wooded areas that store carbon) while providing new ones (visually appealing landscapes); it eliminates some wetlands that function to filter water and mitigate flooding, although the in-filling of such wetlands destroys mosquito habitat, thereby improving human health. Agricultural policies affect land management and use, thereby incentivizing activities that have both negative and positive externality effects.

We address the theory behind the measurement of externalities in agriculture with the aid of Figure 6.14. In the absence of incentives to address externalities, the agricultural sector (whether livestock or crop) will produce an amount Q^* at price P^* in Figure 6.14(a). This is where the demand and supply curves for agricultural commodities intersect. One can think of the demand function as the marginal willingness to pay (WTP) for agricultural output (essentially food) and the supply function as the private marginal cost ($MC_{private}$) of producing it. The private marginal cost function does not take into account the negative externalities associated with agricultural activities. It is the social marginal cost (MC_{social}) that takes into account both the private costs of farming plus their (negative) social impacts. This is illustrated in Figure 6.14(a), where the social equilibrium is Q_x, while the social price of food—the price that includes these spillover costs—is given by P_x.

What then constitutes the proper measure of the externality costs? If externality costs are ignored, consumers of agricultural commodities realize a consumer surplus given by ($\phi+\delta+\sigma+\gamma$), while producers realize a quasi-rent to set against fixed costs that is given by ($\alpha+\beta+\varepsilon$). After correcting for the externality, the new consumer surplus is area ϕ, while the quasi-rent is ($\beta+\delta$). That is, consumers are worse off by ($\delta+\sigma+\gamma$), while agricultural producers gain δ, which is a transfer from consumers, but lose area ($\alpha+\varepsilon$). The net loss to the agricultural sector is given by ($\alpha+\varepsilon+\sigma+\gamma$)—the area between the MC_{social} and $MC_{private}$ functions bounded by the demand function. This is the cost to society of reducing agricultural externalities to their socially desirable level. Of course, the benefits to society of reducing these externalities presumably exceed these costs, although this is something to be settled in the political realm.

Figure 6.14 Measuring the costs of externalities in agriculture

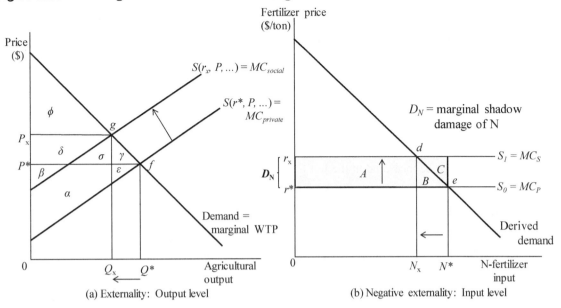

(a) Externality: Output level   (b) Negative externality: Input level

The problem is this: How do we measure these costs given we do not have all of the information to determine the demand and supply functions in Figure 6.14(a)? To do so, we must first realize that agricultural externalities occur upstream from the market for agricultural commodities. It occurs at the farm level where too many inputs are employed than socially desirable; that is, the farm sector uses too much fertilizer, pesticides, herbicides, and land. It is the intensity of input use that causes negative externalities.

It is the input markets that are of greatest relevance. Consider the market for nitrogen fertilizer in Figure 6.14(b). The demand function for fertilizer is derived from the demand for fertilizer by the agricultural sector. The supply function for fertilizer is assumed to be infinitely elastic (horizontal supply), which is identical to assuming that the agricultural sector is a price taker in the (international) market for fertilizer.[4] If no action is taken to address negative externalities, N^* amount of fertilizer will be applied, but then excessive nitrogen enters ground and surface water. One way to incentivize farmers to take negative externalities into account is to tax chemical pollutants or greenhouse gas emissions, thereby shifting $S=MC_P$ (private MC) upwards to $S=MC_S$ (social MC), increasing the input price of N fertilizer from r^* to r_x, and reducing fertilizer use from N^* to N_x.

Given that government already supports farm incomes, taxes are difficult to implement. Instead, the authority will regulate the use of certain chemicals or specify a standard for water quality that must be met, with a failure to meet the standard addressed using fines or stringent on-farm (best-practice) requirements. However, the result is the same: fertilizer use is limited to N_x, with the use of tradable permits one option for

---

[4] This is a crucial assumption for measurement because, if the supply function for inputs is upward sloping, changes in upstream markets (e.g., petroleum refining, transportation, machinery production) will also need to be considered. This is avoided by the assumption of infinitely elastic supply functions in agricultural input markets, as discussed in Chapter 4.3.

ensuring that the restricted quantity is optimally allocated. Whatever mechanism is used, the marginal shadow damage resulting from fertilizer use equals $r^*-r_x = D_N$, which represents the cost of the externality. The value of D_N can be determined by using a benefit transfer method based on a nonmarket valuation method, as described in Chapter 3.

An increase in the price of fertilizer causes the supply function in the agricultural output market to shift upwards and to the left, as indicated in Figure 6.14(a). Indeed, if excessive use of the fertilizer input was the sole cause of agricultural spillovers, then the increase in fertilizer price alone would reduce farm output from Q^* to Q_x.[5] Importantly for measurement purposes, the reduction in quasi-rent in the agricultural commodity market can be measured in the fertilizer market by the reduction in consumer surplus; that is, area $(\delta–\alpha–\varepsilon)$ in panel (a) is identical to area $(A+B)$ in panel (b). If there were more inputs responsible for negative externalities in the agricultural sector, then it would be the sum of the lost consumer surplus areas in the various input markets that would equal the lost quasi-rent in the market for agricultural commodities.

The welfare measure used in the US and UK studies is given by the shaded area in Figure 6.14(b)— the observed level of fertilizer use N^* was simply multiplied by the marginal shadow damage D_N to obtain the externality cost associated with fertilizer use, namely, area $(A+B+C)$. This overstates the loss in quasi-rent by triangle C. Further, it neglects the loss in consumer surplus in the market for agricultural commodities; that is, it ignores the negative impact on consumers of an increase in food prices.

If consumer surplus is ignored, the net loss to the agricultural sector is identical to the reduction in quasi-rent (or net value-added), which is identical to $(A+B)$, and is (over)estimated by shaded area C in panel (b). This implies infinite elasticity of demand so that consumers are price takers, and only the change in producers' welfare or quasi-rent needs to be measured. This is illustrated in Figure 6.15, where the demand function is horizontal rather than downward sloping as in Figure 6.14(a). Area $(M+H)$ in Figure 6.15 equals $(A+B)$ in panel (b) of Figure 6.14. This then is a theoretically correct estimate of the cost to society of reducing agricultural externalities to their socially desirable level.

Positive externalities also need to be considered, some of which are related to the agricultural commodity market in the same way as fertilizer. However, unlike with fertilizer, too little of the input is employed. For example, too little lime might be applied to lands that are acidic. Again assuming infinite elasticity of demand for the output and an infinite elasticity of supply of lime, economic theory in this case would lead one to multiply the marginal (shadow) price by current lime use to obtain an estimate of the social benefit from expanding its use. In the context of Figure 6.15, the shift in the supply function would be to the right rather than the left (as with a negative externality), so then $(M+H)$ would constitute a measure of the positive externality.

---

[5] Supply in the commodity market is a function of the input price. Thus, the increase in the price of fertilizer shifts the supply curve in the commodity market upwards from $S(r^*, …)$ to $S(r_x, …)$.

Figure 6.15 Measuring costs of externalities in agriculture at the output level, with infinite demand elasticity

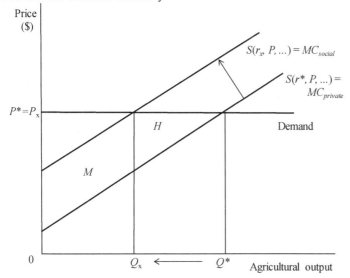

Recall, however, that it is in the input markets represented by Figure 6.14(b) where measurement occurs. In that figure, a positive externality would be equivalent to a downward shift in the input price (from r_x to r^*) but measurement would use N_x in this case rather than N^*. N_x would represent the current level of lime use, whereas it would be optimal to use N^*. Thus, the area used to measure the positive externality would consist of area A only, so, unlike with a negative externality, this method underestimates the positive benefit (by area B).

In addition to the demand for food, citizens are willing to pay directly for some positive externalities—the visual amenities provided by the agricultural landscape (e.g., livestock grazing in a field, rapeseed in bloom), habitat and food for some species of birds, and so forth. In Figure 6.16, the horizontal axis measures environmental amenities, with E^* equal to the environmental amenities associated with the level of agricultural output Q^* in Figure 6.15. Private demand for environmental services equals D_0, while society's demand is given by D_1. At private provision E^*, society's marginal value of the environmental services equals P', while the cost of producing them equals P^*. Society is willing to pay for more environmental services from the agricultural land. In the absence of other considerations, it would be socially optimal to incentivize farmers to increase production of environmental services to E_{pos}. In that case, the added cost to agricultural producers is given by the area bounded by points (E^*kbE_{pos}), while the benefit to society from expanding agricultural activities is given by (E^*abE_{pos}). The net benefit to society in this case is measured by the triangle (kab). This area represents a measure of the welfare loss—the loss in society's well-being—of producing at Q^*.

Farmers would need to be subsidized to produce more environmental amenities. The government can pay agricultural landowners to modify their practices so as to provide certain environmental services. Some examples include incentivizing farmers to protect wetlands and not drain them, delay mowing hayfields to facilitate breeding of certain meadow birds, plant trees to sequester carbon, and practice zero-till agriculture to prevent soil erosion while storing carbon. Payments for environmental services (PES) are increasingly used to incentivize landowners to take into account the WTP of citizens for environmental amenities or services. Of course, society could require farmers to implement certain practices in return for farm payments (known as cross compliance), thereby obtaining desirable levels of ecosystem services.

Society's WTP for positive externalities (Figure 6.16) is generally unknown and difficult to assess. One way around the measurement issue is to assume that the political process reflects society's preferences. Suppose the authority incentivizes the landowner with a payment for the environmental service equal to PES_0, and we then observe that the payment increases environmental services from E^* to E'. An estimate of the benefit to society is then given by the shaded area in Figure 6.16, although, with the exception of the shaded triangle lying above MC (which constitutes a quasi-rent or surplus to the producer), the payment essentially equals the cost of providing the service.[6] In the figure, society's value exceeds PES_0 as society would prefer more than E' (indeed, preferring E_{pos}). The concern with this approach is the assumption that, if the political process leads to an increase in the availability of some environmental amenity, the benefit will naturally exceed the expenditure required to achieve it. This is blatantly not true because environmental lobbying could lead to greater provision of environmental amenities than socially optimal.

Figure 6.16 Agricultural production and environmental services: Positive externalities

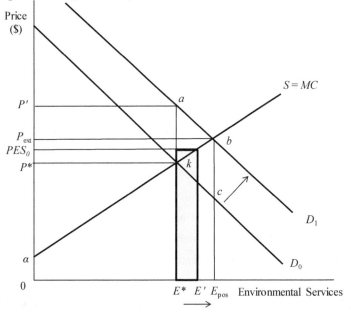

Based on the above theoretical foundation, a Dutch study found that total value-added benefits from intensive agriculture are estimated to be €10,604 million annually. The annual externality costs are estimated to be €1,868 million, while gross annual externality benefits are estimated to be some €263 million. Using

---

[6] Notice that suppliers of environmental services always earn a producer surplus (quasi-rent) when they receive a payment for environmental services, but this payment is required to cover fixed costs.

all available information, total average annual net benefits from agriculture in the Netherlands are calculated to be €8,736 million per year for the period 2005–2012. Nonetheless, net externality costs are equivalent to €849 per ha of arable, horticultural, and pasture land, and, not unexpectedly, are high relative to estimates found for other countries, because Dutch agricultural land produces a value-added of more than €30,000/ha.

6.7 Concluding Discussion

The purpose of economics is to provide guidance to decision makers, to point out the welfare gains and losses, and income transfers, that result from implementing agricultural policies. Often economists are able to point out consequences that were unanticipated by the policy maker. As shown in subsequent chapters, one of the most important contributions of policy analyses has been that of identifying the unanticipated costs and subsequent distorting impacts that various policies have had on the environment. In Chapters 7 and 8, we examine the costs of agricultural policies in various countries, investigating the history of farm support policies in three select countries and the largest trading bloc in the world, namely, the European Union. Although other or additional jurisdictions could have been selected, these are chosen because they are representative of the main approaches that policy makers have employed. Then, in Chapter 9, we examine an alternative approach to supporting agricultural producers that relies primarily on the management of risk.

Guide to Literature

Discussions of the farm problem and programs are provided by Gardner (1987), Pasour (1988), and Rausser (1992). Classic references for the analyses presented here are found in Just, Hueth, and Schmitz (1982, 2004), Schmitz, Furtan, and Baylis (2002), Schmitz et al. (2010, 2021). Analyses of buffer fund storage models under demand uncertainty originate with Waugh (1944) and Oi (1961), while those under supply uncertainty are due to Massell (1969); reviews and extensions are found in van Kooten and Schmitz (1985) and van Kooten, Schmitz, and Furtan (1988). Good economic analyses of the quota are found in Veeman (1982) and van Kooten and Taylor (1989); welfare analyses of the dismantling of quota regimes relies on van Kooten (2017a, 2020).

Information on the Consultative Group on International Agricultural Research comes from the group's website: https://www.cgiar.org/. Benbrook (2012) and Mortensen et al. (2012) are two excellent sources for information on genetic modifications in agriculture.

Studies measuring the externality costs of agriculture include Tegtmeier and Duffy (2004) for the US; Pretty et al. (2000, 2001, 2005) and O'Neill (2007) for the UK; Pillet, Zingg, and Maradan (2002) for Switzerland; and Porter et al. (2009) for Denmark. Much of the analysis in section 6.6 comes from Jongeneel, Polman, and van Kooten (2016), who use this theoretical framework to calculate the externality costs of Dutch agriculture and to compare cost measures used by other studies.

Food for Thought

6.1. What is the "farm problem"?

6.2. What are the main factors that contributed to the expansion of agricultural output during the period of the so-called green revolution (from about 1960s through the early 2000s)?

6.3. If the consumer price index was 120.4 in 2011 and 128.3 in 2018, calculate the annual rate of inflation between 2011 and 2018.

6.4. Why is global food security threatened? What are the potential threats to food security?

6.5. Consider a small country that is deciding between implementing an import tariff and an import quota in an industry that is experiencing falling marginal costs. Draw a diagram that illustrates the effects of a decrease in marginal costs in the case of an import tariff and another diagram that illustrates the effects of a decrease in marginal costs in the case of an import quota. What happens to domestic production, consumption, prices, and imports in each case?

6.6. Assume that the elasticity of supply $\xi_s = 1$, the demand function is given by $pD = 50 - q$, and the market clears at $q = 35$.

(a) What are the (i) consumer surplus, (ii) producer surplus, and (iii) total surplus?

(b) Suppose a quota is set at $\bar{q} = 28$. In that case, what is the:
    (i) loss in consumer surplus;
    (ii) reduction in quasi-rent;
    (iii) value of the quota rent; and
    (iv) overall gain or loss of the agents that get the quota rent?

6.7. In Figure 6.4, we examine the case of a buffer fund that would store grain when supply was high and sell grain when supply was low, thereby holding price constant. Assuming the supply curve was S_0 (abundant) in one period and S_1 (scarce) in another with equal probability, it was shown that the buffer agency would increase the overall (two-period) income of producers, increase variability of producer incomes, and reduce consumer well-being. Now suppose that uncertainty is not due to supply but to demand uncertainty, with each of two demand functions occurring with equal probability of ½. If the buffer fund agency stabilized price, who would gain and who would lose? In other words, what are the overall welfare impacts under demand uncertainty?

6.8. You are given that the elasticity of demand is -0.5 ($\varepsilon_d = -0.5$) and the elasticity of supply is 1.0 ($\varepsilon_s = 1.0$). In addition, the observed price and quantity are $50 per hectoliter (hl) and 1,000 hl, respectively.

(a) Find the equations for the demand and supply functions.

(b) Draw a diagram showing the derived S and D. Identify the consumer surplus and the producer surplus on the diagram.

(c) How much is the consumer surplus? How much is the producer surplus?

(d) Suppose a dairy marketing board is set up so that the supply is restricted to 800 hectoliters (1 hl = 100 l). Illustrate the situation on the diagram and identify the consumer and producer surpluses and the policy-induced scarcity rent.

(e) How much are each of the following: consumer surplus, producer surplus, rent, and deadweight loss to society?

(f) What is the efficiency of the income transfer from producers to consumers? That is, what must consumers pay for every dollar that producers gain?

6.9. In Figure 6.7, the economics of supply management is examined without consideration of the need for a tariff rate quota. How would the analysis change if you take into account the TRQ?

6.10. What determines the value of land and how might a government subsidy be capitalized into land values? Show how an output price support, in the product market, can affect the price of land (use a vertical model with graphs for the final product and the land market).

6.11. *True, False, or Uncertain? Make sure to indicate why*. Price stabilization is an optimal policy because net welfare gains to society will result.

6.12. One agricultural support policy is to set a support price above the market clearing level. This policy has been used in the US (see Chapter 7). It has also been used in the EU and is currently used for rice and wheat in China (see Chapter 8). Using a partial equilibrium graph, show how a price support above the market clearing level affects the production, consumption, and government purchases of a commodity. Explain your graph briefly. You can graph the case where there is only one country (autarky) or the case where trade is possible at a fixed world price.

6.13. In Figure 6.10, we provide a mechanism for dismantling dairy quota. The EU was a dairy exporter, while Canada was an importer of dairy products after the implementation of a quota scheme. For these situations, demonstrate how the authority might want to dismantle the dairy quota program and provide producers with compensation similar to that in Figure 6.10.

6.14. Suppose the current market price for wheat is $3 per bushel and that 10 billion bushels are currently marketed domestically and offshore. Given the following market shares and own-price elasticities of demand for domestic and export markets, answer the following:

(a) What would happen to domestic wheat producers' total revenue if the quantity they supplied to the market increased by 3% (compared to current revenues)?

(b) Would domestic consumers of wheat products be better or worse off economically than they were before the decrease in supply? Why? Illustrate the answer with a diagram.

Market	Market share	Own-price elasticity of demand
Domestic	40%	−0.20
Foreign	60%	−2.00

7

AGRICULTURAL POLICIES IN

THE UNITED STATES AND CANADA

Agricultural programs that support farmers' incomes are primarily a rich-country phenomenon, although in recent years developing countries have increasingly provided support to their farm sectors. Governments in developing countries have often viewed the agricultural sector as a source of revenue, taxing farmers rather than subsidizing them. Given an increasingly urban population, however, those same governments have implemented policies to keep food prices low to avoid civil unrest, thus subsidizing farm imports and even banning agricultural exports on occasions when global prices are high. Based on the experience of rich countries, many developing countries now recognize that it might be beneficial to support agricultural incomes, encourage economies of scale that would result in fewer but larger farms, and make use of the resulting surplus labor in other sectors that compete in global markets.

In this chapter, we begin by examining in greater detail the extent to which countries support their agricultural sectors. Perhaps not surprisingly, countries have historically emulated the farm programs of rivals, especially programs that have been viewed as "successful," although what constitutes success might change over time. More recently, convergence of program types, although not levels of support, has come about as a result of international efforts to decouple agricultural production from farm payments. Countries recognize the need to create programs that do not incentivize production, thereby distorting international markets. As argued in Chapter 5, much of this has come about in an effort to resolve agricultural trade disputes within the context of major trade negotiations. Therefore, we review the agricultural policies of the largest trading blocs—the United States and the European Union. With the exception of Canada and some developing countries, particularly China and India, we will mention other countries and regions only in passing because, although important producers of agricultural commodities, the experiences of these five jurisdictions with various agricultural programs are sufficient that other countries can only emulate and learn from them.

Modern agricultural policy developments began in the United States. In section 7.2, therefore, we provide a historic overview of US agricultural policy, focusing particularly on how to employ tools of applied welfare economics to analyze various programs and why those programs were reformed over time. Because Canada's economy is heavily dependent on that of the US, we also discuss Canada's agricultural policy here. This is done to highlight how the agricultural policies in countries with a common language and colonial heritage differ because one is a global agricultural powerhouse and the other is a small open economy with little influence over global prices, except perhaps with respect to softwood lumber and durum wheat. In Chapter 8 we analyze agricultural policies in the European Union and two developing countries, China and India, both of which have a population greater than the EU and a large agricultural sector, and are the developing world's largest and most vibrant economies. We begin, however, by examining the extent of agricultural support across jurisdictions and agricultural sectors.

7.1 Agricultural Support: A Brief Overview

To compare support for agriculture across sectors and countries, some agricultural economists prefer to use the Nominal Rate of Assistance (NRA) measure. The NRA is the percentage by which the domestic producer price is above (or below if negative) the border price of a similar product, net of transportation costs and trade margins. The NRA is thus an estimate of direct government policy intervention. The NRA to agricultural producers in the European Union exceeded that provided to US producers by a significant amount during much of the period 1962–2011 (Figure 7.1). Exceptions occur in the early 1970s, when the US NRA exceeded that of the EU, and more recently as NRAs of the EU and the US have fallen toward zero. From Figure 7.1, we find that Canada's support for farmers over the period 1962–2011 was generally higher than that provided by the US, but below that provided by the EU (at least for the period 1986–2008). China's level of support was significantly below that of other regions until it began to rise in 2008, at the same time as levels of support in other regions began to decline.

Figure 7.1 Nominal rates of assistance to agriculture, selected countries and regions, 1962–2011

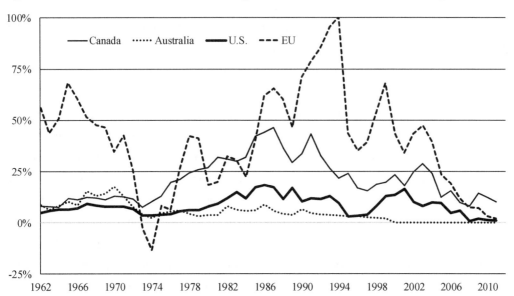

Source: Based on Anderson et al. (2013), who developed a Nominal Rate of Assistance index for the World Bank. Data not available after 2011 nor are data available for many countries, such as China. Work continues at the World Bank on the development and dissemination of data on distortions in agriculture (https://datacatalog.worldbank.org/dataset/estimates-distortions-agricultural-incentives [accessed January 9, 2020]).

An alternative measure of the support received by agricultural producers in various jurisdictions is provided by the Organisation for Economic Co-operation and Development (OECD), which comprises 35 countries and is headquartered in Paris. The OECD defines agricultural support as:

> *the annual monetary value of gross transfers to agriculture from consumers and taxpayers, arising from governments' policies that support agriculture, regardless of their objectives and their economic impacts. Support estimates are measured in monetary terms and as a share of GDP, or as a share of gross farm receipts. ... The Percentage Producer Support Estimate (%PSE) represents policy transfers to agricultural producers, measured at the farm gate and expressed as a share of gross farm receipts.*

Support measures are also available for individual crops. The single commodity transfer is similarly defined, with the farmer required to produce the designated commodity to receive the transfer. In this case, the percentage share refers to the share of gross farm receipts attributable to the specific commodity. One drawback of the %PSE measure is that gross farm receipts vary greatly from one year to the next because commodity prices tend to be quite volatile.

The %PSE measures of support for the selected jurisdictions in Figure 7.1 are provided in Figure 7.2 for the period 1986–2019 (NRA data are available only to 2011). These indicate that the EU provided much greater relative support to agriculture than the US or Canada throughout the period, while Canadian support generally exceeded that of the US except for eight years (1999–2002, 2014, 2015, 2018, 2019). Meanwhile, Chinese agricultural support increased (but not steadily) from no support in 1999 to just over 14% in the five years 2015–2019. In contrast, agricultural support in the US declined from about 25% to about 10% of gross farm receipts, Canadian support from 35% to 8%, and EU support from 45% to 19% over the same period.

If one considers more countries/regions than those shown in Figures 7.1 and 7.2, one finds an even greater disparity in support levels. In Table 7.1, producer support estimate levels, measured in millions of US dollars (and available as well in Euros), are provided for a broader selection of countries and for the OECD and the EU-28. Japan, Norway, and other countries not shown, such as Switzerland, provide high levels of support to farmers for food security reasons. These countries have a comparative disadvantage in the production of agricultural commodities and thus incentivize farmers to produce in agricultural regions that are marginal from a global standpoint. Turkey might fall into this category to some extent, but demographics (a high proportion of the population still engages in agriculture), institutions, and governance, such as corruption (see Chapter 5, especially Figure 5.1), are potentially important factors leading to high levels of support for agriculture. China (14%) and Russia (12%) provide relatively high levels of support to farmers as well, but much less than the EU (19%), Canada (8%), or the US (10%). Among industrial countries, Australia and New Zealand provide much lower levels of support, certainly well below the OECD average (18%). Among developing countries, Brazil and South Africa provide little support for agricultural producers, while Ukraine actually collects more from the farm community than it provides in support.

Figure 7.2 Producer support estimates, percent of farm receipts, select countries or regions, 1986–2019

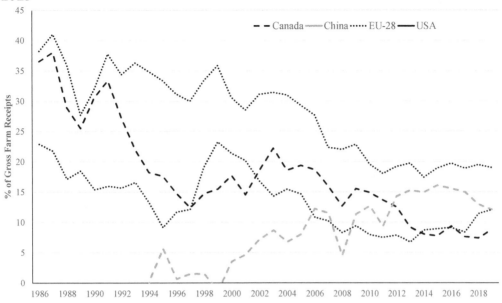

Source: OECD (2020)

Table 7.1 Producer support estimates in agriculture for selected countries or regions, 2019

Country/region	Amount (US$×10⁶)	% of gross farm receipts
Australia	$796.0	1.89
Canada	$4,289.3	9.70
Japan	$37,645.2	70.36
New Zealand	$139.7	0.71
Norway	$3,025.6	136.01
Turkey	$6,695.0	15.64
USA	$48,927.1	13.74
Brazil	$1,747.2	1.13
China	$185,912.7	13.77
India	-$23,091.9	-4.74
Russia	$7,943.6	10.15
South Africa	$876.4	4.83
EU-28	$101,251.5	23.48
OECD (Total)	$231,769.0	21.58

Source: OECD (2020)

Lastly, we can examine the support provided to individual crops. In Table 7.2, we provide the single commodity transfers that measure the support to an individual commodity group as a percentage of the total gross receipts for that commodity. The values are an average of support levels over the period 1995–2019.

In the discussion of agricultural policies in individual jurisdictions, we provide additional details concerning changes in individual-commodity producer support estimates over time. As indicated in Figure 7.2, the data in Table 7.2 confirm that the EU has provided the highest levels of support for farmers; across commodities but with exceptions, support levels in the EU tend to be on the high side compared to other countries. Milk producers in Canada and China, sugar producers in the US, and beef and veal producers in the EU received the greatest levels of support among all commodity producers; support to the milk sector ranked only fifth after beef and veal, sugar, poultry, and rice in the EU. The data also indicate that two of Canada's supply-managed sectors, dairy and eggs, are much more heavily subsidized than those in other countries, but poultry is less subsidized than in Europe and China even though it too operates under a quota regime. An examination of support provided in India indicates that support varies considerably from one year to the next, and from one commodity to another, with average support payments generally falling on the negative side of the ledger.

Table 7.2 Agricultural policy support for various agricultural commodities, average for the period 1995–2019, % of gross commodity receipts

Commodity	USA	EU-28	Canada	China
Wheat	7.65	3.56[a]	2.48	14.23
Barley	5.14	6.73	3.56	n.a.
Maize	5.00	14.17	5.25	15.17
Oats	n.a.	9.85	4.00	n.a.
Sorghum	9.49	n.a.	n.a.	n.a.
Rapeseed	n.a.	0.14	1.79	20.32
Rice	9.69	25.69	n.a.	1.71
Soybeans	5.61	0.37	3.69	10.31
Sugar	39.76	34.39	n.a.	26.99
Milk	25.50	21.48	47.54	27.55
Beef & veal	0.07	42.83	2.29	4.94
Poultry	0.15	26.46	7.86	10.14
Eggs	0.40	2.29	13.50	-2.30
Cotton	18.30	n.a.	n.a.	27.89
Potatoes	n.a.	9.71	1.27	n.a.

[a] For common wheat, whereas it is 19.77 for durum wheat
n.a. = not available from the OECD.
Source: OECD (2020)

7.2 US Agricultural Policy

Government intervention in agriculture began in the United States in the late 1800s with the Homestead Act of 1862. It allocated lands that had come under federal domain to private landowners who were willing to farm the land. At the same time, the US passed the Morrill Act (1862) that created the land-grant colleges, so named because each institution was given 30,000 acres (about 12,150 hectares) of federal land. The land grants were extended to the Confederate states under the 1890 Morrill Act. Then the Hatch Act (1887) created the Agricultural Experiment Stations and the Smith-Lever Act (1914) created the cooperative extension service, both of which came to be located in the various state land grant colleges. Finally, in 1916 the Federal Farm Loan Act was passed to facilitate lending to agricultural producers. However, efforts to stabilize and support farm incomes did not come until 1929 when the first farm bill, the Agricultural Marketing Act, was passed. The legislation created a Federal Farm Board tasked with forming cooperatives in an attempt to stabilize prices—the board cost some $500 million. Agricultural legislation took on greater urgency with the coming of the Great Depression.

As part of Roosevelt's New Deal, the Agricultural Adjustment Act of 1933 sought to stem the Depression-era decline in net cash farm income, which fell from $5.2 billion to $1.4 billion between 1929 and 1932, thereby affecting the one-quarter of the labor force employed in agriculture. The 1933 legislation was challenged in court and declared unconstitutional in 1936. However, with the Agricultural Marketing Agreement Act of 1937 and the Agricultural Adjustment Act of 1938, which replaced the 1933 legislation, the federal government encouraged voluntary marketing agreements, with handlers and processors licensed to enforce marketing arrangements. In essence, these acts encouraged monopoly behavior and price discrimination that were prohibited under the Sherman Antitrust Act (1890) in other sectors of the economy. Price discrimination and supply restrictions using acreage allotments and marketing quotas were employed and taxes were levied on processors to fund expenditures. This was done to reduce production of basic commodities in an effort to increase farm gate prices, and thereby farm incomes.

The Agricultural Adjustment Act created the Commodity Credit Corporation (CCC) and introduced non-recourse loans for cotton and corn (maize). As a result, a corn or cotton producer could take out a loan from the CCC based on the amount harvested, which, together with the size of the loan, determined the commodity's implicit price. The implicit price was the floor or support price. If the farmer defaulted on the loan, the CCC would accept the physical commodity and store it, hopefully selling it when prices rebounded (recall Chapter 6.2). These initiatives resulted in substantial intervention in commodity markets while redistributing income from taxpayers and consumers to agricultural producers.

The problems associated with these programs became apparent once the war-related, high commodity prices of the 1940s and early 1950s subsided, and as technological innovation and non-farm economic growth induced massive labor migration out of agriculture. This left fewer farmers who were better able to organize to lobby government for favorable income transfers. Thus, these early policies persisted into the 1960s and continue in one form or another to this day, although, as we shall see, they have been largely transformed in ways that have eased market interventions and reduced efficiency losses.

After the initial farm bills, the United States would pass a new farm bill approximately every five years, along with other legislation affecting the agricultural sector in many years between the so-called farm bills (Table 7.3). Farm bills subsequent to the 1949 Farm Bill contained a sunset clause—a date when their provisions expire and "permanent law" comes into force. Permanent law refers to non-expiring farm commodity programs based on the 1938 and 1949 farm bills. Therefore, a temporary suspension of permanent law has been included in recent farm bills, with a reversion to permanent law if the suspension expires. Congress seeks to avoid this situation because "permanent" commodity support programs are fundamentally different from current policy and inconsistent with today's farming practices, marketing system, and international trade agreements. They are also viewed as potentially very costly to the federal government.

Table 7.3 US Farm Bills, 1929–2018

1929 – Agricultural Marketing Act
1933 – Agricultural Adjustment Act of 1933
1938 – Agricultural Adjustment Act of 1938
1948 – Agricultural Act of 1948
1949 – Agricultural Act of 1949
1954 – Agricultural Act of 1954
1956 – Agriculture Act of 1956
1965 – Food and Agricultural Act
1970 – Agricultural Act of 1970
1973 – Agricultural and Consumer Protection Act
1977 – Food and Agriculture Act
1981 – Agriculture and Food Act
1985 – Food Security Act
1990 – Food, Agriculture, Conservation, and Trade Act
1996 – Federal Agriculture Improvement and Reform Act
2002 – Farm Security and Rural Investment Act
2008 – Food, Conservation, and Energy Act
2014 – Agricultural Act of 2014
2018 – Agricultural Improvement Act

Source: Adapted from National Agricultural Law Center (https://nationalaglawcenter.org/farmbills/ [accessed January 9, 2020])

The general purpose of farm legislation between 1933 and 1970 was fourfold: (1) reduce rural poverty; (2) promote soil conservation—encourage a shift from soil-depleting (erosive) crops to legumes, grasses, or trees, and promote contour plowing; (3) provide farmers with crop insurance; and (4) make available credit to agricultural producers. These objectives arose from Depression-era shocks to the sector. Since then, agricultural policies have become more nuanced, primarily because farmers have been successful in lobbying for higher levels of support, while greater emphasis has been placed on the environmental impacts of agricultural operations as a result of environmental lobbying (see Chapter 6.6). At the same time, consumers have become increasingly concerned about food safety and food security (including fear of depending on unreliable foreign producers).

Food safety issues relate mainly to fear of food contamination (e.g., pathogens like *salmonella* and *E. coli* that can be found in beef and poultry products as well as on fresh lettuce and spinach), certification of organic and genetically modified foods (see Chapter 6.5), and livestock diseases such as foot and mouth disease and bovine spongiform encephalopathy (BSE)—also known as mad cow disease. It is believed that domestic agricultural products are somehow safer, which influences policies concerning food security and bilateral and multilateral trade negotiations.

As the number of farmers and farm workers fell dramatically after World War II, from nearly one-quarter of the labor force in the mid-1930s to less than 2% today, the ability of farmers to organize and lobby legislators increased significantly. As a result of rent-seeking on the part of agricultural producers, subsidization under the guise of stabilization began in earnest in the late 1970s, partly as a response to the EU's Common Agricultural Policy (CAP). Taxpayers on the other hand lacked the incentive to oppose large farm subsidies because the costs of agricultural programs to any one taxpayer are small. Further, citizens accepted transfers to agriculture out of concerns for food safety and security and a desire to protect a rural lifestyle. Only the negative environmental impacts of farming remained a concern, although these were subsequently dealt with in various ways, as discussed below. Finally, when funding for the Food Stamp Program, which provided assistance to the urban poor, fell under the farm legislation after 1964, rural and urban legislators were united in promoting their constituencies via farm bills. All these factors facilitated rent-seeking behavior and played a significant role in agricultural policy after 1970.

To address environmental spillovers, as early as the 1965 Farm Bill, farmers were required to set aside a portion of their cropland to be eligible for subsidies. Set-aside land was to be put into grasslands (permanent pasture), perennial crops, or forest. As discussed in Chapter 5.2, this red-ticket conservation policy came to be known as cross compliance: It was a red-ticket policy because it forced farmers to comply with environmental standards in order to receive subsidies. In contrast, a green-ticket conservation policy would directly incentivize landowners for meeting or even exceeding certain environmental standards.

7.2.1 Analysis of US Price Support Programs

The Agricultural Act of 1970 introduced three components that continue to influence farm programs to the present (and maybe beyond):

1. Although previous farm bills had included a support price, the 1970 Farm Bill established a target price (TP) for agricultural commodities as the mechanism to support farm incomes.
2. A loan rate (LR) was first introduced in the 1937 legislation as a support price, but later it became the price floor. At the time of harvest, farmers could take out a non-recourse loan on grain at the LR price. If the market price exceeded the LR, the farmer would sell the grain on the open market and repay the loan. If the LR exceeded the market price, the farmer would deliver the grain to the Commodity Credit Corporation to repay the loan. Thus, the loan was referred to as non-recourse because only delivery, not repayment of the loan, was required.
3. In addition, a direct payment was made to farmers based on their historical acreage and yields. The farmer would be paid the minimum of TP – LR, or TP – P, where P is the market price. This payment was referred to as a deficiency payment.

Both the loan rate and target price were predetermined, set by Congress for the period that the Farm Bill was in effect.

Not surprisingly, the interplay between these three components of the 1970 Farm Bill did not go according to plan. The legislation anticipated that farmers would determine output on the basis of the loan rate, while adjustments in the target price could be used to provide a direct subsidy (deficiency payment) that had no impact on agricultural output. It was reasoned that output decisions were *decoupled* from (unaffected by) the target price because the deficiency payment was based on a three-year moving average of the farmer's past yields. Farmers should then base production decisions on the loan rate and not the target price, but they often appeared to make output decisions in anticipation of the target price.

The interplay between the loan rate and target price is illustrated with the aid of Figure 7.3. In the figure, the expected non-intervention price and quantity are p^* and q^*. Suppose that output is truly decoupled from the target price. Given a loan rate P_L for corn, farmers would respond by producing q_L, except for differences due to production risks associated with weather variability, for example. In this case, historic yields would converge to q_L, since farmers would use the loan rate to guide decisions. The deficiency payment would be given by the shaded area $(P_T k x P_L) = (P_T - P_L) \times q_L$. In practice, the CCC performed a buffer fund function by holding stocks when market prices were below what Congress deemed desirable (say, p^*); that is, the loan rate and target price are politically determined and open to rent-seeking by farm lobby groups.

Figure 7.3 Operation of the target price and loan rate under US legislation

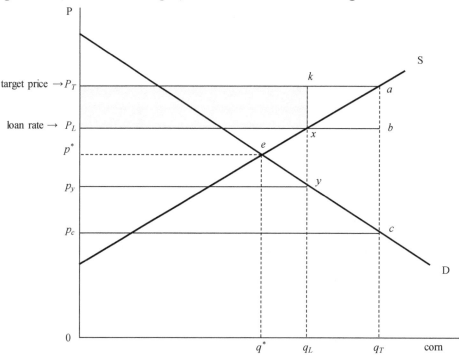

The large subsidies triggered by the target price/loan rate policy were partly prompted and partly a response to growing agricultural subsidies in the EU, resulting in a subsidy trade war. Of course, the intent of the US policy was to remove incentives to overproduce. As illustrated in Figure 7.4, farmers were not really incentivized to produce q_T rather than q_L. Why? The deficiency payment is based on historical yields, with q_L determined as a three-year moving average yield for the crop in question—the reference yield. In that case, the price that producers use to make production decisions might not be the loan rate, nor might it be the target price.

Farmers will likely employ some expected price that lies between P_L and P_T, and this will lead them to increase their average reference level of production from the current q_L to some higher level. Thus, while the legislation sought to hold output at q_L to prevent farmers from increasing output to q_T (as indicated by the upper arrow in Figure 7.4), as long as the expected price $E(p)$ is greater than the loan rate P_L, output can be expected to rise to $E(q)$ (lower arrow in Figure 7.4). Thus, the farmer's historical reference production used to determine the deficiency payment would increase. In the extreme, farmers' yields would converge on q_T, with the deficiency payment slowly converging upon $(P_T ab P_L) = (P_T - P_L) \times q_T$ in Figure 7.3. This would then lower the market price (p_c versus p_y in Figure 7.3), resulting in a higher CCC payment than expected ($P_L bcp_c$ rather than $P_L xyp_y$).

Figure 7.4 Interplay between target price and loan rate: Output effect of expectations

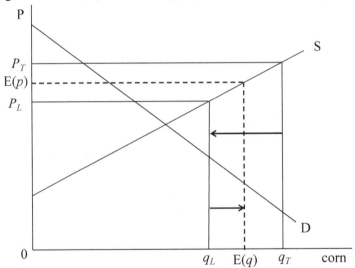

Because the United States is the largest agricultural producing country in the world and commands a large share of export markets in grains, the loan rate is effectively the world price. The loan rate causes other countries to expand their production with the support of the US Treasury. This is illustrated in Figure 7.5. Assume that, in the absence of government intervention and abstracting from shipping and handling costs, the world price is P_E. Then the equilibrium quantity sold internationally is $Q_E = q^E_s - q^E_d$. Under the loan rate, US domestic purchases fall from q^E_d to q^L_d while foreign purchases fall from Q_E to Q^L_d. To maintain price at the loan rate, the US would have to buy up $Q^L_s - Q^L_d = (q^E_d - q^L_d) + (q^L_s - q^E_s)$. This increases the burden to the US Treasury, but also increases the world's surplus grain. Again, it is clear that disposal of grain is a problem.

Figure 7.5 Impact of the US loan rate on the international market

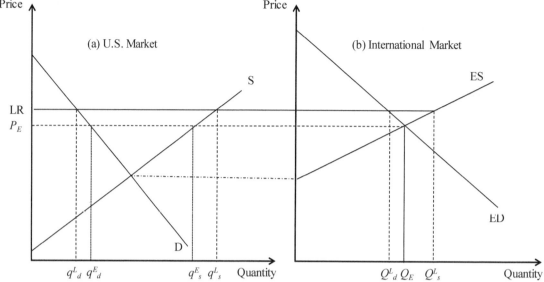

7.2.2 Reducing Production and Disposing of Excess Grain

As a result of the loan rate/target price dichotomy introduced in the 1970 Farm Bill, overproduction led to the accumulation of large government-held stocks of grain. During the period 1981–1986, 3 billion bushels of wheat went into the CCC loan program while CCC payments exceeded $6 billion. Government stocks put a damper on world grain prices as these were released whenever prices rose above the loan rate. Therefore, in the 1985 Food Security Act, the government introduced a Conservation Reserve Program (CRP) and two temporary programs to reduce government grain stocks and their growth: the Export Enhancement Program (EEP) and Payments-In-Kind (PIK). The CRP remains in place, while EEP was in place for 1985–1995 and the PIK program for an even shorter period.

The CRP was established by a provision to retire highly erodible land for a period of 10–15 years. The government identified eligible, highly erosive lands and owners bid to include lands in the Reserve. The objectives of the program were to (1) reduce soil erosion, (2) reduce output to increase prices, and (3) bolster net farm income. To protect rural communities, however, no more than 25% of land in any county could be removed. Per acre payments were used, but payments were limited to $50,000 per farm enterprise. The intent was to reduce crop acreage by 40–50 million acres (16.2–20.2 million ha), but targets were never met: 38 million acres were enrolled in the CRP in 1991, 34 million acres in 2000, and 32 million acres in 2008. In the initial enrollment, the majority of land in the CRP came from the Great Plains, because these were the least valuable lands and bids to enter the CRP were lowest. Subsequently, to increase CRP lands in the Midwest, the 1990 Farm Bill emphasized water quality in determining CRP eligibility, while the 1996 Farm Bill included wildlife habitat conservation as a criterion. By converting row crops to grasslands, soil erosion is reduced and wildlife habitat enhanced. The overall effect of the CRP was to increase world grain prices as a significant portion of US cropland was nonetheless removed from production.

The EEP was designed primarily to match subsidized EU prices and reduce accumulating US grain stocks. Wheat was the most important crop to receive EEP benefits, with $1.15 billion paid to companies to export wheat under the EEP in 1994. The applied welfare implications of EEP are examined using Figure 7.6. Assume that the US supply function includes all production plus stocks, so that P_F is the world price of wheat in the absence of the EEP. A company applies to the government to export $W_E - W_F$ quantity of wheat. Since the US is the largest exporter of wheat, the increase in US wheat exports causes the world price to fall from P_F to P^*, but it also leads to an increase in the domestic price to P_F from P_E. The reason is that $W_F - W_E$ = $(q^S_E - q^S_F) + (q^d_E - q^d_F)$ is removed from the domestic market. The EEP bonus is the difference between the new domestic price and the new world price, or $P_E - P^*$, which is paid by US taxpayers. The cost to the US Treasury equals the EEP bonus × quantity shipped, namely $W_E - W_F$. What are the other welfare implications?

Figure 7.6 Impact of the US export enhancement program

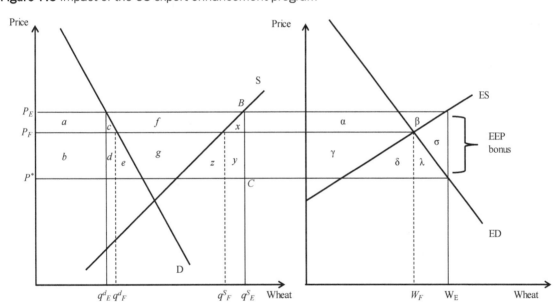

In Figure 7.6, the EEP led US taxpayers to pay the area bounded by $(P_E BCP^*)$; meanwhile, US producers gain $(a+c+f)$ and US consumers lose $(a+c)$. The net loss to the US amounts to the sum of the two triangles represented by $(c+d+e)$ and $(x+y+z)$. Foreign consumers gain, while foreign producers lose, with consumers gaining more than producers lose; the net gain to foreign countries is given by $(\gamma+\delta+\lambda)$. Notice that the deadweight loss σ in the rest of the world is indirectly paid for by the US.

The EEP was an example of unanticipated consequences. In particular, the program actually encouraged greater production because the domestic price had increased; this reduced world prices more than expected. Indeed, the EEP reduced the world price of barley to such an extent that the US on one occasion actually imported barley since the domestic price was so much higher than the world price. The built-in incentive to increase production led to additional changes in subsequent farm bills, and efforts to reduce the loan rate and decouple production from prices (although deficiency payments remained in place). One immediate consequence was a reduction in the loan rate in 1986, which reduced the world price of wheat by approximately $1 per bushel. Another was greater reliance on payments in-kind.

In contrast to the EEP, the PIK program was designed solely to reduce production via acreage set-aside provisions, thereby complementing the CRP. PIK allowed farmers to remove 10%–20% of their acreage from production in return for commodity credits—95% of reference yields for wheat and 80% for other commodities. That is, a farmer would get a commodity credit with the CCC for 95% of the wheat crop (80% of other crops) that would otherwise have been grown—a credit for crops not grown. These credits were based on a farmer's past yields and took the form of commodity certificates redeemable at the CCC. As an alternative, a farmer could bid for the percent of in-kind yield credit to retire the entire farm. The PIK program identified 231 million acres (94 million ha) as eligible for this program, and ended up retiring 188 million acres (76 million ha). Consequently, wheat and corn production each declined by 25%, thereby reducing costs of agricultural programs to the US Treasury in the late 1980s and significantly lowering government stocks of wheat and corn.

7.2.3 Decoupling

Instead of export enhancement payments and paying farmers not to produce (something many taxpayers and legislators oppose), the US next sought to reduce production by decoupling payments from output. As noted earlier, the idea behind decoupling is to remove the link between agricultural support payments and production. With subsidies completely decoupled, output with and without subsidies should be equal. But production is indirectly impacted because a flat-rate payment based on a historic reference output results in an *insurance effect*, as it provides an effective lower bound on a producer's income, and a *wealth effect*, because it increases a farmer's wealth and thus reduces risk aversion that leads to greater production. Decoupled payments do not affect price variability and thus are not expected to have an insurance effect. Wealth effects are likely small and producer specific, because they only occur when a farmer becomes less risk averse as the expected payoff increases.

A first step towards decoupling was taken in 1996 with a farm bill that reflected the new WTO Agreement on Agriculture (see Chapter 5.3). Acreage set-aside authority was eliminated, but the CRP and other conservation-based programs continued. Instead of deficiency payments based on target prices, farmers received fixed annual payments based on past production, but not dependent on annual price levels. Since the deficiency payment disappeared, farmers were compensated for their loss. The 1996 Farm Bill allowed for a seven-year transition period. Farmers were paid declining annual market transition payments based on historic plantings and yields. Importantly, payments were not tied to the market prices that prevailed during those years, or to the producer's planting decisions (i.e., the crops she now planted). With payments no longer tied to prices, planting flexibility was extended to all base acres, although fresh fruits and vegetables could not be grown while retaining payment eligibility because such crops had not previously benefited from price or income interventions. The 1996 US reforms were opportunistic from the farmers' perspective, because the move to fixed payments allowed farmers to capture support that otherwise would have disappeared when market prices temporarily rose above the target price. While the United States had a more market-oriented, non-distortionary agricultural policy that met WTO mandates, the policy reforms had simply shifted payments from one exempted category to another. The deficiency payment fell into the blue box until set-aside authority was ended; once this occurred, the fixed payment that replaced the deficiency payment fell into the green box.

Because agricultural commodity prices were relatively high during the mid- to late 1990s, it was easy for legislators to introduce policies to decouple production from support payments. When farm prices dropped again in the late 1990s, farm incomes fell and loan deficiency payments soared. Fixed payments were expanded and reauthorized. Not unexpectedly, a counter-cyclical payment (CCP) program was brought in to address lower agricultural prices in the 2002 Farm Bill. In theory a CCP is truly decoupled, as illustrated in Figure 7.7.

Figure 7.7 Counter-cyclical payment program

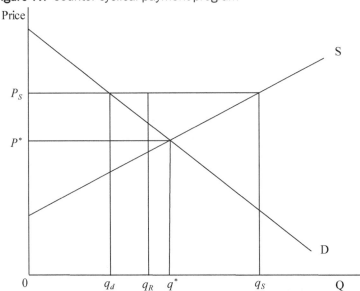

In Figure 7.7, P_S is the support (or target) price at which farmers will produce q_S while only q_d will be demanded, leading to excess production of q_S–q_d and, thereby, the disposal problems discussed earlier. To avoid this, we let the market clear at the free market price and quantity, P^* and q^*, respectively. A reference quantity, denoted q_R, is established (it could equal q^*) and the producer receives a deficiency (counter-cyclical) payment given by $(P_S–P^*)\times q_R$, regardless of how much is actually produced. The market clearing equilibrium price (P^*) will of course vary with changes in supply and demand, as will the counter-cyclical payment. If the price is high, the CCP will be low; if price is low, the CCP will be high. The payment is counter-cyclical and has no influence on how much is produced, and thus the CCP is classified as green box.

In practice, the CCP of the 2002 Farm Bill employed a modified variant of the deficiency payment program found in earlier legislation, thereby restoring target prices and price-dependent deficiency payments on fixed-base acreage and yields, with some options for base acreage and yield updating.[1] But the deficiency payment was based on only 85% of base acres at historical yields and the dates used to determine the history of yields were fixed (see also Chapter 9.2). Further, unlike the earlier programs, the farmer did not need to plant the crop for which payment was received as payments were based on historical yields as opposed to actual plantings. In this way, the deficiency payments across years no longer depended on input use so they remained decoupled.

7.2.4 Moving Forward

The 2008 Farm Bill was similar to the 2002 Farm Bill except that it established a lower limit on the total program payouts that an individual or a farm could receive, although this simply incentivized division of farms among family members. The 2008 bill also extended program payments to include some specialty crops, particularly peas and lentils, and spelled out changes in target prices and loan rates. Finally, it introduced a new disaster relief program and an important innovation: an optional revenue guarantee program known as the Average Crop Revenue Election (ACRE) program, which constituted a form of whole farm revenue insurance.

ACRE was meant to protect farmers against shallow (small) losses in income as opposed to deep losses, which were hedged using more traditional crop insurance. Indeed, modern crop insurance began in the US with the Federal Crop Insurance Act of 1980. Crop insurance evolved over time from crop yield protection into crop revenue protection, while subsidy rates on premiums rose so that crop insurance and shallow protection programs, such as ACRE, became the principal means of stabilizing farm incomes and subsiding producers (see Chapter 9.2). By the time of the 2008 Farm Bill, yield or revenue decline had to be demonstrated before farmers were eligible for a subsidy.

Stronger market conditions after 2007 reduced deficiency payments and made crop revenue insurance the main pillar of US farm support, because higher crop prices resulted in higher nominal levels of insurance premium subsidies and indemnities. The direct payments program introduced in 1996 proved politically unpopular when farm prices and incomes were high; it was similar to the EU's single farm payment (SFP; see Chapter 8.1), but was seen as a form of welfare for farmers. In the 2014 Farm Bill, the relatively non-distorting direct payments program, once envisioned to herald an end to farm support, was ended instead; it had become unsustainable.

---

[1] The CCP provided payments if the effective commodity price was below the target price based on historical prices and yields. The effective price was the greater of the loan rate and season average price. There was a payout under CCP if the effective price was less than the target price minus the direct payment rate.

The 2014 legislation reauthorized the federal crop insurance program and the loan rate program for major row crops. It also introduced two new programs for which all farmers who had been eligible for the direct payments program could qualify, except cotton producers. One choice was a deficiency payments program, now referred to as Price Loss Coverage (PLC); but target prices (now termed *reference prices*) were set at higher nominal levels than previously. A second choice was a new revenue program known as Agriculture Risk Coverage (ARC). Enrollment in ARC was over 90% for corn and soybeans, largely because the reference revenue was a moving average that reflected the high prices during 2007–2013. Wheat enrollment in ARC was about half, while producers of several other crops, particularly rice and peanuts, chose PLC. Since payments under ARC and PLC are determined by current-year market prices and yields, these programs fall in the amber box category of WTO subsidies. These programs are discussed in more detail in Chapter 9.2.

For cotton, an earlier WTO ruling against US support programs in a case brought by Brazil resulted in the replacement of the traditional support program by heavily subsidized insurance (see Chapter 5.3). Cotton farmers could receive support payments if they grew other crops on their old cotton base acres. Subsequent to the 2014 Farm Bill, cotton growers lobbied for new support, mainly to categorize cotton as an oilseed crop. In April 2018, seed cotton was classified as an oilseed thereby making cotton growers eligible for the ARC/PLC programs, although this was in violation of the US–Brazil agreement.

Both ARC and PLC made substantial payments as prices (and revenue) fell after the 2014 Farm Bill was enacted. Nonetheless, only 15% of the US Department of Agriculture's (USDA) budget of $151.5 billion for the 2018 fiscal year, or $22.7 billion, was meant to support agricultural initiatives. This amount was then spent on programs as indicated in Figure 7.8. Payments for conservation programs and R&D, amounting to $7.1 billion, fell in the WTO's green box, but the remaining $15.6 billion fell in the amber box category and was thus charged against the US's *de minimis* amount, which is currently capped at $19.1 billion. However, crop insurance or ARC/PLC payments made to cotton or corn growers that are viewed as distortionary (and in the amber box category) might be targeted by other countries even though they would fall within the *de minimis* aggregate measure of support. Such a dispute could be brought forward under the Agreement on Subsidies and Countervailing Measures, which deals with sector-specific subsidies and countervailing actions (see Chapter 5.3). It is helpful to recall, however, that the bulk of the USDA budget is designated for administration, rural development, data collection, nutrition programs (e.g., food stamps), and other programs not supporting farm payments or agricultural R&D. Compared to the entire USDA budget, agricultural support payments remain a small component.

Due to extensive lobbying by the sugar industry, the US sugar program has become perhaps the sector that relies most on price supports and loan rates rather than risk management. Not surprisingly, the sugar program includes a TRQ to prevent imports (see Chapter 5.4 on TRQs). The loan rate on sugar was set at 18.75¢ per pound (lb) for 2011 and 2012, but by mid-2010 the sugar price was 22¢ per lb due to drought in India and changes to EU sugar policy.[2]

---

[2] The US sugar sector received the highest rate of subsidy of any agricultural sector (Table 7.2).

Figure 7.8 Spending on agricultural subsidy and R&D, 2018, total $22.7 billion

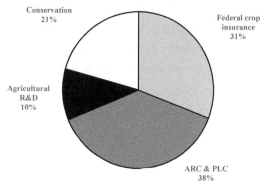

Source: data from Smith (2018)

With ethanol requirements, US and world prices were expected to remain high, but world prices subsequently fell as production in India rebounded and EU output expanded due to the reform of its sugar policies (see Chapter 8.1). Thus, in the 2014 Farm Bill, an in-quota tariff of 0.625¢/lb was mandated, while the over-quota tariff was 15.36¢/lb of raw sugar and 16.21¢/lb of refined sugar. As the world price for raw sugar in 2014 was some 16–18¢/lb, the tariff effectively prevented any imports above the 1.1 million tonnes of raw cane sugar the US was required by the WTO to import from developing countries. Consequently, the domestic US price was slightly more than double the world price over the period 1999–2015. Since sugar is the most important input in the confectionary sector, companies moved their operations to countries such as Mexico and Canada where sugar prices were much lower. At the same time, high sugar prices encouraged the substitution of high-fructose corn syrup for sugar on a grand scale, which appears to be linked to rising rates of obesity and greater insulin resistance to sugar. Until domestic US production of sugar cane and beet is reformed, the US will continue to see jobs exported to other countries to take advantage of lower global sugar prices, and negative health outcomes.

Many subsidy, conservation, trade, rural development, and other programs authorized under the 2014 Farm Bill were scheduled to sunset after September 30, 2018. As a result, Congress passed the Agricultural Improvement Act of 2018, which was signed by the president on December 30, 2018. It is clear that the ARC and PLC programs will remain in place, although farmers will be given greater leeway to shift a crop from the ARC to the PLC program. Based on projections by the Congressional Budget Office, total payments under these programs will fall from $7.88 billion in 2018 to $5.33 billion in 2019, $4.79 billion in 2020, $6.19 billion in 2021, and $5.42 billion in 2022. A major change will enable farmers to update their reference yields to the most recent five-year period, which will cause producers to increase current production and thereby ensure that these programs fall in the amber box category.

We conclude this section with an examination of the trends in commodity support estimates for the period 1986–2019. Trends in commodity-level support are shown in Figure 7.9 for an average of four grains (wheat, barley, corn, and sorghum), rice, milk, and cotton. Data for these commodity groups indicate that support levels have generally declined in response to international trade negotiations under the WTO's

Agreement on Agriculture. The variability in support from one year to the next reflects the policies enacted in the farm bills as discussed earlier in this section. Trends for individual grains show much greater variability than the trend for the four grains combined because prices play a large role in the measure used and because the support mechanisms may have changed from one farm bill to another; although not shown, oilseeds exhibit a similar trend (see Table 7.2). Dairy support payments have declined most dramatically, followed by cotton (although support for milk has risen since 2013). Meat products are not included in Figure 7.9 because there is little support for beef, poultry, and pig producers (see Table 7.2).

Figure 7.9 US commodity support payments as percentage of gross receipts for the commodity, rice, other grains, milk, and cotton, 1986–2019

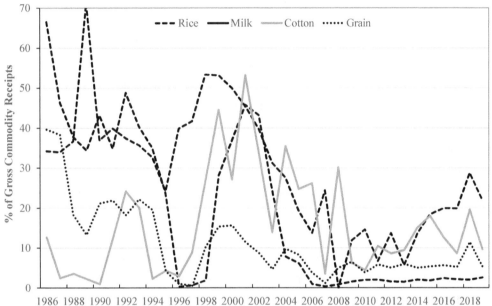

Source: OECD (2020)

In summary, the focus of agricultural support has shifted away from direct payments and price supports to crop revenue insurance and the ARC/PLC programs. That is, US agricultural programs have shifted toward business risk management, a topic discussed more broadly in Chapter 9.2, along with a more detailed discussion of US agricultural business risk management programs.

7.3 Canadian Agricultural Policy

Canada's agricultural policies differ greatly from those in the United States, partly because Canada does not have the fiscal and political wherewithal to keep pace with support levels in the US and the EU. Another important reason is Canada's unique political institutions. Under the constitution, agriculture is a "shared jurisdiction," meaning responsibility is shared between the provinces and the federal government. This implies that agricultural support payments, if not actual policies themselves, will differ among provinces—a farmer in one province might receive more support than an identical farmer in another province. The reason is that agricultural programs in Canada are paid for in one of several ways:

- The most common mechanism is for provincial and federal governments plus the producers to share the costs of a program. The term "tripartite" is used to denote such an arrangement, although costs tend not to be shared equally among the three parties.
- Program costs are shared by the provincial and federal governments; although costs tend to be shared equally, this is not always the case.
- More rarely, costs are shared between one level of government and the producers.
- In some cases, such as feed freight assistance and protection against catastrophes, costs are borne by one level of government only.

The first agricultural stabilization legislation in Canada was the 1958 Agricultural Stabilization Act. This agricultural program was fully funded by the federal government, guaranteed farmers 90% of a three-year moving average price for all commodities (later changed to a five-year moving average), and covered grain and livestock commodities in all provinces. Payouts under this legislation remained low until 1975 when they rose rapidly; the largest payout of $450 million occurred in 1988, but this amount could have been much greater except that the Western Grain Stabilization Act of 1976 had removed grains produced on the prairies (northern Great Plains) from the Agricultural Stabilization Act. Further, dairy, eggs, and poultry had also been removed in the early 1970s due to supply management in these sectors.

Other institutions that played a role in Canada's approach to agricultural stabilization were crop insurance, which began in 1959, state trading and pooling of revenues in the form of the Canadian Wheat Board, and transportation programs, especially the Crow's Nest Pass statutory freight rate on grains. While these programs have now been eliminated or changed beyond recognition, they did inform subsequent programs and, therefore, are briefly discussed below. Today Canada relies primarily on business risk management programs rather than agricultural support programs. The background to this aspect of Canada's farm programs is discussed below, followed by greater detail in Chapter 9.3.

7.3.1 State Trading: The Canadian Wheat Board (1935–2012)

An act of Parliament in July 1935 created the Canadian Wheat Board (CWB) as a single-desk seller of Western Canadian grains. As a result, the CWB was also a monopsony buyer because farmers were required to sell wheat and barley, the two crops under the board's control, to the CWB. At the time of planting, the CWB would announce an initial per acre (= 0.404686 ha) quota for eligible acres, which were based on the area of cultivated land on a farm. The eligibility condition had a perverse impact on the environment as it provided an incentive for farmers to eliminate wetlands and convert permanent grasslands or forest into cropland, thereby increasing the area eligible for quota.

Suppose the farmer had 100 acres of eligible land, that the starting quota was 20 bushels per acre (bu/ac), and the announced price was $2.20/bu. While the price received by the farmer would not go below this, the final price would depend on the CWB's success at marketing the grain. The farmer would eventually receive a pooled price that depended on final sales minus delivery and marketing costs. Leaving aside the question of final price for now, suppose the farmer knew from past experience that the final quota would be 25% higher, or 25 bu/ac, but that the expected yield was 40 bu/ac. Thus, the farmer would expect to deliver 2500 bu at the end of the season, but she could grow this amount on 62.5 ac, leaving 37.5 ac fallow or planted to another crop, such as oats, peas, or lentils. In some cases, farmers would leave land fallow to conserve moisture that would aid crop growth in the following year (although it led to soil erosion). Meanwhile, agricultural producers in the US Palouse region of western Idaho and eastern Washington were keen on knowing something about CWB decisions. The Palouse is a major pea- and lentil-producing region so prices there would depend on how much land Canada's farmers might potentially plant to these crops.

Another problem with the CWB system was related to its marketing approach, specifically grading of grains. The prices received for wheat and barley in international markets depends on the quality or grade of wheat/barley, with the grade of a grain determined from its protein and moisture content. Grades range from feed grain to grains with high protein content, and contracts specify protein and moisture content. While US grain traders such as Cargill would blend various grades of wheat, say, to achieve the precise percentage of protein called for in a contract, no more and no less, the CWB had a reputation for selling higher quality grain for the lower standard price. That is, as a marketing strategy to maintain or perhaps increase market share, the CWB often sold wheat with a higher protein content than called for in a contract.

With the new millennium, some farmers wished to sell wheat and barley outside the CWB system despite some of the obvious benefits of pooling and marketing provided by the board. A variety of questions were raised: Could the CWB really obtain higher prices in export markets? Did it have monopoly power? Did it operate to the benefit of Canadian farmers? Were farm gate prices higher? Was the CWB operating as a monopsony buyer, with prices at the farm gate actually lower than otherwise? Did the CWB sell higher grades of wheat at lower grade prices? Were grade distinctions too coarse and was insufficient effort made to blend various grades of wheat to meet contract obligations? In the end, given their experience marketing non-CWB grains, many farmers felt it was time to end the CWB monopsony over Western grains. The federal government ended the CWB system with the Marketing Freedom for Grain Farmers Act (2011), and the Wheat Board ceased to be the sole marketer of Western wheat and barley in 2012. It was subsequently privatized in April 2015, when a joint venture between a Bermuda company headquartered in the US and a Saudi agricultural firm, known as the Global Grain Group, purchased a 50.1% stake and changed the name of the CWB to G3 Canada Limited.

7.3.2 Crop Insurance

Crop insurance was introduced in Canada via the Crop Insurance Act of 1959. It allowed provinces to establish provincial crop insurance schemes with financial support from the federal government; crop insurance was a joint federal–provincial program. Crop insurance was based on individual farm yields and covered grains, pulses, oilseeds, and forages. Because crop insurance only protects against yield loss and payments depend on output prices, this type of program cannot support farm incomes when prices are depressed. The United States and many other countries also have some form of crop insurance. Since crop insurance is part of the agricultural business risk management suite of programs, it is discussed in Chapter 9.

7.3.3 Western Grain Stabilization Act (1976)

The Western Grain Stabilization Program (WGSP) was created in 1976 to help prairie farmers stabilize income, because CWB quotas on wheat and barley were considered too constraining to do this. The WGSP was established as a result of a 1969 Federal Task Force on Agriculture that recommended replacing the ad hoc programs that had by then come into existence in Western Canada with a single income stabilization program. The ad hoc programs included acreage payments, domestic price targets, and a Temporary Wheat Reserve (1955–1970), which was a major program compensating farmers for on-farm storage of grain resulting from overproduction due to price supports.

The WGSP focused only on farmers' incomes. It was fully funded by equal contributions from producer participants and the federal government, and was viewed as complementary to existing prairie crop yield insurance programs. The idea was that WGSP would stabilize the net cash flow for specific grains while crop insurance would smooth yields. Together these two programs were expected to stabilize the incomes of agricultural producers. Two problems arose: First, increasing yields offset lower prices, with the result that payouts were also reduced. Second, the calendar year was used rather than the crop year, which meant that farmers might not receive payouts when they most needed them. Amendments in June 1984 dealt with both these issues. One problem remained, however: the WGSP incentivized an increase in grain production—an outward shift in Western Canada's grain supply function.

WGSP payouts were not large until the agricultural trade wars between the US and EU began in 1985. The WGSP payout in 1987 amounted to $800 million (recall that the largest payout under the Agricultural Stabilization Act occurred in 1988). As a result, the program faced a huge deficit in the late 1980s so that the WGSP was no longer actuarially sound; yet, the program provided little support to farmers. Consequently, as a result of the trade wars and subsequent low prices in 1986, an extra $1 billion was paid to grain producers beginning in 1987 under the ad hoc Special Canadian Grains Program created in 1986 as a result of lobbying by the then premier of Saskatchewan, Grant Devine. After several years, Canada was forced to abandon these high levels of income support as it constituted too large a drain on the treasury, while program benefits simply ended up being capitalized in land values.

The WGSP was rolled into the Farm Income Protection Act (FIPA) of 1991, which eventually led to a suite of business risk management programs in the new millennium under the rubric of Growing Forward (GF). That is, Canadian agricultural programs were directed towards business risk management rather than income support per se, although by subsidizing premiums, farmers' incomes were indirectly supported. Again, agricultural business risk management programs are discussed further in Chapter 9.

7.3.4 Transportation Programs and Subsidies

Canada's population is concentrated along the coasts and US border, its rural population is sparsely distributed, and agricultural commodities must be transported over long distances to reach export position. In some cases, the lowest cost of transporting grains is through US ports. It is little wonder that transportation policies are important to the agricultural sector. Two programs have had a particular impact on the location of processing facilities, especially livestock production: Feed Freight Assistance and the Crow's Nest Pass Freight Rate, known as the "Crow Rate."

The Feed Freight Assistance Program

This program began in 1941 and was eventually terminated in 1995. It was fully funded by the federal government and provided a subsidy for feed grains shipped from the prairies to livestock producers in British Columbia and Central and Eastern Canada. The program distorted the location of livestock producing and processing sectors by increasing the price of feed grains at the farm gate while reducing them near the population centers—thus, for example, hog production located in British Columbia's Fraser Valley near Vancouver rather than in rural Alberta or Saskatchewan. Disposal of hog manure became an environmental problem in BC's lower mainland, which would not have been the case in Alberta where spreading of hog manure might have provided a positive benefit to farmland in the way of added organic matter. Despite the fact that the program has now been terminated, livestock processing facilities remain in the locations incentivized by the original feed freight subsidies.

The Crow Rate

In the late 1800s, prairie farmers were unhappy with the monopoly power exercised by the railroads. At the same time, the federal government sought to build a transcontinental railway to facilitate British Columbia's joining the Canadian Confederation. The Crow's Nest Pass Agreement of 1897 constituted a compromise that provided lower freight rates in exchange for a $3.4 million subsidy to the Canadian Pacific Railway for building a rail link from Lethbridge, Alberta, to Nelson, BC, to prevent movement of minerals from southeastern BC through the US. Further, the freight rate on grain sold through Lake Superior ports was also lowered by 20%. Then, the Railway Act (1925) made the freight rate statutory ("statutory rate") in perpetuity and extended the Crow Rate to the new Canadian National Railway. In 1927, legislation extended the statutory Crow Rate to cover exports of grain and flour through the ports of Vancouver and Prince Rupert in British Columbia, and through Churchill, Manitoba. Over time, the statutory rate was extended to other commodities, including oilseeds, dehydrated alfalfa, and pulses.

The Crow Rate remained unchanged from 1897 to the early 1980s. Inflation during the 1970s caused the costs of transporting grain to increase significantly. As a result, the railways no longer invested in transportation infrastructure because returns from moving grain were too low. Estimates suggested that more than $1 billion in grain export sales were lost or deferred as a result of inadequate transportation capacity. In response, the federal government provided large operating subsidies to the railways and supplied them with new hopper cars to encourage increased movement of grain. As well, the Western provinces and farmers (through the CWB and provincial grain marketing pools) purchased new hopper cars and gave them to the railways. Yet these measures were only a stopgap.

Attempts to change the Crow Rate system were opposed by prairie grain producers, as well as by livestock producers outside the prairie provinces. The reason was simple: Like feed freight assistance, the Crow Rate subsidy increased the farm gate price, while inhibiting the growth of livestock production on the prairies and shifting it to central Canada and southwestern BC. Livestock producers argued that their investments, made as a result of the distortionary freight rates, were now locked in.

Nonetheless, "forever" ended with the 1983 Western Grain Transportation Act. It institutionalized a subsidy—the Crow Benefit—that was paid annually to the railways to ensure they would make capital improvements and not allow the grain component of the railway system to deteriorate. Freight rates were allowed to increase, but not by more than 10% of the world grain price. Meanwhile, Alberta introduced a Crow offset program in 1985 to help livestock producers, which Manitoba and Saskatchewan were forced to follow in 1989.

The Crow Benefit was initially calculated at $658 million (Canadian dollars). For 1989–1990, the Crow Benefit was set at $720 million, with farmers covering the remaining 30% of the total freight costs. Arbitrary reductions were made to the Crow Benefit during the 1990s because of the federal government's fiscal problems. The payment finally fell to $565 million with farmers covering half of the transportation costs. Then in 1995 the Crow freight rate subsidy was eliminated, with a one-time payment of $1.6 billion to farmers as compensation for lost land values, and $300 million to offset some adjustment costs, although some agricultural economists had argued that the payment should have been $8.5 billion. The legacy of the Crow Rate was that it had been the longest running agricultural subsidy program in the world.

7.3.5 Supply Management

A major feature of Canada's agricultural programs is supply management (SM). Supply management in Canada's dairy sector began with the establishment of the Canadian Dairy Commission in 1966. This was followed in 1970 by a National Milk Marketing Plan to control supply, with Quebec and Ontario along with the federal government as the original participants. The enabling legislation for SM in agriculture was not passed until two years later when the Farm Products Agency Act (1972) became the enabling legislation; in addition to SM in dairy, it also led to the establishment of SM boards in eggs (1973), turkey (1974), chicken (1978), and chicken hatching eggs (1986)—the so-called feather industries. Although SM remains the identifying characteristic of these sectors, the focus here is on dairy because it receives the largest support of any agricultural commodity in Canada, as evident from Table 7.2 and Figure 7.10.

Figure 7.10 Canadian commodity support payments as percentage of gross receipts for milk, poultry, eggs, and grains, 1986–2019

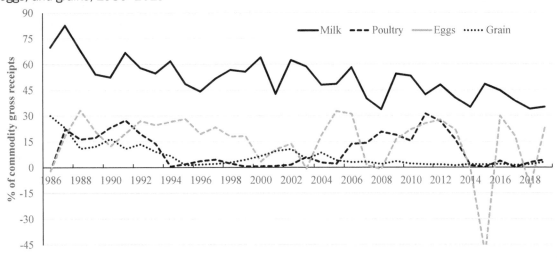

Source: OECD (2020)

Commodity support levels are provided in Figure 7.10 for three supply-managed sectors and for an average of the support payments for six grains (wheat, barley, oats, corn, soybeans, and canola). Dairy support payments accounted for slightly more than 80% of gross commodity receipts in 1987, but declined in fits and starts to some 35% by 2019. Support for the poultry sector reached a high of about 33% in 2011 but has generally been quite a bit lower (also see Table 7.2). Although average support in the supply-managed eggs sector exceeded that of poultry, there were years when support was negative, particularly in 2015 when the price farmers received for eggs greatly exceeded costs, although subsidization in following years more than made up for the losses. As discussed earlier in this section, grains benefited greatly from government payments in the latter part of the 1980s (exceeding 30% in 1986) but declined rapidly thereafter, with support not exceeding 5% after 2005. In this section we focus on SM in dairy because it receives the greatest level of support of any agricultural sector.

By 1974, all provinces except Newfoundland had signed onto supply management in the dairy sector. Subsequently, Australia and the European Union also adopted SM in dairy, but they later abandoned this regulatory regime. The theory underlying SM was previously discussed in Chapter 6.3, and a stylized description of how the EU dismantled its quota regime and compensated producers is provided in Chapter 8.1. Canada maintains a stronghold on its supply-managed agricultural sectors, despite the opposition of many agricultural economists. In 2005, the House of Commons unanimously passed a motion asking the government not to give up any protection for the supply-managed sectors in international trade negotiations; this was re-affirmed in the government's 2011 Speech from the Throne and by all parties in the House of Commons in 2018 as a result of discussions pertaining to renegotiation of the NAFTA trade agreement between Canada, Mexico, and the US (see Chapter 5.3).

As feared, SM has trade implications. First, the US, Australia, and New Zealand have targeted Canada's SM sectors at the WTO. Second, agricultural policy distortions account for nearly 65% of all policy-induced trade distortions, and some 80%–90% of these are tariffs and TRQs. Since Canada had earlier been required to identify TRQs for its SM sectors, ongoing WTO negotiations inevitably seek to eliminate TRQs by increasing quota levels and reducing tariffs on imports above the quota. Third, the Comprehensive and Economic Trade Agreement negotiations and the NAFTA renegotiation had also targeted SM, especially in dairy. Clearly, trading partners will chip away at Canada's supply management programs until it opens them up to greater competition, especially the dairy sector as it is the most subsidized Canadian agricultural sector.

This has already been happening. Under the Comprehensive and Economic Trade Agreement (CETA), the industry gave up 2% of its domestic market, followed by another 3.25% under the Trans-Pacific Partnership excluding the US (see Chapter 5.3). During the renegotiation of NAFTA, Canadian dairy producers lobbied the prime minister and other leaders, with all parties in Parliament again resolving to protect SM. Nonetheless, when the USMCA was signed on September 30, 2018 (although not ratified by the US until July 2020), Canada had agreed to provide the US tariff-free access to 3.59% of its dairy market. More importantly, tariffs on milk protein isolates (MPI), skim milk powder (SMP), and infant formula— previously categorized as Canadian milk classes 6 and 7—were to be eliminated, which satisfied a major US demand that Canada remove its implicit subsidization (via the SM regime) of these categories and the accompanying impediments to imports of milk protein isolates. As the SMP price falls toward the world price, the farm-gate price of milk should decline; farmers receive a blend of the SMP (protein) and butter fat prices, with the final price they receive dependent on the fat versus protein content of the milk they deliver.

As a result of supply management, Canada may have passed up the opportunity to export dairy products at a time when the demand from developing countries for safe dairy products from western countries expanded rapidly. The European Union, particularly the Netherlands and Ireland, remains the biggest player in the global market for dairy products. Not surprisingly, the US is also a large exporter of dairy products, but it ranks below New Zealand, while Australia is also a major exporter. Canada has very little presence in export markets because such exports would lead to charges of dumping. The federal government also abrogated power over trade in dairy products to the provinces, which led to reduced incentives to export milk products. In essence, Canada may be passing up opportunities to profit from rising international demand for dairy and poultry products as per capita incomes in developing countries continue to rise.

Canada's dairy sector might fare quite well should farmers be permitted to participate in global dairy product markets. Cow productivity in Canada is about the same as in the US and much higher than elsewhere. Dairy herds remain small compared to those in other countries, because it is difficult for milk producers to increase herds as milk quota is expensive and difficult to access. Thus, economies of scale may constitute the main obstacle to the creation of a vibrant, multi-billion-dollar export sector. The main reason why SM persists, especially in the dairy sector, relates to the sector's lobbying power and acquiescence by politicians.

The main difference between the EU's dairy quota regime and that of Canada concerns exports. The EU was a net exporter of dairy products before, during, and after SM, while Canada is considered an importer. The EU introduced SM to reduce and control the costs of export subsidies, and then reformed and eventually eliminated SM in dairy because export subsidies were no longer permitted under WTO rules. To examine potential reform of Canada's dairy sector, a stylized model is developed that is similar to models presented in Chapter 6.3 and, more specifically, to a model describing how the EU dismantled its dairy quota system (Chapter 8.1), except modified for the case of imports as opposed to exports. The Canadian model is presented in Figure 7.11.

Figure 7.11 Reforming Canada's dairy supply-management sector

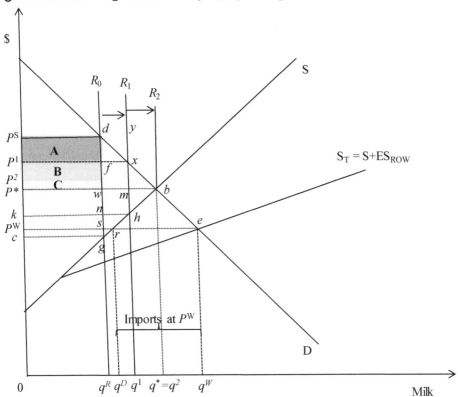

In Figure 7.11, S and D represent the domestic supply and demand functions, respectively. With trade, total supply is S_T, which consists of the horizontal sum of domestic supply S and the excess supply from the rest of the world (ES_{ROW}). Under autarky, price and quantity are given by (P^*, q^*), but under free trade Canadians would consume q^W at price P^W. The dairy marketing board imposed a supply restriction (quota) at R_0 (=q^{R0}) at the support price P^S; to maintain this price, however, imports need to be restricted. To keep the analysis simple, assume that the tariff (some 270%) is sufficient to block all imports. The (annual) quota rent is given by the area ($P^S dgc$), where c is the marginal cost of production. The total value of the quota asset then equals the capitalized value of the quota rent (as discussed in Chapter 6.3).

Suppose the authority wishes to reform or eliminate the quota regime while providing dairy producers with compensation. A stylized description of how this might proceed begins by increasing the quota beyond that needed to maintain price at P^S. Suppose the quota is initially increased from R_0 to R_1, which causes the domestic price to fall to P^1. Denoting the original quota amount as the reference quantity (q^R), the authority compensates producers for the price reduction up to the reference quantity. That is, producers receive (P^S-P^1) × q^R as compensation, which is equivalent to the dark-shaded area denoted **A**. Not only do producers receive **A** as compensation, they also gain area (ghn) as quasi-rent plus the rectangle ($fnhx$) as quota rent since the price still exceeds marginal cost over the increase in production q^1-q^R. Clearly, then, dairy producers are overcompensated for their loss in quota value. Overcompensation can be addressed by compensating only a proportion of the difference (P^S-P^1).

In the second step, the dairy quota is increased to q^2 ($=R_2$), which also happens (for convenience) to equal q^* as drawn here. This time the dairy producers are not compensated the full amount of the price decline from P^1 to P^*, but rather only for part of the difference, namely (P^1-P^2). The total compensation for this increase in quota would amount to only the medium-shaded area denoted **B**, but farmers would also gain (hmb) as quasi-rent, but lose the quota rent ($fwmx$) that constituted part of what they gained in the first step when the price first fell to P^1. Whether they are over or under compensated will depend on whether the shaded area **A** + **B** is larger (overcompensation) or smaller (under compensation) than area (wgb), which is the quasi-rent gained when supply management has been eliminated and there is no international trade.

A reform program would consist of more than two steps, of course, while freeing of international trade would lead to further changes in order to reduce the price to the world level P^W. Each step consists of some compensation at the discretion of the policy maker, although a correct accounting would consider the gains in quasi-rent. Given that it might be difficult to calculate the gain in producer surplus at each stage, it is the policy maker who must determine how much of the drop in price to compensate at each step—the price premium to be provided (using an EU term), if any. However, when a completely free market equilibrium is reached and given that the underlying fundamentals of the market structure in Figure 7.11 remain unchanged (a crucial caveat unlikely to hold if Canadian dairy products are exported), domestic producers will only increase output from q^R to q^D rather than q^*, with an amount $q^W - q^D$ imported from other countries. Producers gain (gsr) but lose (P^SP^Wsd).

Notice the caveat in the above paragraph: The fundamentals of the market structure in Figure 7.11 are unchanged. This is highly unlikely to be the case. Rather, the supply curve is more likely to shift downwards as some dairy producers increase their cow herds to achieve economies of scale, while others will leave the industry (which is why some level of compensation is required from a political perspective). Given that Canada's cows are just as productive, or more so, than those in extant exporting nations, but its cow herds are much smaller, economies of scale might be attainable by expanding dairy herds. Unless this occurs, Canada will be unable to compete internationally and will require continued tariff protection. Milk prices will remain higher than those in other countries with the least well-off citizens bearing the burden of supply management.

Economists have estimated what it might cost to compensate Canada's dairy producers for dismantling the quota system. To use the approach depicted in Figure 7.11 requires knowledge of elasticities of supply and demand and assumptions regarding the functional forms of supply and demand. Recall from Chapter 6.3 that the quota rent consists of a producer component and a consumer component; therefore, upon dismantling SM, milk producers lose the consumer component (a gain to consumers), but the producer component is retained as quasi-rent and there is an increase in quasi-rent as dairy farmers increase output. Assuming linear supply and demand functions and Monte Carlo simulation using various values of supply and demand elasticities, one can calculate the quota rent retained as producer surplus, the consumer rent component of quota rent that is lost, and the producer surplus gained as production increases. Some calculations of the losses and gains to producers are provided in Table 7.4. In this analysis the consumer component of the quota rent turned out to be a great deal smaller than the producer component.

Table 7.4 Annual quota rent and losses, gains and net loss with elimination of quota regime, Monte Carlo simulation of supply and demand elasticities (CAD$ mil)

Year	Retained quota rent as quasi-rent	Consumer component of quota rent lost	Gain in producer surplus	Net loss
2010	2,414.70	372.47	18.48	353.99
2011	2,325.32	345.09	17.53	327.56
2012	2,579.50	396.13	19.61	376.52
2013	2,044.31	251.79	13.52	238.27
2014	2,045.57	253.52	13.66	239.86
2015	2,100.18	262.18	14.17	248.01
2016	933.67	59.71	3.72	55.99
Average	**2,063.32**	**277.27**	**14.39**	**262.89**

Source: van Kooten (2017a, 2020)

Because the estimates in Table 7.4 are annual, it is necessary to discount the stream of future losses to the present to determine the overall level of compensation required. It is likely that buyers of quota recover their costs within a decade or less; this would suggest a discount rate of perhaps 50%, as $1 received 10 years from now would be worth no more than 2¢ today. Further, small businesses tend to require a rate of return of 20% or so in order to survive. Assuming the latter rate of discount, total compensation for the dairy sector would amount to about $1.3 billion (=$262.9 million ÷ 0.2).

Under various trade deals, Canada could lose up to 18% of its domestic milk production by 2024. While the federal government had committed to compensation of $1.75 billion for giving up the domestic market under earlier trade deals, the sector expects additional compensation for losses under USMCA. This level of compensation is greater than the foregoing estimates of what might constitute an appropriate level of compensation. Yet, despite having opened up its dairy markets, Canada remains committed to supply management. However, since much of the market loss relates to milk protein products, SM might need to focus more on the control and pricing of the butter fat component of milk (as quotas are measured in terms of the fat component).

7.4 Concluding Discussion

The United States and, to a lesser extent, Canada have spent billions of dollars supporting the incomes of farmers. Large subsidies have been provided to farmers to protect them from the inherent risks associated with price volatility and the uncertainties associated with drought, hail, and other adverse weather outcomes, potential damage from pests and disease, and even dangers from wildfire. Under the guise of government's helping hand, farmers have not only been able to protect their operations from these risks but, through lobbying, managed to benefit from income transfers from taxpayers and consumers.

The University of California, Berkeley, agricultural economist Gordon Rausser distinguishes between two types of agricultural policies. Policies that reduce transaction costs by correcting market failure, providing public goods, or otherwise improving efficiency he refers to as political-economic resource transactions (PERTs) because of their neutral distributional impacts. In contrast, political economic-seeking transfer policies (PESTs) primarily redistribute wealth while lowering efficiency. One could argue that many early policy innovations, such as the development of agricultural colleges, publicly funded and managed agricultural experiment stations, public extension agencies, and farm credit corporations backed by government were of a PERT nature, because they led to improvements in agriculture that expanded the production possibility frontier.

While other PERTs focused on soil conservation, loss of wetlands, and other environmental externalities, many of the agricultural policies discussed in this chapter and the next might best be classified as PESTs. The ability to distinguish between PEST and PERT policies assumes, however, that economists are able to determine the deadweight loss triangles associated with various agricultural policies; indeed, it is often not possible to determine whether government agricultural programs are welfare enhancing or not. For example, US agricultural policies of the Great Depression were meant to address overproduction of agricultural commodities, which had caused net farm income to fall from $5.2 billion to $1.4 billion between 1929 and 1932, thereby affecting the one-quarter of the US labor force employed in agriculture. These Depression-era policies represented the beginning of farm legislation that eventually led to large annual redistributions of income to the agricultural sector, often to the benefit of well-to-do farmers—what Rausser would refer to as PESTs. Yet, one might regard the Agricultural Adjustment Act (1933) and the subsequent Agricultural Marketing Agreement Act (1937) in a much different light: They may not have increased overall US welfare as measured by economists, but they were necessary to address poverty. The costs of these policies may well have outweighed the long-run (dynamic) benefits to society as a whole, but they were necessary at the time.

The reforms examined in this chapter, and the evidence provided in Figures 7.1, 7.2, 7.9, and 7.10, indicate that governments have reduced subsidies—at least subsidies that distort markets. Farmers have increasingly received subsidies in the form of direct payments that are less distortionary and thereby also somewhat lower than earlier subsidies. By allowing markets to clear, governments no longer have to pay for (public or private) storage, nor do they have to bear the costs of export subsidies and other programs to dispose of excess production; indeed, export subsidies of any form are no longer permitted after the WTO's 2015 Nairobi Ministerial Decision on Export Competition.

Of all the programs investigated in this chapter, supply management in Canada's dairy sector continues to be one of only a very few commodities with high subsidy rates. (The sugar sector is also an example of a highly distorted and controversial agricultural sector.) According to data provided here for Canada and the US, Canadian supply-managed products are the only ones that currently receive more than 45% of gross commodity receipts in the form of subsidies.

One might well ask: Where have all the subsidies gone? In the US they have gone to support business risk management (BRM) programs, where crop insurance and other programs remain heavily subsidized. The same is true for Canada, as we will see in Chapter 9, where we also compare the importance of BRM programs relative to more direct support-type programs. Before doing so, however, we first consider agricultural policies in the EU and the two Asian giants, China and India.

Guide to Literature

Much has been written about US agricultural policies at various times, some of which might be considered interpretations of legislation. Publications relied upon in this chapter include Zulauf and Orden (2014, 2016); Schnitkey and Zulauf (2016); Schmitz et al. (2010); USDA (2012) on the 2008 Farm Bill programs; Babcock (2014); van Kooten, Orden, and Schmitz (2019); and Glauber (2013), Smith and Glauber (2012), and Smith (2017, 2018), who provides excellent reviews of the history and near future of US crop insurance. Monke et al. (2018) provide information regarding how the 2019 Farm Bill will differ from the 2014 Bill based on legislation passed by the House of Representatives and the Senate. Further discussion of US agricultural programs is found in Schmitz et al. (2002, 2010, 2021), with a detailed example of the ACRE program in Schmitz et al. (2010, pp. 137–138). Information on the US sugar program is found in Wohlgenant (2011).

A review of Canadian agricultural programs is provided by Barichello (1995) and Vercammen (2013). A review of quota regimes is provided by van Kooten (2017a). The discussion of the Crow Rate is based on Klein and Kerr (1996). Cardwell et al. (2015) demonstrate that Canadian prices of supply-managed commodities are significantly higher than comparable US prices. Carter and Mérel (2016) make a compelling case that Canada's dairy producers could compete internationally if SM was reformed. Market losses and compensation are summarized by Harding (2020).

Food for Thought

7.1. Describe how the US decoupled its agricultural support program under the 1996 Farm Bill—the Federal Agricultural Improvement Reform (FAIR) Act. Why do you think Congress was successful in getting this Farm Bill passed and why did they revert back to an approach that tied payments to output in the 2002 Farm Bill?

7.2. Between 1941 and 1995, Canada's federal government subsidized the transportation of feed grain from the prairie provinces primarily to BC's lower mainland and central Canada. This program was known as Feed Freight Assistance. What were the economic consequences of this program, including both its private and social consequences?

7.3. Provide a brief explanation of each of the following (use illustrative diagrams where needed):

(a) decoupling
(b) loan rate
(c) cross compliance
(d) PERT

(e) Crow Rate benefit
(f) deficiency payment
(g) PEST

7.4. *True, False, or Uncertain? Make sure to indicate why.* A non-recourse loan sets a floor price on the world price (if it is provided by a large country).

7.5. Compare the effects of different types of trade liberalization on Canadian supply management and the associated marketing boards.

(i) How does SM operate with an import quota? What is the difference between import quota rents and production quota rents? What happens to the sector if the import quota is increased?

(ii) A tariff-only regime would put a ceiling on the domestic price that could prevail with SM. Could SM be practiced if the landed price (i.e., world price plus tariff) is (a) above the domestic price; (b) between the domestic price and the autarky price (i.e., where the supply and demand curves cross); (c) between the autarky price and the marginal cost price; and (d) below marginal cost? Use a diagram(s) to show and explain what would happen in each of these price ranges.

(iii) Using a two-tier tariff (tariff rate quota) graph, describe which of the three components of a TRQ is most likely to affect the volume of imports for Canadian supply-managed sectors and which component would have to be liberalized to have an effect on the domestic industry.

7.6. The Canadian chicken market is currently protected with a tariff rate quota.

(a) Draw a diagram of the Canadian market for chicken (Canada is a small-country importer) where the demand function intersects the effective total supply (domestic plus excess supply of imports) function such that the quota is binding.

(b) The Canadian government is considering increasing the volume of chicken that can be imported at the in-quota tariff rate. Modify your diagram to correspond to this new policy. Label on your diagram and explain what happens to domestic price and consumption of chicken.

7.7. In the past, the US has initiated trade actions against imports of Canadian hogs on the grounds that hog production is subsidized and dumped into the US market. Following on Food for Thought question (4.8), what are the problems with trade remedy law in the context of this type of case? Who benefits and who loses? Is there an alternative measure that results in a more transparent process and would protect US hog producers without presuming guilt on the part of Canadian exporters?

7.8. Suppose that Mexico raises its tariffs on corn imported from the US from zero (free trade) to the WTO bound rate of 37%. Using a partial equilibrium graph, show how imposing a tariff will affect production, consumption, and imports of corn in Mexico. Explain your graph briefly. You can assume Mexico's tariff does not affect the world price at which the US sells corn. In your graph, what are the effects of the tariff on Mexican producer surplus, consumer surplus, government revenue, and net welfare?

7.9. Explain the key features and impacts of the US Conservation Reserve Program.

7.10. Under the Commodity Title of the 2014 US Farm Bill, the two main support programs are Price Loss Coverage (PLC) and Agricultural Risk Coverage (ARC). For one of these programs, describe how payments are determined.

7.11. What is a non-recourse loan? Using a trade diagram, explain how the US loan rate put a floor on world grain prices. Label each axis and explain all relevant information in the graph. What actions did the US government take to make sure that the farm price did not fall below the loan rate? On the graph show what these actions are. What changed in US farm policy so that the loan rate no longer acts as a floor price?

7.12. Approximately 70% of US antibiotic use occurs in livestock production. Low-level antibiotics mixed with feed contribute to rapid growth and avoidance of disease. Graph the likely firm-level supply and market equilibrium responses to an FDA ban on antibiotic use for growth promotion. Suggest how livestock producers might be compensated for the prohibition on antibiotics for growth.

8

AGRICULTURAL POLICY
IN EUROPE AND ASIA

The European Union is the largest trading bloc in the world and, along with the United States, the most important producer and exporter of agricultural commodities. At the same time, the developing world, including China, has become a major export market for agricultural products. Despite efforts to increase domestic production of agricultural products and its increasing role in export markets, China still imports large amounts of grain to feed animals, for example, as well as dairy products from developed countries because they are considered safer and of better quality than the domestic equivalent. Developing countries with large populations also import significant quantities of grain; for example, Egypt is the world's leading importer of wheat, flour, and wheat products (11.5 million tonnes in 2015–2016). In this chapter, we highlight two major agricultural producing regions that are representative of the developed and developing world, namely, the European Union and developing countries as represented by China and India.

Figures 8.1 and 8.2 provide trends in commodity-level support payments as a percentage of gross commodity receipts for the main supported commodities for the EU and China, respectively. OECD data for the EU are available for the period 1986–2019 while they are only available for 1993–2019 for China.[1] For the EU, we provide trends in support payments for milk, meat (an average of beef and veal, pork, sheep meat, and poultry), potatoes, and grains (wheat, barley, oats, maize, rapeseed, soybeans, and rice). For China, we show trends for cotton, meat (beef and veal, pork, and poultry), grains (wheat, maize, rice, soybeans, and rapeseed), and milk.

Since about 2005, there has been a significant decline in EU support for meat, grains, and milk, with the latter two declining to nearly zero by 2019. Although not shown, support for oilseeds (soybeans and rapeseed) had fallen from 55% in 1991 to less than 1% in 1992, remaining close to zero ever since. Support for meat remains relatively high, while that for potatoes has fallen only slightly over time and remains near 10%. This is not to suggest that EU subsidies for agriculture have disappeared. As discussed in the following section, the EU has converted many of its subsidy programs into single farm payments that do not depend on production of any particular commodity.

---

[1] India is not yet an OECD member, but is active in various OECD activities, including development of databases. However, available data for India indicate that it provides very little support to agricultural producers and often collects more in revenue from the farm sector than it provides in subsidies.

Figure 8.1 European Union commodity support payments as percentage of gross receipts for the commodity, milk, meat, potatoes, and grains, 1986–2019

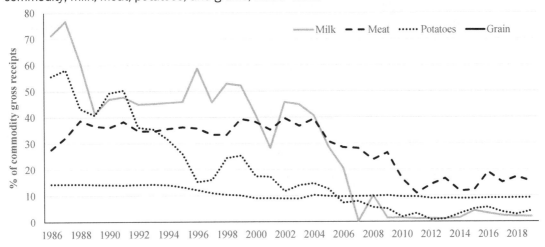

Source: OECD (2020)

Figure 8.2 Chinese commodity support payments as percentage of gross receipts for the commodity, milk, meat, cotton, and grains, 1993–2019

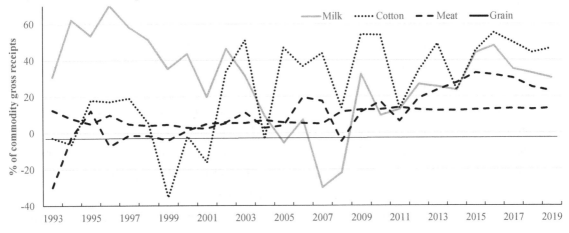

Source: OECD (2020)

In contrast to the US, Canada, and the EU, China's subsidies to producers of grains, meat, and cotton have trended upwards from 1993 to 2019, albeit with ups and downs. The subsidy rate for milk reached 70% in 1996, fell below zero for the period 2006–2008, and then rose to some 40% by the end of 2019. In effect, China currently subsidizes agricultural production to a large extent, and these subsidies distort production. China's agricultural policies along with those of India are examined in section 8.2.

8.1 Agricultural Policy Reform in the European Union

The discussion concerning European agricultural policy inevitably begins with the formation of the European

Union. Because the EU consists of member states that have not relinquished all power over many aspects of governance and the economy to the supranational authority in Brussels, there is some affinity with the way Canada's constitution allocates power across provinces. In both the EU and Canada, power over agriculture is a shared responsibility between states/provinces and the center. Various member states or provinces can provide support to farmers over and above what is provided by the supranational authority. This is unlike the United States where, although states do have some responsibility for agriculture, the federal government (center) is almost exclusively responsible for providing support to agricultural producers. Further, in both the EU and Canada, and unlike in the US, the development of agricultural programs requires agreement among member states/provinces (in economic parlance these are referred to as "agents") and the central government ("principal"), while programs themselves are administered at the member state or provincial level. This implies that the lower level of government can sometimes act contrary to what is desired at the upper level—there is a principal–agent problem that may or may not always be easy to resolve.

8.1.1 Background to the European Union

After World War II, it was relatively easy for European legislators to establish an agricultural policy regime that provided farmers with large subsidies. Many European citizens experienced food shortages during and shortly after World War II, and, further, a large proportion of the population still lived in rural areas in the decade or so after the war. Consequently, agriculture had a great deal of political clout within Europe's legislatures. The European Union first began as the European Coal and Steel Community with the 1951 Treaty of Paris; subsequently, the Treaty of Rome (1957), which actually consisted of two separate treaties, established the European Economic Community (EEC) and the European Atomic Energy Community, or Euratom. Thus, beginning in 1958, what was to become the EU consisted of three separate communities plus guidelines for developing future policies. The original six member countries were West Germany, Italy, France, Belgium, the Netherlands, and Luxembourg. A timeline of EU membership is provided in Table 8.1.

The objective of the EEC was to reduce custom duties among member states, with the eventual goal of a customs union. This would be done by creating a single market for goods, labor, services, and capital. Further, the Treaty Establishing the EEC (a subset of the Treaty of Rome) proposed the development of common policies related to agriculture, transportation, and social welfare, as well as a European Commission. During negotiations on implementation of the EEC treaty, French President Charles de Gaulle pushed for the creation of a common agricultural policy that would protect EEC farmers from outside competition, thereby facilitating European preference for higher-cost French agricultural products.

There is much confusion about the European treaties, the extent to which powers over various policy areas are allocated to the national or supranational level, and the degree to which powers over a jurisdiction are shared. Treaties are the result of negotiations concerning the extent to which economic integration morphs into political union, with countries' willingness to sacrifice independence rising and ebbing over the years. This was particularly true in agriculture, and especially in France.

Table 8.1 Expansion of the European Union and Brexit

Year	Joining members
1956	West Germany, France, Italy, Netherlands, Belgium, Luxembourg
1973	Denmark, Ireland, United Kingdom
1981	Greece
1986	Portugal, Spain
1989	East Germany (integrated into West Germany)
1995	Austria, Finland, Sweden
2004	Slovenia, Slovakia, Poland, Hungary, Malta, Czech Republic, Cyprus, Lithuania, Latvia, Estonia
2007	Romania, Bulgaria
2013	Croatia
	Departing members
2020	United Kingdom

The Treaty of the European Union is also known as the Treaty of Maastricht, as it was signed in Maastricht, the Netherlands, in 1992. This treaty was subsequently amended by the 1997 Treaty of Amsterdam, the 2001 Treaty of Nice (which came into force in 2003), and the 2009 Treaty of Lisbon. Each of the amendments was meant to strengthen integration of the institutions comprising the EU. For example, the Treaty of Lisbon facilitated expansion of the EU to central and eastern Europe: In 2004, the EU expanded from 15 members (EU-15) to 25 members (EU-25). As indicated in Table 8.1, three additional members were subsequently added so that the EU had 28 members (EU-28). However, the United Kingdom left the EU in 2020, leaving 27 members (EU-27).

A parallel treaty to the Treaty of the European Union is the 2007 Treaty of the Functioning of the European Union, which spells out the basis of EU law—the jurisdictions in which the EU has authority and in which it can legislate. Agriculture is one such jurisdiction. Articles 38–44 of the Treaty of the Functioning of the European Union deal with fisheries and agriculture, with Article 39 laying out the objectives of a Common Agricultural Policy (CAP):

> Article 39: 1. The objectives of the common agricultural policy shall be: (a) to increase agricultural productivity by promoting technical progress and by ensuring the rational development of agricultural production and the optimum utilisation of the factors of production, in particular labour; (b) thus to ensure a fair standard of living for the agricultural community, in particular by increasing the individual earnings of persons engaged in agriculture; (c) to stabilise markets; (d) to assure the availability of supplies; [and] (e) to ensure that supplies reach consumers at reasonable prices.

Notice the emphasis in sections (b) and (c) that essentially call on government to support and stabilize farm incomes—i.e., to subsidize agricultural production.

After the Treaty of Rome had established the underlying justification for a CAP, the Conference of Stresa (1958) created the European Agricultural Guidance and Guarantee Fund (EAGF), which emphasized common financial responsibility for market and price policies (the "hard core" of the CAP), and thereby income support for European agricultural producers. A Council of Ministers in 1962 subsequently laid the groundwork for (1) price policy (target prices, threshold prices to prevent imports, and export subsidies), (2) quotas, and (3) direct income support. As a result, payments to agriculture from the EAGF eventually accounted for nearly 90% of the EU's total budget by 1970. Payments continued to rise after 1970, but the share of the EU budget accounted for by agriculture slowly declined to 36% of the budget for the period 2014–2020, and is projected to decline to 28.5% of the EU-27 (sans the UK) budget for the period 2021–2027. The Conference of Stresa also established the framework for Common Market Organizations, much like the 1937 Agricultural Marketing Agreement Act in the US established agencies to encourage orderly marketing of agricultural products. In 1962, organizations for cereals and related products were established, followed in 1964 by Common Market Organizations in milk and dairy products.

As the Agricultural Commissioner of the fledgling European project that eventually became the EU, Sicco Mansholt had been a key figure in the establishment of agricultural policy at the Stresa conference in 1958 and the subsequent Council of Ministers in 1962. However, in 1968, he proposed the so-called Mansholt Plan to reform European agriculture, because he recognized that the CAP would lead to overproduction while doing little to enhance farm incomes. His proposal promoted (i) the consolidation of small farms so as to increase farm size to take advantage of economies of scale; (ii) the removal of more than 2 million hectares of cropland from production (to mitigate overproduction); and (iii) reduced payments for smaller producers (again to increase farm size). These proposals were controversial and opposed by small farm holders and many governments with strong farm lobbies. Attempts to adopt the Mansholt Plan failed and his predictions of oversupply and growing support payments came true during the 1970s. By 1980, the EU embarked on a program to implement some of Mansholt's ideas. In particular, to reduce mounting stocks of butter and skim milk powder, a quota system was adopted in the dairy sector in 1984. Further, in an effort to implement budgetary discipline, growth in CAP spending was to be limited by growth in gross national product; in 1988, it was agreed that growth in agricultural spending would be limited to 74% of growth in gross national product.

By the early 1990s, there was general agreement that the CAP needed to be reformed. However, agricultural reforms would come for reasons that had as much to do with the evolution of the EU—the politics of expansion and greater integration—as they did with agriculture per se. Therefore, in the remainder of this section, three themes are examined: (1) the high and increasing costs of the CAP at a time when politicians wished to allocate more of the limited EU budget to other programs; (2) the integration of new members as the EU expanded from the EU-15 prior to 2004 to the EU-28—more specifically, the implication for the CAP of adding several nations with large, undeveloped agricultural sectors; and (3) increasing environmental concerns that the CAP was perceived to aggravate. Throughout the discussion, analyses of the changes are examined using the tools set out in Chapter 6.

8.1.2 High and Increasing Costs of Agricultural Programs

Even after the CAP had been in place for several decades, large transfers to the agricultural sector continued despite high costs to consumers and/or taxpayers and a declining farm population. There are three reasons why farm payments could continue at high levels despite the obvious strain on the EU budget:

1. Although reduced in numbers, the farm lobby remains strong and is able to influence policy makers to allocate funds in their direction. They have a lot to gain from rent-seeking. Farm program support, on the other hand, is paid for by general taxpayers who lack the incentive to organize to oppose the farmer lobby. The benefit to individual taxpayers is small, while the transaction costs of opposing large transfers to the agricultural sector are high.
2. As the proportion of their income spent on food declines and agricultural support payments fall as a proportion of the total tax bill, consumers and taxpayers become less concerned with the costs of farm programs.
3. Consumers are increasingly concerned with food safety (viz., BSE crisis, pig flu, and hoof and mouth disease), which provides a rationale for continued citizen and government support of agriculture and the food sector.

Shortly after introduction of the CAP, and as Mansholt had predicted, support policies led to growing stocks of wine, butter, milk powder, cereals, and other commodities during the 1970s and 1980s that then needed to be disposed of on world markets. This required subsidies and led to international resentment and retaliation, and became an obstacle to the conclusion of international trade negotiations (recall Chapter 5). One impetus for reforming the CAP, therefore, was to facilitate trade negotiations. Finally, as noted above, EAGF payments gobbled up some 90% of the EU budget in the early 1970s, while politicians began to desire funds for programs besides agriculture.

One initiative that politicians undertook in 1992 entailed a change in priorities from market and income support (dubbed pillar 1) to rural development (pillar 2). The reallocation of program payments for farm support to rural development was termed "modulation"—a shift of agricultural subsidy payments from producers to rural development. Pillar 1 included such things as intervention prices, variable import levies, export restitution (effectively subsidies to promote exports), and public storage. Pillar 2 eventually included payments for environmental goods and services, subsidies to the poorest rural regions in the EU, programs that promoted food quality and higher food safety standards, and programs to improve animal well-being. The budget for market and income support was capped at €48.6 billion, while that for rural development was to rise by €1.2 billion annually.

Although modulation limited direct payments to farmers and enabled politicians to spend money on programs that are more or less related to the agricultural sector, CAP reform was also required to curtail oversupply and its adverse environmental consequences (as discussed in the next subsection). Even so, it would not be easy to tame the proportion of the EU budget going to agriculture, whether directly via pillar 1 or indirectly through pillar 2. This is seen in Figures 8.3 and 8.4. The agricultural component of the budget is no longer referred to by the European Commission as "Agriculture," as it was prior to 2007, but is now referenced in budget documents as "Preservation and Management of Natural Resources." As indicated in Figure 8.3, the budget for agriculture and rural development has risen steadily in nominal dollar terms throughout the new millennium, falling slightly after peaking in 2013. Since 2000, its proportion of the EU budget has fallen, however, from nearly 52% to slightly more than 37% in 2018, and is projected to fall to 28.5% in the Multiannual Financial Framework (MFF) for 2021–2027, which was announced May 2, 2018.

Figure 8.3 EU expenditure on agriculture (left axis) and cap spending as percent of overall EU budget (right axis), 2000–2018

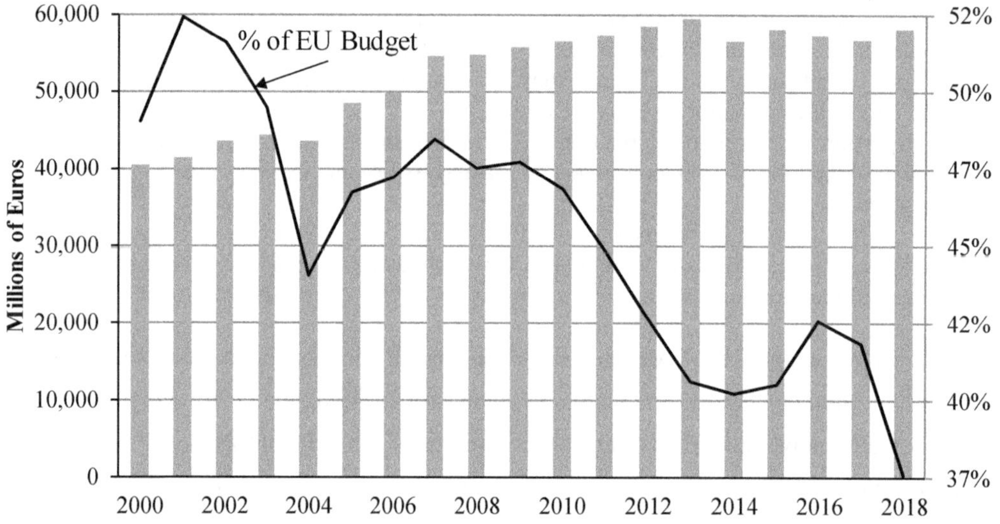

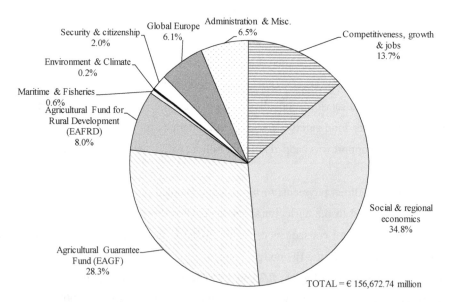

Source: European Commission, http://ec.europa.eu/budget/figures/interactive/index_en.cfm [accessed February 24, 2020]; additional data are from the European Commission, EuroStat, and the St. Louis Federal Reserve (https://research.stlouisfed.org/fred2/)

Figure 8.4 Allocation of the EU budget, 2018

Source: European Commission, http://ec.europa.eu/budget/figures/interactive/index_en.cfm [accessed February 24, 2020]; other data are from the European Commission, EuroStat, and St. Louis Federal Reserve (https://research.stlouisfed.org/fred2/)

Consider the allocation of the EU budget that was adopted for 2018 and provided in Figure 8.4. The European Agricultural Guarantee Fund still gobbles up a whopping 32.5% of the entire EU budget, an increase from 30.7% in 2014. If the EU's Agricultural Fund for Rural Development (EAFRD) is included, it comes to about two-fifths of the budget. To this must be added expenditures on fisheries, although this is a very small component. Interestingly, the monies allocated to climate and environment are tiny, only 0.2% of the budget. Given that the EU is committed by the December 2015 Paris Agreement to reduce emissions of CO_2 by 30% from 1990 baseline emissions by 2030, and has actually a legislated mandate to reduce emissions by 20% from 1990 by 2020, it is surprising that more has not been allocated to this activity. The reason is that the EU has put the onus for meeting climate targets on individual member states, although some monies in the Global Europe and EAFRD funds might also be used to address these targets.

The EU budget for the EU-28 amounted to 1.0% of GDP of all member states, but 1.03% if expenditures of €6.0 billion on the European Defense Fund were taken into account.[2] To address expenditures related to increased security, refugees, and other programs, while retaining adequate funds for agricultural support, some had recommended increasing the budget to 1.11% of GDP. Despite proposals to increase the budget of the Multiannual Financial Framework, CAP funding is expected to decline by about 12% in real as opposed to nominal terms (see 8.1.6 below).

8.1.3 Integration of New Members

Although French President Charles de Gaulle vetoed the United Kingdom's application to join the EEC on two occasions (1963 and 1967) in order to protect French farmers from potential competition from agricultural producers in the British Commonwealth, the UK finally joined the EEC in 1973, along with Denmark and Ireland. Other countries subsequently joined from 1981 through 2013, as indicated in Table 8.1, including East Germany as part of a unified Federal Republic of Germany after the collapse of the Berlin Wall in 1989.

Enlargement after the turn of the new millennium was a stressor for agricultural policy development. As the European Union expanded to include new member states, especially countries in central and eastern Europe in 2004, 2007, and 2013, the agricultural policies of both new and pre-existing members were affected by changes to the CAP, which, in turn, altered the supply and demand conditions for commodities within both the entrant country and each pre-existing EU member. For policy makers, the main concern was the budget implications. To address the ascension of eastern and central European countries whose agricultural sectors were quite large, policy makers had proposed increasing the EU budget for agriculture from 1% of GDP (as noted above).

---

[2] The budget is announced as a percent of gross national income, which equals GDP plus net primary income from abroad plus any product taxes not included in the valuation of output. It is about the same as gross national product (=GDP plus net property income from abroad). For simplicity, the term GDP is used.

There was also a concern about governance. Could the increased complexity in agricultural regulations work in the new entrants where accounting practices were less developed than in the EU-15 and corruption was a greater problem? Given that the CAP had been an obstacle to trade under the GATT, the addition of several countries with large agricultural sectors, most notably Hungary, Poland, and the Czech Republic, and later Romania and Bulgaria, would likely aggravate trade negotiations under the WTO.

To provide some indication of the problem, consider Table 8.2. Although the data are for 2008, they provide a picture of the situation that the European Union faced in grappling with agricultural policy in the face of enlargement. EU policy makers addressed the problem by basing direct payments to farmers on yields and area cropped during the period 1995–1999 (shortly after the demise of communism when yields were particularly low), but not 2000–2002 as with the EU-15. Further, eligibility for full direct farm payments was phased in over a period of 10 years, beginning with 25% in 2004. (Direct payments were phased in by 2013 for the 10 members entering in 2004, by 2015 for Romania and Bulgaria, and 2022 for Croatia.) Overall, the direct payment provided agricultural producers in these countries varied from €300 for small farms in Poland to €40,000 for large farms in Hungary and the Czech Republic.[3] Although average payouts per farm were significantly lower in new member states than in the EU-15 and the original six member states, the citizens of the EU-15 (and original states) contributed more to agricultural support payments than they received in benefits (Table 8.2).

Table 8.2 Expansion of the EU: Population, farmland area, number of farms and farm workers, and expected contributions to and payouts under full benefits, various country groupings, 2008

Grouping	Population (mil)	Farmland (mil ha)	# of farms ('000s)	Farm workers ('000s)	Contribution (€/citizen)	Payout (€/citizen)	Payout (€/ha)	Payout (€/farm)
Original[a]	214.7	60.4	3,334.0	3,116.3	126.4	99.6	353.7	6,411.2
EU-15	336.8	129.4	5,845.0	6,244.4	145.4	138.8	361.0	7,995.0
EU-25	410.9	162.8	9,691.0	9,468.4	126.9	128.7	324.9	5,457.8
EU-27[b]	440.1	182.1	14,482.0	12,564.1	120.0	120.2	290.5	3,652.8

[a] Refers to the original six countries identified in Table 8.1.
[b] Excludes Croatia, which was added in 2013.

The disparity in treatment between the latest entrants to the EU and the EU-15 could not continue, however, because it would destabilize efforts at further political integration. Therefore, the CAP reforms of June 2013 began to deal with the convergence of farm payments between the EU-15, where the average farm payment was €295/ha, and the new members (€187/ha).

---

[3] Collectivization of farms had progressed further in Hungary and the Czech Republic than in Poland, but, when communism ended, the original owners came to an arrangement that accommodated the reality of larger farm sizes, thereby retaining economies of scale.

8.1.4 Reform of the CAP and Increasing Environmental Concerns

Serious reforms to the CAP began in the early 1990s, initially to prevent agricultural surpluses, control growth of the EU budget, and facilitate international trade negotiations. Subsequently, reforms also focused on reducing the CAP's adverse environmental impacts through decoupling and farmland set asides, for example. Government support payments effectively raised the farm gate price of crops, leading to negative environmental impacts at both the intensive and extensive margins. At the intensive margin, higher crop prices led farmers to employ more inputs, resulting in soil depletion and chemical pollution from agriculture (e.g., algae blooms in lakes caused by nitrogen runoff). At the extensive margin, cropland area increased as permanent grasslands and wetlands were brought into crop production, and land shifted out of forestry into agriculture unless prohibited by other laws.

In this subsection, the reforms to the CAP are discussed and evaluated using economic tools of analysis. Differences in programs between the EU and US are highlighted, and we look at how EU agricultural programs affected global markets.

MacSharry Reform (1992) and Agenda 2000 (1999)

Following the failure of the Mansholt Plan, it was nearly a quarter of a century before reforms to the CAP began in earnest. The MacSharry Reform of 1992 affected cereals, oilseeds, protein crops, and beef, and the reforms were phased in over a period of four years. The objectives of the reforms were essentially threefold:

1. They were meant to facilitate conclusion of GATT's Uruguay Round Agreement on Agriculture (AoA) which occurred in late 1994. The 1992 Reform introduced per hectare, fixed direct payments calculated as an Olympic average of 1986–1990 yields. Direct payments were initially placed in the amber box category of the AoA but were subsequently moved to the new blue box category created in 1995. US direct payments under the 1996 Farm Bill were also placed in the blue box (see Chapter 5.3).
2. EU prices were lowered but remained above the world price, with the intervention (internal floor) prices of cereal grains and beef reduced by 30% and 15%, respectively (as can be seen in Figure 8.1). However, farmers were directly compensated for price declines via the direct payments.
3. Land set asides were introduced, although requirements affected only large producers whose annual output exceeded 92 metric tons of grains or oilseeds. Large farms were required to set aside 10% of the previous year's arable land. The set-aside program would remain in effect until 2006–2007.

The MacSharry Reform was followed in 1999 by the so-called Agenda 2000, which was primarily meant to address EU enlargement and the need to move the intervention price even further towards the world price.[4] The guaranteed prices of cereals were reduced by an additional 15%, while the beef price was reduced by 20%; in this case, only half of the loss experienced by producers was compensated via direct payments. Domestic EU prices remained above the world price, with intervention prices for wheat, maize, sorghum, and barley all set at €101.31 per tonne, while the import threshold price was set at 155% of the intervention (floor) price. In addition, the Agenda 2000 reforms extended land set-aside requirements to smaller crop producers, laid the groundwork for future dairy reforms, and limited the CAP budget to €40.5 billion (see Figure 8.4).

Reforms of the Mid-Term Review (2003)

The 2003 Mid-Term Review (also known as the Fischler Reform) followed almost immediately upon the heels of Agenda 2000. The Fischler Reform constituted the first major step towards decoupling production from agricultural support payments. It did so using direct payments rather than support measures for specific products. Payments for specific products were to be replaced with less market-distorting agricultural support whereby decoupled payments were made directly to farmers, conditional upon certain practices but in a way that no longer incentivized production. This was accomplished by introducing a single payment scheme of decoupled income support that combined several pre-existing direct payments into a single farm payment (SFP), with the payment based on average historical commodity-based yields for the period 2000–2002 for EU-15 members but for the period 1995–1998 for new entrants added after 2000. An example of decoupled payments for a representative farm in the Netherlands is provided in Table 8.3. Note that the direct payment varies across crops and is based on area planted to various crops.

Table 8.3 Dutch decoupled single payment scheme based on historic 2000–2002 yields

Crop	Payment
Wheat	€377.5/ha
Barley	€377.5/ha
Seed potato	€0/ha
Edible potato	€0/ha
Sugar beet	€687.0/ha
Onions	€0/ha

Source: Esther Boere (personal communication February 14, 2015)

The 2003 reforms were gradually implemented between January 2005 and January 2007. Direct payments were decoupled from production but linked to eligible farmland, although coupling elements remained in dairy, cereals, sugar beet, and potatoes. In the end, 75% of payments for arable land were decoupled, along with 60% of durum wheat land and 70% of livestock payments. The problem was that, while full decoupling was the default objective, states had some discretion in how they could allocate CAP

---

[4] The intervention price is the price at which the government steps in to prevent prices from falling further; although it is the floor price, it also becomes the EU market price. In contrast, the EU target price operates much like it does in the US—it is used to determine the deficiency payment. Finally, the threshold price is the world price plus the EU tariff. For further discussion see Figure 8.5 below.

funds and, as well, used their own agricultural programs to achieve lower than desired *de facto* decoupling. Elimination of the partial decoupling was accomplished during the so-called Health Check of November 2008. As a result, the share of coupled aid in the total direct aid package fell from 15.0% in 2008 to 14.7% in 2010, 7.6% in 2012, and 6.7% in 2014.

To determine the size of the fixed (direct) payment a farmer would receive, countries could choose one of the following for determining a producer's reference yields:

1. an historic approach with entitlements depending on farm-specific historic reference amounts;
2. a regional approach with entitlements dependent on the region's outcomes for establishing a reference margin; or
3. a hybrid approach that combined the historic and regional approaches.

While the European Commission expressed a preference for the regional approach, the majority of countries opted for the historical one.

Only lands growing specific crops were considered eligible for fixed payments (€/ha) that varied by crop based on historic 2000–2002 yields. Payments were based on farm-specific entitlements, so their size differed significantly by type of farm and across farms, and they were conditional on the cross compliance measures introduced in the Mid-Term Review: To be eligible for farm payments, agricultural producers had to comply with (i) food safety, (ii) animal welfare, and/or (iii) environmental standards. Additionally, farmers could not convert pastureland to arable crops or divert land to non-agricultural uses.

One problem with the 2003 reforms was that countries had quite a bit of discretion as to when they could adopt the reforms—any time during 2005–2007. Further, states could handle the "single payment" scheme in different ways; for example, a country could provide different per ha payments that varied by crop, thereby locking in historical 2000–2002 planting patterns. Frustratingly, they could allocate direct payments in ways that led to undesirable and unpredictable outcomes at the EU level, making for administrative problems. The reason was that countries could provide extra subsidies (up to 10% of previous ceilings) and ones that are tied to production (25% of direct payment for arable crops and 40% for durum).

In dairy, some income support was transferred into a direct decoupled payment; the intervention price was lowered (see Figure 6.10) and producers were provided with a direct payment, known as the dairy premium. The best way to think of the dairy premium (as well as the decoupled payments in the other sectors) is as a deficiency payment, because it was paid only on the previous quota and not the expanded quota. Although the quota system was not yet abandoned, a reduction in price implied that more milk would be consumed, which would require some loosening of the milk quota. A timetable for eliminating the quota system was set in place; the intervention price was slowly lowered toward the world price, while the quota level was increased. By April 2015, the dairy quota had disappeared, and the dairy premium had been converted to a single farm payment (with milk producers receiving payment even if they no longer produced milk). This is discussed further in section 8.1.5.

Finally, there were special provisions for organic farming (an anti-GMO measure), subsidies for growing durum wheat (which hurt durum producers such as Canada; see note on Table 7.2), and subsidies for growing trees to sequester carbon (with some part of the subsidies required to offset CAP support payments). Finally, the greater accounting requirements associated with reforms posed a problem for states that lacked the institutions and qualified accountants to handle the changes to programs, or even the programs themselves, due to corruption and weak rule of law in those states (as indicated in Figure 5.1).

2013 Common Agricultural Policy (CAP) Reform

The 2013 reform of the Common Agricultural Policy, which began to take effect in 2015, provided a single farm payment that was meant to provide the same level of support to every hectare of farmland in a region, independent of the type of farm or crop grown. The SFP is a flat-rate, direct payment (€/ha) that replaced the decoupled payments. In the case of the representative Dutch farm in Table 8.3, the decoupled payments would be replaced by a direct payment of €270/ha in 2015, which is close to the €282/ha that the representative or average farm would receive if it planted the crops indicated by its past history. The 2013 CAP Reform also set 2017 as the date when the sugar production quota would be eliminated (which is analyzed in section 8.1.5).

Producers are also compensated for providing public goods in the form of environmentally friendly farming practices—a so-called greening component added to the single farm payment if farmers are in compliance. The greening component imposes a set-aside requirement referred to as the Ecological Focus Area. The new environmental requirements are costly for farmers as the set asides lead to a minimum 5% reduction in subsidy payments that can be worth more than $200,000 annually to individual farms. The European Parliament and European Commission wanted a mandatory cap on spending, but EU governments agreed only to limit individual payouts to $420,000 per year. Even so, expenditures are still running at more than €60 billion, with €51 billion in direct payments to farmers. Thus, the CAP remains, at 37.0% in 2018, the largest item in the EU's long-term Multiannual Financial Framework (budget plan) for 2014–2020, and remains the largest item in the MFF for 2021–2027 at 28.5% of the EU budget. However, the budget includes plans to reduce the disparity between producers: Producers in Italy, Belgium, and the Netherlands, for example, receive more than €400/ha, while producers in the Baltic states receive less than €160/ha. During budget negotiations in 2013–2014, it was proposed for payments to converge to €196/ha (measured in 2013 euros) by 2020.

One aspect of the 2013 reform was a regulation that allows member states to provide agricultural producers coupled support in certain cases, using some of their national envelope for direct payments. Voluntary coupled support (VCS) payments are meant to incentivize farmers to maintain production in key agricultural sectors or regions. While rules are specific, albeit complex, member states can employ up to 8%–13% of their national ceilings for such coupled support, depending on circumstances. Under some circumstances, these ceilings can be raised; for example, if a country employs 2% or more of its national ceilings to produce protein crops to maintain the autonomy of an animal breeding sector, it can increase coupled support by as much as two percentage points. However, member states decide which sectors and regions to cover by VCS payments, and the level at which sectors are supported.

As of August 2015, five sectors accounted for more than 84% of the VCS budget: beef and veal, dairy and dairy products, sheep and goats, protein crops, and sugar beet. At least 15 member states implemented VCS for each of these sectors, with three sectors accounting for three-quarters of the VCS budget (see Table 8.4). As a proportion of the value of production (evaluated at producer prices), sheep and goat meat, rice, beef and veal, and sugar beet benefit most from a relatively high degree of support.

Table 8.4 Voluntary coupled support (VCS) by sector, EU, 2015

Products	VCS (million €)	Proportion of EU's VCS budget[a]	VCS as % of the production value at producer price	# of states applying VCS
Beef & veal	1,706	41.34%	5.38	23
Dairy	829	20.09%	1.27	19
Sheep & goats	503	12.19%	9.68	19
Protein crops	443	10.73%	< 1	15
Fruit & vegetable	204	4.94%	< 1	18
Sugar beet	174	4.22%	3.81	10
Cereals	87	2.11%	< 1	6
Olive oil	70	1.70%	1.56	1
Rice	57	1.38%	7.42	6

[a] Sectors with a VCS share <1% of total VCS are left out.
Source: Roel Jongeneel (personal communication, September 22, 2017)

Although VCS payments are made on a per hectare basis, their impact is to shift the supply curve downwards in the member state that provides the VCS. For example, sugar beet payments in 2015 varied from €81/ha to over €500/ha, constituting a price subsidy (calculated using average yields) of some 6% to more than 35%. That is, there is an increase in production, but the total VCS payment of €4.1 billion is well within the EU's *de minimis* aggregate measure of support of €98.1 billion allowed under WTO rules (see Chapter 5.3).

8.1.5 Further Analysis of Sector-Level Programs

In this subsection, policy changes affecting the cereal, dairy, and sugar sectors introduced in previous subsections are examined in more detail. The main elements of the common EU agricultural policy during the 1990s might be characterized by:

- price policy consisting of:
  - target prices (payment to producers),
  - threshold prices to prevent imports,
  - intervention prices (floor to internal market price),
  - refunds to reimburse animal producers for higher input prices, and
  - export subsidies;
- quota systems (plus price protection); and
- direct income support that eventually was decoupled from production.

A stylized representation of EU price policy before the most recent reforms were completed is found in Figure 8.5. In the diagram, TP represents a form of target price (because it determines the direct support payment), IP is the intervention price (internal market price), q_d is consumed domestically, q_s is produced domestically, P_w is the world price, and (P^*, q^*) represents the autarkic, non-intervention market price and quantity. Without intervention, the EU is assumed to be a net importer of grain. The cost to the treasury of the support program identified in the figure is the total of the differently shaded areas. The required export subsidy equals the lightly shaded area, assuming that the EU will export any surplus production. Finally, the deficiency (direct) payment related to domestic consumption is given by the darkly shaded area.

Figure 8.5 Stylized diagram of EU policy, circa 1990s

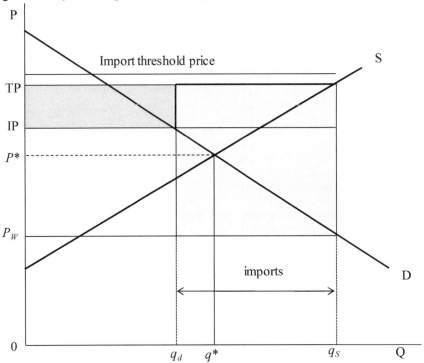

Now consider two situations: (1) the EU is a net exporter under the CAP, so there is no importing of the commodity in question; and (2) the EU is a net importer with and without the CAP, but price support keeps imports below free market levels. These situations are shown in panels (a) and (b), respectively, of Figure 8.6. In panel (a), P_s is the support price (post-intervention) and P_W is the world or free market price. Because the support price leads to overproduction, an export subsidy is needed to export the commodity, as indicated in preceding paragraphs. This would certainly qualify as dumping.

In the case of imports in panel (b), the price floor needs to be supported by a tariff (T). The level of imports falls from $q_d - q_s$ to $q'_d - q'_s$. The welfare effects are as follows: Consumers pay for a price floor enforced with a variable levy. Area A goes to domestic farmers, area B comes out of the EU budget, and areas C_1 and C_2 are deadweight losses.

Figure 8.6 Effect of the CAP depends on whether the EU is an exporter or importer

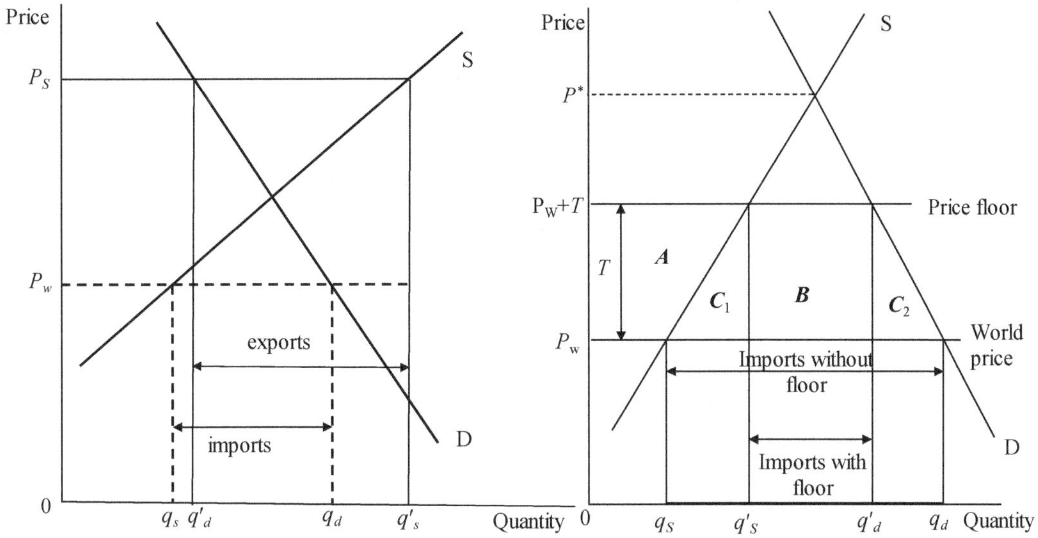

(a) EU as Importer prior to but Exporter after intervention   (b) EU as net importer after intervention

Cereals

The impact of the shift from coupled price support to direct income support in the cereals sector is illustrated with the aid of Figure 8.7. Income support has no effect on price if support is decoupled from production—giving no incentive to produce more; when the incentive is gone, environmental damage is reduced as farming becomes less intensive (e.g., due to reduced fertilizer use). The reforms to the CAP eliminated the target price (TP) but farmers received the darkly shaded area plus area (*kabh*) in the form of a direct income payment based on historical yields given by q_S. Farmers then face only the intervention price (IP), in which case output is reduced from q_S to q_M. This lessens the extent of overproduction thereby reducing the needed export subsidy from the large lightly shaded area (*kdca*) to the smaller area (*hdyx*). Then, the IP can slowly be lowered, thereby reducing q_M and the export subsidy; eventually IP is lowered to the world price P_W and there is no longer an export subsidy. Meanwhile, unless the reference yield is also reduced (e.g., by choosing a new historic period on which it is based), the producer continues to receive the darkly shaded area plus (*kabh*) as a deficiency payment. This direct payment was subsequently transferred into a single farm payment.

Dairy

What distinguished the EU dairy quota regime from that imposed in other countries, most notably Canada, is that the EU was the largest exporter of dairy products in the world, both prior to implementation of a quota regime and thereafter. This has to be taken into account in discussions regarding the process of eliminating quota—the EU simply used supply management to reduce its export subsidies. In addition, the elimination of quota was needed to facilitate further economic integration of EU member states and to integrate the dairy sector into the single farm payment scheme. Finally, the EU super levy did not initially allocate quota across countries in optimal fashion (as discussed in Chapter 6.3). Thus, the description of the EU's dairy sector and its elimination is used only to illustrate the application of applied welfare economics.

Figure 8.7 Shift to direct income support in cereals

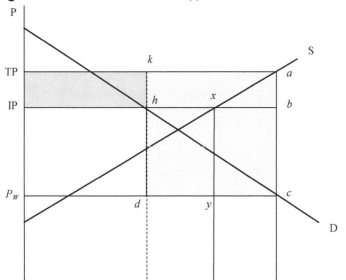

A stylized description of EU dairy policy over the period from establishment of the quota regime in 1984 through its demise in 2015 is provided in Figure 8.8. In this back-to-back diagram, the autarkic price and quantity where there is no trade between the EU and the rest of the world are given by P^* and q^*, respectively, in panel (b). With trade, the relevant demand function facing EU producers is D_T, which is the sum of the domestic demand function (D_E) and excess demand by the rest of the world (ED_R). In the absence of transportation costs, the world price would be P^W, with q^{wd} consumed domestically and the difference $q^W - q^{wd}$ in panel (b) exported to the rest of world—with equivalent imports indicated for P^W in panel (a).

Consider what happens when the EU's dairy producers face support price P^S. Farmers produce q^S but EU consumers would only consume q^D at that price. Since domestic EU consumers pay the higher price, the EU must either store the excess production or subsidize exports. The cost of purchasing the overproduced dairy products, butter and skim milk powder (SMP), is given by the area bounded by points ($ee'q^Sq^D$). The excess production is given by ee' ($=q^S-q^D$), some or all of which can be exported to the rest of the world at price P_0, thereby enabling the EU to recover some of the cost of purchasing the excess production. If all of the excess production is sold on the world market at price P_0, the cost to the EU of subsidizing exports can be lowered to the amount given by area ($ee'k'k$). Of course, export subsidies constitute dumping and quickly draw the ire of trading partners.

Figure 8.8 Stylized diagram of Europe's dairy regime and its demise

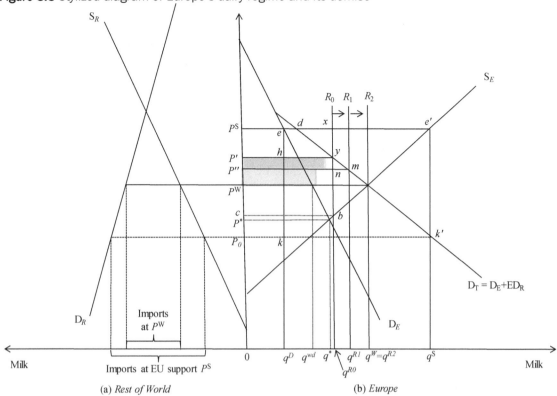

(a) *Rest of World*   (b) *Europe*

To avoid accumulating stocks of dairy products and/or the high costs of export subsidies while still supporting prices, the EU employed a quota beginning in 1984. Assume the quota was initially set at R_0. Dairy farmers would produce q^{R0}, and receive a price (P^S) greater than the marginal cost of production (c), thereby capturing a rent equal to the area bounded by (P^scbx). The price EU consumers pay is still P^S in this case, so the amount ex ($=q^{R0}-q^D$) must still be exported (or stored). The price foreigners pay would be P' with the EU subsidizing exports by an amount given by ($ehyx$), which is much less than the subsidy ($ekk'e'$) when there is no supply management; thus, the introduction of a country-level quota scheme potentially reduced the costs of the EU's dairy support program.

Now consider how the quota system was dismantled. In the stylized version shown in Figure 8.8, the quota is increased in steps to the level that would lead to the free market trade outcome, price P^W and output q^W. In a first step, the quota is increased from R_0 to R_1, which causes the export price to fall from P' to P''. What happens to the price paid to dairy producers? Suppose for convenience of explanation that, in this first stage, the EU permits the support price to fall from P^S to P', with farmers provided annual compensation in the form of a deficiency payment equal to their initial individual quota (denoted their reference quota) multiplied by the price difference, or area (P^sxyP') [$= q^{R0} \times (P^S-P')$]. The effective price difference is referred to as the *milk premium*.

Then, in the second step, the quota is increased to R_2, while the EU lowers the price paid to producers to P''. At this stage, however, the milk premium is set by the authority (EU Commission) to less than the difference P^S–P''. While the price has fallen in this step from P' to P'', farmers are only compensated the darker shaded area rather than area $(P'P''ny)$, as would be the case if they were compensated the full loss in quota rent as in the first step. Thus, the effective milk premium is now less than the difference P^S–P''. After this second step, the EU produces what it would in a competitive global market, but, because it pays farmers more than the world price, it must still subsidize exports by $(P''$–$P^W) \times (q^{R2}$–$q^{wd})$.

Notice that after the second step the marginal cost of producing milk in the EU equals the world price P^W, because S_E equals D_T. In a final step, therefore, the EU lowers the price paid to dairy producers from P'' to P^W, but it now compensates dairy producers for an even smaller component of the quota rent lost as a result of the drop in price; this is indicated by the light-shaded area in Figure 8.8(b).

In practice, the EU had to reduce prices and increase quota over several steps, providing a mechanism for compensating producers along the way. Only butter and SMP were considered eligible for public intervention because these products could be stored (and possibly sold at a later date). In preparation for the phaseout, intervention prices were reduced beginning 2003–2004, as indicated in Table 8.5, but buying was restricted to March 1 through August 31 in a calendar year. There were also limits as to how much the EU would purchase—109,000 tonnes (t) of SMP yearly over the period from 2004 until the quota system ended; for butter, a maximum of 70,000 t would be purchased in 2004, but the amount would decline by 10,000 t annually until it leveled off at 30,000 t/year after 2008, although the commission could purchase more in times of emergency. At the same time, the quota was slowly increased: by 15.5% in 2004–2006, 0.8% in 2006–2007, 3.3% in 2007–2008, 2.3% in 2008–2009, and by about 1% annually thereafter. Compensation for the consequent price reductions was paid in the form of a milk premium that was based on the producer's reference quota. The premium was €8.15/t in 2004, €16.31/t in 2005, and €24.49/t in 2006 and 2007, with the latter premium then converted to a single farm payment by multiplying this final milk premium by the farmer's reference quantity. The dairy quota regime was eliminated entirely in 2015, with producers then receiving a basic payment (equal to the single farm payment) whether they produced milk or not.

Table 8.5 Reductions in intervention prices on butter and skim milk powder, €/100 kg

Year[a]	Butter	Skim milk powder
2003/04	328.20	205.52
2004/05	305.23	195.24
2005/06	282.44	184.97
2006/07	259.52	174.69
2007/08	246.39	174.69
2008 onwards	246.39	169.80

[a] The agricultural year begins April 1 and ends March 31.
Source: Jongeneel et al. (2011)

Sugar Policy

The developed countries of Europe and North America are unable to compete with tropical regions in the production of sugar; sugarcane outcompetes sugar beet. To maintain an ability to produce sugar, developed countries have implemented policies to protect their sugar industries. Nonetheless, a main problem from a political standpoint is that isoglucose and other sweeteners (viz., corn syrup) substitute for sugar in the confectionery industry. How then does one protect sugar beet producers? The US and the EU used tariff rate quotas to protect their domestic industries from outside competition (see Chapter 5.4), with the EU employing a country-level quota regime to shift the costs of sugar policies onto consumers while the US used its loan rate program to subsidize sugar cane and beet producers (Chapter 7.2). For the extent to which countries subsidized sugar, see Table 7.2.

EU sugar policy relied on a traditional quota, but at the country rather than farm level (see Chapter 6.3). Prior to 2006, the only unique feature was that three types of quota were employed, referred to simply as A, B, and C quota. A-quota accounted for approximately 95% of the domestic market; the price of B-quota was historically about 69% of the price of A-quota; and C-quota received the world price. Developing countries were provided access to the EU market through a duty-free TRQ of 1.3 million tonnes. The sugar quota had been in place for about 25 years; the program was self-financing, paid for by a levy of 2% on A-quota holders and consumers paying the remaining costs in the form of higher prices. However, as a result of trade negotiations, this market arrangement came under pressure and, thus, policy reforms began with the elimination of B-quota in 2006.

How the EU sugar quota worked and how it was dismantled is explained with the aid of Figures 8.9 and 8.10 that respectively examine the quota as it existed prior to 2006, and then how it evolved thereafter. Because sugar is a homogeneous product, EU consumers pay the same price for sugar regardless of which of the three types of quota holders produced it or whether it was imported; indeed, an individual producer might even hold more than one type of quota. The authority sets the quota at level Q^R, say, so that the domestic price of sugar is P^Q; since different quotas receive different prices, P^Q is a blended price. Upon setting the quota at Q^R, the authority must simultaneously set the A, B, and C quotas given the import TRQ. Lacking an economic rationale for allocating Q^R among the three types of quota (A, B, and C), an arbitrary choice is made in Figure 8.9; the reason is that this is an income distributional issue, which is by its nature political (at least in the current context). Presumably the authority collects and allocates the politically created quota rents in such a way that no funds come from the Treasury.

In Figure 8.9, the authority sets production at q_A, q_B, and q_C for the respective A-, B- and C-quota holders, while q_M of imports is permitted under the TRQ; thus, $Q^R = q_A + q_B + q_C + q_M$. The prices received by A- and B-quota holders are P^A and P^B, respectively, while C-quota holders and importers receive the world price P^W. The domestic marginal cost of production is given by c, so that domestic sugar producers earn quota rent equal to $(P^Q cvw)$ plus producer surplus of (ckv). The marginal cost of imports is given by c_M, with foreign producers earning a quota rent equal to $(P^W c_M \alpha\beta)$ plus quasi-rent of $(c_M h\alpha)$, and EU authority earning area M as tariff revenue (or as further quota rent).

Figure 8.9 EU sugar policy prior to 2006: Interplay among multiple quota holdings

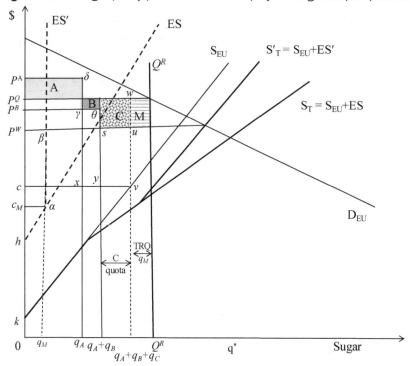

We can now calculate the main income gains to various quota holders and the government. This information is provided in Table 8.6. Again, the overall policy-induced rent available to domestic producers is given by area ($P^Q cvw$). The authority wants to ensure that area (B + C + M − A) ≥ 0, so that no funds are required from the Treasury.

Table 8.6 Income distribution between quota holders, EU sugar policy prior to 2006

Quota holder	Price received	Rent accruing to quota holder (bounded by points)[a]	Gain/loss to authority (shaded area)
A-quota	P^A	($P^A cx\delta$)	−area A
B-quota	P^B	($\gamma xy\theta$)	+area B
C-quota	P^W	($syvu$)	+area C
Importer	P^W	($P^W c_m \alpha \beta$)	+area M

[a] Reference to Figure 8.9. Rent includes quota rent plus quasi-rent.

Figure 8.10 Elimination of EU sugar quota

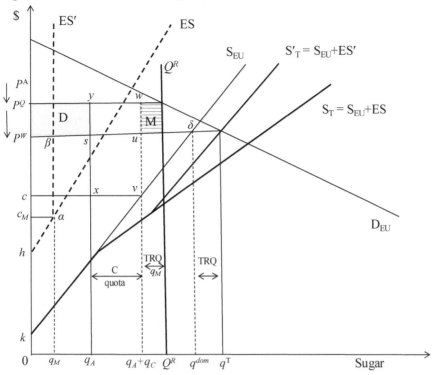

Next consider what happened after 2006. The B-quota was eliminated and then the entire quota regime was dismantled over the period 2011–2017, much as was the case in the dairy sector. In Figure 8.10, the B-quota is gone and the support price for A-quota is reduced by 20%, as indicated by the fall in price from P^A to P^Q, while the quota level remains as before (see Figure 8.9). The quota was made tradeable, however. Since the overall quota target initially remained where it was previously, at Q^R, C-quota expanded to include what had previously been produced by B-quota holders. The TRQ remained in place, so foreign producers continued to produce q_M, realizing a quota rent equal to area ($P^W c_M \alpha \beta$) plus quasi-rent of ($c_m h \alpha$). Again shaded area M is assumed to be captured as a rent because a tariff is presumably not levied on imports from developing countries.

A-quota holders earn a quota rent equal to ($P^Q cxy$), which is smaller than previously by shaded area A in Figure 8.9. C-quota holders receive a rent equal to ($sxvu$) (Figure 8.10), because they only receive the world price; as a group what these quota holders now receive is less than the quota rent they earned previously because the C-quota holders came out of the pool of previous B-quota holders. Area ($ysuw$) is collected by the authority or some intermediary, because sugar is sold at P^Q but C-quota holders only get P^W.

Finally, the EU quota regime in sugar ceased to exist after 2017. The quota restriction Q^R was removed and producers received deficiency payments to cover the lost quota rents. The only loss would be given by area D, because other lost quota rents were recovered by increases in quasi-rent (producer surplus); acceptance of this policy was simpler because the world price of sugar had also risen (partly as a result of new policies promoting ethanol), although subsequently prices fell by half or more. From a practical standpoint, sugar production then came under the EU's single farm (direct) payment scheme.

In terms of Figure 8.10, output expanded from Q^R to q^T, with domestic output expanding to q^{dom}. The quasi-rent accruing to EU producers under free trade (albeit with a TRQ remaining in place) is given by $(P^w k\delta)$. As long as triangle $(uv\delta)$ exceeds shaded area D, producers are better off than previously, although the authority loses $(ysuw)$; however, consumers gain this area along with shaded areas D and M in Figure 8.10, and a triangular area of consumer surplus because price falls to P^W and output expands to q^T.

8.1.6 Brexit

After 52% of British residents voted to leave the EU on June 23, 2016, British exit from the EU (Brexit) formally occurred on January 31, 2020. Since the United Kingdom was the second largest contributor to the EU budget, Brexit impacts the remaining 27 EU member states (EU-27), especially in terms of agricultural policy, as Britain was a net contributor to the CAP. In her 2002 book, *Statecraft*, former British Prime Minister Margaret Thatcher pointed out that Britain was never keen on a European project that required greater integration with increasing sovereignty shifted from London to Brussels. The UK was only interested in a free trade union, not a United States of Europe. Given Thatcher's observations, it should have come as no surprise that the British eventually left the European Union.

Although the UK and the EU agreed to negotiate a new relationship over a period of a year or perhaps more, the implications of Brexit are unlikely to be known for several years, or even decades. The immediate impact is on the Multiannual Financial Framework or budget of the 27 remaining countries. During the period 2014–2020, the MFF constituted 1.16% of EU-27 GDP, once spending on the European Defense Fund is taken into account. This is much higher than the proportion of GDP of the EU-28, indicating that the departure of the UK has major implications for EU spending. This is seen in the various MFF proposals put forward by the departing Finnish EU president in December 2019, the EU Commission, the European Council, and the European Parliament—all summarized in Table 8.7. Clearly, Brexit imposes higher costs on the remaining countries of the EU as Britain had been a net contributor to the European project.

The implications for the agricultural sectors of both jurisdictions are also unknown and one can only guess at what these might be. For one thing, recall that British entry to the EU was delayed by France's concern about losing its share of Germany's agricultural market. Hence, Brexit is likely to increase French access to German agricultural markets, at least relative to that of Britain. To determine the potential impact on agriculture, agricultural economists in Europe have investigated two potential trade scenarios:

1. UK and EU-27 enter into a free trade agreement (FTA) that does not grant the UK the same access as a single market. No tariffs are applied on bilateral trade, but border arrangements to identify country-of-origin, for example, will be required and this will increase transaction costs. The UK would also accord most-favored-nation status to extra-EU nations (e.g., Norway, Iceland) included under the EU's Common Custom Tariff.

Table 8.7 MFF proposals and implications for the CAP budget, EU-27, 2021–2027 (constant 2018 euros, € billions)[a]

Item	2014–2020	EU Commission	Finnish Presidency	European Council	EU Parliament
MFF[b]	1,082	1,135	1,087	1,095	1,324
	(1.16%)	(1.11%)	(1.07%)	(1.074%)	(1.30%)
Agriculture (total)	383	324	334	329	383
EAGF (pillar 1)	286	254	254	257	
EAFRD (pillar 2)	96	70	80	73	
CAP share	35.4%	28.6%	30.7%	30.1%	28.9%
Cohesion[c]	368	331	323	323	378
Cohesion share	34.0%	29.1%	29.7%	29.5%	28.6%
Resources & environment	400	337	347	354	405

[a] Except for the EU Parliament's proposal, amounts include contribution to the European Defense Fund.
[b] Percent of EU-27 GDP provided in parentheses.
[c] Cohesion refers to spending categories that are meant to facilitate greater integration—creation of EU institutions that supersede country-level institutions.
Source: Alan Matthews, President Michel's solution to the MFF conundrum, February 15, 2020, at www.capreform.eu.

2. The default WTO position, whereby UK and EU-27 trade on most-favored-nation terms, as well as with extra-EU nations. However, the EU's import concessions under tariff rate quotas no longer apply so that less is imported and UK prices for those products increase.

As a member, the UK contributed about €7.9 billion to the CAP budget, whereas its farmers received only €3.8 billion. Thus, Brexit could reduce the UK's expenditure on agriculture from between €4.1 billion to €7.3 billion, depending on the extent to which Britain would continue to subsidize farmers. Given that the UK sought to reform the CAP by reducing direct payments to farmers under pillar 1, the UK will likely reduce payments to its farmers. Regarding pillar 2 (rural development), Britain already has well-established policies related to rural development, provision of public goods on agricultural lands, and animal welfare.

An indication of the importance of agricultural trade between the EU-27 and the UK is provided in Table 8.8. The UK's agricultural trade with the EU is less important than agricultural trade with countries outside the EU; 69.8% of the UK's exports go to countries other than the EU-27 and 65.0% of imports come from outside the EU. The Netherlands, Ireland, Germany, France, and Spain are the major suppliers of agricultural commodities to the UK and could be harmed the most by Brexit, although little is known about the effects that Brexit might have on bilateral trade between the UK and individual EU states.

Studies suggest that the impacts on EU-27 countries are likely to be small and may not all be negative; the same is true with respect to the UK. As an illustration, projections of the changes in UK production and prices are provided in Table 8.9 under the two scenarios identified above. Changes in the EU-27 are expected to be smaller due to the difference in size between the UK and EU-27 and because much of the UK agricultural trade is with countries outside the EU. The impact on farmers' incomes depends as much on decisions regarding domestic agricultural policy (e.g., level of direct payments) as it does on the future trade relationship between the UK and the EU-27. For example, Dutch agricultural economists estimated that horticultural, poultry, and hog producers are likely beneficiaries overall, while grain producers will lose or gain depending on final negotiations and UK domestic agricultural policy.

Table 8.8 UK agricultural exports and imports by category, 2016 (% of total)

Item	UK exports to			UK imports from		
	Intra-EU	Extra-EU	World	Intra-EU	Extra-EU	World
Propagation materials	3	2	2	3	1	2
Unprocessed products	10	7	8	8	8	8
Semi-processed products	28	21	25	22	30	24
Final products, not fresh	58	70	63	55	38	50
Final products, fresh	2	1	2	12	23	15
Total (€ billions)	**€16.5**	**€10.8**	**€27.3**	**€42.2**	**€18.1**	**€60.3**

Source: van Berkum et al. (2018)

Table 8.9 Estimated changes in UK prices and production under Free Trade Agreement and Default WTO scenarios, % change in 2025 relative to 2016 baseline

Agricultural product	Free Trade Agreement		Default WTO	
	Price change (%)	Production change (%)	Price change (%)	Production change (%)
Wheat	4	2	25	10
Barley	-5	-3	-4	-19
Sugar beet	5	2	8	1
Tomato	3	0	6	0
Beef	5	-1	46	12
Pig meat	5	1	27	6
Poultry	5	2	11	8
Milk	4	1	26	11
Butter	5	0	74	20
Cheese	5	0	15	-9
Skimmed milk powder	5	17	24	426
Whole milk powder	6	15	49	464

Source: van Berkum et al. (2018)

Another source of aggravation for the UK relates to the fishery. Britain's Exclusive Economic Zone—its 200-nautical mile limit—accounted for 80% of the EU-28's fishing territory. As a member of the EU, the UK found that Brussels and not London set the rules for exploiting the fishery. As a result, Spanish fishermen displaced British ones. Control of the fishery will revert back to the British government as a result of Brexit.

It is important to recognize that the British decision to leave the EU related primarily to its opposition to increasing European integration and accompanying loss of sovereignty. The Brexit decision was not mainly because of dissatisfaction with the CAP per se, despite the fact that the UK was a net contributor to the CAP.

8.2 Agriculture in Developing Countries

In the past, developing countries have tended to tax rather than support their agricultural sectors. Because the farm sector in many developing countries is the most important and often largest sector of the economy, governments in developing countries sought to capture any economic surplus the sector might generate to fund other programs, including the subsidization of food imports to keep food prices low and prevent unrest in rapidly increasing urban centers (as argued in Chapter 6.2 in conjunction with price stabilization and stockholding). Congruently, in many developing countries, land is publicly owned with the tenant not assured of retaining the benefits of any land improvements. Tenancy practices and attempts by government to capture economic surplus (often leading to the capture of quasi-rent needed to pay back investments in fixed assets) led to less than socially optimal use of inputs such as fertilizers, pesticides, and herbicides. Further, lack of infrastructure reduced the availability of many inputs associated with the green revolution (discussed in Chapter 1); lack of transportation infrastructure also impeded the marketing of crops, especially those for export, thereby lowering the prices farmers received. As a result, crop yields lagged those in rich countries, while local concerns about food security increased.

Once government policies were no longer an obstacle to agricultural production, or where policies incentivized production rather than inhibiting it, agricultural output expanded rapidly. This is what happened in China and Brazil, and is beginning to happen in India and other countries. Evidence of this is provided in Figures 8.11 and 8.12. In these figures, we provide five-year moving averages of yields for rice and maize (Figure 8.11) and wheat and soybean (Figure 8.12) for the period 1965–2018. In addition to the three countries mentioned, we include the European Union, landlocked developing countries, and the least developed countries (LDCs)—the poorest countries in the world, most of which are found in sub-Sahara Africa and some regions of central Asia. Of course, not all areas are suitable for achieving high yields of these four crops, although these countries/regions grew these four crops in each of the years indicated.

The important takeaway is that the green revolution has significantly increased the yields of all four crops over the past half century, although other factors (e.g., opening of markets, infrastructure investment, etc.) have also played a role. Maize and wheat yields in China increased fivefold; yields of wheat, rice, and soybean increased by threefold or more in Brazil; maize and wheat yields approximately tripled in Europe; yields of all four crops doubled or more in India and other developing nations, with some exceptions. Further, with the exception of soybean in China and wheat in Brazil, yields in those countries are rapidly converging on those in the developed countries (represented here by the EU). Although lagging behind, crop yields in India are also rising and, with the exception of soybean, can be expected to catch up in the next decade or so. According to the UN's Food and Agriculture Organization (FAO), global cereal production reached a record in 2019 of just over 2,700 million tonnes, but was projected to be even higher in 2020 at 2,790 million tonnes (3% more).[5]

---

[5] Predictions of grain production for 2020 can be found at Grain Central, July 7, 2020, Record Global Cereal Production to Boost Stocks: FAO, https://www.graincentral.com/news/record-global-cereal-production-to-boost-stocks-fao/ [accessed July 14, 2020], and from FAO, July 2, 2020, FAO Cereal Supply and Demand Brief, http://www.fao.org/worldfoodsituation/csdb/en/ [accessed July 17, 2020].

Figure 8.11 Five-year moving average of crop yields for rice and maize, 1965–2018

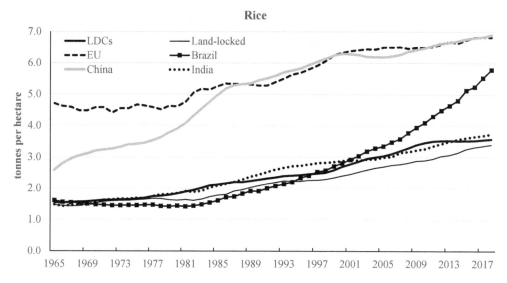

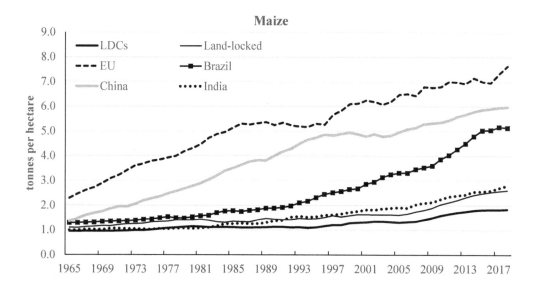

Source: FAO (http://www.fao.org/faostat/en/#data/ [accessed March 2, 2020])

Figure 8.12 Five-year moving average of crop yields for wheat and soybean, 1965–2018

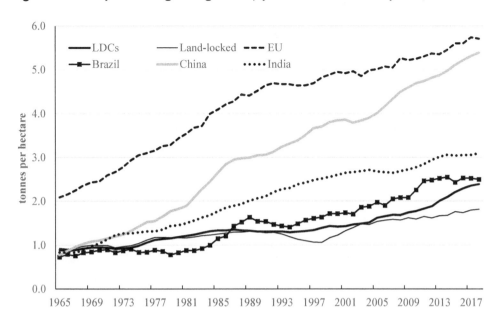

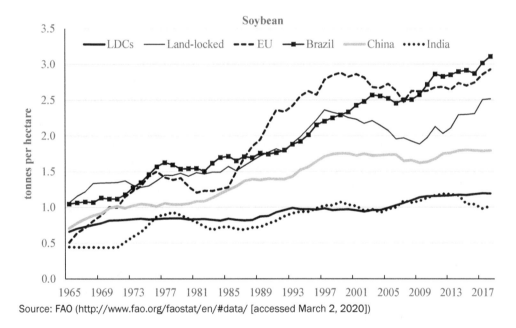

Source: FAO (http://www.fao.org/faostat/en/#data/ [accessed March 2, 2020])

In the remainder of this section, we examine agriculture in China and India, which are the most populous countries in the world by a large margin. At the end of 2019, China had a population of 1.43 billion compared to 1.37 billion in India, although India's population is forecast to surpass that of China by 2024. The third most populous nation is the United States with a population of 330 million, whereas the EU-27 has a population of 445 million (and the UK, 67 million). In the latter half of the twentieth century, food security was a greater issue in China and India than elsewhere. Yet, they are examples of developing countries that have gone from being unable to feed themselves to ones that are leading exporters in some agricultural commodities.

8.2.1 Economy-wide Economic Reform and Chinese Agriculture

By privatizing agricultural production and allowing peasant farmers to compete on global markets beginning in 1978, China went from being a net importer to a net exporter of agricultural commodities at the beginning of the millennium (see Table 1.1). China joined the WTO in 2001 and, for most years thereafter, was a net exporter of grains, primarily maize.

As part of the WTO accession agreement, China was able to implement tariff rate quotas on rice, wheat, maize, cotton, and sugar (as well as many non-agricultural commodities). For rice, wheat, and maize, the agreement called for a tariff of 1% on below-quota imports (although it was 10% on maize) and 65% on above-quota imports; for cotton, 1% was applied to below-quota imports and 40% on imports above TRQ, although China subsequently imposed a sliding scale from 0% to 40% on imports above the cotton TRQ. TRQs for wheat, maize, and rice were set in 2004, respectively, at 9.6 Mt, 7.2 Mt, and 5.3 Mt (half this amount for each of long grain and short/medium grain rice).China began to implement price supports in the 1990s to increase farmers' incomes and ensure food security (see Figure 8.2), because self-sufficiency was a high-level government priority. A minimum purchase price was implemented for rice in 2004 and wheat in 2006, with prices initially set below the world price. If the market price fell below the minimum price, farmers could sell their product to the government. A temporary reserve program was created for maize, soybean, rapeseed, pork, and sugarcane in 2008, and cotton in 2011, and these also guaranteed producers a minimum price. Minimum prices were then allowed to increase in order to protect farmers from rising input prices due in large part to an appreciating yuan; support prices increased annually through 2015, despite a decline in international prices in 2008; and domestic production of wheat, maize, and rice grew by 16%, 35%, and 8%, respectively (Figures 8.11 and 8.12). Imports of grains also increased as the gap between the Chinese domestic price and world price increased, and stocks of grain held by the government began to increase exorbitantly.

By the end of 2015, the Chinese government held stocks of some 63 Mt of rice, 97 Mt of wheat, 113 Mt of maize, and 12.5 Mt of cotton (with cotton holdings nearly double domestic consumption). Meanwhile, China's domestic-to-world market price ratios for the most common grains were at or exceeded 2.0 (double): rice (2.23), wheat (2.00), maize (2.24), and soybean (2.54). Support prices in China for rapeseed exceeded $800/t, soybean more than $750/t, rice more than $450/t, and wheat and maize approached $400/t in 2015. Finally, given high grain prices, low tariffs were used to incentivize livestock producers' purchases of cheap feed grains from abroad; as a result, soybean imports increased from 28.3 Mt in 2005 to 82.4 Mt in 2015, while imports of sorghum, barley, and distillers' dried grain with solubles also expanded.

In addition to price support, direct forms of support for agricultural producers began in 2004 with a payment of ¥10–¥15 per mu for planting grain.[6] Annual expenditures for this program remained relatively stable during the mid-2010s at ¥15.1 billion ($2.22 billion). The Chinese government also subsidized agricultural inputs such as fuel, fertilizer, and chemicals, to the tune of ¥107.1 billion ($15.75 billion) in 2014. A third subsidy program targeted seed improvements, and it cost ¥21.4 billion ($3.15 billion) in 2014. A final program provided a 30% subsidy on machinery purchases and amounted to ¥21.8 billion ($3.21 billion) in 2014. Total agricultural direct support payments from these programs alone amounted to about $24 billion in 2014, which was about double their level in 2008, although they now appear to have stabilized.

Overall, agricultural policies led to the doubling of grain production between 1978 and 2013, but at the cost of the environment. The application of fertilizer increased sevenfold during the same period, so that in 2013, China's average fertilizer use was three times the global average.

By 2015, the pressures created by rising government stocks under China's price support programs prompted policy reform. China began to abandon price supports and temporary reserves, except in rice and wheat. In trial projects in several provinces, target prices were introduced with farmers receiving the difference between the target price and the market price as a deficiency payment, as opposed to delivering grain to the government. At the same time, target prices were lowered. By lowering support prices, there has been a shift to other crops, which then enabled the government to dispose of some surpluses. An exception was soybean, where the target price was raised slightly to incentivize greater production meant to offset imports, although this appears not to have succeeded.

All in all, China is looking to reform its agricultural programs so that it can maintain farmers' incomes, reduce excess stocks of grain, improve the quality of agricultural land (e.g., reduce fertilizer use, prevent cropping on marginal land), and retain sufficient production to satisfy the objective of self-sufficiency. Decoupling agricultural support through direct deficiency payments, cross compliance, and set asides are avenues that will likely be explored. That is, China is likely to follow the US and the EU in terms of programs that could achieve its objectives related to agriculture. Another possibility is for the Chinese government to focus more on agricultural risk management programs such as crop insurance. The roads taken by the US and Canada in this regard are examined in the next chapter.

8.2.2 India and the Rice Economy

The most important crop grown in India is rice, with the country accounting for nearly one-third of global production. Rice is planted wherever there is sufficient rainfall. Nearly 60% of total Indian rice production occurs in five states in the north and northeast: Uttar Pradesh (15%), West Bengal (14%), Andhra Pradesh

---

[6] The mu is an area unit of measurement, with 15 mu = 1 hectare (ha) = 2.47 acres (ac). In June 2017, the Chinese yuan–US dollar exchange rate was US$1 = ¥0.1471. Thus, the subsidy amounted to $22.07–$33.10/ha ($8.93–$13.40/ac). Figure 8.2 illustrates this upward trend in Chinese support for agricultural commodities (see also Table 7.2).

(11%), Punjab (10%), and Orissa (10%). In Punjab (located in the northwest) and western Uttar Pradesh, temperatures are low in winter and rice is grown as a single crop in the May–July to September–October growing season. In the south, irrigation is used to grow rice. In the eastern provinces, on the other hand, rice production depends on the monsoons. In these rice-growing regions, farmers will harvest wheat or some other dryland crop in October and plant rice prior to the start of the monsoon season sometime in November.

Government intervention and storage of rice began in the 1960s in response to market failure caused by grain companies acting as monopsonists, and to encourage greater production to feed a large and growing population. Because small-scale farmers had no means of storing grain once it was harvested, private companies would delay purchases of grain until into the monsoon season knowing that farmers would be desperate to harvest and sell before then, thereby forcing them to sell at a low price. In response to both food security needs and market failure, the government created the Food Corporation of India (FCI) in 1964 under the Food Corporation Act. Its purpose was threefold:

1. to provide effective price support to safeguard the interests of farmers;
2. to distribute food grains throughout the country (public distribution); and
3. to maintain a satisfactory level of grain stocks to ensure the country's food security.

The FCI subsequently played a significant role in India's success in achieving self-sufficiency while also addressing starvation and malnutrition. Its vision was to ensure food security for the country's citizens through procurement of grain at a minimum support price (MSP), and storage and distribution of grain and sugar. The FCI built storage facilities and other necessary infrastructure throughout the country and, by offering to purchase grain at the government-determined MSP, broke the monopsony of the private grain traders. Further, as a policy to address poverty, the government would sell grain cheaply (i.e., well below the MSP) to individuals in the lowest 15% of the income distribution—those in abject poverty; for example, poor people would be able to purchase 20 kg of rice each month at a nominal price. Thus, stocks are held to meet monthly distribution requirements (operational stocks) and to ensure food security (strategic stocks).

As noted in Chapter 1, India is the second largest producer of rice and wheat in the world, and an exporter of these commodities when supply and demand plus stock conditions warrant. Indeed, the FCI has been so successful that, according to the FAO, India has been a net exporter of rice in every year since 1975, with the exception of 1984, 1988, and 1989; net exports have averaged 5.75 Mt per year since 2000. It is clear that India is now able to feed its large population.

It is unclear how the FCI operates its support price and stockholding scheme in practice, although the foregoing discussion indicates that it employs a combination of physical storage and international market transactions. Further, rather than the annual market periods used in previous analyses (e.g., Chapter 6.2), the period used in India's rice economy is likely biannual. A stylized model of the rice policy is provided in Figures 8.13 and 8.14, respectively representing an export position and an import situation. As noted, the export case is more prevalent.

Figure 8.13 Indian price support and storage program: Case of exports

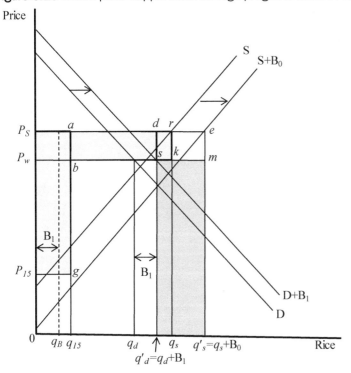

In the figures, S and D represent domestic supply and demand, respectively. In each period, the FCI determines the physical amount of rice that it needs to store until the next harvest of rice becomes available; this is denoted B_1, indicating that it is the current period. This is the stock that the FCI needs to maintain for operational and strategic purposes. The demand for B_1 is added to domestic demand so the effective domestic demand is given by $D+B_1$. Domestic supply is uncertain as is the buffer stock left over from the previous period, which we denote as B_0; this is added to the domestic supply so that the total supply function is $S+B_0$. Finally, P_S represents the support price MSP, P_W is the world price at which the FCI is assumed to sell rice to domestic consumers, and P_{15} is taken to be the price that the poorest 15% of the population has to pay for q_{15} amount of rice. Given that rice is harvested at various times, the model might not necessarily be annual.

Figure 8.14 Indian price support and storage program: Case of imports

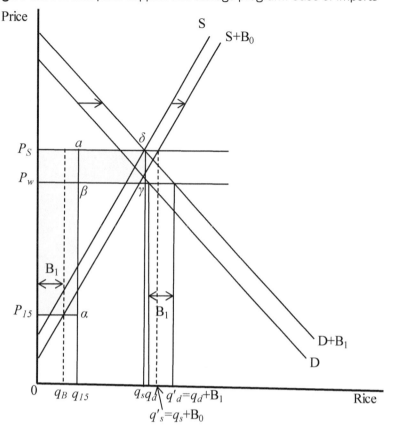

The price support, buffer stock program works as follows. The FCI sets the support price at P_S, so farmers produce q_S amount of rice. The price that domestic consumers pay is set at the world price P_W, although the price paid by the poorest 15% of society is set at P_{15} with q_{15} distributed at that price. The physical buffer stock required by the authority during the period represented by Figure 8.13 is arbitrarily set at B_1, and in this analysis happens to be less than q_{15}, but it could just as easily have been greater. Given that remaining citizens must pay P_W, an amount q_d (which includes q_{15}) is consumed domestically; to this must be added the buffer stock requirement B_1. The demand q'_d $(=q_d+B_1)$ must be met from domestic supply q_s plus any stock left over from the previous period, or q'_s $(=q_s+B_0)$. This results in an excess given by $q'_s-q'_d$ that is then exported at the world price P_W, which requires an export subsidy identified below.

The overall cost to the Indian treasury is given by the light-shaded area $(P_SP_{15}gbkr)$ minus the dark-shaded area $(sq'_dq'_sm)$, which constitutes export earnings. The light-shaded area is composed of $(P_SP_{15}ga)$, which is the cost of the subsidy to the poorest 15% in society, the subsidy to other domestic consumers given by $(absd)$, and the small rectangle $(dskr)$ that constitutes the export subsidy because domestic production in this period, q_s, exceeds domestic requirements in this period, q'_d. The amount B_0 is the stock remaining from the previous period, which equals the stock purchased by the FCI in the previous period minus stock released during that period for whatever reason (e.g., unanticipated extra demand). Importantly, the subsidy required to provide B_0 has already been incurred and does not need to be taken into account in the current period (except for the cost of storage and administration not shown in the figure). Thus, along with excess production, the stock held over from the previous period is sold at the world price earning revenue given by the dark-shaded area ($sq'_dq'_sm$), which is set against the subsidies required in the current period.[7]

Because supply is uncertain, there may be instances where inadequate supply and a drain on stocks in storage results in insufficient supply to meet demand requirements in a given period. This is illustrated in Figure 8.14. In this case, B_0 is less than in the previous figure and domestic supply in the current period is lower than previously. Assuming the support price, world price, and the FCI's demand for rice to store remain unchanged from that in Figure 8.13, India goes from being an exporter to an importer. In this case, $q'_s - q'_d < 0$ so that the country must import the amount $q'_d - q'_s$. Again the overall cost to the treasury is given by the light-shaded area ($P_S P_{15} \alpha \beta \gamma \delta$), which consists of the subsidy ($P_S P_W \gamma \delta$) that pays producers for the difference between the support price and the world price at which the rice is sold domestically, plus a subsidy ($P_W P_{15} \alpha \beta$) to address poverty.

In the analysis above, it was assumed that the FCI accepted the world price of rice as the domestic price. If the domestic price was set higher, the size of the required subsidies would be lower. Conversely, and perhaps more realistically, the FCI would set the price in India somewhat lower than the world price. Then the subsidy required would be higher by the difference between the world price and the domestic price multiplied by domestic consumption. In the case of Figure 8.14, this would imply a subsidy to purchase imports.

Finally, India also took the path toward crop insurance as a means of providing aid to farmers. The Agricultural Insurance Corporation of India was established in 2002 under the administrative control of the Ministry of Finance with operational supervision under the Ministry of Agriculture. The corporation offers crop yield and weather-indexed insurance products to farmers located in some 500 districts. The objective is to protect farmers against all sorts of natural perils, including droughts, hail, landslides, pests, disease, and so forth. These types of insurance products are examined in more detail in Chapter 9. The point of the insurance program is to support farm incomes and enable agricultural producers to recover from a disastrous crop year and continue farming.

Guide to Literature

An excellent source for background information on the EU, including agricultural policy, is provided by Brunet-Jailly, Hurrelmann, and Verdun (2018), while Thatcher (2002, pp. 360–411) makes the case why the UK should not be an EU member state. Alan Matthews's blog site, "CAPreform.eu," provides up-to-

---

[7] Clearly, the cost to the treasury could be quite high in one year and negative in another, depending in large measure on the world price. This is exactly what the OECD's PSE data indicate.

date information on the CAP (see also Matthews 2018). Information about Brexit comes from Jongeneel, Polman, and van Kooten (2016) and van Berkum et al. (2018).

For China's agricultural policy, see Yu (2017), Hejazi and Marchant (2017), and the special issue of *Choices* (2nd quarter 2017) devoted to the impact of Chinese agricultural policies on the US. For information on global rice production and India in particular, see Chauhan, Jabran, and Mahajan (2017). Information on the Food Corporation of India can be found at http://fci.gov.in/aboutUs.php, while information on the Agricultural Insurance Corporation of India is found at https://www.india.gov.in/official-website-agriculture-insurance-company-india-limited [both accessed July 17, 2020].

Food for Thought

8.1. In Figure 8.8, identify the gains and losses to producers and the gains to consumers in each of countries A and B as a result of the elimination of the EU's dairy quota.

8.2. Provide a brief explanation of each of the following (use illustrative diagrams where needed):
(a) modulation between pillars
(b) single farm payment

8.3. Suppose the following respective demand and supply functions:

$P^d = 500 - 0.1\ q$ and $\qquad P^s = 0.05\ q \qquad$ quantity measured in tonnes and price in \$/tonne

(a) What is the equilibrium price and demand? What are the associated producer and consumer surpluses? Build a model in Excel to draw the supply and demand functions and calculate the market clearing price and quantity, and the associated welfare areas.

(b) Suppose there is only a support price (target price) set at \$210/t. How much will farmers produce? Assume no trade and that the market must clear. How much will consumers have to pay? What are the producer and consumer surpluses in this case? What is the cost to the government (the deficiency payment)? What is the deadweight loss?

(c) In the US, a farmer can sell her crops to the Commodity Credit Corporation (CCC) at the loan rate, which is set in advance of the growing season. The farmer takes out a loan and delivers the crop at harvest to repay the loan. If the loan rate exceeds the market price, the farmer will sell the crop to the CCC; if the market price exceeds the loan rate, she will sell the crop in the market and use the proceeds to pay back the loan from the CCC. Introduce a loan rate of \$200/t. How much will farmers produce at the loan rate? What will consumers pay? What are the producer and consumer surpluses, and the deadweight loss? What is the cost to the CCC?

(d) Now impose the target price over and above the loan rate. Assume two cases: (1) where producers make a decision using only the loan rate and (2) where producers make a decision using the target price. For each, calculate:
   (i) What is produced? What is the associated market clearing price?
   (ii) What are the producer and consumer surpluses?
   (iii) What is the CCC payment? What is the deficiency payment?

8.4. Using Figure 8.10, show the changes in welfare accruing to both producers and consumers in going from a quota system to no quota. Discuss the role of the TRQ in the analysis.

8.5. As a result of the 2003 Mid-Term Review (Fischler Reform) of the Common Agricultural Policy, the European Union sought to decouple agricultural output from income support. It began by using a single payment scheme (SPS) that was implemented over the period 2005–2007.

(a) Explain how the single payment scheme works and how it decouples production from support payments.

(b) What was one of the problems with the single payment scheme?

(c) Then, beginning in 2015, the SPS was replaced by a single farm payment (SFP)—the European equivalent of whole farm insurance. How does the SFP differ from the SPS?

(d) How does the single farm payment address the issue of decoupling?

8.6. Consider the evolution of the agricultural policy in the European Union. What are the salient features of agriculture and the unique context in which policy is made in the EU? Historically, what were the primary policy instruments and how have the instruments changed over time? What are the European policies that have the most effect on Western Canada? What pressures are causing change in European farm policy? How is European agriculture policy becoming more like producer support in the United States?

9

AGRICULTURAL BUSINESS RISK MANAGEMENT

More than in any other sector, agricultural producers face sources of risk and uncertainty that threaten their livelihoods and the incomes of those working in the input supply, transportation, and downstream processing sectors. Ultimately, agricultural risk and uncertainty can affect a country's balance of trade. Farmers must manage the risk associated with price variability (prices at planting time differ from those at harvest), commodity storage, adverse weather, potential catastrophe (e.g., floods, drought, disease), issues related to herbicide and pesticide use (e.g., optimal timing and frequency of applications, bans on chemicals such as on neonicotinoids and glyphosate), and uncertainty related to trade negotiations and changes in government policies. Therefore, business risk management (BRM) programs are an important and increasing component of most countries' agricultural policies. In Canada, for example, federal expenditures on BRM for 2020–2021 are budgeted to be $1,506.7 million, or 60.8% of Agriculture and Agri-Food Canada's (AAFC) planned total outlays of $2,477.7 million.

Rather than maximizing farmers' expected net revenue (max ER) in any given year, economists tend to model farmers' behavior as maximizing the expected utility of revenue (max EU). The difference between these ways of viewing farmers' behavior is illustrated by the following relation: max EU = max [ER $- \phi$ $Var(R)$], where ϕ is the coefficient of risk aversion and $Var(R)$ is the variance of returns. The risk aversion coefficient represents a farmer's preference or trade-off between higher expected net returns and the riskiness of those returns. This trade-off can have an important impact on the agricultural producer's decisions regarding the mix of crops to plant, whether to have livestock and how they should be managed, and so on. This is discussed further in the appendix to this chapter.

In previous chapters, we studied the distorting effects of agricultural price support programs on output, economic efficiency, and world trade. Agricultural programs have been an obstacle in trade negotiations, although, with the 1995 Agreement on Agriculture, countries began to dismantle many price support programs while instead focusing on crop insurance and other programs that protect farmers against production and price risk. This was done despite the availability of private crop insurance programs that protect against reduced yields, futures markets, and forward contracts that farmers could use to protect against price risk. For example, a wheat producer could, at planting time, purchase a futures contract on the Chicago Mercantile Exchange (CME) or ICE Futures Canada (ICE) that would guarantee the price of wheat at harvest time. Producers could purchase an over-the-counter (OTC) financial product that would protect against production risk, including crop yield insurance or a weather-indexed insurance product from a financial intermediary. These financial instruments are described in the next section. But few farmers employ such hedges or rely on forward contracts with large companies, such as Cargill, which in turn would protect itself using futures contracts to cover contracts with farmers.

Governments are typically involved in crop insurance programs. Some argue that there is a public role in crop insurance largely because contingent markets are incomplete or there exist information asymmetries, principally *adverse selection* (where farmers who are less likely to make claims fail to participate, thereby raising premiums) and *moral hazard* (where participants in crop insurance fail to take steps to reduce their exposure to risk). Governments can reduce adverse selection by, in some way, coercing farmers to participate in insurance (e.g., making participation mandatory for receiving benefits under other programs), which is a tactic not available to private providers of insurance. Mitigating moral hazard is more difficult, although index insurance (discussed in the next section) solves both problems related to moral hazard and adverse selection. However, even where crop insurance is subsidized, uptake has historically been low because farmers can often self-insure. For example, farmers in developed and even developing countries often rely on off-farm income to protect against losses in farm incomes.

Agricultural producers can protect themselves against many risks using futures markets, forward contracts, crop insurance, and so on, but, as we see in this chapter, they are often unwilling to participate in risk reducing programs without subsidies. Thus, some economists have argued that BRM programs are designed by and benefit farmers, especially the largest producers, at the expense of general taxpayers.

In this chapter, we examine agricultural BRM policies implemented by government to protect farmers against losses in income due to adverse weather, flooding, drought, pests, and, particularly in the livestock sector, disease. In this regard, it helps to distinguish three types of income loss. (1) Shallow losses occur when the reduction in realized income in a given year falls below expected income, but the farmer is still able to earn enough to cover some fixed costs. This usually implies that gross margins (returns minus most variable costs but not fixed costs or interest payments) fall below the expected gross margin by about 25% to 30%—some producer surplus is still earned. (2) Deep losses occur when revenues fall below the variable costs of production (e.g., below the costs of seed, fertilizer, fuel, and herbicides and pesticides) so that the farmer cannot cover any fixed costs including, in some cases, their own labor costs. This occurs when gross margins fall below about 70% of the expected gross margin. In essence, at planting time the producer invests about 70% of the expected future revenue into growing a new crop, including expenses incurred during the growing season (e.g., applying chemicals to control a pest invasion). (3) Finally, catastrophic losses occur when it is not even profitable to harvest a crop because yields are exceptionally low due to flood or drought, or livestock are destroyed because they have been affected by disease. Designing policies to protect agricultural producers from such risks is challenging. One issue of particular interest to the economist relates to the following: Is government intervention to protect farmers against production and price risks welfare improving, or does it lead to reduced well-being?

We focus on business risk management programs in the US and Canada, which rely heavily on such programs as opposed to the EU and China, which are only considering their potential as a means for reforming current support programs. For 75 years following the Depression-era farm legislation, US policy continued to emphasize alleviation of poverty, soil conservation, protection against disaster, and the availability of credit. It was not until 2007 that BRM became a major if not the main pillar of US farm policy—the US government paid out $7 billion in premium subsidies for standard crop insurance in that year, and the 2008 Farm Bill emphasized a shift towards agricultural BRM programs. Likewise, by the beginning of the new millennium, Canada had abandoned subsidy programs, such as Western Grain Stabilization and the ad hoc Special Grains Payment, which had been a response to the US–EU agricultural subsidy war. Transportation subsidies such as feed freight assistance and the Crow subsidy had been abandoned, and single-desk selling of Western grain was done away with in 2012 when the Canadian Wheat Board was privatized. The emphasis of government programs fell primarily on BRM. The EU with its single farm payment has also begun to walk down a similar path, with crop insurance increasingly considered as a mechanism for supporting farmers. China might follow a similar policy trajectory in the future.

9.1 Privatizing Agricultural Hedges: Financial Products versus Insurance

Governments are typically involved in crop insurance, relying solely on public provision (Canada) or more eclectic public–private partnerships (US). Government involvement is needed because contingent markets are incomplete or there exist information asymmetries. One argument for government involvement is that, since insurance companies do not on their own offer multi-peril crop insurance, there must be market failure. However, just because something is not available in the marketplace is not sufficient grounds to argue that this is the result of market failure. Indeed, the evidence indicates that, even with government subsidies, uptake of crop insurance by farmers has been low.

Prior to the early 2000s, participation in US crop insurance was below 50% (see section 9.2), despite average indemnity (payout) to premium ratios that ranged from 1.06 to 2.42 depending on the crop. One argument for low participation rates went as follows: Farmers may avoid crop insurance because premiums are considered to be too high, although they are actuarially sound from the perspective of the insurer. Even a risk-averse farmer might rely on a risky production plan to offset price and other sources of uncertainty, thereby reducing their willingness to pay for insurance. Nonetheless, low uptake despite generous government subsidies suggests that other factors also need to be considered.

Another argument used to advocate for public involvement in the provision of crop insurance is the presence of systemic risk. Insurance companies will not insure farmers against drought, flood, and other risks because, when one farmer in a region is affected by an adverse outcome (e.g., drought), all farmers are impacted. An insurance company may not be able to withstand such large losses. This argument fails to understand that insurance companies hedge against this eventuality through reinsurance, purchasing insurance against such an eventuality from reinsurance companies that are sufficiently large so that agricultural risks constitute a very small component of their overall portfolio.

There are only two explanations for public provision of crop insurance and other risk management tools. First, lobbying by agricultural producers, agricultural transportation and processing companies, and financial intermediaries has led to public involvement in the provision of BRM programs that benefit the agricultural sector. Second, there are efficiency arguments for public provision of crop insurance. These include the ability of the authority to reduce adverse selection (farmers least likely to make claims do not buy insurance) and moral hazard (farmers participating in insurance make no attempt to reduce risks) in ways that are not available to the private sector, but also in terms of the reduced costs related to administration and operation and to reinsurance. Indeed, reinsurance is unnecessary as government budgets are adequate to cover an adverse event affecting a large number of producers simultaneously. For example, recall that requiring all farmers to participate in an insurance program eliminates adverse selection, but at a cost to society.[1] But no crop insurance program can entirely eliminate the problem of moral hazard.

9.1.1 Index Insurance and Derivatives

Index-based insurance is considered a good alternative to crop (yield or revenue) insurance because individual loss characteristics of the producer cannot influence the underlying index—adverse selection and moral hazard no longer apply. Index insurance makes payouts (indemnities) based on an underlying index, such as precipitation or temperature, rather than on the actual loss experienced by the farmer. The several advantages over traditional insurance include: (1) lower transaction costs (e.g., no need for an insurance adjuster to determine the extent of crop loss); (2) fast and transparent settlement of claims; and (3) no adverse selection concerns and a reduced likelihood of moral hazard.

Basis risk is the main challenge in developing commercially viable index insurance. The main problem is that there is often a mismatch between the payout determined by the index and the actual loss on the farm leading to the following possibilities:

- Farmer receives a payout but experiences no loss.
- Farmer does not receive a payout but does experience a loss.

This mismatch is referred to as basis risk. There are three types of basis risk:

1. *Spatial*: the value of the underlying index and the outcome at the farm level differ, because the weather station and the farm are not at the same location.
2. *Temporal*: growing cycles of the crop are not fully considered by the index. For example, high levels of precipitation in the last weeks of the growing season might considerably reduce the value of a berry crop, although total precipitation for the season might be adequate.
3. *Variable*: the wrong variables are used to construct the insurance index.

---

[1] As discussed in section 9.3, requiring farmers to cover a portion and not the total of the deep losses incurred as a result of an adverse event militates against moral hazard. This is known as coinsurance; it encourages a producer to take actions to reduce exposure to risk.

Farmers cannot affect weather outcomes by their cropping decisions, so there exist opportunities for the private sector to provide weather-indexed insurance (or weather-indexed financial derivatives). Hail insurance is the best example as it is generally privately provided. Economists have recommended the use of weather-indexed insurance and financial derivatives in lieu of standard crop yield and revenue insurance. The private sector could provide such products because there is no problem with adverse selection and the problem of moral hazard is mitigated. However, uptake of weather-indexed insurance and use of weather-indexed financial derivatives, much like futures contracting, have not been broadly adopted in the agricultural sector.

Weather-indexed insurance differs from a financial weather derivative. With insurance the concern is to discover actuarially fair premiums, even if these might be subsidized by government or hollowed out by private-sector providers seeking higher profits or reduced exposure to risk. That is, providers of weather-indexed insurance need to determine a premium that would enable them to cover costs and earn a profit. With financial derivatives, there is no search for an actuarially fair premium; there is a speculator on the other side of the market and it is the speculator who willingly takes on some of the farmer's risk. It is up to the farmer to ensure that, given a particular price of the weather-indexed financial product, she is better off with the financial product than without it.

Weather-indexed insurance provides a payout to the farmer when adverse weather is likely to reduce yields. For example, if there are 14 consecutive days without rain during the growing season, or if the number of growing degree days (GDDs; days multiplied by degrees above 5°C)[2] falls below a pre-specified number, farmers might experience reduced yields. An indemnity would be paid to a farmer according to the performance of the weather index rather than on the basis of crop yield, crop revenue, or gross margin (yield × price — certain variable costs), which are influenced by the producer's choices regarding the application of fertilizer and other chemical input amounts, seed variety, and so on.

Financial weather products can be traded over-the-counter (OTC) or in existing markets. A farmer can contract with a financial intermediary to hedge against too little heat or rainfall on the basis of data from the nearest weather station, or on the basis of a weather monitoring station placed on the farm by a company providing this service.[3] This constitutes an OTC contract that blurs the line between privately provided weather insurance and a financial weather derivative. However, the farmer is exposed to credit risk because, if the financial intermediary has a significant number of contracts in a region hit by a drought or unusual cold spell, it may be unable to meet its obligations. To avoid this, the insurance company could in turn hedge its risk with a reinsurer, although this raises the cost of insurance—the premium the agricultural producer has to pay.

---

[2] Suppose the average daily temperatures in three consecutive days are 4°C, 8°C and 15°C. The number of growing degree days over this period are determined as $GDD = \sum Max\,(0, T_d - 5)$, where D refers to the number of days. Then, GDD = 0+3+10 = 13.

[3] Private insurance companies provide weather-based insurance in developing countries. They have found that, when insuring against drought or too little rainfall, farmers cover the gauge used to measure precipitation; however, the insurance providers have found ways to monitor whether this happens (e.g., using satellite data) and will penalize farmers who do this (personal communication, Achmea Insurance, Leiden, Netherlands, Fall 2017).

Cooling degree days (days multiplied by temperature above 18°C) and heating degree days (below 18°C) are financial products that already trade on the Chicago Mercantile Exchange. They are bought by companies seeking to reduce their exposure to weather-related risks (e.g., if it is too warm, an energy provider sees a reduction in revenue). Such financial weather derivatives can complement crop insurance, or take the place of weather-indexed insurance. Again, the advantage of both weather insurance and weather derivatives is that they reduce or eliminate problems of adverse selection and moral hazard, because neither the behavior of farmers nor participation rates can influence weather outcomes. The only drawback relates to basis risk— that the farmer requires a payout, but the outcome of the index suggests otherwise.

9.1.2 Futures Trading and Options

Agricultural risks can be mitigated to varying degrees through market instruments such as futures contracts and options (e.g., weather derivatives). However, a review of literature on financial derivatives for mitigating weather risk results in a variety of questions regarding the broader issue of agricultural risk and the role of government in mitigating such risks. With the exception of some commodity futures trading and even less use of OTC weather products, farmers appear more interested in crop yield and revenue insurance, and protection against catastrophic loss (e.g., a BSE outbreak in cattle), than they are in mitigating risks using existing financial products—the evidence suggests that farmers are not purchasing available financial instruments for optimally hedging risks. An exception is hail insurance. One reason why farmers fail to purchase such financial instruments is continued public subsidization of crop yield and revenue insurance premiums and the associated administrative and operating (A&O) costs (see section 9.2).

Agricultural producers can purchase financial derivatives through one of two markets. First, the *exchange-traded market* enables individuals to trade standardized contracts that have been defined by an exchange, such as cooling degree days on the Chicago Mercantile Exchange or ICE Futures Canada. Second, the farmer can purchase individualized contracts in an OTC market, which consists of a telephone- and computer-linked network of dealers.

Why do people purchase financial derivatives? The reasons vary but three types of traders can be identified. *Hedgers* use financial derivatives (such as options) to reduce the risk that they face from potential future movements in a particular market variable (crop prices, stock values) or even a physical variable (weather). *Speculators* use financial derivatives to bet on the future direction of a market or some financial variable such as stock prices. Finally, *arbitrageurs* take offsetting positions in two or more financial instruments to lock in a profit, and, at the same time, ensure that prices for financial products (sometimes identical products) in different markets do not diverge. For example, arbitrageurs make sure that the US$ to € exchange rate is the same in Frankfurt, Hong Kong, and New York by selling (buying) one currency in one market and buying (selling) it in another.

Forward Contracts

Forward contracts are traded in the OTC market and constitute an agreement to buy or sell an asset at a certain date in the future for a specified price. The forward contract is similar to a spot contract, which is an agreement to buy or sell an asset today rather than at some future date. There are two parties to the contract: One party assumes a *long* position, agreeing to buy the underlying asset on a certain specified future date for a certain specified price, while the other party assumes a *short* position, agreeing to sell the asset on the same date for the same price. For example, a farmer might enter into a forward contract with a large grain company, agreeing to sell a certain amount of grain at a pre-specified price; in turn, the large grain company might enter into a futures contract as a hedge against a drop in price (see below).

A long position obligates the holder of the contract to buy the asset and the payoff is given by $S_T - K$, where S_T is the spot price of the asset at the time of maturity, denoted T, and K is the delivery price, or what the holder of the long contract has to pay for the asset. For example, one party agrees to pay $K per tonne for one unit (1,000 tonnes) of wheat delivered at time T; then, at time T, that party can turn around and sell the unit of wheat (1,000 tonnes of wheat) at $$S_T$ per tonne. On the other side of the contract is the party who is obligated to sell the asset specified in the contract—this agent is in a short position. The payoff to the short position is given by $K - S_T$, which implies that, if the future spot price is greater than the delivery price, the holder of the short position loses; otherwise, the holder gains. It costs nothing to enter into a forward contract, except for an administration fee.

Futures Contracts

Unlike forward contracts, futures contracts are formally traded in an exchange market. A futures contract is an agreement between two parties to buy or sell an asset at a certain time in the future and for a certain price. The unique characteristic of a futures contract that distinguishes it from a forward contract is that it affords the buyer and seller the opportunity to avoid making or taking delivery.

Futures contracting has expanded in the past 50 years, with the number of markets, trading volumes, and types of commodities traded having increased rapidly since the 1970s. The volume on North American exchanges went from 30 million contracts in the early 1970s to nearly 600 million contracts in 2001, and 8.2 billion (not including options) in 2014, representing 36.8% of global futures trading, down from 80% in 1985 as futures contracting is now available in Europe, Asia, and elsewhere. Non-agricultural futures contracts went from 0 to 513 million between 1970 and 2001, and now dominate futures and options trading. The list of exchanges offering futures trading includes Amex, Chicago Board of Trade, Chicago Board Options Exchange, Kansas City Board of Trade, Chicago Mercantile Exchange, ICE Futures Canada, London International Financial Futures and Options Exchange, and Eurex (Zurich), and keeps growing. It now seems that almost anything can be traded: stock indexes, greasy wool, Eurodollars, Canadian dollars, wheat, lean hogs, pork bellies, individual stocks, oil, interest rates, and so on. And there are now categories of futures trading (examples of commodities given in parentheses):

- grains (wheat, corn, soybeans)
- livestock and meat (cattle, hogs, pork bellies)
- food and fiber (cocoa, coffee, sugar)
- metals and petroleum (oil, gold, platinum)
- interest rates (Treasury bonds, Treasury notes)
- indexes (S&P 500 index, DJIA, Nasdaq 100 index)
- currencies (yen, euro, Canadian $).

There are three benefits to futures trading. First, it enables agricultural producers to hedge the risks of planting a crop, say, by insuring the price at harvest time (hedging risk). Second, futures trading enhances price discovery. A commodity firm making a large sale to an overseas buyer can immediately turn around and hedge the sale on a futures market; this has the unexpected benefit that it can transfer information from those who have it to those who do not. Finally, it promotes storage and enhances efficiency. Prior to futures trading, there were wide swings in agricultural prices, but futures trading made storage profitable.

Option Contracts

In addition to futures contracts, options are also traded on both exchange and OTC markets. An option gives a participant in the options market the right to do something. Unlike with a forward or futures contract, the holder of an option contract does not have to exercise the contract; that is, with an option contract, the holder is not obligated to buy or sell the underlying asset as is the case with a forward or futures contract. However, there is a cost to acquiring an option, unlike with a forward or futures contract.

There are two types of options: a *call option* gives the holder of an option contract the right to buy the underlying asset by a certain date for a specified price, while a *put option* gives the holder the right to sell the underlying asset by a certain date for a certain price. The *strike price* is the price at which the contract is exercised, while the *expiration date* is the time at which the option is due, or its date of maturity. American option contracts can be exercised any time up to the expiration date, while European option contracts can only be exercised on the expiration date.

Option trading began in 1973 when call option contracts were created for 16 stocks on the Chicago Board Options Exchange. Put option contracts started trading on the board in 1977. For OTC options, financial institutions often act as market makers (defined below) for the more commonly traded instruments. However, there is one disadvantage to OTC trades in options, namely, potential credit risk—the contract is not honored. Conversely, market exchanges have organized themselves to eliminate virtually all credit risk.

There are two sides to every option contract: There is the investor who takes a *long position* (agrees to buy the option) and the investor who takes a *short position* (agrees to sell or underwrite the option). The payoffs from various option contracts are as follows:

1. long position with call option: $\max(S_T - K, 0)$, as the option is only exercised if $S_T > K$
2. short position with call option: $\max(K - S_T, 0)$
3. long position with put option: $\max(K - S_T, 0)$
4. short position with a put option: $\max(S_T - K, 0)$.

Notice the symmetry between a short position with a call option and a long position with a put option, and between a long position on a call option and a short position on a put option.

The advantage of index insurance, forward trading, futures markets, and options trading is efficiency. Index insurance provides farmers with some protection against production or yield risk, with only basis risk proving an obstacle to better protection. On the price side, in particular, producers can rely on forward contracts, futures trading, and options to hedge price risk. Given that farmers are also able to hedge against production and revenue risks in other ways, most notably through non-farm sources of income but also via farm management choices, these instruments might well be adequate for providing producers with overall protection against the risks they encounter. Nonetheless, governments have stepped in to subsidize this task. How they have done so is discussed for the United States and Canada.

9.2 Agricultural Business Risk Management in the United States

US agricultural business risk management programs began in 1938 when crop insurance was initially introduced, but the early program only applied to a handful of crops and few farmers participated. Modern multiple-peril crop insurance began in 1980, but it did not become a major mechanism for subsidizing agricultural producers until the mid-1990s. And it became prominent only because US legislators made a conscious decision to promote crop insurance rather than deficiency payments as the main pillar of support. Although deficiency-type payments remain (see Chapter 7.2), there are several components to the US suite of agricultural BRM programs. Traditional crop insurance is perhaps the most important program because it insures farmers against potentially deep losses. Other BRM programs enable the producer to hedge against shallow losses that provide some protection against small losses before traditional crop insurance kicks in.

9.2.1 Deep Loss Protection: The Federal Crop Insurance Program

The Federal Crop Insurance Act of 1980 introduced the modern era of crop insurance. Initially, the federal government delivered crop insurance, paying administrative and operating (A&O) costs, as well as the costs of underwriting risks. As a result, premiums were kept low. However, few crops were covered, although crop insurance was available on excluded crops through private insurance companies. But overall participation rates in crop insurance were low. The act mandated expansion of the crop insurance program both in terms of the area and the types of crops that could be covered. Importantly, under pressure from small financial companies selling crop insurance, the act mandated a shift to private delivery and provided for a 30% subsidy rate on premiums for crop yield insurance (see Figures 9.1 and 9.2). The federal government also covered the A&O costs that the private insurance companies incurred; private companies were paid an A&O rate of 33% of total premiums. Despite these subsidies, only 18% of eligible cropland was enrolled in crop insurance.

The 1994 Federal Crop Insurance Reform Act raised the subsidy rate on premiums to 40%, mandated further expansion of the crops and areas covered, and required a catastrophic loading factor of 13.4% on premiums, which increased the actuarially sound premium but was implemented to guarantee long-run underwriting gains. Because A&O payments had risen to $1.4 billion per year, Congress also lowered the A&O payment as a proportion of total premiums to 31%, and eventually to 27%. The 1994 act also mandated development of new crop insurance products, which allowed the Federal Crop Insurance Program to deploy crop revenue insurance in addition to crop yield insurance. This was an important development.

Figure 9.1 Crop insurance subsidy and indemnities (left axis) and subsidy rate (right axis), annual, 1989–2020

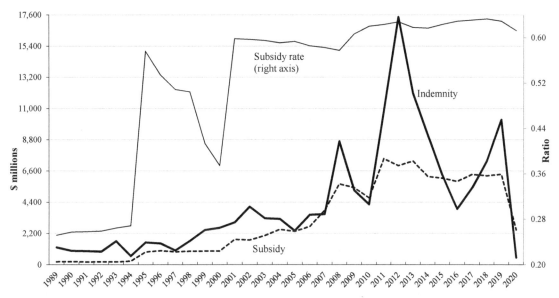

Source: US Department of Agriculture, Summary of Business Reports, https://www.rma.usda.gov/en/Information-Tools/Summary-of-Business [accessed December 4, 2020]

Figure 9.2 Net indemnities (payments) from US crop insurance programs (left axis) and ratio of crop insurance payments to total insurance premiums (right axis) (fiscal year for payments; calendar year for loss ratio), 1989–2020

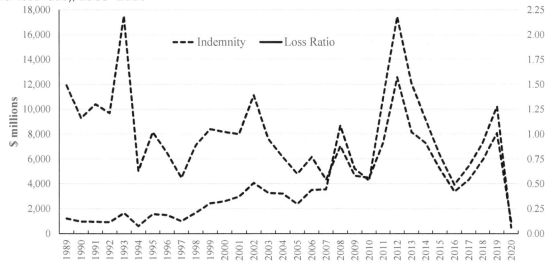

Source: Zulauf & Orden (2014, pp. 8, 12)

The 1994 legislation initially required farmers to participate in crop insurance to remain eligible for deficiency payments associated with other government support programs, but this requirement was removed a year later. In essence, the Federal Crop Insurance Reform Act led to a pronounced shift in government payments to agriculture away from deficiency-type support to crop insurance as the principal mechanism for delivering farm subsidies (Table 9.1).

Table 9.1 Spending by type of US crop program, 1961–2012, annual average based on fiscal year (FY)[a]

Period (FYs)	Total payments	Low price required	Yield or revenue decline required		
			Fixed payment	Disaster	Insurance
1961–1973	$1.7	100%	0%	0%	0%
1974–1995	$7.5	88%	0%	8%	4%
1996–2006	$14.5	49%	35%	7%	9%
2007–2012	$11.6	12%	39%	8%	41%

[a] Low price programs include non-recourse/marketing loans, deficiency payments/CCP, Payments-in-Kind, etc.; fixed payments are programs that employ a fixed unit rate multiplied by historical yields; disaster programs consist primarily of ad hoc disaster relief and Congress-mandated programs of disaster assistance; and insurance refers to indemnities paid to farmers for losses minus premiums they paid.
Source: Zulauf & Orden (2014, p. 4)

Not included in Table 9.1 are payments for conservation and environmental programs. Prior to 1985, such programs tended to be ad hoc because they were primarily designed to reduce output (viz., cross compliance measures and set asides). Since then, however, greater emphasis has been placed on conservation programs, so that the share of US spending on all crop programs increased from 12% in fiscal years 1961–1973 to 38% during the period 2007–2012.

The Agricultural Risk Protection Act of 2000 further increased the premium subsidy so that it averaged 62% (Figure 9.1). That act also increased A&O payments and extended the premium subsidy to take advantage of the Harvest Price Option, namely, the option to choose the higher of the spring planting price or the harvest price when purchasing crop revenue insurance. Although the 1994 act had introduced revenue insurance, the Harvest Price Option helped facilitate a massive shift out of yield insurance into revenue insurance—the proportion of eligible acres in the US covered by yield insurance fell from 93% in 1996 to only 15% in 2013.

In summary, the federal government's share of the premium was approximately 26% for the period 1990–1994, rose to 58% in 1995 but fell to 37% by 2000, and then averaged just below 60% over the next decade. Beginning in 2001, the subsidy rate stayed above 58%, topping out at 63% in 2015, while participation rates also increased so that almost all crop acres were enrolled in an insurance program in 2016. During this period, the federal government covered large A&O costs and performed an underwriting (reinsurance) function.

Clearly, then, crop revenue (and, to a lesser degree, crop yield) insurance subsidies have become the principal means that the US now uses to support farmers. Crop revenue insurance only provides coverage when revenue falls below about 75% of a guaranteed or benchmark revenue (which is the coverage level most farmers choose), thereby enabling farmers to recover their variable costs if a payment is triggered. However, there is no protection in this public–private partnership for shallow losses—the revenue needed to cover the costs of fixed and human capital. Other programs were designed in the 2008 and 2014 Farm Bills to provide such coverage.

9.2.2 Agricultural Business Risk Management Programs in the 2008 Farm Bill

As noted in Chapter 7, the 2008 Farm Bill retained the commodity price supports of the 2002 Farm Bill while introducing an optional revenue guarantee program, known as Average Crop Revenue Election (ACRE), and authorizing a new disaster relief program. To participate in the ACRE program, farmers would agree to (i) forgo price-based counter-cyclical payments (CCP) (see Chapter 7.2), (ii) accept a 20% reduction in their revenue-based direct payments, and (iii) accept a 30% reduction in their marketing loan rate on commodities grown on their farm. Under ACRE, farmers would receive a payment on base acres planted to a program crop if revenue for that crop fell more than 10% below a moving average based on past national prices and state-level yields.[4] It was difficult to determine if a farmer would benefit from ACRE. For years prior to the 2008 Farm Bill, producers would have been better off with direct payments, but after ACRE was implemented, they were likely better off under ACRE because yields fell and prices rose.

While ACRE was a commodity program available to farmers free of charge (no insurance premium was paid), its introduction in 2008 reflected growing interest in crop insurance, and most particularly crop revenue insurance rather than crop yield insurance. In the 1990s, under separate legislation, subsidies for crop insurance premiums had been increased, revenue insurance had become the main form of insurance, and enrolled acres had increased substantially. Annual indemnities for crop insurance remained low until they peaked at just over $4 billion in 2002, then doubled to more than $8 billion in 2008, and doubled again during the droughts that afflicted the US during 2010–2013 (see Figures 9.1 and 9.2). ACRE provided a supplement to growing reliance on crop insurance as it only covered shallow losses—ones that were less severe than those covered by crop insurance. Enrollment was low primarily because the requirements for enrolling in ACRE (exclusion from CPP and a 20% loss in direct payments) were considered onerous.

The 2008 Farm Bill also authorized $3.8 billion for an Agricultural Disaster Relief Trust Fund that financed five separate programs to address agricultural disasters over the period 2008–2011 (when the 2008 Farm Bill was to expire): (i) the Supplemental Revenue Assistance Payments Program (SURE), (ii) Livestock Indemnity Program, (iii) Livestock Forage Disaster Program, (iv) Emergency Assistance for Livestock, Honeybees and Farm-Raised Fish, and (v) the Tree Assistance Program. The SURE program was designed to work with the Federal Crop Insurance Program and the Non-insured Crop Disaster Assistance Program (NAP) to reduce producers' financial risk.[5] As noted earlier, the Federal Crop Insurance Program was

---

[4] State-level yields were employed because of complaints from farmers located in one county who benefited less than a neighbor located in an adjacent county.

[5] NAP was established by the 1994 Federal Crop Insurance Reform Act. NAP applicants pay a $100 service fee and, to receive a payment, must suffer a crop loss of 50% or more, or be prevented by a natural disaster from planting more than 35% of intended area. It pays 55% of the average market price for the covered commodity for losses of 50% or more of normal historic production, with a limit of $100,000 per person. Farmers with a gross revenue greater than $2 million were ineligible.

established in 1980, while NAP was designed to reduce financial losses from catastrophic loss of production (including failure to plant) caused by a natural disaster, and provided coverage equivalent to the USDA Risk Management Agency's Catastrophic Risk Protection insurance.

SURE provided protection against yield loss or crop quality loss, or both, as a result of adverse weather or other environmental conditions. To participate in SURE, a producer was required to carry crop insurance for all insurable crops and NAP coverage for all non-insurable crops where NAP coverage was available. A producer would receive a payout from SURE if her production loss on at least one crop of economic significance exceeded 10% in a county that received a Secretarial Disaster Declaration, or in a contiguous county. For producers not located in an eligible county, they would need to experience a loss of 50% or more to qualify for SURE payments. Since 2008 was an especially poor year for crop producers, the 2009 Recovery Act extended the buy-in period from September 16, 2008, to May 18, 2009, and increased the funding available.

The Congressional Budget Office had calculated that the SURE program would cost $450 million annually, but more than $2.1 billion was paid to 103,000 producers in the 2008 crop year alone. Ensuing drought resulted in severe hardships for farmers without crop insurance. As a result of these developments, in 2012, more than 90% of farmers in the Corn Belt purchased a federally subsidized multiple-peril revenue insurance product at a high level of coverage, mainly incentivized by the price options available under the Harvest Price Option.

The Agricultural Disaster Relief Trust Fund originally focused on livestock and tree fruits. As re-authorized under the 2014 Farm Bill, the Livestock Indemnity Program provides benefits to livestock producers for livestock deaths in excess of normal mortality from adverse weather or predation by animals reintroduced into the wild by the federal government. The Livestock Forage Disaster Program provides compensation to eligible livestock producers who suffer grazing losses on land that is native or improved pastureland or planted specifically for grazing. Emergency Assistance for Livestock, Honeybees and Farm-Raised Fish provides financial assistance to eligible livestock producers for losses due to disease and certain adverse weather events, as determined by the Secretary of Agriculture. Honeybees and farm-raised fish are also covered. Finally, the Tree Assistance Program provides financial assistance to qualifying orchardists and nursery tree growers to replant or rehabilitate eligible trees, bushes, and vines damaged by natural disasters.

9.2.3 Agricultural Business Risk Programs in the 2014 and 2018 Farm Bills

Stronger market conditions had emerged around 2007 and persisted for several years. These reduced counter-cyclical payments and raised the nominal levels of premium subsidies for crop insurance as well as indemnities (due to higher prices), turning crop insurance into the main pillar of US farm support. The 2014 Farm Bill retained target prices (now termed "reference prices") and loan rates, but set them at higher nominal levels than in the period 1996–2008 (Table 9.2), while a revenue guarantee program became more deeply entrenched as an option. Higher prices also played a role in the 2014 Farm Bill: When farm prices and incomes were high, the fixed payments introduced as a reform in 1996 proved unpopular outside the farm sector. Consequently, the relatively non-distorting, fixed-payment support program was eliminated in 2014.

Table 9.2 Loan rates and reference prices by crop under the 2018 Farm Bill (US$)

Commodity	Units[a]	Loan rate	Reference price[b]	Reference price divided by 85%[c]	Max effective reference price[d]
Wheat	bushel	3.38	5.50	6.47	6.33
Corn	bushel	2.20	3.70	4.35	4.26
Grain sorghum	bushel	2.20	3.95	4.65	4.54
Barley	bushel	2.50	4.95	5.82	5.69
Oats	bushel	2.00	2.40	2.82	2.76
Long grain rice	cwt	7.00	14.00	16.47	16.10
Medium grain rice	cwt	7.00	14.00	16.47	16.10
Soybeans	bushel	6.20	8.40	9.88	9.66
Rapeseed/canola	cwt	10.09	20.15	23.71	23.17
Peanuts	ton	355.00	535.00	629.41	615.25
Dry peas	cwt	6.15	11.00	12.94	12.65
Lentils	cwt	13.00	19.97	23.49	22.97
Small chickpeas	cwt	10.00	19.04	22.40	21.90
Large chickpeas	cwt	14.00	21.54	25.34	24.77

[a] Bushel weight varies by commodity; cwt refers to 100 lbs or 45.455 kg; 1 ton is 2,000 lbs or 0.909 tonne (metric ton).
[b] Statutory reference price previously referred to as the target price.
[c] This is the value that the five-year Olympic average price must exceed before the effective reference price is higher than the statutory reference price.
[d] Calculated as 115% of the statutory reference price.
Source: Schnitkey et al. (2019a)

The 2018 Farm Bill kept the same reference prices as in the 2014 Farm Bill, but increased the loan rates. Farmers were again given a choice between a deficiency-type payment program known as Price Loss Coverage (PLC) and a revenue guarantee program (first introduced in 2014) called Agriculture Risk Coverage (ARC), along with a new crop insurance program known as the Supplemental Coverage Option (SCO). Cotton was not covered because of a WTO ruling brought against the US by Brazil (see Chapter 5.3). Rather, a new program, Stacked Income Protection, was specifically designed in 2014 for cotton producers, which protected against shortfalls at the county level. Although premiums were heavily subsidized at 80%, there was a limit on the extent of losses covered. The 2018 Farm Bill did not affect the SCO and Stacked Income Protection programs, but program changes in PLC and ARC did affect these programs. In particular, if producers switch to ARC, they may not purchase SCO coverage for that crop, while Stacked Income Protection coverage may not be purchased if any seed cotton acreage on the farm is enrolled in ARC or PLC.

In the 2018 Farm Bill, the effective reference price is the greater of the statutory reference price (formerly the target price), or 85% of the five-year Olympic national marketing year average (MYA) price, lagged one year. The maximum effective reference price is equal to 115% of the statutory reference price and is provided in the last column of Table 9.2 (although MYA prices would have to increase significantly before the effective maximum reference price is reached).

To provide readers with some notion of the complexity of these programs, they are described in somewhat more detail below.

Price Loss Coverage (PLC)

Price Loss Coverage (PLC) amounts to little more than the earlier price-based counter-cyclical payments program but with a higher trigger price. Compared to 2014, the 2018 Farm Bill permits the effective reference price to be higher than the statutory reference price (target price), potentially resulting in higher PLC payments than under the 2014 Farm Bill if MYA prices are high enough. Under PLC, producers receive a payment if a covered commodity's MYA price is below its effective reference price (Table 9.2). Define the effective price as the maximum of the statutory reference price or 85% of the five-year Olympic national MYA price. Then the payment equals the difference between the effective reference price and the outcome of the MYA price for that year multiplied by the payment yield, but applied to only 85% of the base acres. Suppose the MYA price of corn in a future crop year is $3.40/bu, which is less than the reference price of $3.70/bu, thereby triggering a payment. Assuming a payment yield of 160 bu/ac and 350 acres of corn base area, the payment or indemnity would be:

$$(\$3.70/bu - \$3.40/bu) \times 160 \text{ bu/ac} \times (0.85 \times 350 \text{ ac}) = \$14,280.$$

Agricultural Risk Coverage (ARC)

If agricultural producers opt for Agricultural Risk Coverage, they are no longer eligible for the Supplemental Coverage Option under the 2014 Farm Bill. Under ARC, farmers have the option of choosing individual farm coverage (IC) or county-level coverage. Under ARC-IC, a payment is made if the actual farm revenue from all covered commodities is less than the ARC-IC guarantee or benchmark.

To determine the ARC-IC guarantee, it is necessary to first calculate the most recent five-year Olympic average revenue of each of the covered commodities grown by the producers. Under the 2018 Farm Bill, the Federal Crop Insurance Corporation sets a trend adjustment to determine the average yield, reflecting the fact that average yields have trended upwards—for corn in Illinois, for example, the trend adjustment is 1.71 bu/ac.[6] Then, the benchmark guarantee is a simple weighted average of the individual trend-adjusted crop average revenues, with weights determined by the proportion of the total area planted to each crop. For example, suppose a farmer's five-year Olympic trend-adjusted (and lagged) average revenues for corn and soybeans were $954/ac and $570/ac, respectively, and that the farmer planted 350 ac to corn and 235 ac to soybeans. Then the ARC-IC guarantee would be:

$$(\$954/ac \times 350 \text{ ac} + \$570/ac \times 235 \text{ ac})/(350 \text{ ac} + 235ac) = \$799.74/ac.$$

The revenue for a particular crop in any year is given by the actual yield for that crop multiplied by the maximum of the MYA price or the loan rate. Suppose the yields for corn and soybean are 192 bu/ac and 47 bu/ac, respectively. Further, suppose the MYA prices are $3.40/bu for corn and $9.95/bu for soybean;

---

[6] The trend adjustment is applied as follows: Given a trend of 1.71 bu/ac, the farmer's five-year average would be increased by 5×1.71 bu/ac, or 8.55 bu/ac. Further, yields and prices used in calculating benchmark yields, prices, and revenues are now lagged one year, which was not the case in the 2014 Bill. For 2020, therefore, yields and prices for the period 2014–2018 are used as opposed to 2015–2019. The realized average yield in 2014 is adjusted upwards by six times the trend because it is six years to 2020; the average in 2015 is increased by five times the trend, etc.

both prices are higher than the loan rate (Table 9.2). Then, the current revenue for corn is $652.80/ac and that for soybean is $467.65/ac. We can then determine the ARC-IC revenue as:

($652.80/ac × 350 ac + $467.65/ac × 235 ac)/(350 ac + 235ac) = $578.42/ac.

Since the current year revenue ($578.32/ac) is less than the benchmark guarantee ($799.74/ac), a payment is triggered. However, the ARC-IC program only pays a maximum of 10% of the benchmark guarantee, or $79.97/ac. Since the difference between the benchmark guarantee and current revenue ($221.32/ac) exceeds the allowable payment, it is necessary to use $79.97/ac for calculating the payment. Further, for the individual coverage program, the payment rate only covers 65% of the eligible acres (compared to 85% under the county program); therefore, the payment the farmer would receive is as follows: 0.65 × 585 ac × $79.97/ac = $30,408.59.

With the ARC-county (ARC-CO) option, the revenue guarantees and the realized crop revenues in any given year are both determined using average county yields.[7] The benchmark revenue is given by the benchmark yield multiplied by the benchmark price. Unlike in 2014, county yields are now trend adjusted before calculating the benchmark yield. For 2020, for example, the averages are based on data from the 2014–2018 commodity years and do not include data from 2019, thereby allowing the farmer to know the ARC-CO guarantee and benchmark before the annual enrollment deadline of March 15.

The benchmark yield for a county is determined as a lagged five-year Olympic average of the Risk Management Agency's yield for that county, except that, for relatively low-yielding years, the RMA yield is replaced by a "plug yield" determined as 80% of the county transitional yield (rather than 70% as used in the 2014 Bill). The benchmark price is determined in the same way as under the PLC program—the higher of the reference price or 85% of the five-year Olympic moving average of MYA prices (not to exceed 115% of the reference price). The ARC-CO realized crop revenue is the actual county yield times the higher of the MYA price and the loan rate (Table 9.2). A payment is made if the ARC-CO actual crop revenue is less than the ARC-CO benchmark revenue guarantee.

As an example, suppose the ARC-CO revenue guarantee for corn is determined to be $934.20/ac, based on an Olympic average national MYA price of $5.30/bu and average corn yield of 176.4 bu/ac. However, since the guarantee under the ARC-CO coverage is 86% of the ARC-CO benchmark revenue, the guarantee is only $803.41/ac. Now assume that the current county yield is 189 bu/ac and the MYA price is $3.90/bu, which exceeds the loan rate for corn. Then, the current county-level revenue is $737.10/ac, so that the realized revenue is $66.31/ac below the ARC-CO guarantee. Recall that the farmer is only eligible for a maximum of 10% of the ARC-CO guarantee, or $80.34/ac. Since the realized revenue is less than 10% of the guarantee, the calculated difference of $66.31/ac can be applied to determine the payment, which, in turn, only applies to 85% of the base acreage. Suppose the farmer plants 350 acres to corn, then the payment to be received is: 0.85 × 350 ac × $66.31/ac = $19,727.82.

---

[7] After 2018, yields from crop insurance are given preference in the calculation of county yields, where previously data from the National Agricultural Statistical Service were given priority.

After the 2014 Farm Bill, initial enrollment in ARC exceeded 90% for corn and soybean because the reference revenue used by ARC was a moving average that included the high prices associated with 2007–2012. Wheat enrollment was about half, while producers of several other crops, particularly rice and peanuts, continued to choose the deficiency payment program. Both programs made substantial payments as prices (and revenue) fell after 2014, while lower prices brought down the costs of subsidizing crop insurance. The ARC program began in 2015 and paid $4.377 billion in 2015 and $5.940 billion in 2016, with payments expected to reach $5.380 billion in 2017.

In summary, then, ARC was designed by stakeholders/beneficiaries to supplement crop insurance by covering shallow losses—the ARC revenue guarantee covers losses that are less than most farmers cover with revenue insurance. ARC covers losses for 14% to 24% (revenue less than 86% of the benchmark gets covered down to 76%) as most farmers buy revenue insurance for losses of more than 25%.

In general, an agricultural producer would prefer ARC-CO over ARC-IC, primarily because the latter has fewer payment acres (65% vs. 85% of base acres for ARC-CO and PLC). Further, ARC-IC is operationally more complex, and thus harder to explain and understand. Nonetheless, assuming that the farmer has maintained excellent records of yields and revenues, ARC-IC is worth considering if (1) there is high variability in year-to-year yields; (2) the farmer's yields are much greater than ARC-CO and PLC yields; (3) the farm area is planted to fruits and vegetables rather than grains; and/or (4) the farmer runs a very good chance that planting in a given year does not succeed.

Supplemental Coverage Option (SCO)

Under this option, the farmer is no longer eligible for coverage on those crops enrolled under ARC, although she remains eligible for price loss coverage. The farmer chooses between the yield and revenue coverage options. The federal government pays 65% of the premium cost of SCO, but, to participate in SCO, the producer must have an underlying crop (yield or revenue) insurance policy. SCO is truly supplementary coverage in the sense that it covers losses that are not covered by the underlying insurance policy. Even though SCO coverage depends on the liability, coverage level, and approved yield for the farmer's underlying policy, it is possible for a producer to receive an indemnity under SCO while receiving no payment from the underlying insurance, and vice versa. SCO differs from the underlying policy in how a loss payment is triggered. The underlying policy pays a loss on an individual basis and an indemnity is triggered when the farmer has a yield or revenue loss. SCO pays a loss on an area basis, and an indemnity is triggered when there is a county-level loss in yield or revenue.

To illustrate how SCO works, consider an agricultural producer who purchases a crop revenue insurance policy with 75% coverage. This is the underlying policy. Further assume the farmer's benchmark revenue for corn is $765/ac based on expected yield of 170 bu/ac and price of corn of $4.50/bu. Then the underlying policy will protect the farmer up to $573.75/ac (=0.75×$765/ac), leaving her with an expected loss of $191.25/ac in that circumstance. If the producer chooses to buy a SCO policy, it will take the form of revenue insurance, but payments will be based on county-level outcomes. Payment begins when county-level revenue falls below 86% of the county benchmark (expected) revenue (say, based on a five-year Olympic moving average). Full payment will be made for revenue losses that the farmer experiences when the realized county revenue falls within the range of 86% to 75% of its benchmark value. For example, if the realized county revenue is 80% of the benchmark, the farmer will receive: $(0.86 - 0.80) \times \$765/ac = \$45.90/ac$. Once the realized county revenue falls below 75% of the expected (benchmark) revenue, the underlying policy is assumed to come into play. Thus, the most the producer would get under SCO in this case is: $(0.86 - 0.75) \times \$765/ac = \$84.15/ac$. Notice that an indemnity can be paid under SCO even if the producer experiences no decline in revenue. Further, coverage will vary depending on the underlying policy.

9.2.4 Dairy

Dairy producers can also choose to protect themselves against losses. The 2014 Farm Bill included a Margin Protection Program (MPP) for dairy that paid farmers if the margin between the price of milk and the feed cost of producing that milk was considered too small. In particular, if the difference between the price for a hundredweight (cwt) of milk and the feed costs of producing that 100 lbs. (45.6 kg) fell below $4, the producer would receive a payment for the difference. Producers could choose higher margins of protection but would have to pay a premium. The total payment a producer could receive equaled 90% of their highest annual level of milk production for the period 2011–2013, with an adjustment reflecting the growth in total annual milk consumption in the US. By 2017, most dairy producers had enrolled at the minimum $4/cwt coverage. Farmers paid a $100 administration fee to participate but no premiums unless they wished to enroll at a higher level of coverage (beyond $4). However, the dairy-MPP was based on national level outcomes and failed to account for regional or farm-level specifics.

The 2018 Farm Bill replaced the dairy-MPP with a Dairy Margin Coverage (DMC) program that is also voluntary. It provides catastrophic coverage at no cost to producers, except a $100 administration fee and various levels of buy-up coverage. To participate in DMC, producers select a coverage level ranging from $4.00 to $9.50 per cwt (in $0.50 increments) and a coverage percentage of their operation's production history ranging from 5%–95% (in 5% increments). Producers can choose to lock in coverage levels until 2023, and they receive a 25% discount on their DMC premiums if they continued the same coverage as before. The DMC allows for free coverage at a margin of $5/cwt for the first 5 million lbs., while reducing premiums for higher levels of coverage by 75% and reducing the period from two months to one month over which margins would be calculated. Although MPP has paid indemnities of some $265 million annually, payments could be substantially higher under DMC if milk prices happen to be low in a year when corn and soybean prices are particularly high.

9.2.5 Trade Issues

Under existing WTO rules and as argued by the US, direct payments to agricultural producers fall into a green box category because they do not incentivize production and thus do not distort trade (see Chapter 5.3).

There is no limit on the amount that a country can spend on green box subsidies. Subsidization of crop insurance premiums is another matter: such subsidies can affect output and are thus considered trade distorting. The US has indeed recognized that its yield and revenue insurance programs cannot be classified as green box, but must be classified as amber box subsidies. Under the WTO's Agreement on Agriculture, amber box subsidies are trade distorting and are to be reduced or eliminated, while green box programs are exempt from trade reduction commitments.

Each country has a binding limit (*de minimis*) on the level of amber box support it can provide to agricultural producers as given by the measurable subsidy, referred to as the Aggregate Measurement of Support (AMS; see Chapter 5.3); the US AMS limit is currently set at $19.1 billion per year. The shift from direct payments, which were classified as green box subsidies, to the subsidization of amber box insurance programs could potentially create difficulties for US policy makers in the future.

The US government reimburses insurance companies for the costs of administering insurance contracts and provides reinsurance to the private companies at no cost. Together these costs added up to more than $3.1 billion annually in 2008 and 2009; if these costs were added to the premium subsidy provided in 2011, the government subsidy would amount to more than $10 billion. Given the size of subsidies for individual farmers and the SCO, ARC, and other programs introduced in the 2014 Farm Bill, it is likely the US could exceed its AMS limit. Alternatively, the WTO's Agreement on Subsidies and Countervailing Measures (SCM) permits countries to lodge a complaint with the WTO if US subsidies cause losses to the complainant's domestic or foreign markets (see Chapter 5.3). As with the Brazil–US cotton case, this could result in the US government having to make payments to foreigners or face countervailing duties and cease or modify a particular program.

9.3 Agricultural Business Risk Management in Canada

Although crop insurance began in Canada in 1959, business risk management in the agricultural sector really traces its beginnings to the Western Grain Stabilization Program of 1976, which provided some form of protection against income loss (see Chapter 7.3). However, one might trace the true origins of agricultural risk management programs to the National Tripartite Stabilization Program of 1986–1993. This program marked the first time that the federal government and the provinces negotiated a cost-sharing agreement on agriculture, over which the two levels of government share constitutional responsibility. This cost-shared structure remains in place today.

9.3.1 The Shift from Price Support to Risk Management

The modern era of agricultural BRM began in Canada in 1991 with the Farm Income Protection Act (FIPA). Because of declining prices and falling farm incomes, FIPA replaced all three previous agricultural programs—the Western Grain Stabilization Act (1976), remaining remnants of the Agricultural Stabilization Act (1958), and the Crop Insurance Act (1959). FIPA introduced three new programs: the Gross Revenue

Insurance Program (GRIP), the Net Income Stabilization Account (NISA), and crop insurance, which essentially retained ongoing crop insurance programs.

The costs of GRIP were shared equally between the federal government and the provinces, with no farmer contributions. GRIP was meant to complement the crop insurance program and guaranteed farmers a per acre gross return, thereby protecting against deep losses. However, within 18 months GRIP was dismantled, beginning in Saskatchewan, because it was too costly for the province and the program was ill designed; by 1999, only Ontario was left in GRIP.

NISA was designed to protect farmers against shallow losses, and participation was voluntary. Under the program, a farmer could put up to 2% of her annual net farm sales to a maximum of $5,000 into a savings account, receiving a matching subsidy payment that was shared equally between the federal and provincial governments. As usual, provinces could add to programs, with Alberta, for example, unilaterally increasing the amount farmers could deposit with a matching payment to 3% (something referred to as enhanced NISA). When farm income fell below an established minimum, farmers could go to their NISA accounts and withdraw funds. There were two payout triggers: (1) If in a tax year net income fell below 70% of the average of the previous three years, a farmer could withdraw funds from his NISA account; and (2) if net farm income in a given year fell by $10,000 (after 1999, by $20,000), a farmer could choose to withdraw funds from her NISA account. But no NISA accounts could go into deficit.

Finally, crop insurance provided protection against yield risk, with government subsidizing premiums at a rate of 60% and covering operating and administration costs. This is discussed further below.

All these changes led to a reduced federal role in prairie agriculture. The federal role was reduced further in 1995 with the elimination of the Crow Rate subsidy (paid to producers in 1996) and feed freight assistance, along with a 30% reduction in farm income support payments over three years beginning in 1995.

These programs did not last long. In 1998, the federal government passed the Agricultural Income Disaster Assistance (AIDA) Act. It was structured according to WTO guidelines; when net income fell below 70% of a three-year moving average of net income, a farmer became eligible for a payout. Provinces paid 40% of program costs, with the federal government paying 60%. AIDA was subsequently eliminated in 2001 for three reasons:

1. AIDA was considered unfair: A farmer might experience a bad year and thus receive a payout; but a farmer with an even greater absolute and/or relative loss might receive nothing, because her beginning benchmark three-year moving average coincided with unusually poor returns.
2. The program suffered high transaction costs because of the need for auditors and accountants.
3. AIDA discouraged mixed cattle-grain enterprises: Farmers who experienced losses on the grain side that were offset by high returns to beef got no payout, as net incomes would not decline by enough to trigger a payment.

AIDA was replaced in 2001 by the Canadian Farm Income Program (CFIP), which was similar to but corrected the flaws in AIDA. This program also failed to gain traction and was replaced two years later by the Canadian Agricultural Income Stabilization (CAIS) program, which replaced GRIP, NISA, disaster programs, and crop insurance.

CAIS was designed to protect farmers from small (shallow) and large (deep) drops in income by insuring a farmer's reference or expected margin (revenue minus specified variable costs), which was based on an average of historical margins. When the realized margin in a given year fell below the reference margin, a farmer could withdraw money from her NISA-like program account and receive a matching payment according to the extent of the shortfall. The CAIS program received some 55,000 applications per year. In 2004, 44% received no payment; 26% received less than $10,000; and 0.09% received $500,000 or more, with a very small number receiving more than $1 million. During the 2005–2006 fiscal year, Agriculture and Agri-Food Canada (AAFC) spent $1.1 billion Canada-wide on CAIS. Four provinces administered their own CAIS programs, including Alberta, which generally paid farmers more handsomely than other provinces.

Prior to CAIS, Alberta had established a Farm Income Disaster Program (1996) when no national agreement on disaster relief was struck. This program complied with rules established under the WTO's Agreement on Agriculture and paid $309.4 million to farmers in 2000, more than what farmers in Manitoba received under all programs. It was terminated in 2004 when the CAIS program started. In November 2005, Alberta created the Alberta Reference Margins Program Pilot that protected farmers against deep losses, using a producer's financial history to determine a reference margin that consisted of a three-year average of previous margins. This program paid an additional $224 million to Alberta farmers over and above what they received under CAIS. It also paid more to farmers under CAIS in other years: in 2006, $261 million, and in 2007, an additional $70 million. Clearly, Alberta's oil revenues conferred important benefits on its farmers.

Finally, on the livestock side, several ad hoc programs were introduced by the federal government in 2003 to help livestock producers cope with the backlash associated with the bovine spongiform encephalopathy (BSE) crisis, with US producers lobbying to close the border to Canadian cattle.[8] In 2007, grain prices rose dramatically, causing heavy losses in the livestock sector, with more than half of Saskatchewan's hog producers ceasing operations, for example. As a result, in February 2008, the federal government provided $3.3 billion to support hog and cattle producers. This was an example of an ad hoc disaster relief program. Livestock producers were also impacted by country-of-origin labeling introduced in the 2008 US Farm Bill, although it is not entirely clear that its impact was negative. Given government bailouts of the auto and banking sectors during the financial crisis that began in 2007, it is an open question as to whether government should treat the livestock sector differently.

9.3.2 Enter Growing Forward

Following the US procedure of revising farm legislation approximately every five years via farm bills, Canada introduced five-year planning horizons for its agricultural sector beginning in 2008. The federal government and provinces now negotiate five-year policy frameworks that, once established, give provinces

---

[8] It turns out that the cattle industry is too integrated across borders to benefit either side from shutting the border. However, the BSE crisis did reduce exports to the US, causing many producers to sell off cattle prematurely with subsequent large losses in income.

considerable leeway in their implementation. This is more like the situation in the European Union, where member states also have considerable latitude to implement their own risk management programs within the context of the Common Agricultural Policy. Much like member states in the EU, the nature of agriculture varies considerably across provinces so that one size does not fit all. We have seen this with Alberta, which often developed its own programs or added to tripartite ones.

With the advent of a fixed planning horizon, previous programs were eliminated as the first five-year federal/provincial/territorial agricultural agreement, known as Growing Forward (GF), came into effect in 2008. It focused on the following areas: (1) competitiveness, (2) innovation, (3) environment, and (4) business risk management. Pre-existing agricultural BRM programs were overhauled and subsumed under Growing Forward (2008–2013). Under Growing Forward, agricultural risk protection was provided through four "new" programs as follows.

1. *AgriInvest* is a government-matched savings account, similar to NISA, that is intended to address shallow reductions in net farm income—to help producers protect their margin from shallow losses. Each year, a producer could deposit up to 1.5% of their allowable net sales (ANS) into the AgriInvest account, and this was matched by a government contribution. ANS was limited to $1.5 million annually, with the largest matching annual government contribution equal to $22,500. Further, the account balance was limited to 25% of a producer's average ANS, which made sense as the original purpose of the program was to protect against shallow and not deep losses.

2. *AgriStability* is a margin-based, whole-farm program that protects against greater income losses than under AgriInvest—it aims at deep protection. Indemnities under AgriStability were based on the difference between the realized gross margin (revenue minus specified variable costs) in any year and a reference historical margin, with payments triggered when a producer's realized gross margin fell to 85% or less of the reference margin. The reference margin was determined as an Olympic average (lowest and highest margins removed) of realized gross margins over the last five years. Under GF, funds from AgriInvest were meant to cover the first 15% by which the realized margin fell below the reference margin. After that, the coinsurance portion (what the farmer paid) was 30% when the realized gross margin was between 70% and 85% of the reference margin, but was only 20% when it was less than 70% of the reference margin. Producers paid no premiums and incurred only transaction costs and a fixed fee to participate.

3. *AgriRecovery* provides relief in the case of disasters, permitting governments to fill risk gaps not covered by other government programs. This disaster-relief program is offered by the federal, provincial, and territorial governments to assist producers with extraordinary costs of recovering from natural disasters.

4. *AgriInsurance* provides protection to producers from yield losses for specified perils, including economic losses arising from natural hazards, such as drought, flood, wind, frost, excessive rain or heat, and snow, and losses from uncontrollable diseases, insect infestations, and wildlife—it is production insurance. AgriInsurance is an extension of subsidized multi-peril crop insurance that has been available to Canadian farmers since 1959, although the range of agricultural commodities that insurance covered has increased greatly over time. AgriInsurance does not cover livestock producers although they can insure their on-farm feed production.

AgriStability and AgriInsurance are both offered at the farm level; AgriStability is whole-farm and margin-based, whereas AgriInsurance is commodity-specific and yield-based. The GF suite of programs is cost-shared 60%–40% between the federal government and the provinces.

The role of the federal government is essentially hands-off, leaving administration and oversight to the provinces, although AgriStability employs the federal income tax system to determine eligibility and payments to producers—the income tax system is required to determine the cost side of the gross margin (which equals farm revenue minus specified variable costs). Unfortunately, reliance on tax forms and the tax system leads to a great deal of uncertainty for participating producers regarding indemnities, plus delays in receiving payments. Under GF, producers paid no premiums for AgriStability, incurring only the transaction costs of signing up and paying an initiation fee.

The federal government and provinces share the costs of subsidizing insurance premiums (farmers pay only 40% of the actuarially sound premium), although provinces are primarily responsible for the design, rating, and A&O costs of insurance programs. Importantly, they absorb the underwriting gains and losses, although they can employ reinsurance to hedge against a potentially huge insurance claim caused by an adverse event that affects a large proportion of the farmers in a province. While the federal government provides a reinsurance pool for provinces, international financial intermediaries are often employed (see below and the Appendix to this chapter).

In addition, the federal government has an Advance Payments Program that complements but is not a part of the suite of BRM programs described above (nor are Advance Payments Program costs included in the BRM funding envelope). This program helps crop, livestock, and other agricultural producers with cash flow problems (including producers whose principal activity may not be farming); this form of support provides flexibility in the marketing of commodities, thereby enabling a farmer to sell product based on market conditions and not just on a need for cash flow. The Advance Payments Program provides a loan to producers of up to $400,000, of which $100,000 is interest free, depending on the size of their enterprise. Producers can take out the loan at any time but must repay it within 18 months (24 months for cattle and bison producers).

9.3.3 Shift from Growing Forward to Growing Forward 2

Canadian agricultural BRM programs were subsequently revised under Growing Forward 2 (GF2), which ran from April 1, 2013, through March 31, 2018. In particular, GF2 made changes to two programs—AgriInvest and AgriStability—while leaving the other programs unchanged from GF. In going from GF to GF2, the producer contribution limit under AgriInvest was increased from 1.5% of allowable net sales to 100% of ANS, but only 1% (down from 1.5%) was matched by the government. Further, the government's annual matching contribution was now limited to $15,000, down from a maximum of $22,500 under GF (although provinces could raise this). However, the balance limit that could be held in a farmer's AgriInvest account was increased from 25% of historical average ANS to 400%. As a result, AgriInvest could also provide protection against deep and not just shallow losses.

The changes to AgriInvest were required partly because of the changes made to the AgriStability program. Compared to GF, GF2 simplified the AgriStability payment calculation by harmonizing multitier compensation rates that existed under GF to a single level (70%), but the level of program margin necessary to trigger a payout was reduced from 85% of the reference margin (benchmark) to 70%, with a 30% gap rather than 15% now to be covered by AgriInvest. Under GF2, the coinsurance component is 30% (payouts are based on 70% of the coverage of the eligible decline) regardless of the degree to which income falls (as was the case with GF). Again producers would employ AgriInvest to cover shallow losses and, potentially, the coinsurance component of AgriStability.

For livestock producers who grow feed grains and participate in crop insurance, there is a Western Livestock Price Insurance Program that cattle and hog producers in Canada's four Western provinces can use to manage the risk of falling prices. The program protects producers against an unexpected drop in cattle and hog prices over a period of time. (Poultry producers are not covered because poultry is a supply-managed sector.) In essence, it protects against market volatility by providing a floor for cattle and hog prices. Program premiums are determined much like option prices (see section 9.1), with the premium depending on the strike price, current price, period, and amount of coverage desired. A similar program does not appear to exist outside the four Western provinces.

When it comes to funding, the federal government spent $2.36 billion for the BRM component of GF2 over the last two years of the program, 2016–2018 (a significant increase compared to GF), with the agricultural BRM programs cost-shared 60:40 with the provinces. This constituted 51.4% of government's entire Agriculture and Agri-Food Canada budget. In addition, the federal government contributed to domestic and international marketing of agricultural commodities, and to science and innovation, programs that helped facilitate economic growth in the agricultural sector. The federal government is the sole funder of such programs, including AgriInnovation, AgriCompetiveness, and AgriMarketing, although costs are shared with the private sector and universities. Federal expenditures were planned to be $820.3 million for 2020–2021.

The amount paid by farmers is difficult to determine as it depends on enrollment in various BRM programs. To participate in AgriStability under GF2, farmers now had to pay $3.15 each year for every $1,000 of reference margin protection (based on coverage of 70% of the margin), with a minimum payment of $45; in addition, there is an annual administrative fee of $55. This helps explain why the participation rate for AgriStability fell from 57% under GF to 42% under GF2—under GF, producers paid no premium. For AgriInsurance, insurance premiums are shared as follows: federal government (36%), provincial government (24%), and producers (40%). AgriRecovery is paid by the federal government and AgriInvest provides a subsidy to farmers for which they do not pay.

In summary, then, Canada provides protection against deep losses through the AgriStability and AgriInsurance programs. AgriStability provides protection of farm-level gross margins (revenue minus certain allowable variable costs): If a farmer's gross margin falls by 30% or more from the benchmark (expected) revenue, she receives an indemnity equal to 70% of any loss below 0.7 times the benchmark. For example, if the expected gross margin is $1 million, a payment is triggered if the realized gross margin falls below $700,000. Suppose that the realized margin is $600,000. Then, the payment would equal: 0.7 × ($700,000 – $600,000) = $70,000, with the farmer's coinsurance component equal to the remaining $30,000. However, the farmer would have paid $3.15 per $1,000 of reference margin protection and a $55 fee to participate; this implies a cost to the farmer of $3,205 (= $3.15/$1000 × $1 million + $55). If the farmer also has a crop insurance policy under AgriInsurance, she might be eligible for additional payments depending on the level of coverage she had chosen. For crop insurance, the farmer would only have paid 40% of the actuarially sound premium and none of the A&O costs.

The Canadian government provides additional deep coverage through AgriRecovery. This program is paid for solely by the federal government, with farmers paying no premiums. AgriRecovery is simply a form of disaster protection—protection against major drought or flood, pest/disease outbreaks (e.g., BSE in livestock), and other catastrophes.

9.3.4 Evaluation of Canada's Agricultural Business Risk Programs

Before providing some remarks concerning Canada's BRM suite of programs and the future direction of these programs, consider the role that such programs have played in supporting farm incomes. In Figure 9.3, government payments to the Canadian agricultural sector are allocated by type of program. Crop insurance benefits and those provided by hail insurance are considered separately, as are payments provided by various provincial government programs. Payments related to AgriInvest are combined with those of its predecessor program, the Net Income Stabilization Account; similarly, AgriStability payments are combined with those of its GRIP predecessor. Finally, Western Grain Stabilization payments, extra-supply management dairy payments, and a plethora of other government transfer payments are summed together under "Other" (see Chapter 7.3 regarding some of these programs). Notice that total annual program payments rose during much of the 1980s and flattened out during the 1990s, when payments averaged $3.0 billion ($2017); payments averaged $3.9 billion during the period 2000–2019.

Figure 9.3 Government direct program payments by type of program, Canada, 1980–2019 ($2017 billions) ("Other" plotted on right axis)

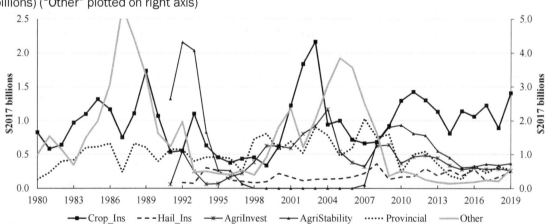

Direct payments from a variety of provincial and other programs have historically been an important source of revenue for farmers. For example, in the mid-1980s, major funding for grain farmers came via the Western Grain Stabilization Act and the Special Canadian Grains program, while in 2007 provincial programs provided farmers with $1.0 billion ($2017) with other federal government programs providing $2.5 billion.

The University of British Columbia agricultural economist James Vercammen (2013) compiled a list of 204 direct payment programs in Canada for the period 1981–2010. He found that Canadian programs had an average weighted lifetime of 8.7 years and provided an annual average payment of $63.5 million ($2017), with 27 programs providing an average of some $367.7 million ($2017) per year (Table 9.3). Approximately 60% of all payments to agricultural producers over the period 1981–2010 came through some type of business risk management program; remaining transfers were pure income support and included the Special Canadian Grains Program, feed freight assistance, input rebates, direct payments from provincial programs, and so on. After 2010, BRM program payments played an even greater role.

How effective was Growing Forward in terms of stabilizing and supporting farmers' incomes? A University of Alberta study by Jeffrey, Trautman, and Unterschultz (2017) calculated the expected net present values (NPV) of a representative Alberta farm enterprise under no BRM programs, and then under GF and GF2. The results are summarized in Table 9.4. These indicate that, compared to the situation where there are no federal BRM programs, GF increased a crop producer's expected net returns by $38.10/ha, an increase of nearly 53%. The subsequent changes made in the implementation of GF2 reduced expected income by $3.38/ha compared to GF—a reduction of only 3%. More importantly, the variability of income was reduced as evidenced by the coefficient of variation, although the standard deviation of income increased slightly. Growing Forward clearly led to higher expected net returns and lower downside risk.

Many provinces created crown corporations to operate agricultural financial services as a cost-cutting budgetary measure. A University of Guelph study by Ker et al. (2017) argued that the crown corporations act too much like private insurance companies as opposed to public delivery agents, and rely too much on private reinsurance despite holding quite large reserves. Alberta, Saskatchewan, Manitoba, Ontario, and PEI paid $108 million in premiums to private reinsurance companies in 2014, while holding $3.65 billion in reserve. Reserves as a percentage of liabilities averaged more than 23% in 2014 for the six provinces that used a crown corporation, from a high of 46% in Alberta to a low of 8% in Manitoba. It was estimated that it would take more than 8,000 years to deplete the reserves held by crown corporations in Alberta and Ontario. Given that the agricultural sector is small relative to the rest of the economy, there is no reason for provinces to rely on private reinsurance, especially since the federal government already provides reinsurance for pooling risks.

Table 9.3 Top agricultural programs providing direct payments to Canadian farmers, average annual payments over the period 1981–2010

Program	Average ($ mil/yr)[a]	Start year	Finish year	Duration (years)
Canadian Agricultural Income Stabilization (CAIS)	1,210.2	2004	2010	7
Crop insurance	774.9	1981	2010	30
AgriStability	736.6	2007	2010	4
Special Canadian Grains Program	662.6	1987	1990	4
Farm income payment	629.5	2005	2006	2
Gross Revenue Insurance Plan (GRIP)	535.0	1991	2001	11
Provincial stabilization programs	499.3	1981	2010	30
AgriInvest	431.1	2008	2010	3
Net Income Stabilization Account (NISA)	430.0	1991	2009	19
Transitional Industry Support Program (TISP)	353.5	2004	2006	3
Grains and Oilseeds Payment (GOPP)	328.2	2006	2008	3
Farm Support and Adjustment Measures II	324.5	1991	1993	3
Farm input rebates	310.1	1981	2010	30
Dairy subsidy	273.0	1981	2002	22
Special drought assistance	254.5	1989	1992	4
Western Grain Stabilization Act	248.2	1981	2001	21
2003 Transition Funding	232.1	2003	2005	3
Farm Income Assistance	225.2	1990	1992	3
CAIS Inventory Transition Initiative (CITI)	213.3	2006	2010	5
AgriRecovery	190.2	2008	2010	3
Beef cattle and sheep support	184.7	1982	1982	1
Canadian Farm Income Program (CFIP)	157.2	2001	2005	5
BSE recovery	151.1	2003	2006	4
Agricultural Income Disaster Assistance (AIDA)	144.9	1999	2004	6
Tripartite payments	136.3	1986	1998	13
Freight Cost Pooling Assistance Program (FCPAP)	134.2	1997	1997	1
Canada–Saskatchewan Assistance Program (C-SAP II)	130.5	2001	2002	2

[a] Real 2017 Canadian dollars.
Source: Data provided by James Vercammen and were part of the background data for Vercammen (2013).

Table 9.4 Estimates of the per hectare benefits from participating in Business Risk Management (BRM) programs under GF & GF2, Alberta

Item	No BRM programs	BRM suite (GF)	BRM suite (GF2)
Mean NPV	$931,960	$1,425,386	$1,381,693
Mean annualized NPV	$71.97	$110.07	$106.69
Standard dev. of annualized NPV	$28.82	$29.88	$31.25
Coefficient of variation	0.40	0.27	0.29

Source: Jeffrey et al. (2017)

Based on evaluations of GF and GF2, several changes regarding how Canada operates its suite of BRM programs can be identified. (1) It is unnecessary for Canadian insurance agencies to rely on private reinsurance to pool risks. Compared to provincial government budgets, agricultural insurance is small and governments can easily handle the risk of adverse outcomes. If pooling of risks is desired nonetheless, provinces could rely on federally provided reinsurance. (2) Canada should not rely on private firms to supply crop yield and/or revenue insurance to farmers, as is done in the United States, because provincial crown corporations and agricultural ministries can supply these products more efficiently than the private sector. (3) Governments are risk averse, require lower rates of return, and can use various policy levers to incentivize farmers to engage in on-farm, risk-reducing activities—reducing moral hazard. Moral hazard can also be mitigated to some extent through coinsurance, requiring agricultural producers to share some of the deep loss against which they hedge. This is already done when it comes to shallow losses, but can also be implemented in the AgriInsurance program. (4) Finally, the AgriStability program is poorly designed because the calculation of gross margins requires knowledge of input use and costs, and these can only be determined from a farmer's tax receipts. Because the tax system is needed to resolve the indemnity a producer would receive, this leads to uncertainty regarding the payment farmers can expect, and to long delays before payment is received. As a result, participation rates are low. It should be replaced by commodity-specific revenue insurance because revenue is much easier to measure and track than gross margins, because the latter require detailed information on costs.

9.3.5 Going Forward: Canadian Agricultural Partnership

In the lead up to the expiration of GF2 on March 31, 2018, the federal and provincial governments appeared intent on continuing with a similar program to start the day after GF2 concluded. There seemed to be no intention to privatize the current approach to agricultural BRM, except to encourage greater participation by the private sector beyond hail insurance and a reinsurance function. The creation of new BRM tools that might be provided by the private sector, such as weather-indexed insurance and consulting services that facilitate greater use of existing risk management tools (e.g., futures markets, enhanced crop and whole-farm management), are encouraged, but remain a minor component of agricultural BRM in Canada. The introduction of new risk products would undoubtedly require government subsidies, so it would be unlikely that crop yield or revenue insurance would be taken over by the private sector. One exception is hail insurance, which has traditionally been provided privately, because premiums and indemnities are unaffected by adverse selection and moral hazard, and the determination of a payment is simple, requiring only a visit by an insurance adjuster, much as is the case with automobile or house insurance. Further, there remains a limited role for private companies in reinsurance, management of farmers' AgriInvest accounts, provision of farm management tools, and so forth, and even in the provision of some types of crop insurance. So, what replaced Growing Forward?

Growing Forward 2 was replaced on April 1, 2018, by the Canadian Agricultural Partnership. Growing Forward's BRM suite remains essentially intact, as is seen in the comparison of Canada's BRM programs provided in Table 9.5. Despite criticism of AgriStability, only two changes were made to the AgriStability program compared to GF2: an adjustment to the reference margin limit and the introduction of a late participation option. Thus, with the exception of minor changes, the Growing Forward program discussed above remains intact as the Canadian Agricultural Partnership, which emphasizes the tripartite nature of Canada's agricultural policies.

Table 9.5 Key features of AgriStability under different policy frameworks[a]

Item	GF	GF2	Canadian Agricultural Partnership
Reference margin (RM)	5-year Olympic average of gross margin (GM) (=allowable income – allowable expenses)	Same as GF	Same as GF
Reference margin limit (RML)	n.a.	The lower of the RM & average of allowable expenses for the corresponding years used to calculate RM	Similar to GF2, but RML is set to no less than 70% of the RM
Trigger	< 85% of the RM	<70% of the RM or RML (if applicable)	Same as GF2
Payment	Multitier: 70% of margin decline when realized GM is 70% to 85% of RM; 80% if realized GM is 0% to 70% of RM; 60% of negative margin	70% of margin decline when the realized GM is below the trigger	Same as GF2
Late participation	n.a.	n.a.	Benefits reduced 20%; provincial & territorial governments can trigger

[a] Data from Agriculture and Agri-Food Canada; RM refers to reference margin; n.a. means not applicable.

9.4 Concluding Discussion: Lessons for Agricultural Business Risk Management

In this chapter, it was argued that private crop yield or revenue insurance will not be provided on a large scale without government subsidization. Of course, the private sector will be present in niche markets such as hail insurance, crop insurance offered to producers meeting specific criteria (e.g., through cooperatives), and some types of index insurance. For the most part, however, farmers appear reluctant to pay enough to cover an actuarially sound premium that also covers an insurance company's A&O and underwriting costs, and provides an adequate rate of return. It is likely that many farmers can self-insure against reductions in crop revenues, perhaps through diversification of production (e.g., growing a variety of crops, mixed livestock-crop enterprises) but more likely through off-farm income. Some (maybe even many) farmers can withstand losses because they owe no debt on their most important input, land. Finally, farmers are protected against disastrous losses by governments that provide ad hoc disaster relief to producers without charge.

Evidence from the US suggests that if private companies require a premium that exceeds the actuarially fair premium by more than 10%, few farmers are likely to participate in the scheme. Private insurance companies generally require premiums that greatly exceed 10% of the actuarially sound premium in order to remain in business. The situation is aggravated by the fact that when participation rates are low, premiums will also need to be higher as only the high-risk farmers enroll (an example of adverse selection).

As to futures markets and over-the-counter financial derivatives, producers tend to shy away from these for whatever reason (e.g., lack of financial awareness and computer skills), although operators of larger farms will employ financial advisers to facilitate use of forward contracts and even futures and options trading. For the most part, however, it is often easier for farmers to lobby for government support programs than determine how best to participate in private-sector options. Subsidization of insurance premiums and A&O costs occurs because politicians wish to employ BRM programs to support farm incomes as opposed to using price supports, for reasons alluded to Chapter 7.4 and section 9.1.2.

9.4.1 Do Agricultural BRM Programs Distort Production?

While price support programs were demonstrably inefficient and distorted production (see Chapters 6 through 8), programs that subsidize crop insurance premiums also distort production. This is seen in Figure 9.4, where the derived demand for crop (yield or revenue) insurance is given by $DD_{insurance}$. If farmers are charged the actuarially correct premium P^* (excluding A&O and other costs), they would purchase q^* insurance contracts, which represents a certain area in crops. When premiums are subsidized so that the farmer pays P^0, more insurance contracts are purchased ($q^0 > q^*$) and more crop area is covered. Because risks have been reduced, more is produced as well. Now, if A&O costs were to be recovered, the premium required might well be P^1, which exceeds the choke price k so that no producer buys insurance. This is likely the case with private insurance.

Figure 9.4 Market for crop insurance

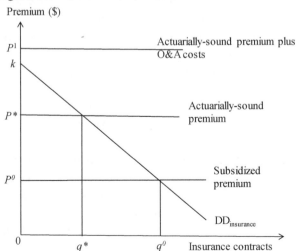

From the perspective of the WTO, an important question concerning crop insurance is the following: Do crop insurance programs affect production decisions? Crop insurance and other programs that protect farmers against risk truncate a producer's net income probability distribution, thereby increasing the expected unit returns for each enterprise and reducing the variance of returns. Together this creates an incentive to grow riskier crops, and likely encourages farmers to take more risks in other aspects of the farm enterprise, such as taking on more financial risks. Further, it is an obstacle to on-farm diversification.

9.4.2 Comparison of US and Canadian Approaches to Risk Management

It is possible to learn something by comparing the US and Canadian approaches to agricultural BRM. Canada provides protection against *deep losses* through the AgriStability and AgriInsurance programs, and to a lesser extent through AgriInvest. AgriStability provides protection of farm-level gross margins, AgriInsurance provides protection against yield losses on a crop-by-crop basis, and AgriInvest incentivizes savings. For AgriInsurance and AgriStability, premiums are subsidized, with government covering 60% of crop yield insurance premiums and the A&O costs (while actual subsidy rates for AgriStability are higher). In addition, AgriRecovery protects against ad hoc disasters such as drought, flooding, disease, pests, and the like, for which the producer pays no premiums—it is a 100% federally funded program.

Deep protection in the US is delivered through private insurance companies whose A&O costs are covered by the federal government. Both crop yield and crop revenue insurance are available (with the term "crop insurance" here referring to yield or revenue insurance); in recent decades, farmers have gravitated to crop revenue insurance. The federal government also covers 60% or more of the actuarially sound premiums (see Figure 9.1). In addition, the government provides ad hoc and other disaster protection much like in Canada.

There are several important differences between the Canadian and US programs of deep coverage:

1. Canadian farmers can insure their total farm net revenue (i.e., gross margin) through AgriStability, while US farmers can only insure gross revenue and then on a crop-by-crop basis. In practice, a US farmer can effectively protect total farm revenue as a weighted average of (eligible) crop plantings. Since revenue is protected rather than gross margin, indemnity determination is more transparent and delays between determination of losses and indemnities are shorter.
2. Canada offers crop yield insurance in addition to gross margin protection. The US crop insurance program offers farmers an option to choose yield or revenue protection.
3. The majority of farmers opt for coverage under crop insurance at a rate of 80% or more, compared to about 75% for US farmers. That is, Canadian producers would receive a payment when realized yield falls below 80% of expected yield compared to 75% for the average US producer.
4. Crop insurance in Canada is delivered by provinces through crown corporations or directly by a Ministry of Agriculture. Many provinces then employ private reinsurance to protect against potentially large losses despite the fact that the provinces and/or the federal government can easily underwrite such risks without using private reinsurers. In the US, crop insurance is delivered by the private sector, but the federal government is the underwriter. Some agricultural economists argue

that public delivery of crop insurance is more efficient than private delivery, but this remains a debatable issue.

5. Canada employs coinsurance to mitigate some moral hazard. Because only 70% of a shortfall in income is covered by AgriStability, with the remainder to be covered by the farmer, there is greater incentive for farmers to take actions that reduce risks. The use of coinsurance in the US depends on the particulars of the plethora of programs available to farmers.

There are problems with both approaches. AgriStability protects gross margin, but requires information only available from tax returns to determine whether an indemnity is warranted and how much it should be. This leads to uncertainty and delays in payments, and much dissatisfaction with the program. Meanwhile AgriInsurance provides only yield protection on a crop-by-crop basis. A better option might be to eliminate AgriStability and provide revenue insurance on a crop-by-crop basis, while keeping the coinsurance provision of AgriStability to mitigate moral hazard. After all, deep protection is also provided by AgriRecovery. The US relies on the private sector to deliver crop insurance, but, in Canada, public delivery was determined to be less expensive, although concomitant use of private reinsurance is considered costly and unnecessary as government finances are more than sufficient to underwrite crop insurance.

When it comes to coverage of *shallow losses* in income, the US employs several options—Agricultural Risk Coverage (ARC) and a Supplemental Coverage Option (SCO). Both programs are meant to protect a farmer against revenue losses of about 14%–25% from expected revenue. Farmers can choose among options that include the use of individual or county revenue benchmarks, the extent to which program premiums are subsidized (100% for ARC, 65% for SCO), and whether the program permits the farmer to remain eligible for a deficiency payment. There are no deficiency payment programs in Canada.

Canada protects farmers for shallow losses through AgriInvest. The federal government allows farmers each year to invest 1.5% of their annual net sales into a tax-free savings account (no income tax is levied on interest), matching producer contributions up to 1% with a maximum annual subsidy of $15,000. Further, producers are permitted to invest up to four times their annual net sales as a safety net to protect against shallow reductions in income (there are conditions under which funds can be withdrawn), although funds could be adequate to protect against deep losses as well. This limits the government's exposure to risk. This approach puts the onus on producers to protect themselves from shallow losses and is less costly than the use of a plethora of insurance-type programs as in the US.

Finally, the federal-provincial-territorial agreement on agricultural risk management in Canada, now known as the Canadian Agricultural Partnership, seeks to limit annual government expenditures. Under GF2, for example, the government sought to limit expenditures to about $0.7 billion annually, but they exceeded $1 billion in the last two years of the program. Yet, this is quite a bit lower than expected expenditures on agricultural risk management in the US, where premium subsidies cost about $6 billion annually with A&O costs adding nearly a further $1.5 billion. Surprisingly, the US taxpayer is spending approximately the same on federal agricultural risk programs as the Canadian taxpayer (approximately US$22 in both countries), although this excludes the provincial contribution to agricultural BRM programs in Canada.

Inevitably, the choice to provide agricultural BRM programs is a political choice that needs to take into account two factors: (1) the extent to which the authority wishes to subsidize farmers, and (2) the efficiency (or perhaps the effectiveness) of the risk management suite that is chosen. In the absence of government intervention to subsidize risk programs, crop yield or revenue insurance is unlikely to be provided by the private sector, at least not on the scale envisioned and required to ensure high rates of participation. The same is likely true of index insurance. Once the administrative and operating costs of providing insurance are added to the actuarially sound premiums, farmers will not generally participate.

Any risk management program will require government intervention, with the extent to which premiums are subsidized determining participation rates. Evidence from Canada and the US suggests that, in order to get participation rates above about 80%, the subsidy rate on premiums must be 60% or more, with A&O costs covered as well. Therefore, before deciding upon a course of action with regards to the choice of risk management programs, a decision needs to be made regarding the funds that the authority is willing to transfer from general taxpayers to the agricultural sector for this purpose. This decision is the object of rent-seeking by various agricultural stakeholders, including private insurance companies (see Chapter 7.2). Although one suspects that US institutions are more susceptible to rent-seeking than Canadian ones (except perhaps in the dairy sector), the overall per capita cost of agricultural programs appears to be similar, as measured by producer support estimates (see Chapter 7.1).

Finally, the role of the supra authority versus the regions differs between the two countries. The reason relates to the Canadian constitution. In the US, states do not participate in the subsidization of agricultural income support or BRM programs, although they are active in providing extension to farmers. In Canada, the provinces are very active in the funding and especially the administration of agricultural programs.

Appendix 9.A: A Brief Look at the Economics of Risk and Risk Aversion

Agricultural production is characterized by risk and uncertainty. As noted in the text, economists attempt to model the behavior of farmers so that they can analyze the effect of various agricultural policies and aid decision makers in designing policies most appropriate for addressing political objectives. The most basic assumption is that agricultural producers will choose an enterprise mix, a livestock management program, or to allocate land to various crops in a manner that maximizes the farm operator's expected net revenue (max ER), defined here as total revenue minus identifiable variable costs. In addition to models that assume farmers maximize expected net revenue, economists have developed alternative models that take into account risk aversion on the part of producers. Such models maximize expected utility (max EU) rather than expected net revenue. In this appendix, we focus on the economics of risk and risk aversion, although this will require the use of some mathematics.

9.A.1 Systemic versus Idiosyncratic Risk

Economists distinguish between systemic and idiosyncratic risk, where the latter risk relates to investment risk, uncertainties, and potential problems that are endemic to an individual asset, group of assets, or a specific class of assets. Agriculture falls into the latter category. Idiosyncratic risk is also referred to as specific risk or unsystematic risk. Thus, systemic risk refers to broader trends that affect almost all investments, such as increases or decreases in interest rates, recessions, changes in exchange rates, and so on. Agricultural business risk management programs are aimed at protecting farmers against idiosyncratic risks rather than systemic risks per se, although some BRM program components might provide a certain degree of protection against systemic risk.

No distinction is generally made between risk and uncertainty. In theory if not practice, risk is associated with known sources of potential variation in crop prices and yields, prices and potential diseases affecting livestock, and so forth. Thus, insurance agencies are able to use probability distributions about such risks to develop actuarially sound premiums for crop insurance, say. Contrariwise, uncertainty refers to events that are not readily predictable and/or so-called black swan events that are totally unknown. With uncertainty, it is not possible for an insurance company to develop actuarially sound premiums because there is little or no experience and information about such events to construct a probability distribution concerning their impact on agricultural outcomes. Farmers are protected against such idiosyncratic occurrences by disaster relief programs—by federal governments seeking to prevent the demise of a major portion of the farm sector.

Presumably, the farm sector is treated differently from other sectors of the economy because the idiosyncratic risks in agriculture are unusual and quite different from those in other sectors. If that were not the case, it would be difficult to justify large public expenditures on agricultural BRM programs that are not available elsewhere.

9.A.2 Expected Income Maximization and the Risk Aversion Coefficient

We distinguish between maximizing expected revenue (max ER) and maximizing expected utility (max EU), where a risk aversion coefficient represents the agricultural producer's attitude toward risk—the preference for (trade-off between) revenue and the variability of revenue. In general, a reduction in the variability of returns comes at the cost of a lower expected revenue. Here the distinction is clarified.

First consider max ER. The gross margin associated with crop k, denoted R_k, is given by the crop yield multiplied by the farm-gate price of the crop at harvest minus variable costs specific to the production of crop k. Consider a farmer who has to allocate available land to several types of crops. We assume a farmer seeks to maximize her expected net revenue, ER, by allocating land to various crop activities, subject to a fixed amount of land and exogenous input and output prices. The objective function can then be written as:

$$\text{Maximize } ER = E\left[\sum_{k=1}^{K} R_k\right] = E\left[\sum_{k=1}^{K} (p_k y_k - c_k) x_k\right],$$

where E is the expectations operator and $E[R_k]$ is the farmer's expected overall net revenue (\$/ha) from planting crop k; there are K crops that can be planted in any period; and x_k denotes the number of acres allocated to the production of crop k. Further, $p_{k,t}$ (\$/tonne) and $y_{k,t}$ (tonne/ha) represent, respectively, the output price and yield for crop k in period t; and c_k is the per unit-area variable cost (\$/ha) of producing crop k. Given that the expected net revenue is known for each crop, the optimal allocation of land to crops using the max ER criterion leads to the planting of one crop—the crop that yields the highest net expected return per ha. In practice, however, we find farmers allocate land to a variety of crops, including crops that have lower expected net revenue.

A farmer plants multiple crops for a variety of reasons, including biophysical ones. For example, good agronomic practice might require growing several crops in rotation. Even if this is taken into account (by constraining the optimization by a rotational requirement), the crop mix identified by a max ER model often falls short of the observed number of crops that are planted. An alternative approach recognizes that farmers are risk averse and concerned as much about the variance of returns as the mean expected return. In that case, a model is required that maximizes the utility of expected net returns.

Agricultural business risk management models employ max EU rather than max ER. The maximization of EU is equivalent to the maximization of the certainty equivalent (CE) which is approximated by CE = μ − ½ $[U''(W)/U'(W)]$ σ, where μ and σ are the mean and standard deviation of the distribution of wealth, W. The standard linear mean-variance model, denoted EV, begins by assuming that wealth W is normally distributed and that the utility function is a negative exponential function of W: $U(W)=1-e^{-\phi W}$. For this utility function, $-U''(W)/U'(W) = \phi$, which is the constant absolute risk aversion (CARA) coefficient.

Assume that the agricultural producer's initial or non-random wealth is given by W^0 and that the decision to allocate land to crops results in a random change in wealth with expectation given by $E[\sum_{k=1}^{K} R_k]$, where R_k refers to the net return accruing to crop k and is random because price p_k and yield y_k are stochastic variables, although costs c_k are assumed to be deterministic. Then, maximizing the expectation of the negative exponential utility function is approximately equivalent to maximizing CE subject to technical constraints. The max EU problem that assumes CARA is given by:

$$\text{Maximize CE} = W^0 + E[\sum_{k=1}^{K} R_k] - \frac{1}{2}\phi V(R),$$

where $V(R)$ refers to the variance of net returns and ϕ is constant.

Rather than CARA, we could assume decreasing absolute risk aversion (DARA). The logarithmic utility function, $U(W) = \ln(W^0 + \sum_{k=1}^{K} R_k)$, has the DARA property, although relative risk aversion $[= -W \times U''(W)/U'(W)]$ remains invariant to wealth. For the logarithmic utility function, $\phi = \frac{-U''(W)}{U'(W)} = \frac{1}{W^0 + E[\sum_{k=1}^{K} R_k]}$, which is substituted for ϕ in the above equation.

Unfortunately, max EU models are not always able to duplicate the actual planting decisions of farmers, regardless of whether CARA or DARA is assumed. As a result, economists have turned to positive mathematical programming as a means of calibrating a mathematical programming model to duplicate exactly the observed crop mix that a farmer plants. The calibration should ideally determine the parameters of an assumed (usually quadratic) cost function and the risk aversion coefficient, but doing so is extremely difficult and controversial. Some argue that, upon calibrating a model using positive mathematical programming based on maximizing expected net returns, the calibrated model parameters (the parameters of the cost function) actually take into account risk aversion on the part of producers. Even so, the calibrated parameters are not the same across producers, nor are they applicable over time for the same producer.

Finally, instead of max ER or max EU, some look to prospect theory to construct farmland allocation models that take into account producers' risk attitudes and, importantly for prospect theory, their current wealth and how current decisions affect future wealth.

Guide to Literature

For background on futures markets and financial derivatives, Carter (2003) and Zhang (1995) are easy to read. There is a vast and growing literature on weather-indexed insurance and derivatives; general readings include Jewson, Brix, and Ziehmann (2005) and Zapranis and Alexandridis (2012); applications to agriculture include Turvey (2001, 2012), Vedenov and Barnett (2004), and Musshof, Odening, and Xu (2011).

Much has been written about US agricultural policies at various times, some of which might be better considered interpretations of legislation. Publications relied upon in this chapter include Zulauf and Orden (2014, 2016); Schnitkey and Zulauf (2016); Schmitz et al. (2010); USDA (2012) on the 2008 Farm Bill programs; Babcock (2014); Sterly et al. (2018); and van Kooten (2017b). Glauber (2013), Smith and Glauber (2012), and Smith (2017) provide excellent reviews of the history of US crop insurance, while Chambers (2007) provides an interesting argument for observed low participation rates in crop insurance. The description of shallow loss programs under the 2014 Farm Bill, along with examples, come from Olson (2014a, 2014b, 2015) and USDA (2016). Crop insurance and trade issues are discussed by Zulauf and Orden (2012) and Zacharias and Paggi (2016). For data see USDA's statistics at https://www.ers.usda.gov/ and USDA's Risk Management Agency (RMA) at http://www.rma.usda.gov/data/sob.html.

For information on what's new in the 2018 Farm Bill, see https://www.rma.usda.gov/farmbill [accessed February 20, 2020]. Latest information on dairy coverage can be found at https://www.fsa.usda.gov/ programs-and-services/dairy-margin-coverage-program/index [accessed February 18, 2020]. Information on US Price Loss Coverage and Agricultural Risk Coverage programs is available from Schnitkey et al. (2019a, 2019b) and Brown, Griffith, and Zoller (2019). These publications also provide excellent examples of how programs function.

Budget and expenditure data for Agriculture and Agri-Food Canada are found at http://www.agr.gc.ca/eng/about-us/planning-and-reporting/departmental-results-reports/2017-18-departmental-results-report/?id=1536950956460 and http://www.agr.gc.ca/eng/about-our-department/planning-and-reporting/departmental-plans/2019-20-departmental-plan/?id=1551989243153 [accessed February 17, 2020].

Reviews and analyses of Canadian business risk management policies are provided, among others, by Ker et al. (2017), Antón, Kimura, and Martini (2011), Vercammen (2013), Barichello (1995), and van Kooten (2017c). The latest information on the Canadian Agricultural Partnership program is found at http://www.agr.gc.ca/eng/about-us/key-departmental-initiatives/canadian-agricultural-partnership/canadian-agricultural-partnership-business-risk-management-programs-effective-april-2018/?id=1500475317828 and http://www.agr.gc.ca/eng/about-us/key-departmental-initiatives/canadian-agricultural-partnership/?id=1461767369849 [accessed February 17, 2020].

For discussion of EU business risk management programs, see European Commission (2017) and van Asseldonk et al. (2019). Information in the appendix comes from a blog by James Chen, https://www.investopedia.com/terms/i/idiosyncraticrisk.asp, and from Liu, Duan, and van Kooten (2020).

Also see Chapter 10 in Schmitz et al. (2021).

Food for Thought

9.1. Private companies have never provided crop yield or revenue insurance on a large scale without government subsidies. In Canada, crop insurance is provided by provincial governments, while, in the US, it took legislation that mandated private provision before crop insurance was delivered by the private sector.

(a) What are some reasons why private crop insurance companies have not provided multi-peril crop insurance on a large scale without subsidization of some form?

(b) In light of your answer to (a), why has the private sector not provided index insurance on a large scale in lieu of crop yield or revenue insurance?

(c) Which approach to provision of crop insurance might be better: public delivery as in Canada or private delivery as in the US? Discuss.

9.2. What is a production margin in the context of AgriStability?

9.3. Explain the following:
(a) What is the difference between a futures contract and a forward contract?
(b) What is the difference between American option contracts and European ones?

9.4. Provide a brief explanation of each of the following terms:

(a) gross margin
(b) basis risk
(c) put option
(d) long position in futures market
(e) coinsurance
(f) adverse selection
(g) AgriStability program
(h) NISA program

(i) multi-peril crop insurance
(j) forward contract
(k) cooling degree days
(l) growing degree days
(m) call option
(n) moral hazard
(o) reference margin

9.5. In an article in a magazine for farmers, a financial analyst recommended that soybean producers consider purchasing a soybeans futures put option for September/October 2018, at least for some of their grain. On October 28, 2017, the spot price was around $13/bushel, while the futures price for September 2018 was $12/bu. Farmers would have to pay a premium of $0.75/bu for the option. Discuss what is meant by the analyst's suggestion and how the farmer might benefit.

9.6. Outcomes of a trading day in gold futures options are provided in the *Wall Street Journal* and duplicated in the table below (recall: calls are on the left; puts on the right). Consider someone who wishes in January of the year in question to purchase a put option.

Gold (CMX)

100 troy ounces; $ per troy ounce

Price	July	Aug	Oct	July	Aug	Oct
300	12.40	13.50	17.30	1.10	2.30	5.30
305	8.70	10.30	13.80	2.40	4.00	6.80
310	5.10	7.40	10.40	3.80	6.10	8.30
315	3.40	5.60	8.70	7.10	9.30	11.60
320	2.50	4.20	7.30	11.20	12.90	15.10
325	1.70	3.20	6.00	15.40	16.90	18.70

Est vol 3,800 Wd 2,303 calls 1,320 puts

Op int Wed 112,810 calls 54,036 puts

(a) If the purchaser chooses a strike price of $310 per ounce and an August expiry date, what is the premium paid to the option seller per ounce?

(b) What is the premium for one put option?

(c) What financial right does the put option give to the holder? That is, what has the buyer of the put option purchased?

(d) Suppose the price of gold falls before August. What should the holder of the put option do?

9.7. What is meant by a financial weather derivative?

9.8. Discuss why index-based insurance is preferred to crop insurance. What might be the major drawback of index-based insurance?

9.9. Canada's Advance Payments Program helps agricultural producers with cash flow problems. Provide an example of how this might benefit farmers.

9.10. In the United States, the acreage and value of commodities enrolled in crop insurance programs has increased since the 1990s. Describe two costs that the government incurs to support (or incentivize) the purchase of crop insurance by farmers.

9.11. Producers respond differently under certainty than with uncertainty. What is risk aversion and how does it affect a producer's supply function? A deficiency payment should reduce the price risk faced by a producer. Using a diagram, show the impact of deficiency payment to a risk-averse producer on the welfare of producers, consumers, taxpayers (government expenditures), and the net benefits to society. You can assume a closed economy with no trade. Label each axis and all relevant information on the graph. Show the gains and losses to each of the agents.

9.12. Food safety has come to dominate farm policy discussions. What is the importance of food safety from a policy perspective? Why would governments become involved in food safety? How do they get involved? How does public regulation relate to private safety regulations? How do food safety and its regulation relate to the supply chain? What is traceability and why is it important? How do international institutions interact with domestic regulations with respect to food safety?

10

CLIMATE CHANGE AND APPLIED
WELFARE ECONOMICS

Adverse weather is perhaps the greatest risk to agriculture and the main reason for agricultural risk management policies; and it is the primary sectors, agriculture and forestry, that are probably the most vulnerable to climate change. These sectors are impacted by climate change but they also offer potential to mitigate climate change through carbon policies, especially through the uptake of carbon in soils and vegetation. The role of forestry and land use in the mitigation of climate change is examined in this chapter (section 10.6). Before doing so, however, it is relevant to consider the application of applied welfare economics in the context of climate change. This requires a somewhat broader type of analysis because the methods discussed in this book are likely not up to the task of evaluating policy in the context of climate change. Indeed, there are various problems in bringing the tools of applied welfare economics to bear on climate change, three of which are as follows.

The first and foremost concern relates simply to the fact that there is a great deal of uncertainty when it comes to climate change. As discussed in the next section, there is uncertainty regarding: (1) the contribution of human activities (mainly burning of fossil fuels but also land-use changes) versus natural factors (viz., changes in the sun's activities) as determinants of global warming; (2) the projected increase in average global temperatures—how warm the Earth will get; and (3) the regional changes in climate that might be expected. Measurement of past temperatures and the conclusions to be drawn from trends of past temperatures are controversial, while projections based on climate models are not without their own problems.

Second, there is a great deal of uncertainty regarding the potential damages from future climate change, which, in turn, constitute the benefits of mitigating (avoiding) climate change. Many estimates of the potential economic damages from a warmer world relate to the environment—think of damage to health and lost biodiversity. Estimates of such damages are usually based on evidence from nonmarket valuation studies; but, as noted in Chapter 3.5, there remain questions regarding the validity of such estimates, particularly if they involve changes on the scale envisioned by climate change.

Finally, the validity of economic measures of surplus—consumer surplus, quasi-rent, and resource rent—is questionable in the context of policy related to climate change. The reason is that the changes to the world's economies that are required to mitigate climate change—to prevent temperatures from rising by no more than 2°C, or even 1.5°C, from pre-industrial times—are on such a scale that standard welfare measurement no longer applies. What is envisioned to stop or slow climate change is a (rather rapid) restructuring of the global economy! At the same time, climate change is projected to change the characteristics of natural resources and thereby the rents available from those resources. This puts enquiry beyond the realm of standard methods of economic analysis, which is why economists have opted for integrated assessment models (IAMs). These are best described as sophisticated, computer-simulated storylines.

The United Nations' Intergovernmental Panel on Climate Change (IPCC) is charged with understanding the risk underlying anthropogenic climate change from the perspective of the latest available science—to find the human footprint. Therefore, its priority is to discover the extent to which humans are responsible for climate change, and only secondarily the best means to mitigate humanity's role in causing climate change. Of course, the latter presupposes that climate change is both anthropogenic and that it can and should be avoided. In that case, a third task of climate research is to determine the cost of permitting climate change to continue unabated—that is, determining that the damages from potential global warming exceed the costs of mitigating it. Lastly, and only as an afterthought, does the IPCC examine possible strategies for adapting to climate change, even though the best strategy may well be to do nothing about climate change but rather focus on reducing global poverty by encouraging economic growth, thereby better enabling people to adapt to a warmer world.

In the following sections, we first examine the uncertainty prevalent in the subject of climate change (section 10.1). Uncertainty is found at every stage—there is uncertainty about the science and the economics. But uncertainty here is not the same as risk, because one cannot construct probability distributions about the variables of interest, particularly future weather events. Indeed, there may even be a black swan event sometime in the future—an example cannot be given because any example is no longer a black swan event. There is little to go on except some form of educated speculation; it is impossible to remove the uncertainty and replace it with probability distributions. This is the dilemma facing policy analysts, although reliance on integrated assessment models makes the educated speculation explicit (albeit difficult to follow unless one is schooled in the mathematical equations that are at the heart of such models). Nonetheless, we consider the role of economics and, particularly, integrated assessment models in more detail in section 10.2.

Given the state of knowledge at the big picture level, we illustrate the problems at the more pedestrian level by focusing on the economic impacts of climate change on agriculture and implications for future food security in sections 10.3 and 10.4, respectively. Then, in section 10.5, we return to the issue of discounting, arguing that urgency in addressing climate change can only be reflected in the rate used to discount future flows of carbon and not by the intergenerational discount rate discussed in Chapter 2.6. Finally, we examine climate mitigation activities in agriculture and forestry. The purpose is simply to provide an example of what the majority of practicing economists might encounter at the policy level. Unfortunately, it is more uncertainty and more modeling; such analyses are likely to be just as speculative as are the storylines we find in the climate literature.

10.1 Anthropogenic Climate Change and Its Impact

The most important greenhouse gas (GHG) is carbon dioxide (CO_2), so much so that the impact of other GHGs is translated into CO_2 equivalence (sometimes simply denoted CO_{2e}, although we continue to use CO_2 in reference to this broader interpretation). Scientists have come to the conclusion that the correlation between rising CO_2 emissions from fossil fuel use and concentrations of atmospheric CO_2 constitutes evidence that rising global temperatures are the result of human activities, even though the increase in temperatures and the rise in atmospheric CO_2 concentration are weakly correlated, if at all; there is no straightforward causal relation between human fossil fuel use and temperatures (although this remains an area of contention). Computer models are the mechanism that scientists rely upon to forecast future increases in global temperatures. Model outcomes have not been tested against actual outcomes, nor are climate models calibrated to real-world data. One question that needs to be addressed if we are to evaluate the costs and benefits of mitigating climate change is this: Can one base predictions of future climate (let alone future economic losses) on models that are not validated by observational data?[1]

While climate models are indeed based on well-known equations of physics, they also contain a lot of ad hoc parameters (such as the equilibrium climate sensitivity parameter discussed below) and relationships based on weak empirical foundations (e.g., transfer of heat between the atmosphere and oceans, and across various ocean layers). Further, models are nonlinear and difficult to solve, and do not guarantee that any solution is anything more than a local optimum. In other words, a numerical solution to a climate model could get trapped at a local point, known as an "attractor," as it often does; an entirely different solution can be found by slightly changing one or more of the model parameters, or the starting value needed in the algorithm to find a solution. In many cases, the highly nonlinear equations in climate models need to be linearized around some point near where the model builders expect the solution to lie, because the nonlinearities are too complex for even a high-powered computer to find a numerical solution. The climate modeler must make a value judgment as to whether a model solution is reasonable given the entered storyline. As a result, climate modeling is as much art as science and has come under increasing scrutiny (e.g., see Hourdin et al. 2017; Millar et al. 2017; Lewis 2018; McKitrick and Christy 2020).

10.1.1 Climate Sensitivity

One of the many parameters in the model that the modeler needs to set is the equilibrium or effective climate sensitivity (ECS). Climate sensitivity refers to the expected increase in temperature from a doubling of the atmospheric concentration of CO_2. In climate models it is the critical ECS parameter that converts a rise in atmospheric CO_2 into an increase in temperature. Values of the climate sensitivity parameter used by the

---

[1] The famous philosopher of science Karl Popper argued that the predictions of any theory or model must be verified by actual data; even if the actual data verify the predictions, this would still not guarantee that a model is correct. Indeed, one can only determine whether a theory or model is false (one can never prove it true), and that occurs when model predictions do not stand up to observation.

IPCC have ranged from a high of 4.5°C to a low ranging from 2.5°C to 3.0°C. While earlier IPCC reports were much more assertive about the size of the ECS parameter, stating a likely range of 2.0°C to 4.5°C with a best estimate of 3.0°C, the 2014 Fifth Assessment Report (AR5) is much less certain about the ECS parameter, reducing its lower likely bound to 1.5°C and offering no best estimate. Yet, the IPCC expressed greater confidence that global warming is anthropogenic in nature than ever before; as of 2014, the IPCC is 95% certain that warming is caused by humans, up from 90% in 2007, 66% in 2001, and only 50% in 1996. These certainty values are frightening for the simple reason that they are speculative, determined from climate models using various storylines regarding future trends in population growth, technological change, increases in per capita income, convergence of per capita incomes between poor and rich countries, energy use, and so forth. The ECS values used by the IPCC are not based on observations—i.e., not based on science.

The extent of global warming hinges on the role of feedbacks. If increases in atmospheric CO_2 increase water vapor in the atmosphere without increasing cloud cover, then there is a positive feedback that serves to amplify the initial warming. However, if increased water vapor leads to increased cloud cover, there is a negative feedback caused by the cloud albedo (reflectivity)—reflecting solar radiation back into space before it can warm Earth's surface. This offsets the initial increase in warming caused by CO_2 rather than amplifying it. The good news is that empirical evidence, as opposed to climate models, shows that climate sensitivity to CO_2 is much less than originally anticipated—that human activities, while contributing to global warming, are less likely to lead to dangerous global warming. Recent studies have found much lower values of the ECS parameter, some even reporting ECS values of 1.0°C and less.

We can examine the implications of the ECS parameter for economic policy making by examining the social cost of carbon (SCC), which is the marginal damage from emitting another metric ton of CO_2 (tCO_2) into the atmosphere. If economic damages increase with temperature, then the SCC will rise over time. Estimates of the SCC are available from IAMs, two of which are open source—William Nordhaus' Dynamic Integrated Climate and Economics (DICE) model and Richard Tol's Climate Framework for Uncertainty, Negotiation and Distribution (FUND) model. Integrated assessment models are discussed in more detail in section 10.2, but here, as in Chapter 2.6, we use the DICE model to illustrate the sensitivity of the social cost of carbon to the ECS parameter only (see also Table 2.1). The results are provided in Figure 10.1.

The marginal damage from climate change is given by the SCC. Then, to determine the appropriate carbon tax, it is necessary to multiply the marginal damage by the inverse of the marginal cost of public funds, which is a measure of the scarcity of public funds. The marginal cost of public funds measures the loss incurred by society in raising additional revenues to finance government spending due to the distortion of resource allocation caused by taxation. The social marginal cost of public funds differs by jurisdiction and the type of tax used to raise revenue (income, corporate, or sales tax), with estimated values ranging for about $1.15 to well over $2.00. With an ECS of 3.0°C, the SCC estimated by the DICE model amounts to $35/tCO_2$ in 2035, rising to $100/tCO_2$ by 2060; conversely, if the ECS is 1.0°C, the SCC is $7/tCO_2$ in 2035, rising to no more than $43/tCO_2$ by 2100.

Figure 10.1 Effect of assumptions about the equilibrium climate sensitivity (ECS) on the social cost of carbon (SCC)

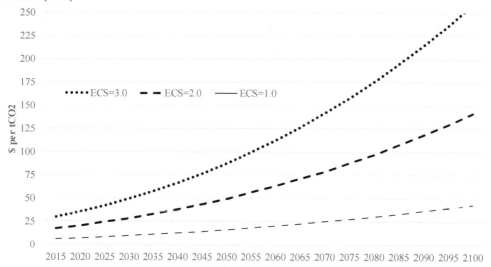

Source: Author's calculations using the DICE model

A carbon tax based on an ECS of 3.0°C would, therefore, need to be set at $17.50 to $30.40 per tCO$_2$ in 2035, depending on the marginal cost of public funds, and $50–$85 in 2060. However, if the ECS is assumed to be 1.0°C, the carbon tax should be set at $3.50–$6.10 in 2035 and some $22–$38 in 2100. The path of carbon taxes associated with an ECS of 2.0°C would fall somewhere between these. Clearly, the debate about the ECS should be settled before decision makers impose high carbon taxes.

10.1.2 Damages

Now consider the economic side of the ledger (although it was implicitly taken into account in the construction of Figure 10.1). The benefits of mitigating climate change are the damages purportedly prevented. What are the expected damages from global warming? The list of potential damages includes those from sea level rise, more frequent and more intense storms, heat waves and drought, increased risk of disease, increasing acidity of the oceans, loss of biodiversity, increased international tensions and climate refugees, and even psychological damage. Upon investigating the potential damage from each of these possible effects, one is struck by two things. First, many simply do not exist. There is no evidence that storm frequency or intensity is increasing. Rather, the available observational evidence suggests that the incidence and accumulated energy of storms have actually declined over the period of greatest anthropogenic global warming—the 40 years since about the mid-1970s (see, e.g., Alexander 2020; Klotzbach et al. 2018). While damages from various storm events may have increased over time, this cannot be attributed to more frequent or severe storms. Instead, if storm damages have increased, it is because more people and more valuable property are in harm's way.

Nor is there evidence to indicate that climate change is causing sea levels to rise, although one might expect this if oceans expand as a result of warming and the melting of glaciers on land (as melting sea ice does not increase sea levels). The problem is that some coastal areas are subsiding (partly due to groundwater withdrawal), while others are lifted up due to natural forces. Measurement of changes in sea level is also a problem as gauges are affected by storm surges, subsidence, et cetera. The point is that, without better evidence, one is left to speculate, which is unscientific.

Likewise, fears that oceans are becoming acidic due to greater absorption of CO_2 is misleading because, based on the pH scale, the ocean is alkaline unless its pH falls below 7.0. The current pH of the oceans is about 8.1, having fallen from a pH of 8.2 in pre-industrial times. This is hardly anything to fear.

With regard to health, the most frequently cited example concerns malaria, which hypothetically would spread as tropical temperatures shifted pole-ward. But malaria (like dengue fever) is not a tropical disease but a disease of poverty. Malaria was present in Europe and North America as recently as the 1960s and was eradicated in these regions through mosquito control, draining of swamps, and public health efforts. Indeed, the greatest malaria outbreak in modern times occurred in Siberia (not noted for its tropical climate) in the 1920s and 1930s, infecting 9.5 million and killing over 600,000; meanwhile, malaria remains a problem in North Korea, but not in South Korea. Effective vector control and the quality of health care, as more recent virus outbreaks—Ebola, Zika, and coronavirus—have shown, are more important than lower temperatures in the prevention of disease. One can only conclude that the health of the globe's population would best be served by economic development that lifts people out of poverty.

Historical data indicate that the frequency and intensity of wildfires has declined dramatically since the 1920s and show no increase in the period since about 1980.[2] This appears to be true not only for the US but for the globe more generally. The reasons likely have to do with fire management, fire suppression, and technology more than climate. Certainly, it is not possible to blame climate change for an increase in wildfires for which there is no evidence.

Other links between changes in climate and economic outcomes are interesting but also controversial. An increase in the atmospheric concentration of CO_2 improves agricultural productivity, enabling crops to better utilize nutrients including water, thereby making them less susceptible to drought. While droughts might increase in some regions of the globe, overall a warmer fSourceatmosphere will hold more moisture leading to increased rainfall. Some argue that, as temperatures continue to rise beyond an increase of 2˚C, say, the CO_2-fertilization effect will be offset by too much heat, with precipitation evaporating before it hits the ground. These arguments are accepted with no empirical support, perhaps because there are few studies that have investigated what happens to crop yields when a higher atmospheric concentration of CO_2 is combined with temperature increases of more than 2°C. The impact of climate change on agriculture and how it might be measured is discussed further in section 10.3.

---

[2] Data are from the US National Interagency Fire Center for 1926–2019 at https://www.nifc.gov/fireInfo/fireInfo_stats_totalFires.html [accessed December 7, 2020]. Canadian data are found at http://nfdp.ccfm.org/en/data/fires.php [accessed December 7, 2020] for 1990–2019. See Arora and Melton (2018) for a reduced trend in wildfires at the global scale.

Higher concentrations of atmospheric CO_2 also enhance tree growth, enabling greater production of wood products from a smaller forested area and thereby increasing natural habitat or wild spaces. This would offset potential losses in biodiversity and might even enhance global biodiversity. Conversely, climate mitigation policies that lead to greater use of wood biomass to produce energy will have the opposite effect and reduce biodiversity. Biodiversity loss is difficult to measure, while valuing such losses likely poses an even greater challenge. The methods used to determine nonmarket values, which play prominently in many evaluations of the costs and benefits of mitigating climate change, are problematic, especially if values measured locally are applied at a global scale (see discussion in Chapter 3.4). Questions regarding the use of nonmarket valuation apply not only to biodiversity but to environmental economics more broadly as the damages avoided by reducing pollution, for example, are estimated using the same techniques.

Polar bears are the poster child of biologists—the harbinger of climate change's negative impact on biodiversity. Yet polar bear populations seem to be increasing and not decreasing as a result of declining sea ice. Finally, mortality from cold weather events currently exceeds that from hot weather. Therefore, as the globe warms, deaths might actually decline.[3]

It may well be true that unprecedented global warming will lead to large damages as envisioned by climate scientists. The point here is simply that there remains uncertainty about the physical science, the validity of future climate projections, and the economic damages that might be forthcoming. While economists have investigated a scenario where the probability of damages from global warming are high (the case of "fat tails" on the probability distribution) the analysis is speculative at best. A catastrophic climate event is comparable only to the possibility that Earth is struck by a devastatingly large object from outer space.[4] Such catastrophic natural events are beyond the realm of economic and scientific analysis, but fall more in the realm of philosophy and religion.

10.2 Economic Evaluation: The Role of Integrated Assessment Models

What role is there for economic analysis? As pointed out, there is a great deal of uncertainty regarding the extent of future climate change. If the climate sensitivity parameter is 0.5°C to 1.5°C rather than 2.5°C to 4.5°C, then the threat of climate change has essentially disappeared (see Figure 10.1), and it would make little sense to implement expensive climate change mitigation strategies. Likewise, if natural causes trump anthropogenic ones as the culprit behind global warming, little can be done to prevent warming. Again, no action should be taken beyond what might make sense for other reasons. Further, climate models are unreliable and unable to predict 100 years into the future with any sort of accuracy, leaving us with nothing more than speculative scenarios of future climate, some of which might be plausible. Therefore, if we should do anything (and that is not certain), it makes sense to rely on a simple tax perhaps that might vary over time

---

[3] Crockford (2018) provides an excellent review of polar bear issues, including the potential effect of climate change on population trends.

[4] One might include here a thermonuclear holocaust, but many aspects of such an event are more predictable than those of climate change, and are probably more catastrophic as well.

as more information becomes available, rather than legislate large structural changes to the economy through regulations, subsidies that shift technology in a particular direction, carbon trading that is open to corruption, and high carbon taxes that harm the poor more than the rich.

Perhaps the most difficult challenge for applied welfare analysis comes in the arena of climate change. How do we evaluate projects at this scale? Clearly, many of the assumptions underlying CBA are violated, most notably the assumption of small scale—that prices remain constant and that the fundamental equation of applied welfare economics (equation 2.4) can straightforwardly be applied. As a result, economists instead employ integrated assessment models (IAMs) to address the welfare economics of global warming. IAMs constitute quite a different approach to applied economics than has been examined in this book.

10.2.1 Climate Models and Policy Models

What are the linkages between climate models and economic policy? How do projections of future climate change affect economic modeling efforts? Well, economic types of models enter into the analysis of climate change quite early. The process of translating climate projections into economic policy variables proceeds in three steps:

1. Storylines are developed and used to determine future emissions of CO2 (recalling that other greenhouse gases are included in this measure as used here). Storylines are then converted into emissions scenarios using one or more IAMs.
2. Emissions scenarios are translated into future climate scenarios using various climate models.
3. Finally, IAMs that differ from those employed in step 1 are used to determine the economic impact of climate change. These IAMs (DICE and FUND, for example) are used to derive optimal policies for mitigating (or perhaps adapting to) global warming.

Prior to its 2014 report, the IPCC essentially employed four storylines to imagine the changes that will occur in the future—an attempt to project what the world will look like in 100 years. These storylines were described in the IPCC's *Special Report on Emission Scenarios* of 2000 and were referred to as A1, A2, B1, and B2. Some of the storylines were not at all realistic, because the assumptions underlying them were the result of a political process that involved the United Nations and member countries. For example, the stated goals of rich countries were to maintain their own growth while ensuring economic development in poor countries, namely the least developed countries, so that the LDCs would eventually "catch up" with the richer nations—a concept known as convergence. At the same time, since developed countries could not neglect their own citizens, there is an emphasis on continued economic growth to prevent recessions that could result in high unemployment and social unrest. Meanwhile, the millennium goals of the United Nations and World Bank had committed rich nations to reduce poverty in developing countries. Overall, these political objectives were (and still are) reflected in the emission storylines.

Prior to its Fifth Assessment Report (AR5) in 2014, the IPCC's *Special Report on Emissions Scenarios* was superseded by Representative Concentration Pathways (RCPs). The RCPs describe various climate futures, all of which are considered possible. They depend on the concentration of GHGs in the atmosphere, measured in parts per million by volume (ppm) of CO_2, with other GHGs measured in CO_2 terms. Rather than emissions, as in previous assessments, the focus in AR5 was the concentration of atmospheric CO_2. Four pathways were identified: RCP2.6, RCP4.5, RCP6.0, and RCP8.5, where the number identifying the pathway representing the expected radiative forcing for the year 2100, measured in W/m^2. The four pathways of atmospheric CO_2 are provided in Figure 10.2.

Figure 10.2 Paths of atmospheric CO_2 and equivalent concentrations for four RCPs

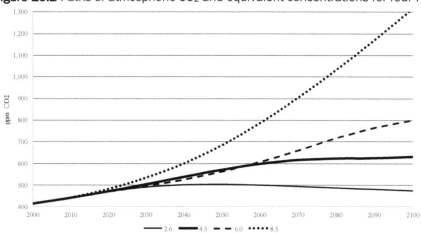

Source: Author's calculations using the DICE model

Although these RCPs were initially used in the AR5, they are now being augmented by Shared Socioeconomic Pathways (SSP) to provide more flexible descriptions of possible futures within each RCP. The SSPs consist of five narratives (storylines) depicting future socioeconomic trends. These narratives are briefly described as follows:

1. SSP1: "Sustainability: Taking the Green Road"
    •   Low challenges to mitigation and adaptation
    •   A world of sustainably focused growth and equality
2. SSP2: "Middle of the Road"
    •   Medium challenges to mitigation and adaptation
    •   A world where trends broadly follow historical patterns
3. SSP3: "Regional Rivalry: A Rocky Road"
    •   High challenges to mitigation and adaptation
    •   A world of resurgent nationalism
4. SSP4: "Inequality: A Road Divided"
    •   Low challenges to mitigation and high challenges to adaptation
    •   A world of ever-increasing inequality
5. SSP5: "Fossil-fueled Development: Taking the Highway"
    •   High challenges to mitigation and low challenges to adaptation
    •   A world of rapid and unconstrained growth in economic output and energy use

As before, the IAMs used to develop these pathways focus on the energy sector because they are used to develop emissions scenarios.

Modern climate models are aptly described as complex, integrated ocean-atmosphere-terrestrial energy circulation models. Not all climate models include a highly developed terrestrial component, and some models consist only of an atmosphere; in these cases, the ocean and/or terrestrial components are taken into account through some sort of exogenous parameterization that might be derived from a relevant stand-alone model. The climate models have a resolution that varies from 5km × 5km to an even finer 2.5km × 2.5km. The models use emissions information from the IAMs based on the above RCPs (and informed by the SSPs) to project the future course of global temperatures.

Ultimately, climate models are expected to answer some simple questions: If anthropogenic emissions of greenhouse gases cause climate change, what will the average global temperature do in the future? Will the Earth's temperature rise and to what extent? Are there non-anthropogenic and external factors that affect the Earth's temperature and to what extent? All of the basic questions can be answered using a "simple" energy balance model—an accounting of the energy arriving and leaving the Earth, and its effect on temperature. Large climate models look at energy exchanges within the various atmospheric columns, from one column to its neighbors (albeit at various vertical levels), and exchanges with the land and oceans, with each of the terrestrial and ocean systems modeled separately. Although this adds tremendous complexity in the way of mathematics and computing needs, the essential elements remain the radiation flux coming from the sun, the energy retained by the Earth, the energy flux from the Earth to outer space, and the factors that affect these fluxes (e.g., volcanic eruptions), especially anthropogenic emissions of greenhouse gases.

For the most part, climate models are superfluous to economic models, as the output from climate models is too detailed for use by economists. Numerical economic models do not use the output from climate models to estimate damages and analyze policies to mitigate climate change. Climate models only serve to inform the climate modules employed in economic models; basically, the policy models exploit information on the exchange of CO_2 between the atmosphere and the ocean, and the relation between the rise in atmospheric concentrations of CO_2 and average global temperature increases. Economic models generally seek to maximize the discounted value of the utility of consumption over a specified time horizon; include a carbon-temperature module; specify simple relationships between a policy variable, temperatures, damages, and time; and add technical and economic constraints to address things such as investment in various capital goods, improvements in technology over time (perhaps even through investment in research and development), population growth, resource constraints, and so on. Depending on the particular IAM, the model might choose the optimal level of consumption and the value of the policy variable in each period, investment in a (technology) variable that mitigates climate change, investment in capital goods, and so forth. The value of the objective function (the discounted utility of per capita consumption) constitutes the measure of welfare gains or losses associated with climate change and policies to mitigate it.

Two IAMs that are used for policy analysis are open source—DICE and FUND. These models, and similar ones, have been criticized by both economists and climate scientists. The models are considered to be too ad hoc, with outcomes highly sensitive to assumed parameter values (as demonstrated in Table 2.1 and Figure 10.1). The parameterizations of the carbon-climate components of these models have been questioned, but such questions are raised with respect to the climate models as well. Despite such critiques, IAMs offer one of the only ways that economists can provide policy advice that is informed by the findings of the climate models and the storylines that are used to determine future CO_2 emissions. Such advice may only be as believable as the storylines themselves.

10.2.2 Carbon Price as a Policy Variable

The major policy instrument in assessment models that integrate climate change and the economy is a carbon price. Economic models provide information about the marginal damages associated with CO_2 emissions, which, in turn, informs the setting of a carbon tax or CO_2 emission targets (with price determined through trading in a carbon market). Economists generally prefer taxes over emissions trading, partly because emission trading involves the use of carbon offsets in lieu of actual emissions reductions, and because offset trading can facilitate corruption. Taxes have been lauded because they could result in an added benefit ("dividend") if the tax revenue is used to reduce distortionary taxes elsewhere in the economy, thereby leading to an efficiency gain over and above the environmental benefit from reducing CO_2 emissions. However, where carbon taxes have been implemented, governments have preferred to redistribute some of the tax revenue as lump sum payments to low income earners (including students) rather than reducing or removing distortionary taxes elsewhere. Further, governments have a predilection to favor particular technologies over others through subsidies and the use of regulations to reduce CO_2 emissions in certain sectors of the economy, but not others. This leads to more distortions rather than less. Overall, carbon trading and government intervention can increase mitigation costs to the extent that adaptation may be preferred.

If a carbon tax is employed, it should be set equal to the social cost of carbon, which measures the marginal economic damage, but then divided by the marginal cost of public funds (as noted above). Economists use temperature (not CO_2 levels) to determine economic damages and thus the social cost of carbon—i.e., integrated assessment models relate economic damages to changes in global temperatures, thereby connecting an economic policy variable (viz., a carbon tax) to the path of global temperatures. For example, Nordhaus's well-known and oft-used DICE model employs a simple causal relationship between global average temperatures and economic damages, and recommends the carbon prices needed to incentivize economic activities that reduce CO_2 emissions.

Nordhaus has certainly not been afraid to make the case for a carbon tax, advocating a tax that rises gradually as atmospheric concentrations of CO_2 increase. The tax is designed to increase in response to the supposed increase in damages from rising CO_2 levels (Figure 10.1). A tax helps to achieve the objectives of a climate policy (reduce fossil fuel consumption) and, as Nordhaus has argued, has some additional advantages.

- It has the potential to raise substantial revenue to set against a nation's debt.
- It is well understood.
- It increases economic efficiency as it tackles undesirable CO_2 emissions.

- It has potential health benefits, because reducing emissions of CO_2 will also reduce emissions of other harmful pollutants, assuming nothing else changes.
- It displaces regulatory inefficiencies associated with attempts to regulate greenhouse gas emissions and useless subsidies to produce ethanol or protect standing forests, for example, when both these policies have been shown to have little or no impact on overall greenhouse gas emissions (due to release of other GHGs and/or leakages).
- A carbon tax can be harmonized across countries, reducing overall distortions.
- A carbon tax leads to fewer opportunities for corruption compared to a cap-and-trade scheme, especially if carbon offsets are permitted, as has been the case in practice.

The other advantage is that a carbon tax is the simplest policy instrument; other policy instruments—such as mandatory fuel standards for automobiles or subsidies for renewable energy, for example—cannot be built into the types of models economists use to study the economics of climate change. Policies regarding these types of regulations are difficult to analyze using existing IAMs.

One drawback of a carbon price/tax is that it results in income redistributional effects. In some countries, carbon policies have occasioned energy poverty: people can no longer afford to pay the higher costs of energy, requiring them to reduce their consumption of essentials such as food, clothing, and energy. For elderly people in some countries, such as the UK, a reduction in the consumption of heating services during the coldest periods of the year has led to higher rates of illness and mortality. Indeed, a carbon tax as low as \$25 per tCO_2 could increase the cost that a household pays for electricity by 150% (if it is generated using coal), while the price of gasoline could rise by more than 15%.

10.3 Economic Impacts of Climate Change on Agriculture

In this section, we examine the impact of climate change on agriculture. Economists have employed two methods to estimate the potential damages of climate change in the primary sectors. The first method uses regression analysis to determine how growing-season variables, such as precipitation and especially temperatures (heat units), affect crop yields or farmland values. Once a regression model has been estimated, projected changes in rainfall and heat units from climate models are applied to determine the expected climate-induced yield or land value. Under the second method, economists use mathematical programming models to mimic a representative farmer's behavior given the economic, policy, and biophysical constraints (including climate constraints) that she faces.

10.3.1 Land Rents and the Regression Approach

Rising food prices lead to an expansion of agricultural production onto marginal land that could not be profitably cultivated at a lower price. At the margin, farmers would earn enough to cover all expenses, including an adequate return on capital investment. When marginal land is brought into production, owners of better land—land that is more fertile, experiences better weather outcomes, or is situated nearer markets—will earn a differential rent, also referred to as Ricardian rent after the nineteenth-century economist David Ricardo (as discussed in Chapter 2.2 and shown in Figure 2.2). The idea is illustrated with the aid of Figure

10.3, where three crop choices are available to a farmer, and the factor determining differential rent is the expected annual number of growing degree days (GDDs; defined in Chapter 9.1). When expected GDDs are low (say, G_0 in the figure), the best crop choice in terms of the greatest rent is durum wheat. It is possible to grow maize, but the maize does not ripen and can only be made into silage for animal feed. Likewise, sorghum yields are inadequate and prices are too low; sorghum is a poor choice compared to durum wheat or maize.

Figure 10.3 Impact of changing heat units on crop choice

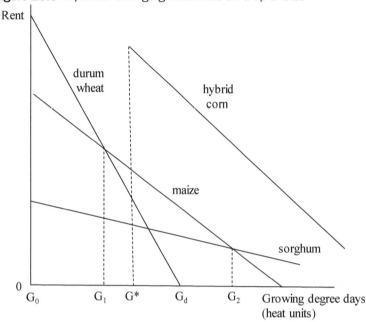

Now suppose temperatures rise and thus the number of GDDs during the growing season rises. If GDDs increase beyond G_d, for example, it is too hot for the landowner to plant durum wheat—the combination of yield and expected price is too low to cover costs of planting and harvesting. Point G_d represents the *extensive margin* for wheat, since rents are zero at this point; at G_d, the landowner would receive just enough to earn a rate of return on investment that is comparable to what she could earn if she sold the land and invested the proceeds in a money market instrument. Even before the Earth warms by enough to realize G_d growing degree days at the site of the farm in question, the landowner would shift from planting wheat to planting maize, which requires more heat units; if GDD is greater than G_1, the farmer would no longer choose to plant wheat, but would switch to maize. Thus, G_1 represents the *intensive margin* of land use. Finally, should GDDs exceed G_2, the farmer would switch to sorghum. G_2 represents the intensive margin between maize and sorghum.

Thus far it is assumed that the landowner only experiences lower rents as warming occurs, which is a basic assumption employed by many analysts. However, suppose there is a crop, referred to here as hybrid corn, that is available to the farmer once the expected growing degree days exceed G^*. This crop will yield large rents, much larger than those from durum, maize, or sorghum. In that case, as warming occurs, landowners will switch to hybrid corn, thereby realizing higher rents than they would without global warming.

A hedonic model estimates farmland values as a function of climate variables, such as GDDs and precipitation, and various control variables (soil quality, latitude, nearness to an urban area, population density, nearby open spaces, presence of irrigation, etc.). The climate and control variables constitute the explanatory variables or regressors of interest. The land-rent regression model has the following general functional form:

$$z_{it} = \hat{a}_{1,it}\, \Delta h_{1,it} + \hat{a}_{2,it}\, \Delta h_{2,it} + \ldots + \hat{a}_{n,it}\, \Delta h_{n,it} + \hat{b}_{1,it}\, k_{1,it} + \hat{b}_{2,it}\, k_{2,it} + \ldots + \hat{b}_{m,it}\, k_{m,it} + \varepsilon_{it}, \qquad (10.1)$$

where z_{it} is the dependent variable—the value of land in crop i in year t. It might consist of actual sales data, yield data (which is multiplied by price to obtain value), assessed values (used for tax purposes), or even self-reported land values.

The explanatory variables on the right-hand side of (10.1) are heat units h and control variables k. Heat units are measured as the amount of time (say, hours) during the crop-growing season in year t that crop i is exposed to temperatures that fall within a small interval j denoted $\Delta h_{j,it}$. There are n such j intervals, where the initial j interval, Δh_1, might be the number of hours that the crop is exposed to temperatures <1°C; the second interval, Δh_2, would be the hours the crop is exposed to temperatures from 1°C to 2°C; and so on. The control variables might include region-level precipitation, longitude and latitude, distance to a city, and so forth. An important variable such as precipitation may be ignored in such models because rainfall can vary greatly even between neighboring farms, so instrumental variables such as average regional precipitation or a drought index might be used instead. Finally, ε_{it} represents the error term, which is often assumed to be normally distributed about a mean of zero.

Once the parameters of the model (a_1, ..., a_n, b_1, ..., b_m) are estimated, as indicated by the hats ($^\wedge$) on the parameters (in which case the ε_{it} should not really be shown), it is possible to forecast the impact of changes in the Δh_j on the dependent variable. The changes in Δh_j are derived from climate forecasts that provide the future pattern of temperatures. If future climate affects one of the k variables, it too will need to be changed to derive a forecast of z_i.

Assuming the dependent variable is farmland value, then, once the model parameters have been estimated for a sample of farms, the results are used first to predict farmland values across an entire study region or country. Then the climate variables are changed to reflect the projected change in climate, with the same model parameters now used to predict farmland values for that region or country under global warming. The model implicitly assumes that if landowners face different climate conditions, they will choose the agricultural land use (crop and technique) that maximizes their net returns. The differences between farmland values in the current climate state and the projected future climate regime constitute the costs (if overall farmland values fall) or benefits (if values rise) of climate change.

Using hedonic econometric analyses of land-use values, research results have been mixed. One study projected a small increase in US GDP as a result of global warming, but others have found that climate change would unambiguously impose net costs upon the US agricultural sector if the average global temperature rose by 2.5°C or more above pre-industrial levels, although some northern states could gain. For Canada, results varied from a marginal gain of only $1.5 million per year to projected average gains in land values of more than 50% in the short term (to 2040) and upwards of 75% or more in the longer term (to 2060), based on projections from climate models. Canadian agriculture could well benefit from global warming, as most likely would that in Russia, but most other regions for which similar analyses were performed would tend to lose once temperatures rose much beyond 2°C. Many commentators would argue that beyond a temperature increase of 5°C, say, a catastrophe is likely; it is the potential cost associated with a possible catastrophe that is considered to be the only worthwhile cost of climate change to take seriously.

There are some drawbacks to these types of models, however. First, if a crop had not been previously grown in the region for which the hedonic regression model is estimated (viz., hybrid corn in Figure 10.3), a crucial benefit of climate change is overlooked. Second, forest use of land needs to be taken into account, but forestlands are often ignored because there is little information on private forestland prices (much is owned by institutional investors) or the forestland is owned by the government and no price data are available. Further, there is no reason to suppose that the estimated parameters will continue to hold under a changed climate regime, which might be the case if growing conditions under a future climate regime are outside observed values (which increases uncertainty of predicted values); it is also difficult to use hedonic models estimated for a current period to project how the same land might be used some 50 to 100 years later. Ricardian models do not take into account technological, biophysical, and economic changes that might occur, nor can they be expected to do so. But they also fail to take into account the fertilizer impact of CO_2, which is discussed below. Despite these flaws, the land-rent method is one of the few statistical approaches that can be used to determine potential damages from global warming, and it is solidly rooted in economic theory.

10.3.2 Mathematical Representation of Landowner Decisions

Mathematical programming models of the agricultural and/or forest sectors are similar to IAMs as they both seek to optimize an economic objective function subject to biophysical, political, and economic constraints. The main differences relate primarily to detail—mathematical programming models are detailed sector-level models that initially replicate observed crop allocations, input use, or other primary sector activities. Models are then used to investigate the impacts of exogenous price shocks, introduction of a carbon tax, changes in crop or livestock insurance schemes, introduction of new crops or crop varieties (e.g., resulting from genetic engineering), and such. Models seek to optimize gross margins (gross returns minus certain variable costs), land values, the utility of a representative landowner, or some other relevant economic variable subject to various economic, social, climate, biophysical, and technical constraints. The constraints represent the crop production technology, but somewhere (usually in the production constraints) climate factors are a driver. Parameters in these models are often based on information from other studies. Since mathematical programming models can focus solely on the allocation of land among uses, they can provide detailed information about how climate change affects the agricultural sector. To determine the costs (or benefits) associated with climate change, the calibrated model is solved with the current climate conditions, and subsequently re-solved with the projected future climate conditions. Differences between the base-case objective function and the future scenario (or counterfactual) constitute an estimate of the costs or benefits of climate change.

Upon comparing econometric results with those from mathematical programming models, we find that the Canadian results and those for the northern US states are in line with earlier studies (late 1980s) by Canadian agricultural economists. The researchers found that even if farmers only adopted crops suitable to the changed climate, Western Canadian farmers could benefit by planting corn rather than wheat and barley. At around the same time, agricultural economists from various agricultural universities in the western US used crop simulation and economic models to conclude that climate change in that country could lead to an overall increase or decrease in well-being, but that such changes were generally small. Indeed, results depended on which of several climate models was employed, but the researchers were unambiguous in finding that the distributional impacts of climate change were the largest and most important aspect.

Likewise, in the mid-1990s, a group of USDA economists linked a global land-use model to a computable general equilibrium model to estimate the global welfare impacts of climate change as it affected output in the primary sectors (Darwin et al. 1995; Schimmelpfenning et al. 1996). They found that global GDP would increase by 0.2%–1.2% depending on which climate model's projections was employed. Another such study (Stevenson et al. 2013) examined past agricultural land-use decisions, finding that increases in atmospheric CO_2 led to a fertilization effect that reduced the area needed to produce the globe's food supply. Over the period 1965–2004, this prevented the conversion of some 18–27 million hectares (ha) of forested land into agriculture. Further, Stevenson et al. (2013) found that, in the absence of crop productivity improvements associated with the green revolution, greenhouse gas emissions would have been 5.2–7.4 Gt higher than observed in 1965–2004.

Overall, the consensus from the regression models, and perhaps to a lesser extent from the mathematical programming studies, suggest that agriculture would benefit from a rise in global mean temperature of a few degrees, buoyed in particular by a CO_2-feritilization effect, but could be greatly harmed beyond this. Further, crop regions in the northern latitudes would likely benefit from global warming in terms of higher yields and the opportunity to plant more valuable crops, while farmers in the midlatitudes could experience a decline in incomes. But what about global food security?

10.4 Climate Change and Food Security

Does climate change lead to greater food insecurity? This is a difficult question to answer. Food security might be compromised at the regional level, but not at the global level, or it might be compromised at both scales. Analysis of this issue is plagued by uncertainty, although the case will be made that the agricultural sector is sufficiently resilient that, with appropriate incentives, climate change is unlikely to result in food insecurity.

We begin by first considering climate change and food security in the context of historical crop yields. Consider trends in yields (measured in t/ha) for four grain crops—maize, rice, wheat, and soybeans—and for selected crop-producing regions in the developed and developing world. These trends were provided in Figures 8.11 and 8.12 for the EU, China, Brazil, India, landlocked developing countries, and least developed countries (LDCs) for the period 1961–2018. As indicated in Chapter 8.2, yields of all four crops have increased severalfold throughout the entire time horizon in almost all areas. Crop yields have steadily advanced since the 1960s, making food insecurity a rarity that results more from bad policies than from vagaries in the weather, or climate change. Average global yields of maize have increased by 2.0% annually, rice by 1.7%, wheat by 2.1%, and soybean by 1.6% (yields of sorghum increased by 0.9% per year). Although not shown in the graphs in Chapter 8.2, the United States has the highest yields of maize, rice, and soybeans; when it comes to wheat, however, US yields are close to the global average, and well below those of the European Union and China.

Given concern about the quality of food consumption, a graph of yields of fresh vegetables is provided in Figure 10.4. Again the US had the highest yields of fresh vegetables (not shown in Figure 10.4), with yields exceeding those of any other region by a factor of four or more. Yields of fresh vegetables are lowest in the least developed countries (6.8 t/ha) compared to the EU (17.2 t/ha); annual average growth rates were also lowest in the LDCs at 0.5 percent, compared to an annual growth rate of 0.6% in the EU, 0.5% in China, 1.2% in India, 1.0% in landlocked developing countries, 1.8% in the US, and 2.3% in Brazil, and a global average of 0.9%. It is difficult to compare yields of fresh vegetables across jurisdictions, however, without further knowledge about the types of vegetables that are grown, use of irrigation, and applications of fertilizers and other chemicals. Nonetheless, there has been steady growth in the yields of all types of crops over the past half century or more, especially in Brazil.

In summary, when it comes to historical crop yields, it is difficult to find evidence to suggest that climate change would result in lower yields. Indeed, once adverse weather events are taken into account, which is done using a five-year moving average of yields, it is easier to argue that technological improvements and, to a lesser degree, rising CO_2 levels (and potentially their interaction) have increased agricultural productivity.

Now consider what might happen with global warming. There is, first off, a CO_2-fertilization effect that needs to be examined. Increasing concentrations of atmospheric CO_2 can improve agricultural productivity, enabling crops to better utilize nutrients, including water, and ward off pests and disease. Higher levels of CO_2 make crops less susceptible to drought. While droughts might increase in some regions of the globe, overall a warmer atmosphere holds more moisture, potentially leading to increased rainfall. Nonetheless, there remains a fear that, as temperatures continue to rise with increasing CO_2, the CO_2-fertilization effect will be offset by too much heat—that crop yields will decline.

Figure 10.4 Five-year moving average of fresh vegetable yields, selected countries or regions, 1965–2018

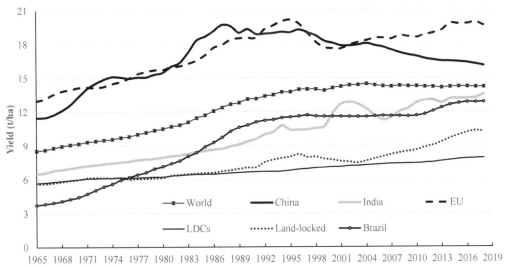

Source: FAO (http://www.fao.org/faostat/en/#data/QC [accessed June 11, 2020])

An increase in average global temperatures does not affect all crops in the same way, nor does it impact different crop regions in the same way. At the regional level, greater humidity and precipitation could be offset by the negative impacts of higher temperatures. Although higher CO_2 in the atmosphere makes plants more drought tolerable, there are limits; crops simply do better in higher temperatures if they also have adequate water.

The most prevalent food crops are C3 plants, which include wheat, rice, barley, oats, many vegetables, and even important tree crops (e.g., apples). C3 crops are expected to do better under projected climate change than C4 crops, the primary ones of which are maize, sorghum, and sugar cane—crops that are also best suited to produce biofuels. There are proportionally more C4 plants among perennial weeds, which implies that they do less well under climate change than C3 plants; for example, C3 weeds would likely develop herbicide resistance more easily than C4 weeds as CO_2 increases (so it is a good thing most weeds are C4 plants and not C3). As an adaptation strategy to greater weed infestations (if any), genetic engineering can be used to increase the ability of crops to compete with weeds, whereas biological and chemical research can lead to improved herbicides and other agronomic practices for combatting weeds. Since crops are mainly C3 and many weeds are C4, C3 crops might outcompete weeds for valuable nutrients as CO_2 levels rise, with genetic engineering potentially able to provide food crops with an additional advantage over weeds. While keeping these adaptation options open, there is evidence that crop yields of non-engineered crops will increase as atmospheric CO_2 levels and temperatures rise.

Before considering the effect of climate change on yields, it is important to note that too little atmospheric CO_2 could lead to starvation: photosynthesis would shut down if the atmospheric concentration of CO_2 fell to some 150 to 200 ppm. As the concentration of atmospheric CO_2 increases, crop production (yield and biomass) can be expected to increase. Indeed, evidence indicates that the twentieth century increase in atmospheric CO_2 has contributed about 16% of the increase in cereal crop yields, and may have been responsible for upwards of one-fifth of the yield increases associated with the green revolution. Crop yields are positively correlated with CO_2 levels, which explains why Dutch farmers will grow crops in greenhouses with an atmosphere of 1,000 ppm CO_2 and hydroponic operations often run at 1,400 ppm.

What is the implication for the future? This is both unclear and controversial. The land-rent studies provide some evidence to suggest that the agricultural sector will be worse off under a changed climate, which would suggest that crop yields will be lower. Conversely, one can find numerous studies finding that crop yields will increase with global warming. Higher CO_2 *reduces* leaf stomatal pores that take in CO_2 and release water vapor, enabling plants to better withstand drought, higher temperatures, and even noxious air pollutants. A number of studies have linked higher levels of atmospheric CO_2 to increased crop yields even if precipitation is lower. Studies have determined that there will be no CO_2-induced change in the relationships between predator-herbivore and prey-plant.

Given the importance of wheat to the global economy, consider the impact that climate change might have on this crop. One study found that wheat yields increased by 44%–52% (depending on variety) when CO_2 concentrations went from 335 ppm to 477 ppm, while the same increase in CO_2 accompanied by a 1°C increase in the average growing season temperature still resulted in an 8%–38% increase in yields. Another found that the wheat plant's biomass increased by 73%–145% in going from 330 ppm to 700 ppm CO_2, despite limited phosphorous (needed for plant growth) in both situations. A more recent study concluded that atmospheric CO_2 enrichment positively impacted wheat growth and yield, even when growing conditions were not ideal; very high temperatures that were 7°C to 15°C above normal air temperatures reduced the CO_2-enrichment benefits in one year (though the impacts were still positive) but maintained them in another.

The story with regards to other crops is similar. Early studies found that yields of rice, wheat, barley, oats, and rye could increase by upwards of 64%; potatoes and sweet potatoes by as much as 75%; and legumes (including peas, beans, and soybeans) by 46% at higher levels of CO_2. Studies find that even maize yields (which is a C4 crop) improve with warmer weather. Overwhelmingly, nearly all plants experience increases in biomass in response to atmospheric CO_2 enrichment, with trees maturing many years earlier than otherwise. In addition to yields, a meta-analysis of 57 studies that examined the effect of enriched CO_2 growing conditions on the nutritional value of vegetables found that plant nutritional enhancements outweighed any CO_2-induced plant nutritional declines.

Agricultural productivity in tropical countries might be under greater threat than in temperate countries. A meta-analysis of 1048 observations from 66 studies focused on the separate impacts of adaptation, change in temperature, change in CO_2, and change in precipitation on crop yields in tropical and temperate regions. The study found that, unless farmers adapted to the changed climate conditions, productivity would generally be adversely affected. With adaptation, wheat, maize, and rice yields in temperate regions would increase as a result of higher temperatures, all else remaining constant, but production of maize and wheat would be adversely affected by higher temperatures in the tropics. Importantly, the analysis also showed that, while rice yields in the tropics would be unaffected by temperature increases between 0°C and 3°C, rice yields would increase by 10% or more if temperatures rose by upwards of 5°C, *ceteris paribus*. Indeed, temperature was the dominant explanatory factor explaining changes in rice yields, with precipitation and CO_2 fertilization playing a minor albeit yield-enhancing role (contributing less than 15% of the overall change in crop yields).

Reductions in crop yields in tropical countries could well be due to lack of institutions (e.g., rule of law, property rights) and public infrastructure. In this regard, the case of Brazil might be instructive. Brazil is a country that has become an agricultural superpower due to large investments in technology and farmland. As a result, this tropical country has become increasingly competitive with the United States in agricultural export markets. For countries that are vulnerable to climate change, Brazil's experience provides hope that food insecurity can be managed if there exists a political will and proper institutions (including agricultural research stations, extension programs, etc.). First off, Brazil is now the world's largest exporter of sugar, coffee, beef, and poultry; the second largest exporter of soybeans; the third largest exporter of corn; and the fourth largest exporter of cotton. It is also the largest producer of sugar and coffee, has the largest commercial cattle herd in the world, and is a leading grain producer because much grain is fed to livestock, particularly poultry.

Further, temperatures in tropical regions are projected to rise more slowly under climate change than temperatures in higher latitudes. What implication would this have for food security? Can other tropical countries duplicate Brazil's success, or are Brazil's circumstances, political institutions, geography, and climate so unique as to preclude a similar rise in agricultural productivity?

The website for the Center for the Study of Carbon Dioxide and Global Change (www.co2science.org) provides an inventory of studies that find positive impacts of global warming on crop production, along with critiques of those that find the opposite. In contrast, the IPCC's Fifth Assessment Report (AR5) reviewed 782 studies, finding an overall median reduction in crop yields of 4.8% and average change of −5.9%; indeed, "the grand mean of the five [Assessment Reports] (−4.0%) and the overall median (−0.92%) show a worrying change in food production for a range of scenarios of climate change, locations, crops, and levels of adaptation" (Porter, Howden, and Smith 2017, p. 681). To add to the confusion, the US National Climate Assessment report projects mid-century (2036–2065) yields of commodity crops to decline by "5% to over 25% below extrapolated trends broadly across the region for corn, and more than 25% for soybeans in the southern half of the region" (USGCRP 2018, p. 882). Notice that the report does not suggest that crop yields will fall; rather, US crop yields are expected to continue trending upwards, but productivity growth will be below what it would be in the absence of climate change.

One can only conclude that the evidence regarding the impact of climate change on agriculture is a matter of interpretation, dependent on which studies are chosen to support one's viewpoint, and how the evidence is presented. While crop yields are likely to continue increasing even if the atmospheric concentration of CO_2 were to rise well above 1,000 ppm, temperatures may not be an impediment to yields; of course, precipitation has a significant role to play, but climate models are less able to project future precipitation than temperature. Even so, it may be possible to develop new crops that can adapt to climate change using standard breeding techniques or, more likely, genetic engineering. In addition, techniques related to the harvesting of water from fog in coastal desert areas, innovative agricultural practices (such as increased use of drones), and new financial instruments (e.g., weather-indexed insurance) will help society and farmers adapt to climate change.

In conclusion, it may well be true that unprecedented global warming will lead to large damages as envisioned by climate scientists, but dire warnings that climate change will lead to dangerous reductions in future crop yields and increasing incidence of famines are simply not warranted on the basis of currently available evidence. Overall, there remains too much uncertainty about the potential impact of climate change on future crop yields, and too little confidence in plant breeding and genetic engineering of crops, to warrant concluding that food insecurity will increase in the future.

10.5 Discounting and Climate Urgency

In Chapter 2, we discussed how applied welfare analysis often requires us to discount future monetary flows to a common date. This is required to determine whether an investment made today (cost incurred today) is worth undertaking—i.e., whether the stream of future net benefits exceeds the current capital cost. Discounting simply reflects the notion that benefits (measured in monetary terms) accruing in the distant future are valued less than those accruing in the near future—funds invested today are more highly valued than the same funds received in the future. This idea pertains even where actions or investments taken today affect future generations. With policies that involve intergenerational redistributions of resources and income, an ethical issue arises, which we considered in the context of the Ramsey discounting formula (Chapter 2.6). In the Ramsey context, how low should the discount rate be to reflect the interests of the future generation?

The Ramsey approach to discounting is misleading if a physical entity such as carbon is considered. With climate change, we are interested in reducing CO_2 emissions or removing CO_2 from the atmosphere through growth of trees, for example. If there is some urgency in addressing climate change, society would want to focus more on actions that reduce CO_2 emissions or ones that sequester carbon from the atmosphere today as opposed to those in the near or distant future. Greater urgency requires a higher discount rate on carbon as a physical entity than the discount rate suggested by the Ramsey process. The intergenerational ethical rate of discount and the physical carbon rate of discount differ. This idea is further discussed in the next subsection, followed by a concrete example related to the use of biomass in lieu of fossil fuels in generating electricity.

10.5.1 Discounting Carbon

Weighting or discounting of physical flows according to when they occur is an acceptable practice in the conservation economics literature. Conservation and depletion policies are defined according to their effect on the time profile of use rates: A redistribution of use rates toward the future is defined as *conservation*, while a distribution towards the present is *depletion*. Use rates (or rates of extraction of a resource) under current policy might remain constant over time. Under one alternative policy, they might increase and then decrease, while under another alternative policy, use rates might first decrease and then increase. The two alternative time profiles of use rates need to be weighted to determine whether they represent conservation or depletion relevant to the baseline profile of use rates (constant extraction rate). This notion of discounting physical entities is related to, yet different from, the discounting concepts discussed in Chapter 2.6. Perhaps this is due to the fact that the concept of weighting or discounting physical fluxes to when they occur seems to have been lost on economists.

Discounting of physical flows is most important when it comes to the timing of CO_2 emissions to or removals from the atmosphere. The projected increase in global temperatures is delayed (1) if CO_2 emissions occur later rather than earlier in time, and (2) if removals of CO_2 from the atmosphere through carbon sequestration in forest ecosystems (or in oceans) occurs sooner rather than later. If climate change is an urgent problem, then future CO_2 emissions to (removals from) the atmosphere are less of a concern than current ones. That is, the more urgent the problem, the more future CO_2 flux should be discounted relative to today's CO_2 flux. In essence, this implies we should discount future CO_2 fluxes more or less harshly (using a higher or lower discount rate) depending on how important it is to avoid putting more CO_2 in the atmosphere.

Three discount rates come into play: the monetary rate used in the private sector, the social discount rate used in an intergenerational context, and the rate used to discount physical carbon fluxes. The social and monetary discount rates only come into play if carbon is priced since the current value of future carbon (say, carbon offset credits traded in a market) is discounted at one of these rates, depending on whether one views the analysis from a social or private perspective. But it is important to distinguish between these two rates of discount and the rate used to discount physical units—the rate on future benefits and costs versus that on net CO_2 flows to the atmosphere. The monetary discount rate is determined in money markets, while the social discount rate can be determined empirically or ethically; but the weighting of physical flows is a policy variable.

Consider an example related to tree planting and carbon removals from the atmosphere. Suppose a tree-planting project results in the reduction of five metric tons of carbon (tC) emissions (= 18.33 tCO_2 emissions[5]) per year in perpetuity. Further assume the project has a permanent sink component that results in the storage of 10 tC per year for 10 years, after which time the sink component of the project reaches an equilibrium. How much carbon is stored? Suppose the present value of project costs are annualized so that the discounted stream of the equal annual costs is the same as the calculated present value of costs. If costs and carbon uptake are compared on an annual basis, does one use 5 tC or 15 tC per year? Suppose the discounted project costs $10,000, or $400 on an annualized basis if a 4% rate of discount is used ($400/0.04 = $1,000). The costs of carbon uptake are then estimated to be either $80.00/tC ($21.81/tCO_2) if 5 tC is used as the annual uptake, or $7.27/$tCO_2$ if the uptake is 15 tC per year.

---

[5] Based on atomic weights, a CO_2 molecule weighs 44/12 as much as a carbon molecule.

Suppose instead that we divide the present value of project costs by the sum of all the carbon that eventually gets removed from the atmosphere. Since carbon is removed each year in perpetuity, the total amount sequestered is infinite, so that the cost of carbon uptake is essentially $0. Therefore, in the absence of discounting physical flows, an arbitrary planning horizon needs to be chosen. If the planning horizon is 30 years, 250 tC are sequestered and the average cost is calculated to be $10.91/tCO_2$; if a 40-year planning horizon is chosen, 300 tC are removed from the atmosphere and the cost is $9.09/tCO_2$. Thus, cost estimates are sensitive to the length of the planning horizon. Unfortunately, the length of the planning horizon is not usually made explicit in studies that estimate costs of carbon uptake by forests, although a 100-year cutoff is most commonly used (in which case the cost would be $16.66/tC, or $4.54/tCO_2$).

Cost estimates that take into account all carbon sequestered plus the timing of uptake can only be achieved if carbon fluxes are discounted. The total discounted carbon saved via our hypothetical project equals 339.83 tC if a discount rate of 2% is used and the correct estimate of costs is $8.03/tCO_2$. If carbon is discounted at a rate of 4%, the project results in costs of $13.23/tCO_2$. Finally, if removals of CO_2 from the atmosphere beyond 15 years are considered too late to prevent warming, a discount rate of 20% might be appropriate because removal of one tCO_2 15 years in the future has the same impact on global warming as 65 kg CO_2 removed today. But the cost is now $149.42/tC, although this translates into a cost of only $40.75/tCO_2$ which is well below the $50/tCO_2$ tax that has been implemented in some jurisdictions. What discount rate should be applied to physical carbon? This is a decision that falls in the political realm.

10.5.2 Economics of Wood Biomass Energy: Climate Urgency and Discounting

To meet their renewable energy goals, developed countries have invested heavily in wind and solar energy. Despite these efforts, the proportion of total energy consumption from these sources remains small. In 2019, 83.3% of total primary energy consumption in the United States came from fossil fuels (39.1% from petroleum, 32.2% from natural gas, 12.0% from coal), 8.0% from nuclear power, 2.6% from hydro, 2.9% from wind, 1.0% from solar, and 0.7% from biomass and geothermal sources. In the European Union that same year, 2019, 74.2% of total energy consumption came from fossil fuels (38.4% from oil, 24.6% from natural gas, 11.2% coal), with 10.7%, 4.3%, 1.8%, 5.6%, and 2.6% coming from nuclear, hydro, solar, wind, and biomass and other renewables (including non-renewable wastes), respectively.[6] The US relies more on natural gas because of low gas prices resulting from the application of fracking technology that is opposed in Europe, where natural gas prices are much higher. Along with ambitious targets and lucrative incentives for renewables, EU policy led to greater investment in wind, biomass, and solar energy. Nonetheless, the fuel mixes in consumption are similar, with fossil fuels dominant.

While capacity investments in wind and solar are expected to continue, the intermittency problem associated with these sources of energy eventually limits their role in consumption—investments in capacity

---

[6] Information for the US and EU comes from the BP Statistical Review of World Energy 2020 (June 2020) found at https://www.bp.com/en/global/corporate/energy-economics/statistical-review-of-world-energy.html [accessed December 7, 2020].

of intermittent resources do not necessarily translate into the same relative growth in consumption. As a result, countries are increasingly looking to other renewables, primarily wood biomass, for future energy needs. EU countries originally agreed to a binding target requiring 20% of total energy to come from renewable sources by 2020, but, in early 2014, the European Commission proposed a more ambitious EU-wide renewable energy target of 27% by 2030. Although this will lead to more investment in wind and solar energy, at least one-half of the renewable energy target will need to come from biomass, with member states individually having adopted various domestic policies to promote biomass energy. European consumption of wood pellets is expected to grow substantially, which will require significant imports of pellets from outside the EU. Likewise, the US and Canada are replacing some coal generating capacity with biomass, as biomass is considered "carbon neutral." For example, two large-scale coal plants in Ontario, Canada, have been retrofitted to run on biomass. The question is: Is biomass truly carbon neutral? What are its climate change mitigation benefits?

Logging and sawmill residues, and coarse woody matter on the forest floor, are considered the main sources of wood biomass for burning. Two factors determine the availability of this material: the cost of removing coarse woody material and logging residues from the forest floor and transporting them to a mill, and competition for sawmill residues. Costs of transporting residuals can be so great that, in regions of northwestern Canada and the US, logs are trimmed to fit onto trucks for transport to the mills, thereby reducing transportation costs; the wood waste is left at the roadside and burned. Logging residues provide important nutrients for the next generation of trees, and habitat and food for various animals. In any case, studies indicate hauling logging residuals and roadside wastes to a power generating facility is not economically viable.

The focus in the Pacific Northwest is on sawmill residues, as these can be used to produce wood pellets for export to Europe. Sawmill residues are also burned for heat and power in sawmills and used to produce oriented strand board, medium fiber board, pulp for paper, and other products. Thus, residues have value; they are not a free resource. Any subsidies or requirements to use these residues to produce electricity comes at a cost. Nonetheless, it is the release of carbon into the atmosphere by the burning of pellets that is of concern, because the carbon could otherwise have been stored in wood products.

The other problem relates to the timing of CO_2 fluxes. When wood biomass is burned to produce electricity, more CO_2 is released to the atmosphere than if that same electricity was produced using coal or gas. The only difference is that the CO_2 released by burning biomass can be recovered from the atmosphere by growing new trees; however, it takes time to recover this CO_2 depending on how fast trees grow. Meanwhile, the material burned to produce electricity could have been used to make products, with CO_2 subsequently stored for a period of perhaps 100 years or more and the growth of a new forest again sequestering carbon. Ecologists do not advocate use of whole trees for generating electricity, focusing instead on logging and sawmill residues (and roadside wastes), because these wood residues would decay and release carbon to the atmosphere if they were not burned. Therefore, the recovery of carbon from the atmosphere would be much shortened compared to using whole trees to make lumber.

It is important when managing forests for climate change mitigation to consider the timing of carbon fluxes. This is illustrated with the aid of Figure 10.5. Suppose that electricity is generated by a coal-fired power plant. In that case, an amount 0F of CO_2 enters the atmosphere and remains there indefinitely, as indicated by the horizontal dashed line. Suppose instead that the power was generated by burning wood biomass rather than coal. In that case, an amount 0K > 0F of CO_2 enters the atmosphere at time 0, thereby creating a carbon deficit equal to KF (= 0K–0F). If trees are planted at t=0, the trees will begin to remove CO_2 from the atmosphere and store it in wood biomass, with the cumulative amount of CO_2 removed determined by the growth function as indicated by the S-shaped curve in Figure 10.5. At t=M, the amount of CO_2 left in the atmosphere as a result of burning wood biomass at t=0 equals the amount that would have been in the atmosphere if coal had been burned instead. Then, at t=N, the CO_2 that had been released by burning biomass will have been completely removed. Between t=M and t=N, the biomass option has resulted in a carbon dividend or benefit relative to the coal option. This is generally what is meant when biomass burning is declared to be carbon neutral.

Figure 10.5 Carbon flux profile for biomass energy versus business-as-usual fossil fuel energy

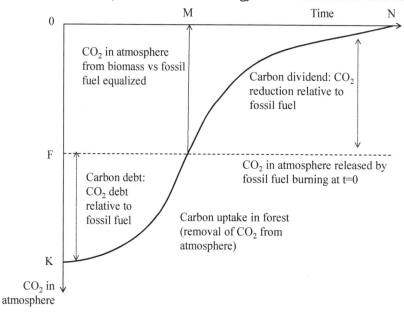

Source: Johnston and van Kooten (2015)

When it comes to biomass energy, the time that incremental carbon is in the atmosphere may be measured in decades, in which case it contributes to climate forcing. Thus, if there is some urgency to remove CO_2 from the atmosphere to avoid climate forcing, the timing of emissions and removals of carbon are important, with current emissions of CO_2 and removals from the atmosphere by sinks more important than later ones. This implies that carbon fluxes need to be weighted as to when they occur, with future fluxes discounted relative to current ones.

The rate used to discount carbon fluxes can be used in the policy arena to put into practice the urgency with which society needs to address climate change. Clearly, if global warming is not considered a problem, the economist might use a zero discount rate, in which case it really does not matter if biomass growth removes CO_2 from the atmosphere today, 50 years, or even thousands or millions of years from now—it only matters that the CO_2 is eventually removed. In that case, coal and biomass are on a similar footing and, since coal is more energy efficient, it would be preferred to biomass.

Conversely, suppose that global warming is already widespread and consequential and that the once distant concern is now a pressing one as future climate change is largely determined by today's choices regarding fossil fuel use. Then we want to weight current reductions in emissions and removals of CO_2 from the atmosphere much higher than those in future years. This is the same as discounting future uptake of CO_2, with higher discount rates suggesting greater urgency in dealing with global warming. Figure 10.6 depicts such urgency; in the figure, the level of urgency is sufficiently high that burning of biomass for energy never leads to carbon neutrality. Indeed, if one were to accept that climate change is a more urgent matter (a relatively high discount rate), substituting biomass for fossil fuels may actually lead to a net increase in atmospheric CO_2 emissions.

Figure 10.6 Carbon flux associated with fossil fuel and biomass energy production over time: Comparing lesser and greater urgency to address climate change

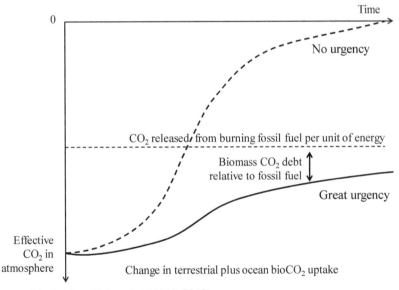

Source: Adapted from Walker et al. (2010, 2013)

In Figure 10.6, forest carbon uptake is discounted to such an extent that carbon uptake in the more distant future is of little value today. As a result, the discounted future uptake of CO_2 from the atmosphere (regardless of the sink) is too small to offset the additional increase in CO_2 emissions when biomass substitutes for fossil fuels in power production. The change in the cumulative CO_2 or carbon flux from substituting biomass for coal will depend on the relative emissions intensity of coal; the fossil fuel emissions related to the mining (harvesting) of coal (timber), processing (if any), and transportation to the power plant; the tree species or other types of crops (e.g., straw, hemp) used as fuel; the geographic location; and other economic and biophysical variables.

Carbon dioxide released from burning coal and wood varies greatly by the quality of coal and biomass. For example, on average across all types of coal, 0.518 tonnes of coal are required to produce 1.0 megawatt hour (MWh) of electricity, thereby releasing 1.015 tCO_2 per MWh. However, for bituminous coal, which is used most commonly in power plants, only 0.397 t of coal are required per MWh, releasing 0.940 tCO_2 per MWh. When it comes to wood biomass, on the other hand, approximately 0.658 t are required to produce 1.0 MWh of electricity—nearly twice the weight required for bituminous coal, which requires more fossil fuel emissions just to transport the extra material. Further, trees and/or plant material require a large area to produce energy, thereby competing directly with other land uses such as agriculture. Meanwhile, the average emissions intensity of wood biomass varies between hardwoods (1.170 tCO_2 per MWh) and softwoods (1.242 tCO_2/MWh). Thus, biomass releases significantly more CO_2 into the atmosphere per unit of energy than coal, and even more so when compared to natural gas.[7]

10.6 Mitigating Climate Change

10.6.1 International Action to Mitigate Climate Change

At the twenty-first Conference of the Parties to the UN's Framework Convention on Climate Change held in Paris in December 2015, countries agreed to reduce their emissions of CO_2 and related greenhouse gases so as to keep the global temperature from rising more than 2°C (or to keep the atmospheric concentration of CO_2 at less than 450 parts per million, while it is currently already above 400 ppm). In the run-up to the Paris Agreement, countries provided their intended nationally determined contributions—their individual contributions to the global objective. Many developed countries indicated that they would reduce their CO_2 emissions by 30% in the next 15 years, while aiming to reduce emissions by 80% by 2050 compared to 1990. Then, following a report by the IPCC that recommended reducing emissions to prevent a 1.5°C rise in temperature compared to pre-industrial times, developed countries are looking to reach zero emissions by 2050.

Realistically there is no way for the United States, Europe, or any country to meet these stringent targets and retain their present standards of living. Reductions in CO_2 on that scale are simply not achievable without severely impoverishing people. The last time the United States had CO_2 emissions that were 80% below 1990 levels was around 1905, when it had less than a fifth as many people as now, and their average income was about 13% of current incomes.

Even emission reductions of as little as 25% from 2015 emissions would be difficult and costly to achieve. They would require huge investments in nuclear power generation, massive changes in

---

[7] The conversion to biomass of a 120-megawatt capacity coal plant that operates at an average capacity factor of 83.3% increases emissions by 300,000 tCO_2 annually and requires a forested area of 1,000 to 1,500 ha to support it. This is demonstrated as an exercise at the end of the chapter. Conflict between forestry and other land uses is discussed in the following paragraphs.

transportation infrastructure, and impressive technical breakthroughs in everything from biofuels to battery technology. Yet even if the developed countries are successful in reducing their emissions of greenhouse gases, the overall impact on climate change will be small. Growth in emissions by developing countries, especially China and India, will easily and quickly exceed any reduction in emissions by rich countries. Fossil fuels are abundant, ubiquitous, and inexpensive relative to alternative energy sources; therefore, any country would be foolish to impair its economy by large-scale efforts to abandon them. While the efforts of rich countries to reduce emissions of CO_2 will have no impact on climate change, they will have an adverse impact on their own citizens—and such citizens will vote those governments out of office. Whether anthropogenic global warming is real or not, whether the climate model projections are accurate or not, fossil fuels will continue to be the major driver of economic growth and wealth into the foreseeable future.

10.6.2 Agricultural Role in Mitigating Climate Change

As a sector, agriculture is the third largest emitter of greenhouse gases after fossil fuel burning for electricity and heat, and transportation. Emissions of methane account for about half of total agricultural emissions, nitrous oxides for 36%, and CO_2 for 14%. While emissions from agriculture have been increasing, agricultural activities could contribute to a reduction in GHG emissions. By growing energy crops (viz., corn for ethanol), agriculture can reduce reliance on fossil fuels. Finally, by changing cropping practices, carbon can be stored in soils. Yet, the contribution that the agricultural sector can make towards mitigation of CO_2 emissions is likely limited.

Although GHG emissions from agriculture have been rising, agricultural output has been increasing at a faster rate. Methane emissions are the result primarily of enteric fermentation, or the digestion of organic materials by livestock, predominantly beef cattle. Nitrous oxide emissions are associated with manure spread on fields as organic matter and fertilizer. Both sources of emissions are increasing as incomes grow and people demand more animal protein in their diets. Some progress has been made to reduce methane emissions through improved animal feed and capturing animal wastes, using the resultant methane gas and solid matter as fuel for use on and off the farm. More drastic measures are attempts to reduce demand for meat and develop substitute products.

One source of CO_2 emissions is fossil fuel burning associated with the operation of equipment (tractors, trucks, combines, etc.) and for heating (e.g., drying grain to improve its quality and marketability). But the main source of CO_2 emissions is deforestation for the purpose of agriculture. Land-use change may be driven by climate change policies, however. Incentives to produce energy crops raise the price of farmland, which, in turn, causes forestland to be converted to agriculture or, in the tropics, to the production of palm oil, thereby releasing large amounts of CO_2. Governments sometimes devise incentives that encourage such changes in land use because landowners have lobbied policy makers to support policies that promote biofuels.

The point here is simply that one has to be careful in designing policies that affect land uses. For example, the EU has incentivized the use of wood pellets for power production. This should lead to an increase in forested area, but has actually increased the pressure on old-growth forests in eastern Europe and the southern US, which are increasingly harvested to provide biomass for generating electricity. If crop yields decline (as some predict) and population continues to grow, it will be nearly impossible to shift farmland into forestry without subsidies; indeed, if food prices increase, the economics are likely to result in shifting land out of forestry into agriculture, which makes the production of electricity from biomass more expensive. In essence, then, ethanol subsidies need to be larger than otherwise since they would need to offset subsidies to plant trees.

It is also possible to mitigate climate change by removing CO_2 from the atmosphere and storing it as soil carbon. This can be done by switching from conventional tillage (CT) to conservation tillage or zero-tillage, simply referred to as no-till (NT) agriculture. Estimates of carbon uptake by soils in the northern Great Plains as a result of going from CT to NT vary from 100 to 500 kg carbon per ha (C/ha) per year. To this must be added the reduced emissions from employing less tillage operations, which saves some 30 kg C/ha per year. Assuming farmers do not go back to CT, the total savings in shifting from CT to NT will depend on the rate used to weight the future stream of carbon fluxes—that is, the rate used to discount physical carbon. This is shown in Table 10.1, where carbon has been converted to CO_2 (1 tC = 3.667 tCO_2). Total carbon uptake due to agricultural operations varies from about 14.7 tCO_2/ha to at most 45.8 tCO_2/ha. The amount of carbon that can potentially be prevented from entering the atmosphere via a dramatic change in agricultural practices is small compared to the carbon sequestered by forests.

Table 10.1 Expected annual and total carbon savings from adopting zero-tillage practices in Canada's prairie provinces (tonnes of CO_2 per ha)

Assumed annual carbon uptake in soil organic matter during first 20 years after adoption	2% Discount rate		4% Discount rate	
	Total	Annual	Total	Annual
200	21.8	0.4	15.3	0.6
300	29.8	0.6	21.5	0.8
400	37.9	0.8	27.7	1.1
500	45.9	0.9	33.9	1.4

Source: Derived from data in van Kooten and Folmer (2004)

Continuous cropping and NT may increase production costs (because more chemical inputs and/or greater investments in specialized equipment are required), and potentially lead to lower yields. High rates of adoption of NT indicate that the savings in tillage operations exceed the costs associated with increased use of chemicals and lower yields, if any. As a result, NT may be an inexpensive means for sequestering carbon. By reducing the intensity of tillage, soil organic matter will increase, resulting in an increase in carbon storage plus greater retention of moisture, which could result in a reduced need for irrigation. However, reduced tillage also has negative environmental impacts associated with greater use of pesticides for control of weeds, fungus, and insects. This may have negative spillover effects on ecological systems and water quality, which is why use of some chemicals, especially inexpensive glyphosate, may potentially be banned, thereby threatening carbon stored in soil organic matter.

Data on the costs of sequestering carbon through agricultural activities are based on two meta-regression analyses to determine the costs of sequestering carbon using NT. First, 52 studies examining the costs of conventional versus zero-tillage were compared. The studies found that conventional tillage yielded higher net returns, except in the US Corn Belt (corn and other crops) and Canadian prairies (wheat). A meta-regression analysis based on 24 studies was then used to determine the carbon-uptake benefits of employing NT. The results depended on the depth of measurement of the soil, because, with conventional tillage, organic matter is plowed under. Thus, soil organic carbon content is higher under NT than CT if measurement is confined to the plow layer, but it is less under NT if measurements are made to a greater depth. The estimated costs of sequestering carbon through changes in agricultural practices are provided in Table 10.2 for zero- or no-till agriculture. The results indicate that costs of removing CO_2 from the atmosphere and storing it as soil carbon by changing tillage practices range from about $47/tCO_2$ to $120/tCO_2$.

Table 10.2 Net costs of carbon sequestered under no-till agriculture[a]

Region	Crop	Cost per tC at 25 cm	Cost per tC at 50 cm
Great Plains	Wheat	$129.85	***
	Other crop	$115.91	$163.40
Corn Belt	Wheat	$49.04	$64.30
	Other crop	$66.10	$67.93

[a] Costs in 2016 US dollars for crops harvested in 1986 (the sample mean) after 20 years of NT *** indicates that under those conditions, NT is not expected to result in net carbon sequestration compared to CT.
Source: Adapted from Manley et al. (2005)

Finally, the agricultural sector can aid in mitigating CO_2 emissions by producing energy crops that substitute for fossil fuels in transportation or production of electricity. Sugar beets, sugar cane, corn (maize), and sorghum can be used to produce ethanol, while soybeans and canola (rapeseed) are used to produce biodiesel. Farmland can also be used to produce hybrid poplar, with trees harvested within a short period (<10 years) and used as biomass for producing electricity; similarly, crop residues can be used to produce electricity in lieu of fossil fuels. The problem is that, when farmland is diverted to the production of energy crops, land and food prices increase, which can lead to deforestation. The rise in food prices disproportionately harms the world's poorest citizens. Further, production of ethanol from corn (rather than sugar cane) and biodiesel from canola might actually increase rather than decrease GHG emissions, mainly because farmers apply chemicals to produce energy crops, just as they do with food crops, but the production and application of chemicals releases GHGs. The use of crop residues (or even wood residues from logging) reduces soil organic matter and the amount of carbon stored in an ecosystem. It also lowers nutrients available to the next crop, thereby requiring their replacement by fertilizers and other chemicals from off site.

10.6.3 Managing for Carbon: Carbon Pools and Fossil Fuel Substitution

In their nationally determined contributions under the Paris climate agreement of 2015, countries with significant forestlands included forestry activities as a major means for meeting their emission reduction targets. For example, China plans to increase its forest stock volume by some 4.5 billion m^3 between 2005 and 2030, thereby removing some 3,300 Mt of CO_2 from the atmosphere, or 132 Mt CO_2 annually (representing approximately 1.9% of annual US emissions). Canada intends to reduce or eliminate coal-fired power (replacing a significant portion with wood biomass) and otherwise rely on forestry activities to reduce greenhouse gas emissions (but will ignore emissions from natural disturbances); Brazil will rely on forest conservation; and 40%–55% of Russia's commitment is to come from forestry, including activities that protect, maintain, and regenerate the forest. Renewable energy is to account for 27% of the EU's total energy production, with 30% (or 8% of total energy) coming from wood biomass.

Given the importance of forest activities in the global strategy for mitigating climate change, two issues are considered in this section. These issues pertain to the use of wood biomass to generate electricity and the management of forest ecosystems to maximize the benefits landowners can obtain from creating carbon offsets. Since forestry activities result in a stream of CO_2 fluxes over time, we begin by focusing on how one might discount physical flows to a common date at which time they are monetized.

Rather than focusing only on bioenergy and forest activities that reduce emissions from deforestation and forest degradation, it is also necessary to examine the carbon that enters into various pools within the forest ecosystem and postharvest wood product pools. Economic incentives are the best way to encourage public and private forestland owners to consider the climate impacts of forest management decisions. Economic agents need to know how many carbon offset credits they can expect to earn or be required to purchase as a result of the decisions they make regarding harvest utilization and logging methods (including logging residuals left on site), transportation (roadside waste left behind), processing of fiber into products, and regeneration, among others.

Subject to technical and institutional constraints, price signals determine how much timber a rights holder will harvest and how much lumber, plywood, wood chips, et cetera, are produced. Whether through the issuance of offset credits for sale in carbon markets or through a tax/subsidy scheme, carbon prices signal agents to alter their harvesting practices, choice of product mix, and overall use of wood fiber to take into account carbon flux. In the case of carbon markets, agents need to know the carbon credits they will receive at each stage. They need to know whether and how many offsets they will earn when wood substitutes for fossil fuels in electricity generation, or when wood substitutes for concrete and steel in construction. They need to know how much carbon is credited to their account in each period if trees are left unharvested, or if they plant faster-growing trees. That is, economic agents need to know the rules of the game, and that may require the use of models that establish the carbon fluxes associated with various forestry activities.

Technical advances in engineered wood products have enabled the construction of multistory wood buildings and state-of-the-art, multipurpose (even irregular shaped) buildings. Engineered products, such as cross-laminated timbers, can be used in the construction of high rises as tall as 40 or more floors. Engineered products are now much less vulnerable to fire and pests, while wood buildings require less energy to heat or cool, thereby further reducing CO_2 emissions. A carbon price incentivizes investment in wood buildings.

To overcome issues related to measurement and monitoring, issuance of carbon offset credits for removals of CO_2 from the atmosphere, or required purchases to offset emissions, can be based upon a forest management (growth and yield) model to which all parties agree, and observed changes in land use. The forest management model would specify the annual carbon uptake in the various components of the forest ecosystem from the time trees are planted until they are harvested, if at all. Each year, the landowner would receive carbon offset credits (or subsidies) for the carbon removed from the atmosphere, which would depend on rates of tree growth, species, soil, and other characteristics of the site that are determined in advance. At the time of harvest, the owner would purchase offsets (or pay a tax) based on the amount of CO_2 released from decaying residues left on the site, decaying residues resulting from processing and manufacturing, and decaying short- and long-lived products. It will, however, be necessary to determine how much roundwood and other biomass is harvested and how this wood is utilized. Decay rates for each carbon pool can be established a priori and the carbon fluxes resulting over infinite time can be discounted to the time of harvest to determine the emissions to be taxed (or offset credits to be purchased) at that time. In addition, it is possible to specify and provide a credit for the CO_2 emissions avoided when biomass is burned in lieu of fossil fuels, or the credits for emissions avoided from producing non-wood materials when wood is substituted for steel or concrete in construction.

This approach was used by determine the optimal management strategy for a forest in southeastern British Columbia. The forest in question had been regularly harvested, but at a low level so that significant stands of mature timber remained, as well as recently harvested, young stands. Mature stands sequester little if any carbon, but newly regenerated and young stands sequester significant amounts of carbon for a long period if unmanaged and assuming no wildfires. As alternatives to retaining the forest in wilderness (an unmanaged state), the researchers considered conservation management, which would prevent degradation of the forest while harvesting small amounts of timber in support of this goal, and a management regime that sought to maximize net commercial benefits plus revenues from the sale of carbon offset credits. Commercial management did not mean untrammeled exploitation; because forest management practices on the land needed to be certified if the timber were to be sold commercially, sustainable development criteria needed to be satisfied.

Carbon flux outcomes depended on the management regime chosen, which, in turn, were contingent on the price of carbon. Further, the carbon offset credits that were assigned depended on the rate used to discount (or weight) carbon as to when it occurred. Finally, the carbon flux was impacted by the extent to which wood substitutes for non-wood in construction and the accreditation of CO_2-emission reductions, and the emissions savings when wood biomass is burned to produce energy in lieu of fossil fuels. Other parameters included decay rates for organic matter left on the forest site after harvest and for the various post-harvest carbon pools, plus financial discount rates; costs of harvesting, gathering, and hauling biomass to downstream facilities; costs of processing and manufacturing; and rates of CO_2 emissions at each stage of the stump-to-products process. Some illustrative results are provided in Table 10.3.

Table 10.3 Annualized carbon sequestered in a southeastern British Columbia forest under different management regimes, '000s tCO_2[a]

Forest management method	Substitution parameter[b] (tCO_2/m^3)	Discount rate on carbon					
		0%		2%		4%	
		Price of carbon $/tCO_2$					
		$0	$10	$0	$10	$0	$10
Unmanaged		91.7	91.7	100.2	100.2	99.1	99.1
Conservation	0.25	-25.5	-23.0	-14.0	-12.5	-8.8	-8.3
	0.75	-7.2	-4.7	4.2	5.7	9.7	10.3
Commercial	0.25	8.1	22.4	57.1	60.3	77.3	80.2
Management	0.75	186.3	193.3	238.1	243.9	265.8	271.4

[a] Assumes a monetary discount rate of 4%.
[b] Credit for emissions avoided producing concrete/steel when wood substitutes for non-wood in construction.
Source: Derived from data in van Kooten Bogle, and de Vries (2015).

The results show that the unmanaged forest could generate more carbon offset credits than a forest managed for conservation, or managed simply to prevent degradation. This follows because the CO_2 emissions from the small harvests, and from maintenance of the forest in a non-degraded state, reduce the ecosystem sequestration and post-harvest carbon storage benefits. Essentially, the CO_2 released during activities to manage the forest for conservation exceed the gains in ecosystem carbon storage as there are insufficient economies of size in commercial-type activities. In the case of the unmanaged forest, the presence of young stands along with discounting of carbon fluxes leads to greater CO_2 sequestration than if the forest is managed for conservation that removes only a small amount of timber as part of a conservation management plan. This was true even if a credit of 0.75 tCO_2/m^3 was provided to any harvested timber to take into account the reduction in CO_2 emissions from not producing steel and concrete that is replaced by wood in construction.

It turns out that a commercial operator who responds to incentives to create carbon offset credits (i.e., reduce carbon flux), especially early in the time horizon (due to discounting), lowers atmospheric CO_2 to a much greater extent than the conservationist. Of course, the commercial operator must certify that the forest is sustainably managed in order to be able to sell timber. The commercial operator manages the forest to maximize income not only from the commercial sale of forest products but also the revenue from storing carbon in the ecosystem through sequestration and silvicultural management, and producing long-lived products with the lowest possible rates of decay.

Nonetheless, as is the case when the forest is managed for conservation that also permits limited harvests, there are situations where the unmanaged forest with young stands of trees can sequester more carbon than a commercially managed forest because CO_2 emissions are unavoidable when harvests occur. This is true for a low substitution parameter; but, if the substitution parameter is higher than about 0.3 tCO_2/m^3, commercial management does better than an unmanaged forest in terms of carbon benefits, as indicated in Table 10.2. If the substitution parameter exceeds 1.0 tCO_2/m^3, which is not unusual as substitution rates vary from 0.3–3.3 tCO_2/m^3, then commercial management will be preferred as a means of mitigating climate change in all circumstances.

10.7 Discussion

An important question regarding climate change that has yet to be satisfactorily answered pertains to the primary sectors. It is clear that climate change will impact agriculture and forestry, and the consensus appears to be that global warming will have a negative effect on these sectors—that crop yields will decline and that there will be less forestland. This conclusion is fraught with uncertainty, partly because it ignores the potential for increased crop and timber yields due to a CO_2-fertilization effect, but also because it neglects technological improvements related to machinery and management methods and crop breeding, including development of genetically engineered tree and crop varieties that withstand drought, grow better in a more concentrated CO_2 atmosphere, and protect against pests, disease, and even wildfire. Surprisingly, policy makers appear to be more confident that technological advances in wind turbines, solar photovoltaics, and batteries will take place than that technical changes should come in the primary sectors. Except that the former technological improvements relate to mitigation and the latter deal with adaptation, it is not clear why advances in one field are more likely than those in another, nor why government should promote the one and neglect the other.

Likewise, it is not clear why policies are implemented to encourage planting of energy crops for transportation (ethanol, biodiesel) and use of wood biomass for generating electricity. Both promote environmental damage by bringing wild spaces into commercial production (expanding cultivation at the extensive margin) and deepening crop production and silviculture through greater use of chemicals at the intensive margin. These policies increase land prices and divert land from growing food to energy production, thereby increasing food costs that harm the least well-off in global society. Yet, evidence presented here and elsewhere indicates that these policies do very little if anything to reduce the concentration of CO_2 in the atmosphere, and may even increase it.

Incentives to increase production of energy crops has one major benefit: it reduces the costs to the treasury of farm payments, because prices are higher. However, once these added benefits are capitalized in land values, the farm sector will again clamor for agricultural programs that protect them from production and price shocks.

When it comes to the primary sectors, one again wonders why climate change mitigation policies that are questionable in terms of their ability to forestall global warming (e.g., subsidies to biofuels and wood biomass power generation) are preferred to "adaptation" policies, such as genetic engineering and new management methods, which would ensure adequate food supplies in the future. The reasons surely have to do with institutions and governance and which groups are better able to lobby for their preferred solutions. It is all about who can capture the most government largesse at the expense of taxpayers and consumers.

Guide to Literature

The literature on climate change and climate models is vast. McGuffie and Henderson-Sellers (2009) provide a primer on climate models, but it is not helpful to those interested in how the models are technically put together. A summary of climate modeling, temperature data, economics, and other issues is found in van Kooten (2013, pp. 104–112). The latest report of the Intergovernmental Panel on Climate Change is the Fifth Assessment Report or AR5 (IPCC 2014). See https://www.youtube.com/watch?v=sC1N1-Okm1c [accessed January 11, 2019] by the Heartland Institute for further information on the science of global warming.

William Nordhaus and Richard Tol have developed IAMs for analyzing the economics of climate change (Tol 2014; Nordhaus 2010, 2013; Nordhaus & Boyer 2000), while Ross McKitrick has disputed the link between CO_2 and temperature (McIntyre and McKitrick 2005; McKitrick and Michaels 2007; McKitrick and Nierenberg 2011; McKitrick and Vogelsang 2014). On climate sensitivity see Lewis and Curry (2015, 2018) and Mauritsen and Pincus (2017); on social cost of carbon see Pindyck (2013) and Dayaratna, McKitrick, and Kreutzer (2016); on the marginal cost of public funds see Dahlby (2008), Dahlby and Ferede (2011), and Sandmo (1975, 1998). McKitrick (2011) provides a simple pricing rule for addressing global warming, a carbon tax that is contingent on global average temperature and its rate of increase. Stevenson et al. (2013) used a mathematical programming model to show the importance of CO_2 fertilization. Moore et al. (2017) used the FUND model.

Information on storylines is found in IPCC (2000). See van Vuuren et al. (2011) for information on the Representative Concentration Pathways; and Riahi et al. (2017) for information on the Shared Socioeconomic Pathways.

For a discussion of the economics of biodiversity, see van Kooten and Bulte (2000). Many scientists have argued that climate models are running too hot—that they predict much higher temperatures than observed and need to be re-parametrized downwards. An admission of this is by Santer et al. (2017). See Steele (2020) on ocean acidification. On polar bears, see Crockford (2018). A reflection on uncertainty in the case of climate change is found in Randall (2017).

Studies of the effect of climate change using similar regions or farm management models include, for Canada, Arthur and Abizadeh (1988), Mooney and Arthur (1990), and Arthur and van Kooten (1992), and, for the US, Adams (1989), Adams et al. (1990, 1996), and Kaiser et al. (1993). Mendelsohn, Nordhaus, and Shaw (1994), Schlenker, Hanemann, and Fisher (2006), Schlenker and Roberts (2009), Chen, McCarl, and Thayer (2017), and Arunanondchai et al. (2019) used hedonic-type methods (see Chapter 3.2) to examine the effects of global warming on US agriculture, with many finding negative effects. The Canadian study using the Ricardian approach is by Weber and Hauer (2003). Darwin et al. (1995) and Schimmelpfenning et al. (1996) examined climate impacts on global agriculture using mathematical programming methods. Further discussion on this topic and CO_2-fertilization impacts is found in van Kooten (2013).

See Idso (2001), Stevenson et al. (2013), and Idso et al. (2014) regarding CO_2 fertilization and the green revolution; Long (1991), Bettarini, Vaccari, and Miglietta (1998), Gifford (2004), Long et al. (2004), and Goklany (2015) regarding lower precipitation and higher CO_2 levels; Morgan et al. (2011) regarding the ability of crops to withstand pollution with higher CO_2; in the atmosphere; Prakash et al. (2017), Pandey, Lal, and Vengavasi (2018), and, especially, Macabuhay et al. (2018) on the ability of wheat to withstand global warming; Xie et al. (2018) and Zheng et al. (2018) regarding climate change and maize yields; Boullis, Francis, and Verheggen (2018) regarding predator-herbivore and prey-plant relationships; Levitt and Dubner (2009, p. 185) regarding use of higher CO_2 levels in greenhouse operations; Arunanondchai et al. (2019) on climate change effects on bioenergy crops; Dong et al. (2018) for a meta-analysis of nutritional values; Wittwer (1995) for information on early studies and tree growth; Challinor et al. (2014) for a meta-analysis demonstrating adverse effects of climate change on crop yields in tropical countries; and, for example, Ebert (2017) on the GMOs in agriculture.

The literature on the economics of conservation begins with Ciriacy-Wantrup (1968, original 1952) and Scott (1973, original 1955). In his classic book on conservation, Ciriacy-Wantrup (1968) defined depletion and conservation in terms of a redistribution of non-renewable resource flows toward the present or future, respectively, but this required weighting flows as to when they occurred (see also van Kooten 1993, pp. 166–168). Likewise, physical carbon fluxes can be weighted (discounted) as to when they occur, as argued early on by Richards (1997); see also van Kooten and Johnston (2016). Johnston and van Kooten (2015) examine the carbon discounting and the urgency to address climate change, while van Kooten (2013) discusses more broadly the inability of bioenergy to mitigate climate change. The notion of limiting the rise of average global surface temperature to 1.5°C is found in an IPCC special report (IPCC 2018). Information on countries' nationally determined contributions for the Paris climate accord are found at http://unfccc.int/focus/indc_portal/items/8766.php [accessed July 20, 2020].

Crutzen et al. (2008) and Searchinger et al. (2008, 2009) made an early case that growing bioenergy crops often results in greater release of CO_2 than warranted by the benefits of reduced fossil fuel use. Data on carbon in soils under different tillage systems are from West and Marland (2001).

On forest management for carbon, see Malmsheimer et al. (2011); Lemprière et al. (2013); Moiseyev et al. (2011); Niquidet, Stennes, and van Kooten (2012), who provide costs of removing logging residues and roadside wastes; Stennes, Niquidet, and van Kooten (2010) on competition for residual fiber; and van Kooten, Bogle, and de Vries (2015) for the example from a forest in southeastern British Columbia. Carbon intensities for fuels are available from http://www.canadianbiomassmagazine.ca/images/stories/table1-2.pdf [accessed December 8, 2020]; data on CO_2 emissions in transportation are from the European Chemical Transport Association's 2011 "Guidelines for Measuring and Managing CO_2 Emission from Freight Transport Operations" at https://www.ecta.com/resources/Documents/Best%20Practices%20Guidelines /guideline_for_measuring_and_managing_co2.pdf [accessed December 8, 2020].

Food for Thought

10.1. Suppose that, once timber is harvested, some proportion of the wood enters a carbon pool that decays slowly, over time releasing its carbon to the atmosphere. Since trees are harvested each year, each year there will be a stream of carbon released from the wood products made in that year. To account for the carbon released at the time of harvest, these carbon releases need to be discounted to the date at which harvest occurs, because that is when the landowner should be granted the carbon offset credits that are earned. Assuming the rate of product decay is denoted δ and the rate used to discount future carbon flux is denoted k, derive a formula for determining the current value of carbon C that is stored in wood products.

10.2. In 2016, the US deficit rose to about $600 billion, some $162 billion higher than in 2015. Proposals to increase government revenue include higher taxes on the rich and a reduction in tax loopholes, most notably removing the write-off of interest payments on mortgages against taxes (which benefits everyone, but the rich the most). Increased taxes on the rich could increase revenue by $800 billion over the next 10 years, while the removal of the mortgage benefit could increase revenues by $2,200 billion over the same period. However, the budget deficit is forecast to be $9,900 billion over the next decade, so the shortfall is about $3 trillion. Given that the US emitted 6,145 Mt of CO_2 in 2010, what effect might a $30 per tCO_2 tax (as in BC) have on the budget deficit? Explain/discuss your answer.

10.3. In 2006, global GDP amounted to $47.267 trillion (measured in constant 2000 US dollars). Global emissions of CO_2 were 29.12 Gt. As a result, the ratio of CO_2 emissions to GDP (C/Y) was 0.616 tCO_2 per $1,000 of GDP, which was lower than the global average of 0.92 tCO_2 per $1,000 GDP in 1980. The lowest C/Y of any country is that of France, which emits 0.30 tCO_2 per $1,000 GDP because of its heavy reliance on nuclear energy. Suppose (probably unrealistically) that in the next

50 years, technological advances will lower the global C/Y to 0.15. Recall that the underlying assumption upon which future warming is projected to occur has real global income increasing by threefold (i.e., multiply the 2006 GDP by 3.0) or by sevenfold (multiply by 7.0). Given these scenarios, will technological advances in energy efficiency and energy conservation prevent global warming from occurring? Why or why not? If not, what is needed and does any of this make sense? Discuss.

10.4. China, India, and Indonesia combined are home to about 40% of humankind. Consider China. In the late 1990s, Vaclav Smit estimated that, if China achieves a modest 2% annual growth per year, it will need an increment of primary energy production equal to the 1990 combined output of Brazil and India, extra electricity equal to that of Brazil's current output, extra steel equal to Italy's production, extra cement and fertilizer equal to Japan's consumption, extra grain equal to all of Africa's current consumption, and extra water equal to Mexico's 1990 consumption. You can imagine the extra pollution that this might cause. While environmentalists in the West are horrified at the thought of the potential environmental degradation, what do you think was the foremost impact on the West? Should steps be taken to prevent the economies of these three countries from developing?

10.5. Suppose a weather station is initially located in a field far from developments. Now the area near the weather station gets paved. The pavement absorbs the sun's energy but also emits heat to its surroundings, even during the day. (To experience the impact, walk on bare feet on a grass field and then on pavement when the temperature is 30 °C or higher.) Which surface thermometer would yield a higher temperature reading—one located in the field or in the paved parking lot? Collect temperature data for any city (there are plenty of sources for such data so you should have no trouble finding something). For this data set, is there any evidence to suggest that temperatures are influenced by non-climatic factors? What evidence might one use?

10.6. The rate used to discount monetary values is determined in the marketplace where the demand for funds and the supply of funds are equated. Is the rate used to discount physical carbon determined in a free market? If not, how would it be determined?

10.7. Suppose a hypothetical forestry project prevented 2 tC from entering the atmosphere each year in perpetuity. In addition, 5 tC were sequestered each year in the ecosystem carbon sink, but only for 10 years, after which the ecosystem sink was saturated (uptake into the sink was offset by release from the sink). Prove that, for this project, the total discounted carbon saved amounts to 147.81 tC if a discount rate of 2% is used.

10.8. Suppose that climate change is considered an urgent concern that policy needs to address immediately. What is the implication, if any, for the weight that we should use to discount physical carbon fluxes as to when they occur?

10.9. Suppose that a small power plant of about 120 MW capacity burns subbituminous coal to produce 1 TWh (= 1 million MWh) of electricity annually. [It is important to distinguish between "power," which is the electricity that can be supplied at any moment and is measured in MW, and "energy," which is power multiplied by time and measured in MWh.] The coal plant is to be replaced by a biomass facility producing the same amount of electricity. Assume that coal was transported by road over an average distance of 20 km, but that biomass is transported over an average distance of 40 km (because the wood needs to be gathered over a large area). The transportation of both coal and biomass is taken to release 62 g of CO_2 per tonne-km (see "Guidelines for Measuring and Managing CO_2 Emission from Freight Transport Operations" at https://www.ecta.com/resources /Documents/Best%20Practices%20Guidelines/guideline_for_measuring_and_managing_co2.pdf).

(a) If 0.40 tonnes of coal releases 0.94 tCO_2 to produce a MWh of energy, while 0.65 t of biomass releases 1.24 tCO_2/MWh, how much more CO_2 is released during the year upon exchanging biomass for coal as a fuel source?

(b) Now assume that wood biomass contains 200 kg of carbon per cubic meter (0.733 tCO_2/m^3). Suppose that a hectare of forest is harvested when the stand's volume of biomass reaches 250 m^3. How much area is required to support the biomass power plant? What is the area of forest required if harvest occurs at 400 m^3?

(c) Suppose the mean annual increment (MAI or average growth) of the forest is 50 m^3/ha (which is attainable in some plantations in the US South). How long does it take before the biomass conversion project is carbon neutral for physical discount rates of 0%, 5%, and 20%? How do the results change if the MAI is 5 m^3/ha, which is more representative of a Canadian forest?

10.10. Using a diagrammatic applied welfare economics approach, demonstrate how incentives to increase ethanol production from corn in the US can reduce the costs of the loan rate payment and even the deficiency payment.

REFERENCES

Acemoglu, D., and J.A. Robinson, 2019. *The Narrow Corridor. States, Societies, and the Fate of Liberty*. New York: Penguin Press.

Adamowicz, W.L., 1995. Alternative Valuation Techniques: A Comparison and Movement to a Synthesis. In *Environmental Valuation: New Perspectives* (pp. 144–159), edited by K.G. Willis and J.T. Corkindale. Wallingford, UK: CAB International.

Adamowicz, W.L., P. Boxall, M. Williams, and J. Louviere, 1998. Stated Preference Approaches to Measuring Passive Use Values: Choice Experiments versus Contingent Valuation, *American Journal of Agricultural Economics* 80(February): 64–75.

Adams, D.M., R.J. Alig, J.M. Callaway, B.A. McCarl, and S.M. Winnett, 1996. The Forest and Agricultural Sector Optimization Model (FASOM): Model Structure and Policy Applications. 60 pp. Portland, OR: US Department of Agriculture, Pacific Northwest Research Station.

Adams, R.M., 1989. Global Climate Change and Agriculture: An Economic Perspective, *American Journal of Agricultural Economics* 71(5): 1272–1279.

Adams, R.M., C. Rosenzweig, R.M. Peart, J.T. Richie, B.A. McCarl, J.D. Glyer, R.B. Curry, J.W. Jones, K.J. Boote, and L.H. Allen Jr, 1990. Global Climate Change and US Agriculture, *Nature* 345(6272): 219–224.

Alexander, R.B., 2020. Weather Extremes: Are They Caused by Global Warming? Report 43. 32 pp. London: The Global Warming Policy Foundation. https://www.thegwpf.org/content/uploads/2020/06/Alexander-Weather-Extremes.pdf [accessed June 4, 2020].

Amacher, G.S., M. Ollikainen, and E.A. Koskela, 2009. *Economics of Forest Resources*. Cambridge, MA: The MIT Press.

Anderson, K., G. Rausser, and J. Swinnen, 2013. Political Economy of Public Policies: Insights from Distortions to Agricultural and Food Markets, *Journal of Economic Literature* 51(2): 423–477.

Antón, J., S. Kimura, and R. Martini, 2011. Risk Management in Agriculture in Canada. OECD Food, Agriculture and Fisheries Papers, No. 40. 88 pp. Paris: OECD Publishing. http://dx.doi.org/10.1787/5kgj0d6189wg-en.

Arguedas, C., and D.P. van Soest, 2011. Optimal Conservation Programs, Asymmetric Information and the Role of Fixed Costs, *Environmental & Resource Economics* 50: 305–323.

Arora, V.K., and J.R. Melton, 2018. Reduction in Global Area Burned and Wildfire Emissions since 1930s Enhances Carbon Uptake by Land, *Nature Communications* 9: 1326.

Arrow, K.J., M.L. Cropper, C. Gollier, B. Groom, G.M. Heal, R.G. Newell, W.D. Nordhaus, R.S. Pindyck, W.A. Pizer, P.R. Portney, T. Sterner, R.S.J. Tol, and M.L. Weitzman, 2012. How Should Benefits and Costs Be Discounted in an Intergenerational Context? The Views of an Expert Panel. RFF Discussion Paper 12–53. 34 pp. Washington, DC: Resources for the Future.

Arrow, K., R. Solow, E. Leamer, P. Portney, R. Randner, and H. Schuman, 1993. Appendix I - Report of the NOAA Panel on Contingent Valuation. *Federal Register* 58(10, January 15): 4602–4614.

Arthur, L.M., and F. Abizadeh, 1988. Potential effects of climate change on agriculture in the prairie region on Canada, *Western Journal of Agricultural Economics* 13(2): 215–224.

Arthur, L.M., and G.C. van Kooten, 1992. Climate Change Impacts on Agribusiness Sectors of a Prairie Economy. *Prairie Forum* 17(Spring): 97–109.

Arunanondchai, P., C. Fei, A. Fisher, B.A. McCarl, W. Wang, and Y. Yang, 2019. How Does Climate Change Affect Agriculture? In *Routledge Handbook of Agricultural Economics* (pp. 191–210), edited by G.L. Cramer, K.P. Paudel, and A. Schmitz. New York: Routledge.

Babcock, B., 2014. Welfare Effects of PLC, ARC, and SCO, *Choices: The Magazine of Food, Farm, and Resource Issues* 29(3): 1–3.

Barichello, R., 1995. Overview of Canadian Agricultural Policy Systems. In *Understanding Canada/United States Grain Disputes* (pp. 37–59), edited by R.M.A. Loyns, R.D. Knutson, and K. Mielke. Winnipeg, MB: Friesen Printing.

Barrett, C.B., R. Carter, and J.-P. Chavas, 2019. *The Economics of Poverty Traps*. Chicago, IL: University of Chicago Press and National Bureau of Economic Research.

Benbrook, C.M., 2012. Impacts of Genetically Engineered Crops on Pesticide Use in the US—the First Sixteen Years, *Environmental Sciences Europe* 24: Article 24. https://enveurope.springeropen.com/track/pdf/10.1186/2190-4715-24-24.pdf.

Bettarini, I., F.P. Vaccari, and F. Miglietta, 1998. Elevated CO_2 Concentrations and Stomatal Density: Observations from 17 Plant Species Growing in a CO_2 Spring in Central Italy, *Global Change Biology* 4: 17–22.

Boadway, R.W., and N. Bruce, 1984. *Welfare Economics*. Oxford, UK: Blackwell Publishing.

Boardman, A., D. Greenberg, A. Vining, and D. Weimer, 2011. *Cost-Benefit Analysis* (4th ed.). Upper Saddle River, NJ: Prentice Hall.

Boullis, A., F. Francis, and F. Verheggen, 2018. Aphid-hoverfly Interactions under Elevated CO_2 Concentrations: Oviposition and Larval Development, *Physiological Entomology* 43: 245–250.

Brink, L., 2014. Commitments Under the WTO Agreement on Agriculture and the Doha Draft Modalities: How Do They Compare to Current Policy? December 2. 89 pp. Paris: OECD Trade and Agriculture Directorate, OECD.

Brown, B., M. Griffith, and C. Zoller, 2019. The Ohio State University's Guide to the 2018 Farm Bill Commodity Programs. AEDE Agricultural Report 2019–2011. November 12. 32 pp. Columbus, OH: Department of Agricultural, Environmental & Development Economics, Ohio State University. https://aede.osu.edu/research/osu-farm-management [accessed February 20, 2020].

Brunet-Jailly, E., A. Hurrelmann, and A. Verdun (eds.), 2018. *European Union Governance and Policy-Making: A Canadian Perspective*. Toronto, ON: University of Toronto Press.

Bulte, E.H., D.P. van Soest, G.C. van Kooten, and R. Schipper, 2002. Forest Conservation in Costa Rica: Optimal Forest Stocks under Uncertainty and Rising Nonuse Benefits, *American J of Agricultural Economics* 84(February): 150–160.

Cardwell, R., C. Lawley, and D. Xiang, 2015. Milked and Feathered: The Regressive Welfare Effects of Canada's Supply Management Regime, *Canadian Public Policy* 41(1): 1–14.

Carter, C.A., 2003. *Futures and Options Markets: An Introduction*. Upper Saddle River, NJ: Pearson Education.

Carter, C.A., and P. Mérel, 2016. Hidden Costs of Supply Management in a Small Market, *Canadian Journal of Economics* 49(2): 555–588.

Chambers, R.G., 2007. Valuing Agricultural Insurance, *American Journal of Agricultural Economics* 89(3): 596–606.

Challinor, A.J., J. Watson, D.B. Lobell, S.M. Howden, D.R. Smith, and N. Chhetri, 2014. A Meta-analysis of Crop Yield under Climate Change and Adaptation, *Nature Climate Change* 4: 287–291.

Chauhan, B.S., K. Jabran, and G. Mahajan (eds.), 2017. *Rice Production Worldwide*. Dordrecht, NL: Springer.

Chen, J., B.A. McCarl, and A. Thayer. 2017. Climate Change and Food Security: Threats and Adaptation. In *World Agricultural Resources and Food Security: International Food Security* (pp. 70–84), edited by A. Schmitz, P.L. Kennedy and T.G. Schmitz. Bingley, UK: Emerald Publishing.

Ciriacy-Wantrup, S.V., 1968 (1952). *Resource Conservation. Economics and Policies* (3rd ed.). Berkeley, CA: University of California, Agricultural Experiment Station.

Clawson, M., 1959. Measuring the Demand for and Value of Outdoor Recreation. RFF Reprint #10. Washington: Resources for the Future.

Coppens, D., 2014. *WTO Disciplines on Subsidies and Countervailing Measures: Balancing Policy Space and Legal Constraints*. Vol. 12. Cambridge, UK: Cambridge University Press.

Costanza, R., R. d'Arge, R. de Groot, S. Farber, M. Grasso, B. Hannon, K. Limburg, S. Naeem, R.V. O'Neill, J. Paruelo, R.G. Raskin, P. Sutton, and M. van den Belt, 1997. The Value of the World's Ecosystem Services and Natural Capital, *Nature* 387: 253–261.

Costanza, R., R. de Groot, P. Sutton, S. van der Ploeg, S.J. Anderson, I. Kubiszewski, S. Farber, and R.K. Turner, 2014. Changes in the Global Value of Ecosystem Services, *Global Environmental Change* 26: 152–158.

Crockford, S.J., 2018. State of the Polar Bear Report 2017. GWPF Report 29. 60 pp. London: The Global Warming Policy Foundation. https://www.thegwpf.org/content/uploads/2018/02/Polarbears2017.pdf.

Crutzen, P.J., A.R. Mosier, K.A. Smith, and W. Winiwarter, 2008. N_2O Release from Agro-biofuel Production Negates Global Warming Reduction by Replacing Fossil Fuels, *Atmospheric Chemistry and Physics* 8(2): 389–395.

Cummings, R.G., D.S. Brookshire, and W.D. Schulze (eds.), 1986. *Valuing Environmental Goods: An Assessment of the Contingent Valuation Method*. Totowa, NJ: Rowman & Allanheld.

Dahlby, B., 2008. *The Marginal Cost of Public Funds: Theory and Applications*. Cambridge, MA: MIT Press.

Dahlby, B. and E. Ferede, 2011. What Does It Cost Society to Raise a Dollar of Tax Revenue? The Marginal Cost of Public Funds, *Commentary* No. 324. 16 pp. Toronto, ON: CD Howe Institute.

Dalhuisen, J.M., R.J.G.M. Florax, H.L.F. de Groot, and P. Nijkamp, 2003. Price and Income Elasticities of Residential Water Demand: A Meta-Analysis, *Land Economics* 79: 292–308.

Darwin, R., M. Tsigas, J. Lewandrowski, and A. Raneses, 1995. World Agriculture and Climate Change: Economic Adaptations. AE Report No. 703, June. Washington, DC: US Department of Agriculture, Economic Research Service.

Dasgupta, P.S., 2002. Discounting: Public vs Private and Constant vs Hyperbolic. Keynote speech, Second World Congress of Environmental and Resource Economists, Monterey, CA, June 24.

Dayaratna, K., R. McKitrick, and D. Kreutzer, 2016. Empirically-Constrained Climate Sensitivity and the Social Cost of Carbon. SSRN Discussion Paper 2759505. http://papers.ssrn.com/sol3/papers.cfm?abstract_id=2759505.

De Soto, H., 2000. *The Mystery of Capital*. New York: Basic Books.

Dong, J., N. Gruda, S.K. Lam, X. Li, and Z. Duan, 2018. Effects of Elevated CO_2 on Nutritional Quality of Vegetables: A Review, *Frontiers in Plant Science* 9: 924. https://doi.org/10.3389/fpls.2018.00924.

Ebert, A.W., 2017. Vegetable Production, Diseases, and Climate Change. In *World Agricultural Resources and Food Security: International Food Security*, edited by A. Schmitz, P.L. Kennedy, and T.G. Schmitz (pp. 103–124). Bingley, UK: Emerald Publishing.

Engel, S., C. Palmer, L. Taschini, and S. Urech, 2012. *Cost-Effective Payments for Reducing Emissions from Deforestation under Uncertainty*. February. 24 pp. Centre for Climate Change Economics & Policy Working Paper No. 82. Grantham Research Institute on Climate Change & the Environment Working Paper No. 72. https://www.cccep.ac.uk/wp-content/uploads/2015/10/WP72_payments-emissions-deforestation.pdf.

Epstein, R.A., 1985. *Takings: Private Property and the Power of Eminent Domain*. Cambridge, MA: Harvard University Press.

European Commission, 2017. Risk Management Schemes in EU Agriculture: Dealing with Risk and Volatility. EU Agricultural Markets Briefs No. 12. September. http://ec.europa.eu/agriculture/markets-and-prices/market-briefs/index_en.htm [accessed September 28, 2017].

European Union (EU), 2016. Doha Development Agenda. Updated April 26. At http://ec.europa.eu/trade/policy/eu-and-wto/doha-development-agenda/ [accessed February 2, 2018].

Evans, M.F., N.E. Flores, and K. J. Boyle, 2003. Multiple-Bounded Uncertainty Choice Data as Probabilistic Intentions, *Land Economics* 79: 549–560.

Fischhoff, B., S. Lichtenstein, P. Slovic, S.L. Derby, and R.L. Keeney, 1981. *Acceptable Risk*. New York: Cambridge University Press.

Fooks, J.R., S.J. Dundas, and T.O. Awokuse, 2013. Are There Efficiency Gains from the Removal of Natural Resource Export Restrictions? Evidence from British Columbia, *World Economy* 36: 1098–1114.

Freeman, A.M. III, 1979. *The Benefits of Environmental Improvement. Theory and Practice*. Baltimore, MD: Johns Hopkins University Press.

Freeman, A.M. III, 1995. Hedonic Pricing Methods. In *The Handbook of Environmental Economics* (pp. 672–686), edited by D.W. Bromley. Cambridge, MA, and Oxford, UK: Blackwell Publishers.

Freeman, A.M. III, 2003. *The Measurement of Environmental and Resource Values. Theory and Methods* (2nd ed.). Washington, DC: Resources for the Future.

Fukuyama, F., 1992. *The End of History and the Last Man*. New York: The Free Press.

Fukuyama, F., 2014. *Political Order and Political Decay: From the Industrial Revolution to the Globalization of Democracy*. New York: Farrar, Straus and Giroux.

Gantz, D.A., 2013. *Liberalizing International Trade after Doha: Multilateral, Plurilateral, Regional, and Unilateral Initiatives*. Cambridge, UK: Cambridge University Press.

Gardner, B.L., 1987. Causes of US Farm Commodity Programs, *Journal of Political Economy* 95(2): 290–310.

Garrod, G.D., and K.G. Willis, 1999. *Economic Valuation of the Environment. Methods and Case Studies*. Cheltenham, UK: Edward Elgar.

Gifford, R.M., 2004. The CO_2 Fertilising Effect—Does It Occur in the Real World? *New Phytologist* 163: 221–225.

Glauber, J.W., 2013. The Growth of the Federal Crop Insurance Program, 1990–2011, *American Journal of Agricultural Economics* 95(2): 482–488.

Goklany, I.M., 2015. *Carbon Dioxide: The Good News*. GWPF Report 18. October 11. London, UK: Global Warming Policy Foundation.

Graham-Tomasi, T., 1995. Quasi–Option Value. In *The Handbook of Environmental Economics* (pp. 594–614), edited by D.W. Bromley. Cambridge, MA: Basil Blackwell Publishers.

Gregory, R., S. Lichtenstein, and P. Slovic, 1993. Valuing Environmental Resources: A Constructive Approach, *Journal of Risk and Uncertainty* 7: 177–197.

Hamilton, J.R., N.K. Whittlesey, M.H. Robison, and J. Ellis, 1991. Economic Impacts, Value Added, and Benefits in Regional Project Analysis, *American Journal of Agricultural Economics* 73(May): 334–344.

Hanley, N., and E.B. Barbier, 2009. *Pricing Nature: Cost-Benefit Analysis and Environmental Policy*. Cheltenham, UK, and Northampton, MA: Edward Elgar.

Hanrahan, C.E., and R. Schnepf, 2007. WTO Doha Round: The Agricultural Negotiations. CRS Report for Congress. OC RL33144. Washington, DC: Congressional Research Service.

Harberger, A.C., 1971. Three Basic Postulates for Applied Welfare Economics: An Interpretive Essay, *Journal of Economic Literature* 9(3): 785–797.

Harberger, A.C., 1972. *Project Evaluation: Collected Papers*. Chicago, IL: University of Chicago Press.

Harding, L., 2020. USMCA: Auto Sector Can Adapt, but Dairy Industry Will Take a Hit, *The Epoch Times*, July 9–15, p. A9.

Hart, O.D., A. Shleifer, and R.W. Vishny, 1997. The Proper Scope of Government: Theory and an Application to Prisons, *Quarterly Journal of Economics,* 112(4): 1127–1161.

Hausman, J., 2012. Contingent Valuation: From Dubious to Hopeless, *Journal of Economic Perspectives* 26(4): 43–56.

Heal, G., 2007. Discounting: A Review of the Basic Economics, *University of Chicago Law Review* 74(1): 59–77.

Heal, G., 2009. The Economics of Climate Change: A Post-Stern Perspective, *Climatic Change* 96: 275–297.

Heilbroner, R.L., 1999. *The Worldly Philosophers. The Lives, Times and Ideas of the Great Economic Thinkers* (revised 7th ed.). New York: Touchstone.

Hejazi, M., and M.A. Marchant, 2017. China's Evolving Agricultural Support Policies, *Choices* 32(2). https://www.choicesmagazine.org/choices-magazine/theme-articles/us-commodity-markets-respond-to-changes-in-chinas-ag-policies/chinas-evolving-agricultural-support-policies.

Horowitz, J.K., and K.E. McConnell, 2002. A Review of WTA/WTP Studies. *Journal of Environmental Economics and Management* 44(3): 426–447.

Hourdin, F., T. Mauritsen, A. Gettelman, J. Golaz, V. Balaji, Q. Duan, D. Folini, D. Ji, D. Klocke, Y. Qian, F. Rauser, C. Rio, L. Tomassini, M. Watanabe, and D. Williamson, 2017. The Art and Science of Climate Model Tuning, *Bulletin of the American Meteorological Society* March: 589–602. https://doi.org/10.1175/BAMS-D-15-00135.1.

Huffman, W.E. 2016. New Insights on the Impacts of Public Agricultural Research and Extension. *Choices*. https://www.choicesmagazine.org/choices-magazine/theme-articles/a-future-informed-by-agricultural-sciences/new-insights-on-the-impacts-of-public-agricultural-research-and-extension.

Idso, C.D., 2001. Earth's Rising Atmospheric CO_2 Concentration: Impacts on the Biosphere, *Energy and Environment* 12(4): 287–310. https://doi.org/10.1260/0958305011500797.

Idso, C.D., S.B. Idso, R.M. Carter, and F. Singer, 2014. *Climate Change Reconsidered II: Biological Impacts*. Chicago, IL: Heartland. http://climatechangereconsidered.org/climate-change-reconsidered-ii-biological-impacts/ [accessed November 1, 2018].

IPCC, 2000. Special Report on Emissions Scenarios. Edited by N. Nakicenovic & R. Swart. Geneva, CH: Intergovernmental Panel on Climate Change. https://www.ipcc.ch/site/assets/uploads/2018/03/emissions_scenarios-1.pdf.

IPCC, 2014. *Climate Change 2014: Impacts, Adaptation, and Vulnerability. Part A: Global and Sectoral Aspects*. Contribution of Working Group II to the Fifth Assessment Report of the Intergovernmental Panel on Climate Change [Field, C.B., V.R. Barros, D.J. Dokken, K.J. Mach, M.D. Mastrandrea, T.E. Bilir, M. Chatterjee, K.L. Ebi, Y.O. Estrada, R.C. Genova, B. Girma, E.S. Kissel, A.N. Levy, S. MacCracken, P.R. Mastrandrea, and L.L.White (eds.)]. Cambridge, UK: Cambridge University Press.

IPCC, 2018. Global Warming of 1.5 °C. Geneva, CH: UN Intergovernmental Panel on Climate Change. http://ipcc.ch/report/sr15/.

Jeffrey, S.R., D.E. Trautman, and J.R. Unterschultz, 2017. Canadian Agricultural Business Risk Management Programs: Implications for Farm Wealth and Environmental Stewardship, *Canadian Journal of Agricultural Economics* 63: 543–565.

Jewson, S., A. Brix, and C. Ziehmann. 2005. *Meteorological, Statistical, Financial and Mathematical Foundations*. Cambridge, UK: Cambridge University Press.

Johnston, C., and G.C. van Kooten, 2015. Back to the Past: Burning Wood to Save the Globe, *Ecological Economics* 120: 185–193.

Jongeneel, R., A. Burrell, and A. Kavallari, 2011. Evaluation of CAP Measures Applied to the Dairy Sector. Final Deliverable. EU Directorate-General for Agriculture and Rural Development under Contract No. 30-CE-0382055/00-63. November. 336 pp. Wageningen, NL: Wageningen University.

Jongeneel, R., N. Polman, and G.C. van Kooten, 2016. How Important Are Agricultural Externalities? A Framework for Analysis and Application to Dutch Agriculture. REPA Working Paper 2016-04. Victoria, BC: Resource Economics and Policy Analysis, Department of Economics, University of Victoria. http://web.uvic.ca/~repa/publications.htm.

Just, R.E., D.L. Hueth, and A. Schmitz, 1982. *Applied Welfare Economics and Public Policy*. Englewood Cliffs, NJ: Prentice Hall.

Just, R.E., D.L. Hueth, and A. Schmitz, 2004. *The Welfare Economics of Public Policy: A Practical Approach to Project and Policy Evaluation*. Cheltenham, UK: Edward Elgar.

Kahneman, D., 2011. *Thinking, Fast and Slow*. New York: Farrar, Straus and Giroux.

Kahneman, D., and A. Tversky, 1979. Prospect Theory: An Analysis of Decision under Risk, *Econometrica* 47: 263–291.

Kahneman, D., and A. Tversky, 1984. Choices, Values, and Frames, *American Psychologist* 39(4): 341–350.

Kaiser, H.M., S.J. Riha, D.S. Wilks, D.G. Rossiter, and R. Sampath, 1993. Farm-Level Analysis of Economic and Agronomic Impacts of Gradual Climate Warming, *American Journal of Agricultural Economics* 75(2): 387–398.

Kay, J., and M. King, 2020. *Radical Uncertainty: Decision-Making Beyond the Numbers*. New York: W.W. Norton & Company.

Ker, A., B. Barnett, D. Jacques, and T. Tolhurst, 2017. Canadian Business Risk Management: Private Firms, Crown Corporations, and Public Institutions, *Canadian Journal of Agricultural Economics* 65: 591–612.

Klein, K.K., and W.A. Kerr, 1996. The Crow Rate Issue: A Retrospective on the Contributions of the Agricultural Economics Profession in Canada, *Canadian Journal of Agricultural Economics* 44: 1–18.

Klotzbach, P.J., S.G. Bowen, R. Pielke Jr., and M. Bell, 2018. Continental US Hurricane Landfall Frequency and Associated Damage: Observations and Future Risks, *Bulletin of the American Meteorological Society* 99(7): 1359–1376.

Knetsch, J.L., 2000. Environmental Valuations and Standard Theory: Behavioural Findings, Context Dependence and Implications. In *The International Yearbook of Environmental and Resource Economics* (pp. 267–299), edited by T. Tietenberg and H. Folmer. Cheltenham, UK: Edward Elgar.

Kramer, R.A., and D.E. Mercer, 1997. Valuing a Global Environmental Good: US Residents' Willingness to Pay to Protect Tropical Rain Forests, *Land Economics* 73(2): 196–210.

Krcmar, E., B. Stennes, G.C. van Kooten, and I. Vertinsky, 2001. Carbon Sequestration and Land Management under Uncertainty, *European Journal of Operational Research* 135(December): 616–29.

Krcmar, E., and G.C. van Kooten, 2008. Economic Development Prospects of Forest-Dependent Communities: Analyzing Tradeoffs Using a Compromise-Fuzzy Programming Framework, *American Journal of Agricultural Economics* 90(4): 1103–1117.

Krcmar, E., G.C. van Kooten, and I. Vertinsky, 2005. Managing Forest and Marginal Agricultural Land for Multiple Tradeoffs: Compromising on Economic, Carbon and Structural Biodiversity Objectives, *Ecological Modelling* 185(July): 451–468.

Krutilla, J.V., 1967. Conservation Reconsidered, *American Economic Review* 57(4): 777–786.

La Porta, R., F. Lopez-de-Silanes, A. Shleifer, and R.W. Vishny, 1999. The Quality of the Government, *Journal of Law, Economics & Organization* 15(1): 222–279.

Landes, D.S., 1998. *The Wealth and Poverty of Nations*. New York: W.W. Norton & Company.

Lemprière, T.C., W.A. Kurz, E.H. Hogg, C. Schmoll, G.J. Rampley, D. Yemshanov, D.W. McKenney, R. Gilsenan, A. Beatch, D. Blain, J.S. Bhatti, and E. Krcmar, 2013. Canadian Boreal Forests and Climate Change Mitigation, *Environmental Reviews* 21: 293–321.

Lesser, J., D. Dodds, and R. Zerbe, 1997. *Environmental Economics and Policy*. New York: Addison-Wesley.

Levitt, S.D., and S.J. Dubner, 2009. *Super Freakonomics: Global Cooling, Patriotic Prostitutes, and Why Suicide Bombers Should Buy Life Insurance*. New York: Harper Collins.

Lewis, M., 2017. *The Undoing Project: A Friendship that Changed Our Minds*. New York: W.W. Norton & Company.

Lewis, N., 2018. Abnormal climate response of the DICE IAM—A trillion dollar error? April 22. https://www.nicholaslewis.org/abnormal-climate-response-of-the-dice-iam-a-trillion-dollar-error/ [accessed November 1, 2018].

Lewis, N., and J.A. Curry, 2015. The Implications for Climate Sensitivity of AR5 Forcing and Heat Uptake Estimates, *Climate Dynamics* 45: 1009–1023.

Lewis, N., and J.A. Curry, 2018. The Impact of Recent Forcing and Ocean Heat Uptake Data on Estimates of Climate Sensitivity, *Journal of Climate* 31(August): 6051–6071. https://doi.org/10.1175/JCLI-D-17-0667.1.

Liu, S., J. Duan, and G.C. van Kooten, 2020. Calibration of Agricultural Risk Programming Models Using Positive Mathematical Programming, *Australian Journal of Agricultural and Resource Economics* 59: 1–23. https://doi.org/10.1111/1467-8489.12368.

Long, S.P., 1991. Modification of the Response of Photosynthetic Productivity to Rising Temperature by Atmospheric CO_2 Concentrations: Has Its Importance Been Underestimated? *Plant, Cell and Environment* 14: 729–739.

Long, S.P., E.A. Ainsworth, A. Rogers, and D.R. Ort, 2004. Rising Atmospheric Carbon Dioxide: Plants FACE the Future, *Annual Review of Plant Biology* 55: 591–628.

Macabuhay, A., A. Houshmandfar, J. Nuttall, G.J. Fitzgerald, M. Tausz, and S. Tausz-Posch, 2018. Can Elevated CO_2 Buffer the Effects of Heat Waves on Wheat in a Dryland Cropping System? *Environmental and Experimental Botany* 155: 578–588.

Malmsheimer, R.W., J.L. Bowyer, J.S. Fried, E. Gee, R.L. Izlar, R.A. Miner, I.A. Munn, E. Oneil, and W.C. Stewart, 2011. Managing Forests because Carbon Matters: Integrating Energy, Products, and Land Management Policy, *Journal of Forestry* 109(7S): 7–50.

Manley, J., G.C. van Kooten, K. Moeltner, and D.W. Johnson, 2005. Creating Carbon Offsets in Agriculture through Zero Tillage: A Meta-Analysis of Costs and Carbon Benefits, *Climatic Change* 68(January): 41–65.

Margolick, M., and R.S. Uhler, 1992. The Economic Impact on British Columbia of Removing Log Export Restrictions, *Journal of Business Administration* 20(1–2): 273–296.

Massell, B.F., 1969. Price Stability and Welfare, *Quarterly Journal of Economics* 83(2): 284–298.

Matthews, A., 2018. *The EU's Common Agricultural Policy Post 2020. Directions of Change and Potential Trade and Market Effects.* Agriculture Issue Paper, November. 39 pp. Geneva: Food and Agriculture Organization of the UN/International Centre for Trade and Sustainable Development.

Mauritsen, T., and R. Pincus, 2017. Committed Warming Inferred from Observations, *Nature Climate Change* 7(July 31): 652–655.

McFadden, D. and G.K. Leonard, 1993. Issues in the Contingent Valuation of Environmental Goods: Methodologies for Data Collections and Analysis. In *Contingent Valuation: Volume 220* (pp. 165–215), edited by J.A. Hausman. Amsterdam: Elsevier Science Publisher B.V.

McGuffie, K., and A. Henderson-Sellers, 2009. *A Climate Modeling Primer* (3rd ed.). Chichester, UK: John Wiley & Sons.

McIntyre, S., and R.R. McKitrick, 2005. The M&M Critique of the MBH98 Northern Hemisphere Climate Index: Update and Implications, *Energy and Environment* 16(1): 69–100.

McKitrick, R.R., 2010. *Economic Analysis of Environmental Policy.* Toronto: University of Toronto Press.

McKitrick, R.R., 2011. A Simple State-Contingent Pricing Rule for Complex Intertemporal Externalities, *Energy Economics* 33: 111–120.

McKitrick, R. and J. Christy, 2020. Pervasive Warming Bias in CMIP6 Tropospheric Layers, *Earth and Space Science* 7: e2020EA001281.

McKitrick, R.R., and P.J. Michaels, 2007. Quantifying the Influence of Anthropogenic Surface Processes and Inhomogeneities on Gridded Global Climate data, *Journal of Geophysical Research* 112: D24S09. https://doi.org/10.1029/2007JD008465.

McKitrick, R.R., and N. Nierenberg, 2011. Socioeconomic Signals in Climate Data, *Journal of Economic and Social Measurement* 35(3,4): 149–175.

McKitrick, R.R., and T. Vogelsang, 2014. HAC-Robust Trend Comparisons among Climate Series with Possible Level Shifts, *Environmetrics.* https://doi.org/10.1002/env.2294.

Mendelsohn, R., W.D. Nordhaus, and D. Shaw, 1994. The Impact of Global Warming on Agriculture: A Ricardian Approach, *American Economic Review* 84(4): 753–771.

Millar, R.J., J.S. Fuglestvedt, P. Friedlingstein, J. Rogelj, M.J. Grubb, H.D. Matthews, R.B Skeie, P.M. Forster, D.J. Frame, and M.R. Allen, 2017. Emission Budgets and Pathways Consistent with Limiting Warming to 1.5°C, *Nature Geoscience* 10: 741–747.

Millennium Ecosystem Assessment, 2003. *Ecosystems and Human Wellbeing.* Vol. 1, *Current State and Trends.* Washington, DC: Island Press.

Millennium Ecosystem Assessment, 2005. *Ecosystems and Human Wellbeing.* Vol. 3, *Policy Responses.* Washington, DC: Island Press.

Mitchell, R.C., and R.T. Carson, 1989. *Using Surveys to Value Public Goods: The Contingent Valuation Method.* Washington, DC: Resources for the Future.

Moiseyev, A., B. Solberg, A.M.L. Kallio, and M. Lindner, 2011. An Economic Analysis of the Potential Contribution of Forest Biomass to the EU RES Target and Its Implication for the EU Forest Industries, *Journal of Forest Economics* 17: 197–213.

Monke, J., R.A. Aussenberg, and M. Stubbs, 2018. Expiration of the 2014 Farm Bill. Report R45341. Updated October 11. Washington, DC: Congressional Research Service. https://crsreports.congress.gov/product/pdf/R/R45341.

Mooney, S., and L.M. Arthur, 1990. Impacts of 2xCO$_2$ on Manitoba Agriculture, *Canadian Journal of Agricultural Economics* 38(4): 685–694.

Moore, F.C., U. Baldos, T. Hertel, and D. Diaz, 2017. New Science of Climate Change Impacts on Agriculture Implies Higher Social Cost of Carbon, *Nature Communications* 8(1): 1607. https://doi.org/10.1038/s41467-017-01792-x.

Morgan, J.A., D.R. LeCain, E. Pendall, D.M. Blumenthal, B.A. Kimball, Y. Carrillo, D.G. Williams, J. Heisler-White, F.A. Dijkstra, and M. West, 2011. C4 Grasses Prosper as Carbon Dioxide Eliminates Desiccation in Warmed Semi-Arid Grassland, *Nature* 476(11): 202–205.

Mortensen, D.A., J.F. Egan, B.D. Maxwell, M.R. Ryan, and R.G. Smith, 2012. Navigating a Critical Juncture for Sustainable Weed Management, *BioScience* 62(1): 75–84.

Musshoff, O., M. Odening, and W. Xu, 2011. Management of Climate Risks in Agriculture: Will Weather Derivatives Permeate? *Applied Economics* 43: 1067–1077.

Navrud, S., 2001. Comparing Valuation Exercises in Europe and the United States, Challenges for Benefit Transfers and Some Policy Implications. In *Valuation of Biodiversity Benefits: Selected Studies* (pp. 63–77). Paris: Organisation for Economic Co-operation and Development (OECD).

Navrud, S., and R. Ready (eds.), 2007. *Environmental Value Transfer: Issues and Methods*. Dordrecht, NL: Springer.

Nelson, R.H., 2010. *The New Holy Wars: Environmental Religion versus Economic Religion in Contemporary America*. University Park: Pennsylvania University Press.

Newell, R.G., and W.A. Pizer, 2003. Discounting the Distant Future: How Much Do Uncertain Rates Increase Valuations? *Journal of Environmental Economics and Management* 46: 52–71.

Niquidet, K., B. Stennes, and G.C. van Kooten, 2012. Bio-energy from Mountain Pine Beetle Timber and Forest Residuals: The Economics Story, *Canadian Journal of Agricultural Economics* 60(2): 195–210.

Nordhaus, W.D., 2010. Carbon Taxes to Move toward Fiscal Sustainability, *The Economists' Voice* (September).

Nordhaus, W.D., 2013. Integrated Economic and Climate Modeling. In *Handbook of Computable General Equilibrium Modeling*, Vol. 1A (1st ed.) (pp. 1069–1131), edited by P. Dixon and D. Jorgenson. Dordrecht, NL: Elsevier. (DICE model found at https://sites.google.com/site/williamdnordhaus/dice-rice).

Nordhaus, W.D., and J. Boyer, 2000. *Warming the World. Economic Models of Global Warming*. Cambridge, MA: The MIT Press.

O'Neill, D., 2007. The Total External Environmental Costs and Benefits of Agriculture in the UK. April 24. 33 pp. London, UK: Environment Agency. http://webarchive.nationalarchives.gov.uk/20140328084622/http://www.environment-agency.gov.uk/static/documents/Research/costs_benefitapr07_1749472.pdf [accessed 19 February 2016].

OECD, 2001. *Valuation of Biodiversity Benefits: Selected Studies*. Paris: Organisation for Economic Co-operation and Development.

OECD, 2020. Agricultural Policy Monitoring and Evaluation. OECD online data at http://www.oecd.org/agriculture/topics/agricultural-policy-monitoring-and-evaluation/ [accessed July 16, 2020].

Oi, W.Y., 1961. The Desirability of Price Instability under Perfect Competition, *Econometrica* 29: 58–64.

Olewiler, N., 2004. The Value of Natural Capital in Settled Areas of Canada. 36 pp. Stonewall, MB, and Toronto, ON: Ducks Unlimited Canada and the Nature Conservancy of Canada.

Olson, K., 2014a. Price Loss Coverage (PLC). Agricultural Act of 2014, Fact Sheet 4 Updated. November. Agricultural Business Management, University of Minnesota Extension. http://dx.doi.org/10.22004/ag.econ.307962 [accessed December 14, 2020].

Olson, K., 2014b. Agriculture Risk Coverage: ARC-County. Agricultural Act of 2014, Fact Sheet 5. March. Agricultural Business Management, University of Minnesota Extension. http://dx.doi.org/10.22004/ag.econ.307961 [accessed December 14, 2020].

Olson, K., 2015. Agriculture Risk Coverage: ARC-Individual (ARC-IC). Agricultural Act of 2014, Fact Sheet 6 Updated. January. Agricultural Business Management, University of Minnesota Extension. http://dx.doi.org/10.22004/ag.econ.307963 [accessed December 14, 2020]

Ostrom, E., 2000. Social Capital: A Fad or a Fundamental Concept? In *Social Capital: A Multifaceted Perspective* (pp. 172–214), edited by P.S. Dasgupta and I. Serageldin. Washington, DC: The World Bank.

Pandey, R., M.K. Lal, and K. Vengavasi, 2018. Differential Response of Hexaploid and Tetraploid Wheat to Interactive Effects of Elevated [CO_2] and Low Phosphorus, *Plant Cell Reports* 37: 1231–1244.

Pasour, E.C., 1988. The Farm Problem, Government Farm Programs, and Commercial Agriculture, *Journal of Production Agriculture* 1: 64–70.

Pearce, D.W., and J.J. Warford, 1993. *World Without End: Economics, Environment, and Sustainable Development*. Oxford, UK: Oxford University Press.

Phillips, W.E., W.L. Adamowicz, J. Asafu-Adjaye, and P.C. Boxall, 1989. An Economic Assessment of the Value of Wildlife Resources to Alberta Department of Rural Economy Project Report No. 89-04. August. 70 pp. Edmonton: University of Alberta.

Pillet, G., N. Zingg, and D. Maradan, 2002. Appraising Externalities of Swiss Agriculture. Bern, CZ: Swiss Federal Office of Agriculture. http://www.academia.edu/19974676/appraising_externalities_of_the_swiss_agriculture_a_comprehensive_view [accessed July 1, 2017].

Pindyck, R.S., 2013. Climate Change Policy. What Do the Models Tell Us? *Journal of Economic Literature* 51(3): 860–872.

Pindyck, R.S., 2017. The Use and Misuse of Models for Climate Policy, *Review of Environmental Economics and Policy* 11(1): 100–114.

Porter, J., R. Constanza, H. Sandhu, L. Sigsgaard, and S. Wratten, 2009. The Value of Producing Food, Energy, and Ecosystem Services within an Agro-ecosystem, *AMBIO: A Journal on the Human Environment* 38(4): 186–193.

Porter, J.R., M. Howden, and P. Smith, 2017. Considering Agriculture in IPCC Assessments, *Nature Climate Change* 7: 680–683.

Prakash, V., S.K. Dwivedi, S. Kumar, J.S. Mishra, K.K. Rao, S.S. Singh, and B.P. Bhatt, 2017. Effect of Elevated CO_2 and Temperature on Growth and Yield of Wheat Grown in Sub-Humid Climate of Eastern Indo-Gangetic Plain (IGP), *Mausam* 68: 499–506.

Prasad, E.S., 2014. *The Dollar Trap. How the US Dollar Tightened Its Grip on Global Finance*. Princeton, NJ: Princeton University Press.

Pretty, J.N., A.S. Ball, T. Lang, and J.I.L. Morison, 2005. Farm Costs and Food Miles: An Assessment of the Full Cost of the UK Weekly Food Basket, *Food Policy* 30(1): 1–20.

Pretty, J.N., C. Brett, D. Gee, R. Hine, C.F. Mason, J.I.L Morison, H. Raven, M. Rayment, and G. van der Bijl, 2000. An Assessment of the Total External Costs of UK Agriculture, *Agricultural Systems* 65(2): 113–136.

Pretty, J.N., C. Brett, D. Gee, R. Hine, C.F. Mason, J.I.L Morison, M. Rayment, G. van der Bijl, and T. Dobbs, 2001. Policy Challenges and Priorities for Internalizing the Externalities of Modern Agriculture, *Journal of Environmental and Management* 44(2): 263–283.

Randall, V., 2017. The Uncertainty Monster: Lessons from Non-Orthodox Economics, *Climate Etc.* https://judithcurry.com/2017/07/05/the-uncertainty-monster-lessons-from-non-orthodox-economics/#more-23186 [accessed July 10, 2017].

Rausser, G.C. 1992. Predatory Versus Productive Government: The Case of US Agricultural Policies, *Journal of Economic Perspectives* 6(3): 133–157.

Ready, R.C., 1995. Environmental Evaluation under Uncertainty. In *The Handbook of Environmental Economics* (pp. 568–593), edited by D.W. Bromley. Cambridge, MA: Basil Blackwell Publishers

Riahi, K., D.P. van Vuuren, E. Kriegler, J. Edmonds, B.C. O'Neill, S. Fujimori, N. Bauer, K. Calvin, R. Dellink, O. Fricko, W. Lutz, A. Popp, J.C. Cuaresma, K.C. Samir, M. Leimbach, L. Jiang, T. Kram, S. Rao, J. Emmerling, K. Ebi, T. Hasegawa, P. Havlik, F. Humpenöder, L.A. Da Silva, S. Smith, E. Stehfest, V. Bosetti, J. Eom, D. Gernaat, T. Masui, J. Rogelj, J. Strefler, L. Drouet, V. Krey, G. Luderer, M. Harmsen, K. Takahashi, L. Baumstark, J.C. Doelman, M. Kainuma, Z. Klimont, G. Marangoni, H. Lotze-Campen, M. Obersteiner, A. Tabeau, and M. Tavoni, 2017. The Shared Socioeconomic Pathways and Their Energy, Land Use, and Greenhouse Gas Emissions Implications: An Overview, *Global Environmental Change* 42: 153–168.

Richards, K.R., 1997. The Time Value of Carbon in Bottom-Up Studies, *Critical Reviews in Environmental Science and Technology* 27(Special Issue): S279–292.

Sandmo, A., 1975. Optimal Taxation in the Presence of Externalities, *Scandinavian Journal of Economics* 77(1): 86–98.

Sandmo, A., 1998. Redistribution and the Marginal Cost of Public Funds, *Journal of Public Economics* 70: 365–382.

Santer, B.D., J.C. Fyfe, G. Pallotta, G.M. Flato, G.A. Meehl, M.H. England, E. Hawkins, M.E. Mann, J.F. Painter, C. Bonfils, I. Cvijanovic, C. Mears, F.J. Wentz, S. Po-Chedley, Q. Fu, and C.-Z. Zou, 2017. Causes of Differences in Model and Satellite Tropospheric Warming Rates, *Nature Geoscience.* https://doi.org/10.1038/ngeo2973.

Schimmelpfenning, D., J. Lewandrowski, J. Reilly, M. Tsigas, and I. Parry, 1996. Agricultural Adaptation to Climate Change: Issues of Long-Run Sustainability. *Agricultural Economic Report* 740. 57 pp. Washington, DC: USDA Economic Research Service.

Schlenker, W., and M.J. Roberts, 2009. Nonlinear Temperature Effects Indicate Severe Damages to US Crop Yields under Climate Change, *Proceedings of the National Academy of Sciences* 106(37): 11594–15598.

Schlenker, W., M.H. Hanemann, and A.C. Fisher, 2006. The Impact of Global Warming on US Agriculture: An Econometric Analysis of Optimal Growing Conditions, *The Review of Economics and Statistics* 88(1): 113–125.

Schmitz, A., W.H. Furtan, and K. Baylis, 2002. *Agricultural Policy, Agribusiness and Rent Seeking Behavior*. Toronto, ON: University of Toronto Press.

Schmitz, A., C. Moss, T. Schmitz, W.H. Furtan, and C. Schmitz, 2010. *Agricultural Policy, Agribusiness and Rent Seeking Behavior* (2nd ed.). Toronto, ON: University of Toronto Press.

Schmitz, A., C. Moss, T. Schmitz, G.C. van Kooten, and C. Schmitz, 2021. *Agricultural Policy, Agribusiness and Rent Seeking Behavior* (3rd ed.). Toronto, ON: University of Toronto Press.

Schmitz, T.G. and A. Schmitz, 2012. The Complexities of the Interface between Agricultural Policy and Trade, *The Estey Centre Journal of International Law and Trade Policy* 13(1): 14–42.

Schnitkey, G., and C. Zulauf, 2016. The Farm Safety Net for Field Crops, *Choices* 31(4). http://www.choicesmagazine.org/choices-magazine/theme-articles/looking-ahead-to-the-next-farm-bill/.

Schnitkey, G., J. Coppess, N. Paulson, C. Zulauf, and K. Swanson, 2019a. The Agricultural Risk Coverage—County Level (ARC-CO) Option in the 2018 Farm Bill, *farmdoc daily* (9): 173. https://farmdocdaily.illinois.edu/2019/09/the-agricultural-risk-coverage-county-level-arc-co-option-in-the-2018-farm-bill.html [accessed February 19, 2020].

Schnitkey, G., C. Zulauf, K. Swanson, J. Coppess, and N. Paulson, 2019b. The Price Loss Coverage (PLC) Option in the 2018 Farm Bill, *farmdoc daily* (9): 178. https://farmdocdaily.illinois.edu/2019/09/weekly-farm-economics-the-price-loss-coverage-plc-option-in-the-2018-farm-bill.html [accessed February 19, 2020].

Scott, Anthony, 1973 (1955). *Natural Resources: The Economics of Conservation*. Toronto, ON: McClelland and Stewart.

Searchinger, T.D., S.P. Hamburg, J. Melillo, W. Chameides, P. Havlik, D.M. Kammen, G.E. Likens, R.N. Lubowski, M. Obersteiner, M. Oppenheimer, G.P. Robertson, W.H. Schlesinger, and G.D. Tilman, 2009. Fixing a Critical Climate Accounting Error, *Science* 326(October 23): 527–528.

Searchinger, T.D., R. Heimlich, R.A. Houghton, F. Dong, A. Elobeid, J. Fabiosa, S. Tokgoz, D. Hayes, and T. Yu, 2008. Use of US Croplands for Biofuels Increases Greenhouse Gases through Emissions from Land-Use Change, *Science* 319(February 29): 1238–1240.

Shaikh, S., L. Sun, and G.C. van Kooten, 2007. Treating Respondent Uncertainty in Contingent Valuation: A Comparison of Empirical Treatments, *Ecological Economics* 62(1 April): 115–125.

Shleifer, A. and R.W. Vishny, 1999. *The Grabbing Hand: Government Pathologies and their Cures*. Cambridge, MA: Harvard University Press.

Smith, V., 1997. Pricing of What Is Priceless: A Status Report on Nonmarket Valuation of Environmental Resources. In *The International Yearbook of Environmental and Resource Economics 1997/1998* (pp. 156–204), edited by H. Folmer and T. Tietenberg. Cheltenham, UK: Edward Elgar.

Smith, V.H., 2017. The US Federal Crop Insurance Program: A Case Study in Rent Seeking. Mercatus Working Paper, 48 pp. Arlington, VA: Mercatus Center, George Mason University.

Smith, V.H., 2018. *US Agricultural Policy Beyond 2018: Implications for the World Trade Organization*. Agriculture Issue Paper, November. 30 pp. International Centre for Trade and Sustainable Development. Geneva, CH: Food and Agriculture Organization of the UN/International Centre for Trade and Sustainable Development.

Smith, V.H., and J.W. Glauber, 2012. Where Have We Been and Where Are We Going? *Applied Economic Perspectives and Policy* 34(3): 363–390.

Stabler, J.C., G.C. van Kooten, and N. Meyer, 1988. Methodological Issues in Appraisal of Regional Resource Development Projects, *The Annals of Regional Science* 22(July): 13–25.

Steele, J. 2020. Ocean Health—Is There an "Acidification" Problem? Paper prepared for the CO_2 Coalition. http://co2coalition.org/wp-content/uploads/2020/06/Steele-Ocean-Health-White-Paper-final-5-28-20.pdf [accessed July 20, 2020].

Stennes, B., K. Niquidet, and G.C. van Kooten, 2010. Implications of Expanding Bioenergy Production from Wood in British Columbia: An Application of a Regional Wood Fibre Allocation Model, *Forest Science* 56(4): 366–378.

Sterly, S., R. Jongeneel, H. Pabst, H. Silvis, J. Connor, D. Freshwater, M. Shobayashi, Y. Kinoshita, G.C. van Kooten, and A. Zorn, 2018. Research for AGRI Committee—A Comparative Analysis of Global Agricultural Policies: Lessons for the Future CAP. 107 pp. Brussels: European Parliament, Policy Department for Structural and Cohesion Policies. https://www.europarl.europa.eu/thinktank/en/document.html?reference=IPOL _STU(2018)629183.

Stern, N., 2007. *The Economics of Climate Change: The Stern Review*. Cambridge, UK: Cambridge University Press.

Stevenson, J.R., N. Villoria, D. Byerlee, T. Kelley, and M. Maredia, 2013. Green Revolution Research Saved an Estimated 18 to 27 Million Hectares from Being Brought into Agricultural Production, *Proceedings of the National Academy of Sciences* 110(21): 8363–8368. doi:10.1073/pnas.1208065110.

Sugden, R., 2003. Conceptual Foundations of Cost-Benefit Analysis: A Minimalist Account. In *Transport Projects, Programmes and Policies, Evaluation Needs and Capabilities* (pp. 151–169), edited by J. Nellthorp and P. Mackie. London: Routledge.

Sugden, R., 2005. Coping with Preference Anomalies in Cost-Benefit Analysis: A Market Simulation Approach, *Environmental and Resource Economics* 32(1): 129–160. https://doi.org/10.1007/s10640-005-6031-5.

Sun, L., and G.C. van Kooten, 2009. Fuzzy Logic and Preference Uncertainty in Non-Market Valuation, *Environmental & Resource Economics* 42(April): 471–489.

Sunstein, C.R., 2005a. *Laws of Fear: Beyond the Precautionary Principle*. Cambridge, UK: Cambridge University Press.

Sunstein, C.R., 2005b. The Precautionary Principle as a Basis for Decision Making, *The Economists' Voice* 2(2): Article 8. https://doi.org/10.2202/1553-3832.1079.

Tegtmeier, E.M., and M.D. Duffy, 2004. External Costs of Agricultural Production in the United States, *International Journal of Agricultural Sustainability* 2(1): 1–20.

Thatcher, M., 2002. *Statecraft: Strategies for a Changing World*. New York: HarperCollins Publishers.

Thrice, A.H., and S.E. Wood, 1958. Measurement of Recreation Benefits. *Land Economics* 34(August): 195–207.

Tol, R.S.J., 2006. The Stern Review of the Economics of Climate Change: A Comment, *Energy & Environment* 17(6): 977–981.

Tol, R.S.J., 2014. *Climate Economics: Economic Analysis of Climate, Climate Change and Climate Policy.* Cheltenham, UK: Edward Elgar.

Turvey, C.G., 2001. Weather Derivatives for Specific Event Risks in Agriculture, *Review of Agricultural Economics* 23(2): 333–351.

Turvey, C.G., 2012. Whole Farm Income Insurance, *Journal of Risk and Insurance* 79: 515–540.

US Department of Agriculture (USDA), 2012. Supplemental Revenue Assistance Payments Program—American Recovery and Reinvestment Act of 2009. Audit Report 50703-0001-31. March 12. Washington, DC: Office of the Inspector General. https://www.usda.gov/sites/default/files/50703-0001-31.pdf [accessed December 2, 2020].

US Department of Agriculture (USDA), 2016. Supplemental Coverage Option for Federal Crop Insurance: A Risk Management Agency Factsheet. Revised October 2020. https://www.rma.usda.gov/pubs/rme/2017sco.pdf [accessed December 3, 2020].

US Global Change Research Program (USGCRP), 2018. *Impacts, Risks, and Adaptation in the United States: Fourth National Climate Assessment*, Vol. II, edited by D.R. Reidmiller, C.W. Avery, D.R. Easterling, K.E. Kunkel, K.L.M. Lewis, T.K. Maycock, and B.C. Stewart. Washington, DC: US Global Change Research Program. https://doi.org/10.7930/NCA4.2018. https://nca2018.globalchange.gov/ [accessed December 7, 2020].

US Water Resources Council, 1973. Water and Related Land Resources: Establishment of Principles and Standards for Planning. *Federal Register* 38(174, 10 December): 24778–24869.

US Water Resources Council, 1979. Principles and Standards for Planning Water and Related Land Resources. *Federal Register* 44(242): 72878–72976.

US Water Resources Council, 1983. Economic and Environmental Principles and Guidelines for Water and Related Land Resources Implementation Studies. 10 March. 137 pp. Washington, DC. Mimeograph.

van Asseldonk, M., R. Jongeneel, G.C. van Kooten, and J. Cordier, 2019. Agricultural Risk Management in the European Union: A Proposal to Facilitate Precautionary Saving, *EuroChoices* 18(2): 40–46.

van Berkum, S., R.A. Jongeneel, M.G.A. van Leeuwen, and I.J. Terluin, 2018. *Exploring the Impacts of Two Brexit Scenarios on Dutch Agricultural Trade Flows*. Report 2018-026. Wageningen, NL: Wageningen Economic Research.

van der Heide, C.M., 2005. An Economic Analysis of Nature Policy. Academic dissertation, Tinbergen Institute and Vrije Universiteit, Amsterdam.

van der Heide, C.M., N.A. Powe, and S. Navrud, 2010. Economic Principles of Monetary Valuation in Evaluation Studies. In *Environmental and Agricultural Modelling: Integrated Approaches for Policy Impact Assessment* (pp. 295–317), edited by F. Brouwer and M.K van Ittersum. Dordrecht: Springer.

van Kooten, G.C., 1993. *Land Resource Economics and Sustainable Development: Economic Policies and the Common Good*. Vancouver: UBC Press.

van Kooten, G.C., 1995. Economics of Protecting Wilderness Areas and Old-Growth Timber in British Columbia, *The Forestry Chronicle* 71(Feb/Mar): 52–58.

van Kooten, G.C., 1998. Benefits of Improving Water Quality in Southwestern British Columbia: An Application of Economic Valuation Methods. In *Economics of Agro-Chemicals* (pp. 295–311), edited by G.A.A. Wossink, G.C. van Kooten, and G.H. Peters. Aldershot, UK: Ashgate.

van Kooten, G.C., 2002. Economic Analysis of the Canada-United States Softwood Lumber Dispute: Playing the Quota Game, *Forest Science* 48: 712–721.

van Kooten, G.C., 2013. *Climate Change, Climate Science and Economics: Prospects for an Alternative Energy Future*. Dordrecht, NL: Springer.

van Kooten, G.C., 2014. The Benefits of Impeding Free Trade: Revisiting British Columbia's Restrictions on Log Exports, *Journal of Forest Economics* 20(4): 333–347.

van Kooten, G.C., 2017a. *The Welfare Economics of Dismantling Dairy in a Confederation of States*. REPA working paper 2017-04. April. 32 pp. Victoria, BC: Resource Economics and Policy Analysis Unit, Department of Economics, University of Victoria. http://web.uvic.ca/~repa/publications/REPA%20working%20papers/Workingpaper2017-04.pdf.

van Kooten, G.C., 2017b. Case Study 7: What Could EU Policymakers Learn from Agricultural Risk Management Policy in the United States? Annex 7 in Study on Risk Management in EU Agriculture. October. 49 pp. Brussels: European Commission. https://ec.europa.eu/agriculture/external-studies/2017-risk-management-eu-agriculture_en.

van Kooten, G.C., 2017c. Case Study 8: What Could EU Policymakers Learn from Agricultural Risk Management Institutions Available in Canada? Annex 8 in Study on Risk Management in EU Agriculture. October. 38 pp. Brussels: European Commission. https://ec.europa.eu/agriculture/external-studies/2017-risk-management-eu-agriculture_en.

van Kooten, G.C., 2020. Reforming Canada's Dairy Sector: USMCA and the Issue of Compensation, *Applied Economics and Policy Perspectives* 42(3): 542–558.

van Kooten, G.C., T. Bogle, and F.P. de Vries, 2015. Forest Carbon Offsets Revisited: Shedding Light on Darkwoods, *Forest Science* 61(2): 370–380.

van Kooten, G.C., and E.H. Bulte, 2000. *The Economics of Nature: Managing Biological Assets.* Oxford, UK: Blackwell.

van Kooten, G.C., and H. Folmer, 2004. *Land and Forest Economics*. Cheltenham, UK: Edward Elgar.

van Kooten, G.C., and C. Johnston, 2014. Global Impacts of Russian Log Export Restrictions and the Canada-US Lumber Dispute: Modeling Trade in Logs and Lumber, *Forest Policy & Economics* 39: 54–66.

van Kooten, G.C., and C.M.T. Johnston, 2016. The Economics of Forest Carbon Offsets, *Annual Review of Resource Economics* 8(1): 227–246.

van Kooten, G.C., E. Krcmar, and E.H. Bulte, 2001. Preference Uncertainty in Nonmarket Valuation: A Fuzzy Approach, *American Journal of Agricultural Economics* 83: 487–500.

van Kooten, G.C., S. Laaksonen-Craig, and Y. Wang, 2009. A Meta-Regression Analysis of Forest Carbon Offset Costs, *Canadian Journal of Forest Research* 39(1): 2153–2167.

van Kooten, G.C., D. Orden, and A. Schmitz, 2019. Use of Subsidies and Taxes and the Reform of Agricultural Policy. In *The Routledge Handbook of Agricultural Economics* (pp. 355–380), edited by G. Cramer, K. Paudel, and A. Schmitz. New York: Routledge.

van Kooten, G.C., and A. Schmitz, 1985. Commodity Price Stabilization: The Price Uncertainty Case, *Canadian Journal of Economics* 18: 426–434.

van Kooten, G.C., A. Schmitz, and W.H. Furtan, 1988. The Economics of Storing a Non-Storable Commodity, *Canadian Journal of Economics* 21: 579–86.

van Kooten, G.C., R.A. Schoney, and K.A. Hayward, 1986. An Alternative Approach to the Evaluation of Goal Hierarchies among Farmers, *Western Journal of Agricultural Economics* 11: 40–49.

van Kooten, G.C., S.L. Shaikh, and P. Suchánek, 2002. Mitigating Climate Change by Planting Trees: The Transaction Costs Trap, *Land Economics* 78(November): 559–572.

van Kooten, G.C., and K.F. Taylor, 1989. Measuring the Welfare Impacts of Government Regulation: The Case of Supply Management, *Canadian Journal of Economics* 22: 902- 913.

van Kooten, G.C., and L. Voss (eds.), 2021. *International Trade in Forest Products: Lumber Trade Disputes, Models and Examples*. Wallingford, UK: CABI Publishing.

van Vuuren, D.P., J.A. Edmonds, M. Kainuma, K. Riahi, and J. Weyant, 2011. A Special Issue on the RCPs, *Climatic Change* 109(SP1): 573–1480. https://doi.org/10.1007/s10584-011-0157-y.

Vedenov, D.V., and B.J. Barnett, 2004. Efficiency of Weather Derivatives as Primary Crop Insurance Instruments, *Journal of Agricultural and Resource Economics* 29(3): 387–400.

Veeman, M.M., 1982. Social Costs of Supply-Restricting Marketing Boards, *Canadian Journal of Agricultural Economics* 30(1): 21–36.

Vercammen, J., 2011. *Agricultural Marketing. Structural Models for Price Analysis*. London and New York: Routledge.

Vercammen, J., 2013. A Partial Adjustment Model of Federal Direct Payments in Canadian Agriculture, *Canadian Journal of Agricultural Economics* 61(3): 465–485.

Walker, T., P. Cardellichio, A. Colnes, J.S. Gunn, B. Kittler, B. Perschel, C. Recchia, and D.S. Saah, 2010. Massachusetts Biomass Sustainability and Carbon Policy Study: Report to the Commonwealth of Massachusetts Department of Energy Resources. Natural Capital Initiative Report NCI-2010-03. June. 182 pp. Brunswick, Maine: Manomet Center for Conservation Sciences. http://www.mass.gov/eea/docs/doer/renewables/biomass/manomet-biomass-report-full-hirez.pdf [accessed July 14, 2017].

Walker, T., P. Cardellichio, J.S. Gunn, D.S. Saah, and J.M. Hagan, 2013. Carbon Accounting for Woody Biomass from Massachusetts (USA) Managed Forests: A Framework for Determining the Temporal Impacts of Wood Biomass Energy on Atmospheric Greenhouse Gas Levels, *Journal of Sustainable Forestry* 32(1–2): 130–158.

Wallace, T.D, 1962. Measures of Social Costs of Agricultural Programs, *Journal of Farm Economics* 44(2): 580–599.

Waugh, F.W., 1944. Does the Consumer Benefit from Price Instability? *Quarterly Journal of Economics* 58: 604–614.

Weber, M. and G. Hauer, 2003. A Regional Analysis of Climate Change Impacts on Canadian Agriculture, *Canadian Public Policy - Analyse de Politiques* 29(2): 163–180.

Weitzman, M.L., 1998. Why the Far-Distant Future Should Be Discounted at Its Lowest Possible Rate, *Journal of Environmental Economics and Management* 36(3): 201–208.

Weitzman, M.L., 1999. *Gamma Discounting*. Cambridge, MA: Harvard University Press.

Weitzman, M.L., 2007. A Review of the Stern Review on the Economics of Climate Change, *Journal of Economic Literature* 45: 703–724.

West, T.O., and G. Marland, 2001. A Synthesis of Carbon Sequestration, Carbon Emissions, and Net Carbon Flux in Agriculture: Comparing Tillage Practices in the United States. Environmental Sciences Division Working Paper. 39 pp. Oak Ridge, TN: Oak Ridge National Laboratory.

Wilson, M.A., and J.P. Hoehn, 2006. Valuing Environmental Goods and Services Using Benefit Transfer: The State-of-the Art and Science, *Ecological Economics* 60(2): 335–342.

Wittwer, S.H., 1995. *Food, Climate and Carbon Dioxide. The Global Environment and World Food Production.* Boca Raton, FL: CRC Press.

Wohlgenant, M.K., 2011. Sweets for the Sweet: The Costly Benefits of the US Sugar Program. Washington, DC: American Enterprise Institute. https://www.aei.org/research-products/report/sweets-for-the-sweet-the-costly-benefits-of-the-us-sugar-program/ [accessed April 9, 2019].

Woodward, R.T., and Y.-S. Wui, 2001. The Economic Value of Wetland Services: A Meta-analysis, *Ecological Economics* 37(2): 257–270.

World Trade Organization (WTO), 2002. United States - Continued Dumping and Subsidy Offset Act of 2000 Report of the Panel WT/DS217/R and WT/DS234/R. Geneva: World Trade Organization.

WTO, 2003a. United States - Continued Dumping and Subsidy Offset Act of 2000 Report of the Appellate Panel WT/DS217/AB/R and WT/DS234/AB/R. Geneva: World Trade Organization.

WTO, 2003b. Subsidies and Countervailing Measures. Paris: WTO.

WTO, 2005. United States - Continued Dumping and Subsidy Offset Act of 2000 Report of the Panel WT/DS217/R and WT/DS234/R. Geneva: WTO.

WTO, 2014a. The Bali Decision on Stockholding for Food Security in Developing Countries. November 27. https://www.wto.org/english/tratop_e/agric_e/factsheet_agng_e.htm [accessed May 13, 2020].

WTO, 2014b. Protocol Amending the Marrakesh Agreement Establishing the World Trade Organization. WT/L/940. November 28. https://docs.wto.org/dol2fe/Pages/SS/directdoc.aspx?filename=Q:/WT/L/940.pdf [accessed May 13, 2020].

WTO, 2015a. Ensuring Safe Trading Without Unnecessary Restrictions. Paris: WTO.

WTO, 2015b. Proposal On Export Competition from Brazil, European Union, Argentina, New Zealand, Paraguay, Peru, Uruguay and the Republic of Moldova. November 16. 13 pp. Committee on Agriculture. JOB/AG/48/Corr.1. http://trade.ec.europa.eu/doclib/docs/2015/november/tradoc_154007.pdf [accessed May 13, 2020].

WTO, 2020. Trade Facilitation. https://www.wto.org/english/tratop_e/tradfa_e/tradfa_e.htm [accessed May 13, 2020].

WTO, n.d.(a). Agreement on Subsidies and Countervailing Measures ("SCM Agreement"). https://www.wto.org/english/tratop_e/scm_e/subs_e.htm [accessed December 4, 2020].

WTO, n.d.(b). Understanding the WTO Agreements. Agriculture: Fairer Markets for Farmers. https://www.wto.org/english/thewto_e/whatis_e/tif_e/agrm3_e.htm [accessed May 13, 2020].

Xie, X., R. Li, Y. Zhang, S. Shen, and Y. Bao, 2018. Effect of Elevated [CO_2] on Assimilation, Allocation of Nitrogen and Phosphorus by Maize (Zea mays L.), *Communications in Soil Science and Plant Analysis* 49: 1032–1044.

Yu, W., 2017. How China's Farm Policy Reforms Could Affect Trade and Markets: A Focus on Grains and Cotton. Geneva: International Centre for Trade and Sustainable Development (ICTSD).

Zacharias, T.P., and M.S. Paggi, 2016. Current Perspective on Crop Insurance Farm Safety, *Choices* 31(3). https://www.choicesmagazine.org/choices-magazine/theme-articles/crop-insurance-in-the-20182019-farm-bill/current-perspectives-on-the-crop-insurance-farm-safety-net.

Zapranis, A.D. and A. Alexandridis, 2012. *Weather Derivatives: Modeling and Pricing Weather-Related Risk.* Dordrecht, NL: Springer.

Zerbe, R.O., Jr., and D.D. Dively, 1994. *Benefit-Cost Analysis in Theory and Practice.* New York: HarperCollins College Publishers.

Zhang, P.G., 1995. *Barings Bankruptcy and Financial Derivatives.* Singapore: World Scientific Publishing.

Zheng, Y.P., R.Q. Li, L.L. Guo, L.H. Hao, H.R. Zhou, F. Li, Z.P. Peng, D.J. Cheng, and M. Xu, 2018. Temperature Responses of Photosynthesis and Respiration of Maize (Zea mays) Plants to Experimental Warming, *Russian Journal of Plant Physiology* 65: 524–531.

Zulauf, C., and D. Orden, 2012. US Farm Policy and Risk Assistance: The Competing Senate and House Agriculture Committee Bills of July 2012. ICTSD Programme on Agricultural Trade and Sustainable Development, Issue Paper No. 44. Geneva, Switzerland: International Centre for Trade and Sustainable Development.

Zulauf, C., and D. Orden, 2014. The US Agricultural Act of 2014: Overview and Analysis. Discussion Paper 01393. December. 63 pp. Washington, DC: International Food Policy Research Institute.

Zulauf, C., and D. Orden, 2016. 80 Years of Farm Bills—Evolutionary Reform, *Choices* 31(4). http://www.choicesmagazine.org/choices-magazine/theme-articles/looking-ahead-to-the-next-farm-bill/80-years-of-farm-billsevolutionary-reform.

INDEX

Costa Rica, 46
cost-effectiveness analysis (CEA), 8, 32–33
Counter-Cyclical Payment (CCP) program, US, 153, 219
counterfactual land use, 96
countervailing (CV) duty, 78, 81, 84–86
county-level coverage, 222–223
crop insurance, 1, 10, 90, 94, 99, 109, 146, 154–155, 158–160, 169, 201, 205, 208–213, 216–245
Crop Insurance Act (1959), Canada, 159, 226
cropland, 8, 25, 26, 54, 96, 111, 131, 147, 151, 158, 176, 181, 216
cross compliance (*see* policy: red-ticket), 96, 98, 136, 147, 170, 183, 201, 218
Crow's Nest Pass Freight Rate (Crow Rate), 9, 161–162, 169–170, 227
cumulative effects analysis, 35

dairy premium, 183
damage function, 50, 51, 53, 64
deficiency payment, 83, 120, 122–123, 147–155, 170, 182–183, 187, 189, 193, 201, 206, 216–218, 224, 239, 245, 283
deforestation, 7, 65, 273–276
degradation, 27, 59, 276–278, 282
demand uncertainty, 112, 137–138
descriptive approach (discounting), 42, 46
direct use value, 22
discount rate, 8, 13–15, 22, 30, 38–48, 116, 120, 167, 247, 266–271, 277–278, 282–283
    private, 8, 16
    real, 38
    social, 23, 40, 267
    utility (*see also* social rate of time preference), 8, 42t
Doha Development Agenda (DDA), The, 100–102
downstream markets, 71–72
durum wheat, 9, 66–70, 75–77, 107, 141–144, 182–183, 258

economic efficiency, 25, 27, 29–34, 63, 65, 81, 92, 208, 256
economic efficiency account, 27, 31, 63
economic integration, 121, 174, 187
economies of scale, 1, 119, 123, 140, 164, 166, 176, 180
ecosystem, 1, 8, 10, 22–23, 26, 46, 53–54, 60–64, 136, 275, 278, 282
    capital, 54

forest, 35, 60, 267, 276–277
    services, 1, 8, 22, 23, 46, 53, 62–64, 136
emissions
    CO_2, 8, 16, 23–24, 26, 35, 49, 104, 132, 248, 256, 266–267, 271–278, 281
    greenhouse gas (GHGs), 21, 35, 104, 133, 248, 253, 255, 257, 261, 272–273, 276
    methane, 104
    reduction, 41, 272, 275, 277
    trading, 253, 256, 257
energy crop, 23, 25, 26, 27, 50, 273, 275, 279
energy project, 17, 19, 33, 34, 37, 45
equilibrium climate sensitivity (ECS), xviii, 43, 44, 248, 249, 250, 252
equivalent surplus and variation, 22, 46
EU Agricultural Fund for Rural Development (EAFRD), 179, 195
European Agricultural Guidance and Guarantee Fund (EAGF), xviii, 175, 177, 179, 195
European Commission, 174, 177, 178, 183, 184, 243, 269
European Economic Community (EEC), 174, 179
European Union (EU), 2, 9, 35, 37, 66, 68, 75–78, 95, 100–102, 105–106, 110, 120–125, 129, 137–144, 147–148, 151, 154–157, 160, 163–210, 228, 240–243, 262, 268–269, 273, 276
    EU-15, 175, 176, 180, 182
    EU-25, 175, 180
    EU-27, 175–176, 180, 194–195, 199
    EU-28, 142–144, 175–176, 179, 194, 196
    Treasury, 191–192, 215
exchange-traded market, 213
existence value, 24–25, 27, 30, 53, 160
expiration date, 215
Export Enhancement Program (EEP), xviii, 150, 151, 152
externality, 16, 27, 35, 41, 49, 50, 63, 90, 93, 96, 104, 130–137
    environmental, 91, 93, 96, 168
extreme events, 8, 36, 37

Farm Bills, US
    1949, 145
    1965, 147
    1970, 147–148, 150
    1990, 150
    1996, 150, 152, 169, 181
    2002, 153
    2008, 154, 169, 210, 219, 228, 243
    2014, 154–156, 218, 220–226, 243